AMERICAN ART ANALOG

VOLUME I
1688–1842

Compiled by
Michael David Zellman

CHELSEA HOUSE PUBLISHERS
in association with
AMERICAN ART ANALOG

1986

Director : Michael David Zellman
Editor : Rebecca Stefoff
Production Management and Coordination : Richard Alan Zakroff
Editorial and Project Consultant : Don Sugarman
Photo Research and Registration : Elizabeth Preston
Computer Operations : Sheila Mulligan
Administrative Assistant : Evelyn Kobler
Production Support : Phil DiPiero

Photographers : James D. Dee
Ali Elai
Theodore Flagg
Robert Grove
Richard Haynes, Jr.
John Kasparian
M.S. Rezny
Clive Russ
Neil Scholl
Paul Wilson

Researchers : Edmond Bassetti
Cheryl Cibulka
Roberta Geier
Joan Irving
Rebecca Rackin
David Sellin
Cynthia Seibels
Michelle Stricker
J. Gray Sweeney
Linda Sykes
Diane Tepfer
Jennifer Way

Designer : Richard Goettel
Typesetting : The Kingswood Group, Inc.
Printed in Japan

Library of Congress Cataloging-in-Publication Data

American art analog.

Includes bibliographies and indexes.
Contents: v. 1. 1688–1842—v. 2. 1842–1874—v.3. 1874–1930
1. Art, American.   2. Art, American—Prices.
3. Art as an investment.   4. Art—Collectors and collecting.
I. Zellman, Michael David.
N6505.A56   1986   759.13   85-29085
ISBN 1-555-46000-3 (set)
ISBN 1-555-46001-1 (Volume I)

CONTENTS

————————VOLUME III————————

ARTWORK CONTRIBUTORS

MUSEUMS AND UNIVERSITIES

Abby Aldrich Rockefeller Folk Art
    Center
Alabama Department of Archives and
    History
Amon Carter Museum
Anchorage Historical and Fine Arts
    Museum
Art Institute of Chicago
Bayly Museum
University of Virginia
Baltimore Museum of Art
Board of Selectmen, Abbot Hall
Boston Athenaeum
Bowdoin College Museum of Art
Brandywine River Museum,
    Brandywine Conservancy
Brooklyn Museum
Butler Institute of American Art
Cahoon Museum
Carnegie Institute
Colby College Museum of Art
Connecticut Historical Society
Corcoran Gallery of Art
Crocker Art Museum
Delaware Art Museum
Detroit Institute of Art
Florence Griswold Museum,
    Lyme Historical Society
Fogg Museum, Harvard University
Gilcrease Institute of American History
    and Art
Grand Rapids Art Museum
Hirshhorn Museum and Sculpture
    Garden
Historical Society of Pennsylvania
Independence National Historical Park
    Services
Indianapolis Museum of Art
La Salle University Art Museum
Los Angeles County Museum of Art
Metropolitan Museum of Art
Montclair Art Museum
Monterey Peninsula Museum of Art
Montgomery Museum of Fine Arts
Morse Gallery
Mount Vernon Ladies Association
Munson-Williams-Proctor Art Institute
Museum of American Folk Art
Museum of Fine Arts, Boston
Museum of the Confederacy
Muskegon Museum of Art
Nassau County Museum of Fine Art
National Academy of Design

National Center of Afro-American
    Artists
National Cowboy Hall of Fame
National Gallery of Art
National Museum of American Art
National Portrait Gallery
Neuberger Museum State University of
    New York
New Jersey State Museum
New York Historical Society
New York State Historical Association
Newark Museum
North Carolina Museum of Art
Oakland Museum
Palm Springs Desert Museum
Passaic County Historical Society
Peale Museum
Pennsylvania Academy of the Fine Arts
Perry Public Library
Philadelphia Museum of Art
Phillips Collection
Princeton University Art Museum
Reading Public Museum and Art
    Gallery
Sagamore Hill National Historical Site
Schomberg Center for Research in Black
    Culture, New York Public Library
Shelburne Museum
Sheldon Memorial Art Gallery,
    University of Nebraska
Smithsonian Institution
Stark Museum of Art
Strong Museum
Studio Museum in Harlem
Vassar College Art Gallery
Walters Art Gallery
Whitney Museum of American Art
William A. Farnsworth Library and Art
    Museum
Winterthur Museum
Worcester Art Museum
Yale University Art Gallery

GALLERIES

A.B. Closson Gallery
ACA Galleries
Adams Davidson Galleries
Andre Emmerich Gallery
Arvest Galleries, Inc.
Balogh Gallery
Borghi Galleries
Braarud Fine Art
Chapellier Gallery
Connecticut Gallery, Inc.

County Store Gallery, Inc.
Daniel B. Grossman, Inc.
Deru's Fine Art
Driscoll & Walsh Fine Art
GWS Galleries
Gallery Schlesinger-Boisante,
    Incorporated
Gerald Peters Gallery (The Peters
    Corporation)
Gimpel & Weitzenhoffer Gallery
Graham Gallery
Grand Central Gallery
Henry B. Holt, Inc.
Hirschl & Adler Galleries, Inc.
James Maroney Gallery
Jeffery Hoffeld & Co., Inc.
Jeffrey Allen Gallery
John H. Garzoli
Kennedy Galleries
Kraushaar Galleries
M. Knoedler & Co., Inc.
Marbella Gallery, Inc.
Martin Diamond Gallery
Maxwell Galleries
Newman Galleries
O.K. Harris Works of Art
Oliphant and Company, LTD.
Oscarsson Hood Gallery
Peter Tillou Gallery
Petersen Galleries
Raydon Galleries
Richard Love Galleries
Robert Elkon Gallery
Robert M. Hicklin, Jr., Inc.
SIMIC Gallery
Schwarz & Son, Philadelphia
Smith Gallery
Sperone Westwater Gallery
Taggart, Jorgensen & Putman, Dealers
    in Fine Paintings
Thaler, Frederic Gallery
Vose Galleries of Boston, Inc.
Whistler Gallery, Inc.
Whitehall Gallery
Wunderlich & Company, Inc.

CORPORATE COLLECTIONS

Chase Manhattan Bank, N.A.
Coca-Cola Company
Early California and Western Art
    Research
George Demont Otis Foundation
Sotheby's
Sterling Regal, Inc.

ESSAY CONTRIBUTORS

Matthew Baigell, Rutgers University
Robert Bishop, Museum of American Folk Art
Thomas W. Bower, National Museum of American Art, Smithsonian Institution
Richard Boyle, Philadelphia College of Art
Patricia Janis Broder

George M. Cohen, Hofstra University
Edmund Barry Gaither, Museum of the National Center of Afro-American Artists
Piri Halasz
Mary F. Holahan, Delaware Art Museum
Robert F. Looney, Free Library of Philadelphia
Henry Niemann

A.J. Peluso
Oswaldo Rodriguez Roque, Metropolitan Museum of Art
David Sellin
J. Gray Sweeney, Arizona State University
Diane Tepfer
Mary Jo Viola, Baruch College, City University of New York

ART HISTORY CONSULTANTS

Roland Elzea, Delaware Art Museum
Jonathan Harding, Boston Athenaeum

Elizabeth H. Hawkes, Delaware Art Museum
Richard Love, Richard Love Galleries

David Sellin
Diane Tepfer

BIOGRAPHY WRITERS

Craig Ruffin Bailey
John Bolles
Jessica Chapin
Sandra Chatfield
Barbara Craig
Robert Cullers
Sondra Donner
Jeanne Doseff Dority
Anne C. Dougherty
Thomas M. Duthie
Randee Dutton
Andrea Fine
Donalyn Frank
Jeanne Gampe

Patricia Gibbon
Jonathan Gross
George M. Harding, Jr.
Joan G. Hauser
Joan Irving
Nina Jaroslav
Evelyn Kobler
Patricia McBroom
Marguerite Morris
Marc M. Narducci
Doris Patterson
Rebecca Rackin
Susan Shiber
Lisa Silverman
Peter Simoneaux

Vic Skrowronski
Yvonne Sobel
William Sokolic
Rebecca Stefoff
Michele Stricker
Donald Sugarman
J. Gray Sweeney
Ruth Tallmadge
Delia Turner
Dan Vitale
Kate Walbert
Deidre Watters
Anne Werner
Steve Witte

FOREWORD

Reference works are shaped by the research needs and methods of a particular time. James Thomas Flexner suggested that an appropriate way to read William Dunlap's history of American art, first published in 1834, is to "put on your slippers, place a drink by your elbow, and resolve to ramble imaginatively with the author through vanished times." The *American Art Analog* is emphatically a product of today, and though its users are more likely to sprint than ramble through its pages, its distinctive features will prompt occasional wanderings.

Included are topical essays in the history of American art; summary biographies of more than 800 painters, many little-known and each represented with a color reproduction; and—most unusual in a general reference work—figures and graphs that illustrate the market activity of paintings by these artists (which also served as the basis of their selection).

Heretofore the only general reference to include prices obtained for works of art was the French dictionary of artists by Emanuel Benezit. Art and the market, a natural liaison in France where art has long been an important part of the nation's economy, have an uneasy association in the United States—where the nation's business is business. The marketplace as an implicit presence in the American art scene comes more sharply into focus with information on recent prices in the *Analog,* revealing fluctuations of American taste over the past decade and confirming the lack of a consistent connection between quality and prices.

Although the ease of slippers and drink may not be appropriate accompaniments for the pace of the scholars, collectors and dealers who will use the *American Art Analog,* this new reference tool, with biographical and illustrative materials set within the context of recent market activity, will stimulate and promote their explorations into untrodden expanses of American art.

Lois Marie Fink
Curator, Office of Research
National Museum of American Art

SECOND FOREWORD

Historically, man has placed value on commodities used for survival and pleasure. After thousands of years, this exchange of value continues in organized as well as haphazard ways. The pure barter system no longer dominates trade; instead, we rely for the most part on regulated promissory and monetary systems of exchange. Today, standardized products are evaluated and forecasted by worldwide networks of professional analysts. The trading of these commodities and futures is complex. It involves sophisticated computer programs and is governed by stringent federal regulatory agencies which require total accuracy. The astute trader, constantly aware of economic nuances, knows that accurate, timely information is of vital importance.

Until now, meaningful information concerning one particular commodity—American art—has been difficult to obtain. Appraisal, valuation and informed decision-making have suffered. In the past decade, we have matured aesthetically where appreciation and preservation of American art are concerned. From a financial or investment viewpoint, not only has the value of American artworks escalated, but this dramatic escalation has created an unsated demand for accurate and comprehensive information. In my opinion, the *American Art Analog* admirably fills this void. In its design and creation, the publishers of the *American Art Analog* have utilized the latest technology and incorporated the current proven thinking of leading authorities from both the art professional and financial communities to create an accurate and excellent product. Unlike any other reference book in its field, the *Analog* devotes great attention to the vast number of obscure artists who are very much a factor in American art history, and whose works very likely represent the undervalued opportunities most visionary investors seek. Now, after painstaking international auction analysis, the *Analog* presents the necessary information in a clear format, enabling the investor to make better-informed decisions.

For philanthropists who may donate works of art for charitable or tax-planning purposes, please be mindful of the new rule and form changes required by the Internal Revenue Service, which now requires valid supportive documentation for non-cash gifts in excess of $5,000. The potential complications may be minimized for recipients, appraisers and IRS staffers alike by the information contained in the *American Art Analog* reference system. Additionally, this information should encourage more appropriate insurance coverage and accurate protection against unfortunate damage or loss.

The purchase of fine art has a distinct advantage over any other type of investment. An artwork pays you a dividend of pleasure each time you look at it ("income-in-kind") and concurrently offers high value appreciation potential. The years of planning, research and devoted effort that have gone into the *American Art Analog* make it an indispensable and wonderful tool for many disciplines, including tax accounting, insurance, estate planning and investing. Undoubtedly it will help you expand your portfolio with quality works by American artists.

Jack Ludwig
Vice President/Financial Consultant
Shearson Lehman/American Express Corporation

INTRODUCTION

At the close of the Second World War, the art world's treatment of American art was poised between neglect and obligatory acceptance. There were few curatorial positions in American art and little space for exhibition. Several courageous galleries represented American art exclusively, but their following was modest. Colleges and universities seldom provided chairs for American art professors. The press championed artists from abroad, and private collectors gave their attention and their dollars to European artists. Although there were exceptions, the wealth of the American art heritage was largely ignored.

The idea that an American painting would ever fetch a million dollars would have been preposterous in the 1950s; in fact, the total of all American art sold at auction during any one year in the early 1950s might not greatly have exceeded that figure. Nearly four decades later, the tide has turned, and the interest in American art is astounding. Museums have expanded their facilities to accommodate growing permanent collections of American art, and curatorial and research staffs, as well as budgetary allocations, have increased. Colleges and universities now offer more art courses than ever, especially in American art. Hundreds of American artists who have remained anonymous for as long as 200 years are at last being discovered.

Concurrently, the private sector's interest in American art has increased dramatically. Million-dollar prices for American masterpieces are almost assured each auction season, and many hitherto unrecognized nineteenth-century artists are fetching prices well into the hundreds of thousands of dollars.

Rising interest creates a demand for information, and collectors of American art soon needed to know more about the artists and their work—and especially about the investment potential of that work. Art dictionaries, monographs, reference books and auction house catalogs were available, but there was no single source for all the information an investor needed. After many years of purchasing, selling, and appraising fine art, I was determined to create a reference source to remedy that deficiency. I consulted art professionals across the nation, who agreed that its critical components would be high-quality color plates, biographical information, and auction performance figures. Out of these conferences grew the *American Art Analog.*

More than 800 artists born from the early eighteenth century through 1930 were selected for the *Analog* based on two criteria: the performance of their work at public auctions during the past ten years and their historical importance. And while any omissions or misjudgments in this regard are deeply regretted, at least 200 more artists will be considered for the second edition.

The *American Art Analog* is the cornerstone of a larger reference system. In addition to the encyclopedic three-volume first edition, the system includes the *American Art Analog Blue Book,* which annually updates the financial data on market activity and includes color plates of record sale paintings. And a sophisticated, highly detailed series of studies called *Special Reports* focuses on all the sales activity of each of the works by any artist in the *Analog.*

An undertaking of this size must be a collective effort. The *Analog* has received encouragement and support from many people, and has had the benefit of an excellent staff and top professionals in the art community for research and consultation. The network of museums and fine galleries nationwide also provided invaluable assistance. In particular very special thanks are due to Henry Holt, of Holt Galleries, Janet Flint, of Hirschl & Adler, and Robert Looney, of the Free Library of Philadelphia, for their counsel in the early stages of the project; to Robert and Susan Pilberg, who created a computer system for the *American Art Analog;* and to Ronald Drucker and Jack Ludwig, who helped with financial planning. Without the contributions of Bill Bianco, Harold Cramer, Lawrence Fleischman, Stanley Merves and Diane Tepfer the *Analog* would not have been possible.

Grateful appreciation is also extended to Linda Bantel, Frederick Bernaski, Laura Borghi, Mildred Cohen, A. Ara Danikian, Bruce L. Dietrich, Anita Duquette, Eleanor F. Fink, Daniel Freeman, Helen K. Fusscas, John Garzoli, Henry Geldzahler, Jonathan P. Harding, Robert A. Harman, Mark Hoffman, Karen Carolan, Richard Love, Kathleen Luhrs, Gayle Maxon, M.P. Naud, Andrew Newman, Bryan Oliphant, Alexander R. Raydon, Robert Schwartz, Patricia Sheeleigh, Michelle Stricker, the late Richard Stuart, Hollis Taggart, Birute Vileises, Abbott Williams Vose, Marcia Latimore Vose, Robert Churchill Vose, Jr., Robert Churchill Vose III, S. Morton Vose II, William Vose, Gerold Wunderlich and Rudolf Wunderlich.

I am also grateful to Ann Adams, Bruce Altschueler, Eva Balogh, Ira Bartfield, Michael J. Bennett, Lillian S. Bristol, Elizabeth Broun, Nicolai Cikovsky, Cecilia H. Chin, Conna Clark, Ted Cooper, Bill Cuffe, Roy Davis, John Driscoll, Charles C. Eldredge, Suzanne Embree, Robert Ewing, Sr., Trevor Fairbrother, Stuart Feld, Debra A. Fillos, Stephen Gaillard, Glenda Galt, Patricia C. Geeson, William Gerdts, Jean A. Gilmore, Frank Goodyear, Martha Heintz, Robert M. Hicklin, Jr., Patricia Hill, John K. Howat, Steven R. Jacobs, Diane McManus Jensen, Carl Jorgensen, Antoinette M. Kraushaar, Sandra Leff, Miriam Little, Cliff Logan, Murray Luterman, Cynthia Jaffee McCabe, Garnett McCoy, Donald Morrison, Edward J. Nygren, Elsie Oliver, Marius Peladeau, Gerald Peters, Sandra L. Petrie, Rosemary Rapp, Sigmund Rothschild, Patricia Smith, Janice Sorkow, Harold Steinberg, Kathleen D. Stocking, Laurie K. Strothman, John Thornton, Peter Tillou, Alexander Walsh, Deedee Wasserman, Ann Watkins, Caroline Wistar, Francine Woltz, Shari Zellman and Judith Zilczer.

Most importantly, I wish to thank my dear wife, Nancy, for her commitment and support. Lastly, this book is dedicated to my father's memory and his belief in freedom of expression.

Michael David Zellman
Director

The three-volume *American Art Analog* contains information about 820 artists. Unlike most other reference works, it does not present its subjects in alphabetical order. Instead they are listed chronologically, so that the *Analog* reflects the overall history of American art and at the same time gives you a close look at each artist. To find the entry for a particular artist, check the Index, which is repeated in full at the back of each volume.

Artists are presented in order by the year of their birth—or, in cases where the birth year is unknown, by the year in which their artistic activity began. Volume I includes artists born from 1688 to the second quarter of the nineteenth century; Volume II, artists born during the second and third quarters of the nineteenth century; and Volume III, those born from the fourth quarter of the nineteenth century through 1930.

In addition to the biographical entries on individual artists, each volume of the *Analog* also contains four or more special essays—concise articles about various periods or types of American painting, written for the *Analog* by expert scholars in the field of art history. They are designed both to introduce the era of American art covered in each volume and to amplify your understanding of the individual artists.

Each of the three volumes includes a glossary of art terms and a bibliographical list of further reading on American art. The Glossary and the Bibliography, like the Index, are repeated in full at the end of every volume.

The biographical entries are the backbone of the *American Art Analog*. Each biography consists of three elements, which together give a succinct picture of the artist's life, work and performance at recent auctions. The three elements are: one or more full-color reproductions of representative paintings; an article giving information about the painter's education and training, important influences, significant works, critical reputation, and the like; and a chart or graph of financial data based on recent sales of the artist's work.

This financial data is unique to the *Analog*. It gives you a quick, clear general idea of the auction performance of the artist's work. From this you can arrive at an approximation of the current auction worth of a painting by the artist, for purposes of investment or valuation.

Because it is impossible to analyze private sales, the values analyzed in the *Analog* are international auction figures, generally regarded by the art-purchasing community as the most reliable guide to value. Although the relationship of these auction-house or wholesale values to the retail value of a painting can vary, certain factors influence the difference between the two figures. Some of the factors which may contribute to a dealer's asking price for a painting are: the value of the dealer's counsel in helping you build a specialized collection, as of the Ashcan School, the Hudson River School, or Western art; conservation or restoration services, which can amount to 25 percent or more of the ultimate asking price; framing costs; scheduled insurance costs; photographic costs, promotional fees and exhibition costs; the cost of researching and creating a properly executed monograph; general overhead expenses; and examination and research by outside experts to determine authenticity.

Perhaps the most important of these factors is authentication: a $50,000 work of art which is obtained for $20,000 is no bargain, if at a later date it is determined to be a forgery.

As a general rule, the markup between the auction and retail values of art is directly related to the asking price. Generally, the lower a piece's value, the higher the percentage of markup—the markup percentage of a $100,000 item is less than that of a $2,000 item.

Of course, many factors affect the value of individual paintings. Such factors include the painting's condition, size and restoration history, the rarity of the artist's work and the period during which he executed the painting, the subject matter and provenance of the painting, and its exhibition history.

The *Analog* financial data represents the percentages of change in auction price based on averages only. With the exception of record sales, they do not identify specific paintings. However, bidding between two aggressive buyers can sometimes drive a particular painting's price well beyond the anticipated estimate, resulting in a mathematical skew. Such skews are greatly reduced in a ten-year analysis, but the possibility exists that some of the values given here reflect these unusual situations.

The *American Art Analog* financial analysis is based on the aggregate surface area of the paintings sold in a given year and the dollars paid for those paintings, as compared with the base year, 1975.

The ten-year financial analysis will appear in the form of either a four-line chart or a chart plus a bar graph (in a very few cases, information on recent sales activity was insufficient or unavailable, so no analysis is given).

The chart consists of four elements (see Example A on the following page). The top line identifies the auction season. (Each auction season actually includes parts of two calendar years, because most auction house sales seasons follow the academic year from September through August.) The second line, "Paintings," gives the number of paintings analyzed for each auction season. The third line, "Dollars," gives the aggregate dollars paid for those paintings.

The bottom line of each chart describes the artist's record sale—the highest price paid for a painting during the decade. It tells you: the price paid for the painting, the auction house which sold it (identified by initials which are explained in the Auction House List at the back of each volume), the date of the sale, and the title and dimensions of the painting.

In cases where sufficient data exists, the chart is supplemented by a bar graph, which appears immediately above it (see Example B). The graph represents the percentage of change in the sales of the artist's work in each season of the decade, taking the 1975-1976 season as the base of comparison for each succeeding season. At the top of the graph, the average change over ten years is given as a percentage. Note that the ranges covered by the graphs differ, depending on the different levels of performance of various artists' work. In cases where the bar rises above or falls below the borders of the graph, the increment shown is a standard one, not necessarily representative of the actual percentage.

In summary, the *American Art Analog* graphs and charts reflect average changes only, and if properly employed can be of inestimable value for the art professional, appraiser, investor, collector, estate specialist, and all others interested in the field of American art. They provide an excellent overview of the gross auction activity of a particular artist.

The financial data in these three volumes is expanded and updated in other elements of the *American Art Analog* reference system. The Blue Book is published annually and adds each new season's auction figures to the ten-year data base. In addition, Special Reports are available for amplified financial analysis of a specific artist, including painting-by-painting sales information.

Ignoti nulla cupido.

Example A

SEASON	75-76	76-77	77-78	78-79	79-80	80-81	81-82	82-83	83-84	84-85
Paintings	1	1		3	5	6	8	2	5	6
Dollars	$2,500	$4,250		$4,950	$6,700	$12,000	$18,950	$2,900	$7,175	$19,675

Record Sale: $11,000, CH, 3/15/85, "Tropical Landscape at Dusk," 24 × 49 in.

Example B

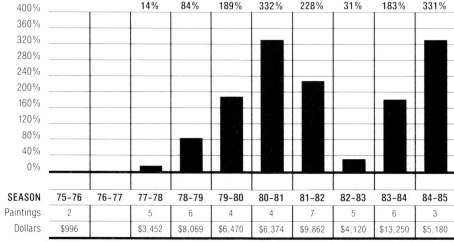

10-Year Average Change From Base Years '75-'76: 155%

SEASON	75-76	76-77	77-78	78-79	79-80	80-81	81-82	82-83	83-84	84-85
			14%	84%	189%	332%	228%	31%	183%	331%
Paintings	2		5	6	4	4	7	5	6	3
Dollars	$996		$3,452	$8,069	$6,470	$6,374	$9,862	$4,120	$13,250	$5,180

Record Sale: $4,200, P.NY, 10/13/83, "Feeding the Ducks," 30 × 41 in.

ESSAYS

COLONIAL AND EARLY REPUBLICAN PAINTING

OSWALDO RODRIGUEZ ROQUE

Thomas Smith, *Captain Thomas Smith—Self Portrait,* 17th century, 24½ x 23¾ in., signed l.l. Courtesy of Worcester Art Museum, Worcester, Massachusetts.

The history of American painting up to about the last quarter of the eighteenth century is really the history of one type of picture—the portrait. Although examples of religious painting and landscape can be found, portraiture absorbed the energies of the great majority of painters working in the then-British colonies. This was especially true in Puritan New England, where a strict religious outlook disciplined whatever frivolity might have been induced by increasing wealth, but it was also generally true of once-Dutch New York, Quaker Pennsylvania and

Anglican Virginia. Portraiture had a useful social role: it not only preserved a likeness for posterity, but did so in the context of strong family alliances. Although lacking a native nobility, America was nonetheless extremely respectful of good ancestry.

The body of seventeenth-century American portraiture is still undefined. Attribution to a given hand, much less to an American one, is frequently problematic. Nevertheless, we know that a number of professionally trained portraitists worked in America, principally in New England,

John Smibert, *The Bermuda Group—Dean George Berkeley (1685-1753) and His Family,* 69½ x 93 in., signed l.c. Courtesy of Yale University Art Gallery; Gift of Isaac Lothrop of Plymouth, Massachusetts.

and that they were responsible for works such as the portraits of *Mr. and Mrs. John Freake* (ca. 1674, Worcester Art Museum), and the likenesses of the Gibbs and Mason children. Fairly stiff and two-dimensional, these paintings reflect the position in which provincial English portraiture found itself at the time, poised between the decorative linearity of the Elizabethan period and the baroque concerns with three-dimensionality and light and shadow of the mid-seventeenth century.

One figure towers above all the American painters at this time, Captain Thomas Smith of Boston, whose self-portrait of about 1690 (Worcester Art Museum) not only alludes to his marine exploits but also includes a rhymed memento mori, the opening lines of which read:

Why, why should I the World be minding
Therein a World of Evils Finding
Then Farewell World: Farewell thy Jarres
Thy Joies, thy Toies, thy Wiles, thy Warres. . . .

Here, as in his other known works, the artist has not only employed fully up-to-date artistic conventions, he has made a real attempt to convey something of the character of the sitter. In doing this Smith emerges as the first in a line of New England portraitists who, despite changing notions of style, centered their art on strong characterization.

The coming of the eighteenth century saw the beginning of interesting developments in American portraiture, all achieved by immigrant artists. In Maryland, Justus Englehard Kuhn located his sitters in fanciful architectural settings that echoed the complex baroque formulas popular in North-central Europe. In South Carolina, Henrietta Johnston worked in a small scale, using pastels and favoring the wispy delicacy of the new rococo style. In New York, several unknown artists, usually called the patroon painters, formed a virtual school of folk-art portraiture, although their frequent reliance on recently published English and continental mezzotint engravings gives their works an oddly urbane air. In Philadelphia, Gustavus Hesselius painted well-crafted baroque-style portraits and tried his hand at allegorical painting. Only in Boston, however, did American portrait painting make a quantum leap toward true professionalism in the person of John Smibert.

Robert Feke, *Thomas Hopkinson,* 1746, 49⅞ x 39⅝ in. Courtesy of National Museum of American Art, Smithsonian Institution, George Buchanan Coale Collection, Washington, D.C.

Trained in England in the late-baroque style of Sir Godfrey Kneller and his followers, Smibert arrived in this country in 1729 as part of an entourage headed by scholar and philosopher Dean George Berkeley. Berkeley had intended to found a college in Bermuda, at which Smibert would be the professor of fine arts. But his enterprise failed when promised funding failed to materialize. Berkeley eventually returned to England, but Smibert decided he could make a more handsome living in America than in the motherland and chose to settle in Boston. His hunch proved right. Soon the elite of New England began deluging him with commissions. He married well, acquired wealth and fame, and became New England's link with the great artistic traditions of the past. His studio—filled with the engravings, casts and art treatises he had acquired, chiefly in Italy, in anticipation of his teaching duties—was America's first atelier. Its contents, preserved as he left them long after his death, influenced many New England painters of the younger generation.

Smibert's masterpiece, *The Bermuda Group* (1729 or 1739, Yale University Art Gallery), depicts the principal members of Berkeley's group, including the painter at the far left and Berkeley on the right. Smibert's compositional skill, his roundly modeled figures and his command of color and drapery are all given full play. The work demonstrated his powers to the fullest and clearly impressed many. Among them was a young Newport sailor, of uncertain artistic background, who would transform Smibert's baroque approach, with its emphasis on painterly execution and chiasoscuro, into a more linear, crisp and taut style.

Robert Feke has long been regarded as the first practitioner of a recognizable American portrait style. In his most ambitious and earliest known work, *The Family of Isaac Royall* (1741, Harvard University Law School), the proud figure of the young merchant displays a decorative two-dimensionality and an intensely defined likeness that already set Feke apart from Smibert, whose formulas he otherwise imitates.

In the next 10 years or so, Feke increasingly employed poses, color schemes and draperies derived from fashionable English portraiture in the popular rococo style. It is

Joseph Blackburn, *Mrs. Alexander Grant,* 50 x 40 in. Courtesy Vose Galleries of Boston, Inc., Massachusetts.

probable that a good deal of this information came to Feke via mezzotint engravings; it is also possible that in his travels the painter-mariner saw actual examples of the up-to-date style. Whatever its sources, however, Feke's work achieved a new sophistication that had immediate appeal. Besides Boston, he worked in Newport and Philadelphia, painting leading citizens in each town. In Boston, his portraits almost certainly enchanted the young John Singleton Copley, whose famed mature style is in many ways a fulfillment of Feke's.

Smibert died in 1751; Feke disappeared from view about the same time. The artistic vacuum left by them in Boston was filled by Joseph Badger, whose unappetizing works are at best a folk-artist's attempt to digest the lessons of Smibert's example, and by Joseph Blackburn, one of two itinerant English painters whose appearance in the American colonies at this time did much to elevate local taste. The other, John Wollaston, worked in New York, Philadelphia and the South, but not in New England. Neither Blackburn nor Wollaston was much at face painting: Wollaston repeatedly turned out mask-like characterizations with almond-shaped eyes, while Blackburn's subjects are frequently rather pathologically misshapen. Yet both were highly accomplished drapery painters and both were fully aware of the compositional conventions of the English rococo style, with its emphasis on informality and movement. Both returned to England after realizing what, judging from the large quantity of surviving portraits, must have been substantial profits.

The itinerant painters' command of the latest fashion in

John Wollaston, *Portrait of Lucy Parry, Wife of Admiral Parry,* 1745-1749, 50⅛ x 40 in., signed l.l. Courtesy of National Museum of American Art, Smithsonian Institution, Museum Purchase, Washington, D.C.

portrait painting was quickly recognized by the two most precocious talents produced in the American colonies, Benjamin West and John Singleton Copley. Blackburn's influence is clearly evident in many of Copley's works of the 1750s, while Wollaston's influence substantially shaped West's style before West left for Europe in 1759.

Without a doubt, the greatest of America's colonial painters, John Singleton Copley, must be regarded as something of a natural phenomenon. As a mere teenager in the 1750s, he demonstrated his ability to absorb the lessons not only of Feke and Blackburn but of whatever engravings and copies might have been available to him in Boston. His stepfather, Peter Pelham, an accomplished mezzotint engraver and dealer, must also have taught him a great deal about painstakingly labored contrasts of light,

used to define volume. But his own sheer talent, ambition and determination elevated Copley to the pinnacle of American colonial painting. After about 1760 he began to produce works whose considerable communicative power seems to emanate, not from the portraits as paintings, but from the sitters as personalities. Copley's saturated colors, his carefully balanced compositions, his meticulously studied likenesses and the poses and expressions with which he depicted his patrons were naturally calculated to achieve this effect.

Copley's approach was not only superior to anything New England had seen in the way of art, it was also profoundly in tune with the world-outlook of people who, as the American Revolution would soon prove, had strong convictions about their way of life. Compared to contem-

7

John Singleton Copley, *Robert "King" Hooper,* 1767, 50 x 39¾ in., signed l.r. Courtesy of The Pennsylvania Academy of the Fine Arts; The Henry S. McNeil Collection.

porary English portraits, Copley's appear somewhat stiff, obsessed with the materiality of objects, and overly strong in coloring. Yet these very qualities are so obviously in tune with the non-aristocratic—but still wealth-oriented—society they mirrored that it is easy for Americans to regard them as the hallmarks of a distinct native style.

As the Revolution approached, and as the constraints on his ambition became increasingly clear, Copley began seriously to consider leaving the city that had made him a rich man for Europe. In 1774 he did so, eventually settling in London. There he was welcomed by Benjamin West, whose reputation and accomplishments in that city were already considerable. West, who opened his home and studio to virtually any American painter looking for some formal European training, extended his hospitality to

Copley. Eventually, however, the two artists became rivals.

West had pioneered a type of painting that dealt with important historic events, including events of the recent past, in a relatively realistic fashion. Copley followed in his footsteps, but turned out to be more technically adept, painting what today are generally viewed as works of higher quality than West's. Copley felt that West, who by all accounts was a popular man and enjoyed the confidence of George III, did not deserve fame as much as he, and he bitterly resented West's election to the presidency of the Royal Academy after the death of Sir Joshua Reynolds in 1792.

West's and Copley's considerable achievements in history painting are America's greatest contribution to the

John Trumbull, *Surrender of Lord Cornwallis at Yorktown,* ca. 1828, 20⅞ x 30⅝ in. Copyright Yale University Art Gallery, New Haven, Connecticut.

development of international art in the eighteenth century. It is clear that their colonial background did much to fire the determination of these artists, and it probably predisposed them to take seriously the much-trumpeted notion that a hierarchy of painting existed and that history painting crowned it.

Ironically, America did not warm up to the idea of history painting, despite the best efforts of accomplished painters who thought they could, as it were, bring it to the land of its creators. The most important of these artists was John Trumbull, who worked under West in his studio but admired Copley's style more. While still in London, Trumbull set about creating a series of works illustrating the leading events in America's struggle for independence. Many of these paintings, such as *The Death of General Warren at the Battle of Bunker's Hill* (1786, Yale University Art Gallery) and *The Declaration of Independence* (1787-1820, same location) are now part of our national iconography, but they brought little financial reward to the artist at the time.

Even though Copley hardly had any contact with America after his departure, the lingering influence of his compelling portraiture largely determined the look of American painting from the 1760s through the 1790s.

John Mare, John Durand, Matthew Pratt and Charles Willson Peale produced portraits that frequently echoed Copley's style, although none of them can be regarded as a slavish imitator. Peale was probably the most accomplished. A highly inventive and versatile man, he was the only artist of note who worked during the Revolution, portraying many of its leaders. He, his brother James, and their children made up an important artistic dynasty in Pennsylvania, and were chiefly responsible for establishing still-life painting in the United States.

Of the accomplished artists who managed to avoid the overwhelming authority of Copley's works, two deserve to be mentioned. One of them, Jeremiah Theus, a Swiss immigrant who worked in Charleston, was clearly familiar with the poses and pastel-like shades of French rococo-style portraiture. He was well-patronized from the 1740s until his death in 1774. Another, Henry Benbridge, studied with the Italian painter Pompeo Batoni in Rome. He had some success in England with a celebrated full-length portrait of Corsican patriot Pascal Paoli which had been commissioned by James Boswell. Back in America in 1770, Benbridge became increasingly eccentric artistically, in his coloring as well as in the rendition of his figures.

A new ideal and a very high level of quality in portrai-

Thomas Sully, *Portrait of Colonel Samuel B. Davis,* 1819, 86 x 60 in., signed l.r. Photograph courtesy of Hirschl & Adler Galleries, Inc., New York, New York.

ture appeared in the recently formed United States of America with the return of Gilbert Stuart in 1793. An American who had worked in London under West, Stuart realized that his talent lay in portrait-painting, something West had never excelled in. He found inspiration in the genteel neoclassical style of Romney, Hoppner and Raeburn, as well as in the late works of Gainsborough, and quickly established a reputation. Stuart had an unerring eye for capturing a likeness and a deft, feathery touch. Had he stayed in England he would have ranked with the finest of English portraitists, but financial irresponsibility drove him first to Dublin, then again to his native land.

His success in the United States was almost instantaneous. He worked in New York, Philadelphia, Washington and Boston, and was swamped with commissions in each city. What Copley did for colonial American portraiture, Stuart accomplished for the art of the early republic. His relatively unpretentious style, with its emphasis on the face, very much reflected the confidence, individualism and sobriety of newly independent America. It strongly influenced a host of painters, among them James Frothingham, Ezra Ames, Thomas Sully, John Wesley Jarvis and Matthew Harris Jouett.

With the arrival of the nineteenth century, American painting gained noticeably in sophistication. Portraiture began to share the stage with still-life and genre painting, and at times even with history painting. The sharply linear style of French neoclassicism, a style that had been foreshadowed in this country by Copley, made its appearance in America in the works of John Vanderlyn, the first American to study in France, and then in the works of Rembrandt Peale. In general, this style did not meet with great favor, probably because it was too antithetical to Stuart's. The romantic outlook of British poets William Wordsworth and Samuel Taylor Coleridge found eloquent expression in the allegories and religious paintings of Washington Allston, who worked in Boston but who was nationally famous. Something of a hero to young American artists who admired his artistic independence, Allston brought to this country, after his return from Europe in 1808, a highly personal style that explored mood and emotion in a deliberately ambiguous way. Ultimately derived from continental Renaissance and baroque precedents, his coloring and brushwork continued the concern with painterly execution that characterized the adventurous and ground-breaking late works of Benjamin West. A looser handling of paint, in fact, was a frequent attribute of English painting in the early decades of the nineteenth century and reached its apogee in the bravura style of Thomas Lawrence. Lawrence's stylish portraits influenced the most important young American portraitist of the time, Thomas Sully, who worked in Philadelphia. Sully's palette, however, was always lighter than Lawrence's, and his brushwork more restrained.

These are, in brief, the major figures and developments of the colonial and early republican periods in American art. About 1825, however, portraiture, which had from the beginning dominated American painting, began to yield its primacy to landscape, which increasingly became the chosen genre for the expression of the nation's cultural values in the years that followed.

Oswaldo Rodriguez Roque is associate curator of the departments of American art at the Metropolitan Museum of Art. He was previously curator of fine arts at the Museum of Art, Carnegie Institute, Pittsburgh, and is the author of *American Furniture at Chipstone* and of the forthcoming *American Paintings in the Metropolitan Museum of Art, Volume One.*

AMERICAN PORTRAIT PAINTING

MARY F. HOLAHAN

John Singleton Copley, *Judge Martin Howard,* 50 x 40 in. Courtesy of Vose Galleries of Boston, Inc., Massachusetts.

Portraits—as personal mementos, signs of status and historical documents—have been a staple of American painting almost since the earliest settlements in the New World.

By 1670, itinerant portraitists, or limners, were active in the colonies. Portraiture was just one of their several mar-

ketable crafts; others were sign painting and house decoration. The limners' portrait formula usually presented the subject frontally, with little or no background. Anatomy and clothing were reduced to simple shapes and colors.

The limner tradition—now considered an aspect of folk

Charles Willson Peale, *Matthias and Thomas Bordley,* 1767. Courtesy of the National Museum of American Art, Smithsonian Institution, Museum Purchase and Gift of Mr. and Mrs. Murray Lloyd Goldsborough, Jr.

art—survived into the nineteenth century, with artists such as Ammi Phillips, Deborah Goldsmith and Erastus Salisbury Field. The folk portraits of these and other artists retained their basic limner-like simplicity but sometimes became very decorative and colorful. Twentieth-century folk artists, such as Horace Pippin and Anna Mary Robertson "Grandma" Moses, continued this portrait tradition, now often referred to as "primitive." Through folk art, the style of these modern primitives is linked to that of America's earliest limners.

In the 1720s and 1730s, several professionally trained European artists brought the more sophisticated continental style of portraiture to America.

Swedish-born Gustavus Hesselius painted middle-class subjects in the Philadelphia area. He depicted his sitters carefully posed and stylishly dressed in the European manner. But, as their frequently plain and age-worn faces show, he did not flatter them unduly; in fact, Hesselius's portraits point toward the realism that characterizes much American portraiture.

Scotsman John Smibert, who had been working in London, arrived in Boston in 1729. His portraits, although rather awkward, have the dignified formality of European baroque court portraiture. Like Hesselius, Smibert did not flatter his subjects. The faces of the people portrayed in *The Bermuda Group* (1729 or 1739, Yale University Art Gallery) are impressive but not beautiful.

In the mid-eighteenth century, many successful American colonists liked to think of themselves as English aristocrats. They patronized portraitists who painted in the English rococo style, such as John Wollaston and Joseph Blackburn. In *Mrs. Samuel Cutts* (ca. 1763, Metropolitan Museum of Art), Blackburn softened the face of his subject, eliminating all imperfections. Her delicate silks and lace seem appropriate for the mistress of an English manor house.

By the 1740s, America had its first well-known native-born artist. The most popular portraitist in the growing city of Boston, Robert Feke painted upper-class colonists who wished to be depicted as proper and prosperous Americans. Despite stiffness of pose, Feke's portraits are quite successful. In *Isaac Winslow* (1748, Museum of Fine Arts, Boston), for example, dramatic brilliance of color and texture overcome other technical defects.

American portrait painting really came into its own with John Singleton Copley, who combined realism with a gift for individual characterization. Copley's strongly modeled and richly colored forms convey depth naturally. The expressions he gave his sitters are relaxed and sympathetic.

Copley frequently showed his subjects caught momentarily at work or leisure. In *Mr. and Mrs. Thomas Mifflin* (1773, Historical Society of Pennsylvania), he communicates the easy mood of the couple, just interrupted at read-

Samuel Morse, *The Muse—Susan Walker Morse,* ca. 1835-1837, 73¾ x 57⅝ in. Courtesy of The Metropolitan Museum of Art, New York, New York. Bequest of Herbert L. Pratt, 1945.

Gilbert Stuart, *Mrs. Edward Tuckerman,* 28 x 22½ in. Courtesy of Vose Galleries of Boston, Inc., Massachusetts.

ing and weaving. Such complexity of composition and self-assured technique are virtually unknown in earlier American portraiture. The political unrest leading up to the American Revolution limited Copley's market, and in 1774 he settled permanently in England, where his style became more fluid and painterly.

Throughout the late 1770s and the 1780s, America's leading portraitist was Charles Willson Peale. Although the Revolution and its aftermath left little time for the fine arts, Peale turned this situation to his advantage and painted portraits of many of the heroes of the Revolution. Peale was a naturalist and inventor as well as an artist, and his portraits express his preference for practical experience. *Washington at the Battle of Princeton* (1779, Pennsylvania Academy of the Fine Arts), although it is dramatic, has no highly refined rococo qualities. His portraits of private individuals are equally reserved and direct, frequently with little emphasis on background. Of Peale's many artist-children, Rembrandt Peale was the one best known for his portraits.

In the early 1790s, American-born Gilbert Stuart returned to New York City after study in England. Under the influence of Joshua Reynolds and Thomas Gainsborough, Stuart had perfected a graceful portrait style that made him the new nation's premier portraitist until his death in 1828. Stuart painted for an age that valued the individual and took pride in its hard-won freedom. His portraits, characterized by fluent brushwork and warm colors, seem to reflect this self-confidence. He frequently simplified or eliminated backgrounds. Often he showed his subjects about three-quarter length, in straightforward and self-contained poses.

Stuart's portraits have often been described as "timeless." They are classical in simplicity but capture a sense of individual character. His several portraits of Washington, especially the *Landsdowne Portrait* (1796, Pennsylvania Academy of the Fine Arts) and the *Athenaeum Portrait* (1796, Museum of Fine Arts, Boston), have in fact served as timeless reminders of the president's likeness.

Stuart's success inspired several followers. At their best, they closely emulated Stuart's adroit brushwork and manner, but many developed more individual styles. Jacob Eichholtz and Chester Harding often gave their sitters a rather harsh appearance, while John Wesley Jarvis and Henry Inman added more liveliness to the Stuart formula. Jarvis's *Washington Irving* (1809, Sleepy Hollow Restorations) presents the author against a neutral background. But his hair is windblown and his dark eyes are unusually penetrating. The style is a romantic one that later became a hallmark of the paintings of Thomas Sully.

Sully was known as the "American Lawrence" for the elegant and dextrous style he had learned from the English master portraitist Thomas Lawrence. A new generation of patrons, encouraged by the American victory in the War of 1812, now enjoyed a national sense of well-being. Generally quite prosperous, they sought out Sully during his long career.

Some of Sully's portraits, especially those of fragile-skinned women, seem prettified. His men are stronger, and often seem to make a direct appeal to the viewer. *Joseph Dugan* (1818, National Gallery of Art), handsome and somewhat idealized, is casually posed, with his necktie informally disarranged. Like many Sully portraits, *Joseph Dugan* is characterized by the emotional and stylistic qualities of romanticism, a movement which became increasingly evident in America between 1810 and 1820. The interest in the individual as hero that had marked Stuart's age took a different turn; painters now tried to capture the private feelings of the individual. At the same time, interest in the expanding frontier's natural beauty made landscape painting paramount. Portrait painting in turn was affected by landscape's dramatic lighting and evocative atmosphere.

Many of the portraits of Samuel F.B. Morse have the hallmarks of fully developed romanticism. His *Marquis de Lafayette* (1826, Art Commission of New York) places the general before a glowing sunset. Nature is present in the wind that billows his cape. Lafayette seems lost in thought. Classical busts recall the faded glories of the past, a favorite romantic device.

John Neagle gained his reputation as a portraitist with *Pat Lyon at the Forge* (1826, Museum of Fine Arts, Boston). His debt to Sully is evident in the warm coloring and animated brushwork. The style is romantic, but the subject, a common worker, adds a realistic element.

Realism did continue to be a strong force in portraiture, as well as in American life. In the 1820s and 1830s, Jacksonian democracy emphasized the common, unvarnished man. Throughout the 1840s and 1850s the daguerreotype and the photograph, both eminently realistic media, gained popularity. During this period, portrait styles ranged from realistic to romantic to any combination of the two. In fact, mid-nineteenth-century artists are sometimes called romantic realists.

National prosperity created a large portrait clientele during the middle of the century. But quantity rather than quality was the chief characteristic of mid-century portraiture. Instead of a few masters like Copley, Stuart and Sully, America now produced numerous and frequently mediocre portraitists. Still, several had quite distinctive styles.

George Peter Alexander Healy became an international artist; at home in the United States, his work was regarded as very fashionable. During his European travels, Healy painted many portraits of notables and royalty, including *Franz Liszt* (1829, Newberry Library) and *Charles I, King of Roumania* (1881, Newberry Library). Despite his realistic attention to detail, Healy's color and mood are usually romantic.

Charles Cromwell Ingham was in great demand for portraits of women and girls. His highly glazed paintings were valued for their porcelain-like charm, which today seems overly sweet.

Charles Loring Elliott had a more energetic, direct style. The homely face of *Mrs. Thomas Goulding* (1858, National Academy of Design, New York) gives credibility

William Merritt Chase, *Mrs. Chase and Dana,* 60 x 40 in., signed l.r. Photograph courtesy of Borghi & Co. Fine Art Dealers, New York, New York.

Thomas Eakins, *The Honorable John A. Thorton,* 1903, 24 x 20 in., signed u.r. Courtesy of Frank S. Schwarz & Son, Philadelphia, Pennsylvania.

to the suggestion that Elliott was influenced by the daguerreotype.

After the Civil War, American contacts with Europe increased. The interchange also worked in the other direction—the Centennial Exposition at Philadelphia in 1876 presented European styles to a large American audience.

At this time, France and Germany were centers of art study; at the academy in Munich, for example, the curriculum emphasized the study of seventeenth-century Dutch and Spanish art, especially Hals and Velasquez. The styles that characterized European academies like the one in

Munich were brought back to the United States by American students and thus influenced American art.

One such student was Frank Duveneck, who adopted the dark palette and broad brushstroke of his German teachers and produced some of the first portraits to strike today's viewer as "modern." The broken planes of color do not so much describe form as create contrasts of light and dark. His *Munich Girl* (ca. 1878, Delaware Art Museum) emerges from a black background, her face defined by vigorous strokes of flesh tones.

William Merritt Chase was also trained in the German style, but he eventually developed a more versatile

Thomas Eakins, *The Cello Player,* 1896, 64⅛ x 48¼ in., signed l.r. Courtesy of The Pennsylvania Academy of the Fine Arts, Philadelphia; Temple Fund Purchase.

approach. His portraits became freer, brighter and more impressionistic than Duveneck's. With Chase the idea of "art for art's sake" enters American portraiture. Color and form serve aesthetic design more than realistic description. In *Miss Dora Wheeler* (1883, Cleveland Museum of Art), a spray of daffodils and a printed curtain backdrop compete for attention with the subject herself.

Thomas Eakins studied not only the paintings of the old masters but—just as important—human anatomy. Strong modeling gives his portraits a convincing physicality. Forms are firmly grounded in space, hands grasp objects with compelling realism, and faces are fully individualized. His portraits of his family and friends and of the intelligentsia of his native Philadelphia are sympathetic and moving. *Mrs. John H. Brinton* (1878, collection of Mrs. Rudolphe Meyer de Schauensee) wears an unreadable expression that makes her portrait seem all the more true-to-life. With Eakins, objective realism overtook the romantic realism of the earlier nineteenth century. He was one of America's great masters of portraiture.

Two stars of the international art world in the late nineteenth and early twentieth centuries were the American-born expatriates James Abbott McNeill Whistler and John Singer Sargent. Both were accomplished portraitists.

Whistler planned his portraits largely in terms of color relationships. The title of the famous painting of "Whistler's Mother" is *Arrangement in Gray and Black No. 1* (1871, Louvre). For his *Symphony in Flesh-Color and Pink: Mrs. F.R. Leyland* (1873, Frick Collection) Whistler chose a dress to harmonize with his subject's hair and a rose-tinted wall to complete the design.

Sargent enjoyed great success as a high-society portraitist. His painstaking method is belied by the appearance of an easy virtuosity. He added psychological insight to his mastery of opulent textures and colors. The extravagant brushwork and stunning whites of *Mr. and Mrs. I.N. Phelps Stokes* (1897, Metropolitan Museum of Art) strike the eye from well across the room. *Padre Sebastiano* (ca. 1905, Metropolitan Museum of Art) shows Sargent's ability to paint a more intimate, informal portrait.

In the last quarter of the nineteenth century, French impressionism affected a number of American artists, most notably Mary Cassatt. As an impressionist, she was chiefly concerned with light and color. Although they are not titled as such, many of Cassatt's domestic and genre scenes are actually portraits. (This became increasingly common as subject matter lost its primacy in painting.) Her *Lady at the Tea Table* (1883-1885, Metropolitan Museum of Art) portrays Mrs. Robert Moore Riddle. Neither the strong design element nor the blue color scheme overcomes the personality of the elderly, rather severe lady.

By the turn of the century, the National Academy of Design in New York City had set conservative standards for all types of painting. But in a New York exhibition of 1908, Robert Henri emerged as the leader of the anti-academic artists, who looked to seventeenth-century Dutch and Spanish art and to Manet for examples. They painted portraits of subjects ranging from wealthy matrons to street urchins.

Henri's *Kevin* (1928, High Museum of Art) and John Sloan's *Will Bradner* (1903, Delaware Art Museum) are typical of the work of these anti-academic painters in their neutral backgrounds, spontaneous brushwork and dark palettes. George Luks caught the rakish demeanor of *Otis Skinner as Colonel in "The Honor of the Family"* (1919, Phillips Collection).

Also in 1908, Alfred Stieglitz began to present the work of current European artists in his New York City gallery. By the time of the famous Armory Show in 1913, several American artists had been influenced by this avant-garde movement. Although portraiture was not their primary concern, some affecting portraits did come from this group during their long careers.

Alfred Maurer painted a cubist portrait of *George Washington* (1932, Portland Art Museum, Oregon). Marsden Hartley honored a Nova Scotia fisherman with the posthumous portrait *Adelard the Drowned, Master of the Phantom* (1938-1939, University of Minnesota, on extended loan from Ione and Hudson Walker). The blocky forms and simplified features of the latter work are clearly expressionistic.

In the 1920s and 1930s a trend toward social commentary, spurred by German art, produced several disturbing portraits. Ivan Albright made all his figures, including his *Self-Portrait* (1935, collection of Earle Ludgin), appear to be decaying. The accusing faces of *Nicola Sacco and Bartolomeo Vanzetti* (1932, Museum of Modern Art) by Ben Shahn are a challenge to American justice.

In another mode, the regionalist painters of the 1930s rejected European trends. Their portraits were less of individuals than of American character types. The best example is Grant Wood's *American Gothic* (1930, Art Institute of Chicago).

Several mid-twentieth-century artists have continued the portrait tradition. Although abstractionism for the most part eliminated the human figure, Larry Rivers painted an almost-abstract portrait of *Joseph H. Hirshhorn* (1963, Hirshhorn Museum and Sculpture Garden), in which Hirshhorn's face comes forth from an arrangement of flat color planes. Andrew Wyeth frequently uses his characteristic tempera or drybrush watercolor technique to depict his sitters in stark rural houses.

Perhaps the most prolific portraitist of recent years was Alice Neel, who painted many subjects from the art world. *Virgil Thompson* (1971, estate of Alice Neel) shows Neel's typical broad color areas and heavy outlining of forms.

For three centuries, then, portraits have preserved the private and public faces of Americans. Portraiture has proven to be both a durable and a durable type of American painting.

Mary F. Holahan is an art historian and registrar of the Delaware Art Museum in Wilmington, Delaware.

AMERICAN STILL-LIFE PAINTING

MARY JO VIOLA

William Michael Harnett, *Still Life: Letter to Mr. Lask,* 1879, 9 x 12 in., signed l.r. Courtesy of Kennedy Galleries, New York, New York.

If one discounts the books, flowers and bowls of fruit that appear as accessories in many colonial portraits, American still-life painting may be said to begin with the aesthetic which valued it least: neoclassicism.

American neoclassical artists at the beginning of the nineteenth century subscribed to a hierarchy of values that reflected not only current English taste but also ideas which could ultimately be traced back to the founding of the French Academy more than two centuries earlier. The hierarchy was headed by historical painting, which was followed by historical portraiture, historical landscape, landscape compositions, marine compositions, architectural paintings and animal paintings. Still life was among the least-valued modes, outranking only sketches and copies. Thus the grand historical canvases of West, Copley and Allston were ranked far above the still-life arrangements that Americans today find so appealing.

From the beginning, trompe l'oeil, a naturalistic "fool the eye" style, was an important aspect of American still-life painting. The Peales, who excelled at it, called it sim-

Charles Bird King, *Poor Artist's Cupboard*, ca. 1850, 29¾ x 27¾ in. In the collection of the Corcoran Gallery of Art, Washington, D.C., Museum Purchase, Gallery Fund and Exchange.

ply a "deception." The technical skill required for this high degree of imitation was admired, but by the time of its exponent William Michael Harnett it was sometimes dismissed as trickery.

In the early years of the nineteenth century, art writers tended to ignore still life, but exhibition catalogues indicate that still-life paintings were frequently shown in many exhibitions in American cities. The strongest tradition at this time was the table-top still life, practiced by numerous members of the Peale family. The "Peale family formula" consisted of an arrangement, on a simple horizontal support, of edibles, generally fruit or vegetables, augmented by china, glasses and knives. The illumination was usually a single source of light which divided the composition diagonally into light and dark halves.

The finest practitioner of this format, and the most neoclassical, was Raphaelle Peale, who may be considered the first master of American still-life painting. Raphaelle Peale favored the sweet fruits of summer, the season when nature is at its peak. On small wood panels and larger canvases, he painted perfect strawberries, raspberries, peaches, grapes and melons, as in *Fox Grapes and Peaches* (1815, Pennsylvania Academy of the Fine Arts). They were constructed with the geometric logic associated with neoclassicism. In addition, the fruit and its accompaniments—such as a small cake, a glass of wine, or a beautiful dish—were rendered with an intense, jewel-like clarity that gives them a power beyond the apparent simplicity and size of the subject.

With James Peale, Raphaelle's uncle, who took up the

John F. Peto, *Still Life: Candle,* 1901, 9 x 6 in., signed u.r. Courtesy of Frank S. Schwarz & Son, Philadelphia, Pennsylvania.

specialty late in his life, American still-life painting entered the romantic age. Painted mostly in the 1820s, the same decade as the early landscapes of Thomas Cole, James Peale's still-life paintings show a similar concern with temporality. In contrast to Raphaelle Peale, James Peale loved the irregular and the imperfect. In his "kitchen pictures," such as *Still Life: Balsam Apple and Vegetables* (ca. 1820, Metropolitan Museum of Art), he joyfully delineated the crinkles and warts of unglamorous vegetables. He preferred the fruits of autumn, apples and pears, and he piled heaps of produce on table-tops in a spirit of neobaroque, but incipiently rotting, abundance. The romantic emphasis on the passing of time is often further personalized by poignant inscriptions that refer to his age.

The still-life paintings of the Peales perfectly embody the modest, yet gracious, elegance that was the ideal in the early years of the American republic. The sustained attention of the Peale family to still life helped set the stage for its eventual acceptance and also created a Philadelphia tradition so strong that its reverberations continued to be felt until the end of the nineteenth century.

Charles Bird King, the Washington-based portraitist best remembered for his American Indian likenesses, was the most significant painter of still life outside the Peale tradition. His niche and cupboard paintings reveal an ironic sense of humor and seem to be precursors of the type of still life which was to become popular at the end of the century in the works of artists such as Harnett and Peto.

John F. Francis, *A Luncheon Table,* 1852, 25 x 30¼ in., signed l.r. Courtesy of Vose Galleries of Boston, Inc., Massachusetts.

In one of these paintings, *The Poor Artist's Cupboard* (ca. 1815, Corcoran Gallery of Art), King comments on the neoclassical hierarchy of painting as it relates to the artist's position in America. A notice for a sheriff's sale listing the contents of the artist's studio mentions *Fall of the Giants* and *View of Paradise,* 16 by 20 feet, subjects and sizes which satirically evoke the ambitions of a history painter. Books whose titles are legible within the jumble of the cupboard—*The Advantages of Poverty, Pleasures of Hope* and *Vegetable Diet*—suggest discontent with an aesthetic whose highest ideals offer the artist such meager financial rewards.

The 1830s saw a lull in still-life painting. Toward the middle of the century, however, although still life was not held in any greater esteem in the literature on art, more still-life paintings were appearing in exhibitions. In the late 1840s, when the American art unions raffled paintings through lotteries, still life prospered because it was an inexpensive—yet, as opposed to portraiture, agreeably impersonal—kind of painting to distribute.

By mid-century, still-life paintings had become larger and more elaborate, reflecting changing tastes and a greater degree of wealth and material comfort in America. Overall, the aesthetic which developed in the years before the Civil War was an optimistic expression of well-being, based on the perception of an abundant nature.

In traditional, yet distinctly individual, ways, John F. Francis and Severin Roesen best exemplify the bountiful mid-century still life. With John F. Francis, rich table-cloths replace the simple plank surfaces used by the Peales. Invitingly healthy fruits are combined with crackers, cheese, nuts, baskets and ornate Victorian china and tableware. Francis's arrangements often suggest a family meal, such as a luncheon—or at least a part of one, as in his "dessert pictures," which emphasize delicious-looking cakes, cookies, berries, sugar and cream served in equally attractive containers. Sometimes, as in *Luncheon Still Life* (ca. 1870, National Museum of American Art), Francis

Severin Roesen, *Still Life: Fruit,* 1854-1855, 30 x 40 in., signed l.r. Courtesy of The Pennsylvania Academy of the Fine Arts, Acquired by exchange through the gift of William C. Williamson and Henry S. McNeil and The Gilpin Fund.

introduced a view through a window onto an Edenic landscape, enhancing the feeling of material well-being.

In contrast to Francis's American vision, German-born Severin Roesen revived, in his multi-tiered fruit and flower pieces, the exuberant traditions of European baroque still life. He adapted these traditions to the Victorian taste for the extravagant.

The second half of the nineteenth century, however, was marked by an increasing sense of dissent, in America as well as in Europe. By the 1860s, American painting had moved in directions that differed profoundly from the norms of the first part of the century.

Americans were confronted in the 1860s with the reality of a divided nation. Although the actual events of the Civil War rarely became a major subject for painters, the war nevertheless had a deep effect on the American consciousness and contributed to a new mood of introspection. Celebrations of natural purpose were no longer convincing, and American painting lost its prewar aura of

optimistic innocence. Instead, artists created images expressive of a growing sense of isolation, sadness and fragility.

By 1870, there was no clear consensus on appropriate style or subject matter. For the rest of the century, still-life painting encompassed a wide variety of personal styles and a range of themes with increasingly private, rather than public, meanings.

One of these changes concerned portrayals of nature, which were influenced by the pre-raphaelite aesthetic philosophy of English critic John Ruskin. Ruskin fostered the study and acceptance of nature with a fervor that necessitated a re-evaluation of the format and status of the still life.

It became apparent that if one truly accepted nature, as Ruskin urged, then nature was manifest in the humble and insignificant, as well as in the grand and beautiful; in weeds, wildflowers and birds' nests, as well as in mountains and waterfalls. In a reversal of previous values, the

George C. Lambdin, *Roses,* 1882, 24 x 18 in., signed l.r. Courtesy of Frank S. Schwarz & Son, Philadelphia, Pennsylvania.

small still life thus became an appropriate vehicle for conveying the highest truths.

At their most intense, Ruskinian artists such as William Trost Richards favored a tight, dry style and close-up views of nature. Painters began to emphasize natural arrangements over manmade manipulations of nature displayed indoors. George Hall placed raspberries on a leaf on the ground; Andrew Way showed grapes still hanging on the vine; George Cochran Lambdin painted roses growing against a garden wall.

Although fruit paintings had predominated in the early part of the century, flower painting was an important specialty by the 1870s. The Victorian flower still life can be loosely allied to a sentimental symbolism, a "language of flowers," that was disseminated through popular literature. Floral dictionaries defined the flowers' meanings: daisies connoted beauty and innocence; hollyhocks, ambition; pansies, tender and pleasant thoughts; forget-me-nots, remembrance; and poppies, forgetfulness. Different varieties and colors of roses conveyed the nuances of love. Theoretically it was possible to construct a bouquet with a message based on the meanings of flowers, as some artists did.

The flower paintings of Martin Johnson Heade are the antithesis of these genteel bouquets of wholesome garden flowers. Heade chose instead to paint the orchid, an exotic hothouse flower fraught with a fragile sensuality, as in *Orchid and Hummingbirds* (Vose Galleries). Orchids had served as aphrodisiacs in antiquity and were considered so indelicate that they never appeared in the flower dictionaries. Heade combined them with hummingbirds and set them against a luxuriant, mist-filled Brazilian forest.

Heade's floral repertoire expanded to include passion-flowers, Cherokee roses and eventually magnolias. These he arranged on lush draped velvet, with a sense of languor that has suggested to more than one writer an odalisque reclining on a couch. Yet Heade's impassioned blossoms also partake of a scientific attitude. They are the heirs of

John La Farge, *Flowers on a Window Ledge,* ca. 1862, 24 x 20 in., signed l.c. In the collection of the Corcoran Gallery of Art, Museum Purchase, Anna E. Clark Fund.

illustrated botanical books and, for all their emotional qualities, they remain descriptive.

A far different attitude is embodied in the flower paintings of John La Farge. Although his style had its roots in realism, La Farge transcends the literal. Through the intermediary of French barbizon painting, La Farge transformed flower painting from description to poetic evocation, in a manner akin to the transformation in landscape painting brought about by his contemporary, George Inness.

Like James McNeill Whistler, La Farge was strongly affected by an admiration for oriental art. He absorbed the Eastern heritage of informed understatement that contributed to a mood of unfathomable mystery in the face of nature's complexities.

In *Flowers on a Window Ledge* (ca. 1862, Corcoran Gallery of Art), La Farge created a haunting image of delicate beauty, an image so deliberately still that a soft breeze seems to carry the perfumed air from the bowl of violets and roses toward the viewer. The dreamy, meditative mood of his water-lily paintings arises, in part, from his choice of the flower itself: the lotus, traditionally associated with mysticism.

The enthusiasm for flowers reached new heights with the impressionist movement. Impressionist painters created table-top flower paintings in a traditional manner, but they also merged the still-life format with landscape in works that celebrate the garden setting. Childe Hassam's *Poppies* (ca. 1890, private collection) pays lyrical tribute to the gardening skills of Celia Thaxter, whose island garden on Appledore, Isle of Shoals, New Hampshire inspired Hassam's paintings.

Flower paintings were concerned with imagery universally accepted as symbolic of the female. Other late-nineteenth-century still-life painters portrayed objects that evoked a male persona.

The most aggressively masculine still lifes are the trophy pictures. William Michael Harnett's rigorously controlled

Martin Johnson Heade, *Orchids and Hummingbirds,* 15⅝ x 20 in., signed l.l. Courtesy of Vose Galleries of Boston, Inc., Massachusetts.

vertical composition *After the Hunt* (1885, Fine Arts Museums of San Francisco) features a display of costly hunter's equipment and an array of dead game. The emphasis on masculine prowess, as well as the dark tonality, made *After the Hunt* (and paintings like it) particularly suitable for hanging in saloons.

Similarly, the hanging trout of Winslow Homer and the paintings of Richard La Barre Goodwin and George Cope suggest the outdoor sportsman's life as well as Darwinian notions of survival. The fish subjects of William Merritt Chase and Emil Carlsen, however, although they depict the catch, suggest more the comforts of unpretentious cookery. They are kitchen pictures in the earthy copper-pot-and-game tradition of Chardin, the eighteenth-century French painter whose works these artists admired.

The personal library as a solitary masculine preserve is a theme addressed by Harnett and his contemporary John Frederick Peto. The books in Harnett's pictures imply a literary antiquarian whose melancholy meditations on the transitory pleasures of life are filtered through classic authors like Dante, Tasso and Shakespeare. But the tattered books with illegible titles in the paintings of Peto indicate a personality at once more down-to-earth and more elusive. For both, the pipes and tobacco cannisters that accompany the books call forth an introspective male presence. This mood of reclusiveness, so characteristic of the post-Civil War period, has parallels in the work and lives of Winslow Homer, Thomas Eakins and Albert Pinkham Ryder.

Both Harnett and Peto painted letter-rack pictures, delineations of the office boards that were customarily hung in places of business. This was a specialty of Peto's; his rack pictures that include photographs of the brooding face of Lincoln convey a mournful sense of personal and national loss.

Emil Carlsen, *Still Life with Roses,* 1885, 26 x 36 in., signed l.r. Courtesy of Henry B. Holt, Inc., Essex Fells, New Jersey.

Harnett and Peto are often compared. At one time, in fact, a number of Peto's paintings, some with deliberately forged signatures, passed for Harnett's. The sensibilities of the two men, however, were very different. Harnett's style was clear and tight; he was master of a magical trompe l'oeil illusionism. Peto's realism, on the other hand, is tempered by a looser handling of paint, which seems deliberately to withhold information, as in the illegible titles of books. Peto's manner creates an atmosphere of mystery that has affinities with the general ambiguities of symbolist painting at the turn of the century.

The twentieth century fostered abstract styles, moving away from the naturalism that had nurtured the growth and acceptance of still life in America. Yet when Picasso made the shift from analytic to synthetic cubism, the change took place in still-life compositions. Still life remained a major vehicle of personal expression for many American modernists. One has only to consider the work of Patrick Henry Bruce, Marsden Hartley, Max Weber, Georgia O'Keeffe, Charles Demuth, Gerald Murphy and Stuart Davis, among others, to realize the intrinsic resilience of the still-life form.

Mary Jo Viola has taught at Hollins College in Virginia and Marymount College in Tarrytown, New York. She is currently at Baruch College, City University of New York, where she co-edited the art-history textbook *A World View of Art History: Selected Readings.* Viola holds an M.A. from the Institute of Fine Arts, New York University and an M. Phil. from The Graduate Center, City University of New York. Her specialty is nineteenth-century American art.

AMERICAN FOLK ART

ROBERT BISHOP AND HENRY NIEMANN

William Matthew Prior, *Unidentified Child,* 26¾ x 21¾ in. Courtesy of Museum of American Folk Art, New York, New York.

American folk art was first recognized and acknowledged by modern artists returning to the United States from Europe immediately after World War I. The artists were soon joined by scholars, art critics and art historians. Their attention was focused on paintings by members of the transplanted European cultures that from the earliest American colonization had perpetuated the social and artistic patterns of the Old World in isolated New World settlements: the English in New England and the South; the Dutch in the Hudson River Valley; the Germans in Pennsylvania; the Swedes in the Delaware River Valley; and the French in what is now Michigan and Louisiana. All these groups created paintings that closely mirrored the artistic conventions of their ancestors.

Portraiture developed as the most significant form of artistic expression in the small colonial towns which dotted the East coast in the seventeenth century. Two distinct styles of portraiture flourished in the declining years of the century.

The older had its origins in early England. Artists

Erastus Salisbury Field, *Portrait of a Mother and Daughter*, 35 x 38⅛ in. Photograph courtesy of Hirschl & Adler Galleries, Inc., New York, New York.

working in a medieval style generally focused on what they considered the essentials of a portrait—the subject's head and facial features. Their backgrounds were simplified and stylized. Some of these portraits, although they seem poorly drawn by academic standards, demonstrate a strong sense of characterization. The sitters often exude a remarkable presence.

A number of immigrant English painters introduced a new style of portraiture toward the end of the seventeenth century. They were familiar with concepts of painting established during the Renaissance, which were brought to England by Italian and Dutch artists who traveled and fulfilled commissions there in the last half of the seventeenth century. Artists working in this new mode

attempted to create accurate, realistic spatial relationships in their compositions.

Most folk painters of the seventeenth century in both New England and the South were English. Their technical abilities satisfied a clientele which, because of its geographic and cultural isolation, was perhaps somewhat less demanding than its European counterpart.

In the eighteenth and nineteenth centuries, many folk painters, who were for the most part self-taught, developed abilities which earned national and international reputations. Benjamin West, John Singleton Copley and other well-known artists began their careers as naive painters whose techniques were developed through personal experiment. In time, varying degrees of formal

Ruth W. and Samuel A. Shute, *Portrait of Eliza Gordon (Mrs. Zophar Willard Brooks)*, 1832-1833, 25 x 19½ in.
Courtesy of Museum of American Folk Art, New York, New York.

training enabled them to cast aside their folkish ways. But thousands of folk painters lacked the luxury of training like that available to West and Copley. Economic, cultural and social considerations prevented these folk artists from attaining the impressive stature of the recognized masters. Still they created art—great art which is only recently beginning to be fully appreciated.

Although much of the work of the untrained painters shows that they lacked technical competence, it demonstrates a power of observation, a brilliant sense of design and a wide range of imaginative vision. The folk art record of America was brushed with penetrating insight. During the nineteenth century, the folk artist caught the many faces of an optimistic, self-confident, expanding country.

Despite the fact that most country people lived simple, modest lives, they did not always lack pretension, and having a portrait painted was sometimes a way of satisfying social pretensions. Within the folk-art idiom, countless portrait artists earned their livings by traveling from town to town, recording the likenesses of all who could afford them. William Matthew Prior, Erastus Salisbury Field, Sturtevant J. Hamblen, J.A. Davis and Ruth W. and Samuel A. Shute are but a few of the better-known among them.

Prior began his career in Bath, Maine in the early nineteenth century; later he moved to Portland, Maine; finally he settled at 36 Trenton Street in Boston, Massachusetts,

Edward Hicks, *Penn's Treaty,* 18 x 24 in. Courtesy of Vose Galleries of Boston, Inc., Massachusetts.

Joseph Hoffman Johnson, *Washington at Valley Forge,* ca. 1850, 27 x 30 in., signed l.l. Courtesy of Raydon Gallery, New York, New York.

Anonymous, *Harbor Scene on Cape Cod,* 1880, 23 x 31¼ in. Courtesy of Museum of American Folk Art, New York, New York.

where he established his now-famous "Painting Garret." Prior adapted his technique to the potential sitter's financial means: a flat likeness "without shade" could be had for about one dollar. For more affluent subjects, he would provide surprisingly realistic portraits at prices as high as 25 dollars. Prior also practiced the art of reverse painting on glass. His likenesses of American Founding Fathers in this medium were exhibited at the Boston Athenaeum, where they were enthusiastically received by a public that marveled at the artist's special skills. Athenaeum officials were so impressed that they allowed him to copy Gilbert Stuart's portraits of George and Martha Washington from the permanent collection.

Most early folk landscapes and seascapes took the form of decorations on utilitarian objects such as fireboards, overmantels and paneled doors. These functional objects were produced throughout colonial America but were especially popular with the Dutch and English settlers. The Dutch brought to the Hudson Valley a love of genre painting, which flourished wherever they settled, and folk landscapes on utilitarian objects also began to appear in small numbers during the final decades of the seventeenth century in the English colonies.

Prints served as the primary design source for the struggling self-taught "landskip" painter. *The Graphice, or The Most Ancient and Excellent Art of Limning,* written by Henry Peachem and published in London in 1612, and *The Artist's Assistant in Drawing, Perspective, Etching, Engraving, Mezzotinto Scraping, Painting on Glass, in Crayons, in Watercolours, and on Silks and Satins, the Art of Japanning, etc.,* originally produced around 1750 by English publisher and print seller Carrington Bowles, provided a visual encyclopedia for the beginning artist who lacked access to formal training.

Although there are many categories of folk painting, historians and collectors have a special appreciation of the art created by the immigrants who, with brushes and paints, celebrated the personal and political freedoms of their adopted homeland. In the late 1700s and early 1800s, these artists rendered idealized portraits of political heroes, such as George Washington, and personifications of Liberty, Hope and Virtue. These were the same artists who painted numerous battle scenes of the American Revolution and the War of 1812 and carved ships' figureheads

Anonymous, *Along the Hudson,* ca. 1900, 16¾ x 23 in. Courtesy of Private Collection, Radnor, Pennsylvania.

in the form of Columbia. They celebrated America and its spirit.

Religion, too, has always been a major inspiration for the folk artist. From the first outpost settlements of the Spanish adventurers near Santa Fe, New Mexico in the late 1500s came a rich outpouring of artistic efforts designed to serve and propagate the Catholic faith. Three-dimensional sculptural pieces, wooden panels and animal hides decorated with painted representations of holy figures were used both in the home and in the church. These were initially created by the Franciscans, who in turn taught the converted Indians to execute religious works depicting Christ and the most important patron saints. Portraiture and landscapes, on the other hand, were rarely attempted in Spanish colonial North America.

In the Hudson Valley, the Dutch settlers between New York City in the South and Albany in the North commissioned an extensive body of highly significant religious art. Many Dutch immigrants adorned their walls with religious paintings based on the illustrations in Bibles brought from Holland. A number of these crude, vital pictures appear to have been executed by itinerant English painters, such as Nehemiah Partridge and other visiting portraitists.

During the opening years of the nineteenth century, culture-hungry Americans of financial means took great pride in their success. They sent their daughters to academies and finishing schools where the polite arts of needlework, music, dancing, writing and painting were major elements of the curricula. At precisely the same moment in history, the French and English romantic movements reached the American shores. Idealized pictures—moody, moonlit landscapes and romantic story paintings—emanated from these schools in astonishing numbers. Delicate watercolors rendered in incredible detail, picturesque landscapes filled with castles, and black-and-white and brightly colored thereoms (stencilled still lifes on canvas, velvet or paper) were also manifestations of the romantic spirit. A renewed interest in "religious" subjects led to untold numbers of watercolor and needlework pictures

Anonymous, *The White House,* 1855, 12¾ x 17¾ in. Courtesy of Museum of American Folk Art, New York, New York.

depicting Hope, Virtue and romanticized biblical scenes.

No discussion of folk painting in America would be complete without an acknowledgment of the contributions made by the furniture decorator. Folk furniture inevitably reflected the European tastes of earlier periods, when a furniture style emerging at an English or Continental court would almost immediately be adopted by the ruling classes. It would then filter down to the wealthier classes and ultimately to the lower classes. Immigrants to America brought with them these styles, which were incorporated into the designs of the leading cabinetmakers in the colonial cities. Once established in America's cosmopolitan centers, these designs were in turn adopted and adapted by rural craftsmen who, with great imagination, developed them into new forms. Folk furniture was almost always painted and very frequently decorated.

Most of the folk art of the twentieth century has been inspired by the same motivations that inspired the folk art of earlier periods. Portraiture has continued to flourish, and naive artists still attempt to record the world which surrounds them. The creation of utilitarian, functional objects which can be embellished and made more beautiful with decoration has certainly been a concern of the contemporary folk artist. Immigrants and the descendants of immigrants still use transplanted exotic designs and motifs which infuse America's artistic heritage with a unique blend of the old and the new.

Will American folk art continue to exist in the twenty-first century, despite the ongoing trend toward worldwide cultural homogenization? It seems almost certain the answer is yes. "Isolate" and "outsider" artists have increased in number; in recent years their paintings have found great favor with scholars and critics. Although magazines, newspapers and especially television have provided these artists with expanded visual references, they ignore the formal lessons of the contemporary art world. With inner vision and burning zeal, self-taught painters like Antonio Esteves, Mattie Lou O'Kelley, Jack Savitsky, Mose Tolliver, Nellie Mae Rowe, Philo Willey ("the Chief"), Sister Gertrude Morgan, John Serl and the Rev-

S. Halberg, *Lower Lake Champlain,* 1903, 11¼ x 16 in., signed l.r. Courtesy of Private Collection, Radnor, Pennsylvania.

erend Howard Finster "make" pictures that bring their private worlds to public eyes. They are sometimes difficult to understand, but these modern-day naives are the folk painters of our time. Their work is today's folk legacy for the future.

Robert Bishop is director of the Museum of American Folk Art in New York City. He has taught at the University of Michigan and New York University and has published several books on American furniture and folk art.

Henry Niemann is a collector of American folk art. He received a B.S. in Education from Hofstra University and an M.A. from New York University, where he is currently a Ph.D. candidate in American folk art studies. He is co-author of *Folk Art: Paintings, Sculpture and Country Objects,* published by Knopf Press.

BIOGRAPHIES

JOHN SMIBERT

(1688-1751)

A house painter at age 20, John Smibert was to become, by age 40, one of the best portrait painters in colonial America. From his base in Boston, Smibert painted some 275 portraits in 17 years, in the style of the old masters. He achieved an excellence rare in the new country.

Smibert grew up in Edinburgh, Scotland, apprenticed to a tradesman. But he had higher ambitions and at 20 set out for London to seek his fortune. He worked first as a coach painter, then as a copyist for London dealers. Through that experience and attendance at Sir James Thornhill's academy, Smibert learned how to draw.

When he went to Italy in 1719, Smibert began to develop his own techniques. For three years, he studied the old masters, copying Raphael and Titian, among others, and returning to London as a mildly successful portrait painter.

Smibert met George Berkeley, later Bishop of Cloyne, who sat for him in London. Berkeley was about to embark for Bermuda to establish a college to "civilize" the American Indians. In 1728 he invited the artist to teach the fine arts. He never reached Bermuda. The group landed at Newport, Rhode Island, the quixotic venture dead for lack of funds. Smibert went to Boston, married an heiress and became an overnight success.

His group portrait, *The Bermuda Group* (1729, Yale University), begun in London and completed in Boston, had no match in the colonies. Smibert's reputation as a leading portrait painter was established.

The painting of eight figures is balanced in composition and baroque in style. A central seated group forms a pyramid, flanked by standing figures on the side, including Smibert's self-portrait. Throughout his career, Smibert

Mrs. Louis Boucher (Sarah Middlecott), 1730, 51 x 40 in. Courtesy of The Henry Francis du Pont Winterthur Museum. Funds for purchase in part a gift of Mrs. Brooks Thayer.

followed the same style. His pose of a woman holding a child in her lap resembles Raphael's *Madonna*. By European standards, the work was imitative, but in America, a country of few artistic resources, Smibert stood out for his high style.

He also opened an artist's shop, imported engravings and casts of Renaissance works, and organized the first American art exhibition. Moreover, he was the architect of Boston's famed Faneuil Hall in 1742. Late in his career, with his eyesight failing, Smibert turned to landscape painting.

SEASON	75-76	76-77	77-78	78-79	79-80	80-81	81-82	82-83	83-84	84-85
Paintings		1	1		1	1		2		1
Dollars		$10,300	$2,865		$2,100	$2,856		$5,615		$6,600

Record Sale: $10,300, C, 3/18/77, "Portrait of Edward Nightingale," 49 × 39 in.

PUBLIC COLLECTIONS
Yale University

43

ROBERT FEKE
(1708?-1751?)

Little is known about the life of Robert Feke, although he was among the most important colonial portrait painters of the generation before John Singleton Copley. It is conjectured that he was born around 1708 in Oyster Bay, Long Island to a Baptist family. His artistic career seems to have spanned merely a decade, from 1741 to his death in around 1751. Some 60 portraits survive.

Feke's early portraits show the influence of John Smibert, particularly with respect to the figures and their poses. An example is the many-figured *Isaac Royall and His Family* (1741, Harvard University), whose composition is clearly dependent on Smibert's *Bermuda Group* (1729, Yale University).

But the *Royall* portrait also reflects the style Feke would develop throughout his career: vivid color; preference for flattened shapes over sculptural ones; emphasis on surface patterns, details and textures of clothes and furnishings; and a compositional style in which taut, delineated forms relate to one another in a flowing, rigorously geometrical way.

Later works, such as *Tench Francis* (1746, Metropolitan Museum of Art) and *Unknown Woman* (1748 to 1750, Brooklyn Museum), demonstrate Feke's mature style. The former incorporates within the landscape background a descriptive view of the subject's home; the latter is an excellent example of the baroque, sensual portraits of women for which the artist became famous.

Generally less a student of character than of design, Feke nonetheless produced a number of psychologically probing portraits, among the best of which are *Reverend Thomas Hiscox* (1745) and *Isaac Winslow* (ca. 1748, Museum of Fine Arts, Boston).

Feke was a decided itinerant. Between 1741 and 1750, he spent time in Newport, Rhode Island; Boston, Massachusetts; Philadelphia, Pennsylvania; and Willingboro, New Jersey. The last record

Margaret McCall, 1749, 49¾ x 39¾ in. Courtesy of Vose Galleries of Boston, Inc., Massachusetts.

of Feke is from 1751, when he attended his nephew's Rhode Island wedding. He then disappeared. In 1767, his family received notice of his death some years earlier.

PUBLIC COLLECTIONS
Bowdoin College, Brunswick, Maine
Brooklyn Museum of Art
Cleveland Museum of Art
Harvard University
Metropolitan Museum of Art, New York City
Redwood Library, Newport, Rhode Island
Rhode Island School of Design, Providence
Yale University

SEASON	75-76	76-77	77-78	78-79	79-80	80-81	81-82	82-83	83-84	84-85
Paintings		1								
Dollars		$445								

Record Sale: $445, B, 2/17/77, "Portrait of Mrs. J. Hedges-Cooper," 37 x 29 in.

JOSEPH BADGER
(1708-1765)

Joseph Badger, an early New England portraitist, was active in Boston during a lull in competition from other painters. The least sophisticated of all the early portraitists, Badger had a fair number of prominent sitters, in spite of his plain style and awkward composition. Authorities assume he prospered when more talented artists left the city or died. (John Smibert became blind one year before Badger began his major work in 1750.)

Badger had no formal training in art. Working as a house painter and glazier, he moved from his hometown of Charlestown, Massachusetts to Boston in 1731. Beginning portraiture as a sideline in 1740, Badger used as models black-and-white mezzotint reproductions of the work of English painters, including Kneller. He adapted these models to his own literal, naive techniques, losing most of the subtleties of the English work; his colors are unsophisticated.

His portraits are three-quarter length, often somewhat wooden. For background, Badger apparently copied from source material, placing a water view here and a clump of trees there, without integrating the details into the overall scheme. Nevertheless, Badger's plain, direct style has a particular appeal in his depiction of elderly subjects. He painted even wealthy women without ornaments or rich drapery, giving the effect of puritanical severity.

Seventy-five portraits by this artist have been identified.

Hannah Kent, 50 x 40 in., Private Collection, Photograph courtesy of Vose Galleries of Boston, Inc., Massachusetts.

PUBLIC COLLECTIONS
Bowdoin College, Brunswick, Maine
Worcester Art Museum, Massachusetts

SEASON	75-76	76-77	77-78	78-79	79-80	80-81	81-82	82-83	83-84	84-85
Paintings				1						
Dollars				$1,900						

Record Sale: $1,900, SPB, 2/2/79, "Mrs. John Marston," 46 × 35 in.

JEREMIAH THEUS
(1716-1774)

Portraits of leading families in late colonial South Carolina and Georgia were the province of Jeremiah Theus.

The artist was born in 1716 in Chur, Switzerland. His family, including two brothers, Christian and Simon, came to South Carolina and settled in Orangeburg Township about 1735. On September 6, 1740, in the *South-Carolina Gazette,* Theus advertised his services as "a Limner" who would draw portraits, "Landskips," and crests and coats of arms for coaches. He was an immediate success—although he had little or no competition in the area.

Although John Wollaston and Henry Benbridge painted some portraits during brief visits, Theus already was firmly ensconced as the region's established artist. For 30 years, he traveled from his Charleston home and studio to paint his subjects at plantations and towns as far north as Georgetown, South Carolina, south to Savannah, Georgia and as much as 100 miles inland.

Theus's portraits are not great, but they are competent, with some distinctive touches—enough to indicate some art training, perhaps in his native Switzerland.

His figures are unrelievedly rigid. Judging from the clothes of his sitters, often identical fold-for-fold, Theus did a great deal of copying from engravings.

The portraits are executed with attention to detail and characteristic uncompromising, often unflattering, candor. There is a sameness in the features of both men and women that makes Theus's work instantly identifiable. The close-set eyes and long noses, the elongated distance between eyes and chin, and the mouths curved in similar tight manner make all of his subjects appear to be close relatives.

In 1744, Theus opened an evening drawing school for "all young gentlemen and ladies inclinable to be taught." He prospered in his long and busy career.

Polly Ouldfield of Winyah, ca. 1761, 30⅛ x 25¼ in. Courtesy of National Museum of American Art, Smithsonian Institution, Museum Purchase.

He purchased a brick house for 2,000 pounds in 1755, selling it later for 8,000 pounds and buying another in 1760. He eventually owned seven slaves.

When he died in 1774, the *Gazette* noted his passing: "On Wednesday last died a very ingenious and honest man."

PUBLIC COLLECTIONS
Detroit Institute of Arts
Telfair Academy of Arts and Sciences, Savannah, Georgia
Joseph Manigault House, Charleston, South Carolina
Minneapolis Institute of Arts, Minnesota
National Gallery of Art, Washington, D.C.

(No sales information available.)

ROBERT EDGE PINE
(1720?-1788)

In 1784, illustrious British painter Robert Edge Pine came to America, intent on becoming the premier visual chronicler of the American Revolution.

Four years later, Pine was dead of apoplexy. Further, an 1803 fire destroyed a great portion of his life's work and contributed to historians' neglect of Pine and his art.

London-born sometime in the 1720s into the artistic family of engraver John Pine, Pine was a soundly trained artist of great ability. By the 1760s, he was a master at luminously rich, dramatic portraits in the grand manner that was then favored. He painted estimable portraits of George III, actor David Garrick, and the Duke of Northumberland, among other notables, and earned prizes for his historical designs.

Pine was a serious rival of Sir Joshua Reynolds, court artist and first president of the Royal Academy. He was conspicuously absent from the list of the Academy's founding members in 1769, possibly because of Reynolds's jealousy and possibly because of Pine's outspoken support of the American Revolution.

Despite his ability, Pine's personal attributes may have worked against him then and later. Contemporaries described him as extremely small, irritable, argumentative and unpleasantly temperamental.

In Bath, England, from 1772 to 1780, Pine turned increasingly to painting historical themes, though in this effort he failed to approach Benjamin West's popularity. After an unsuccessful showing in a 1782 London exhibition, Pine sought introductions to help him establish himself in America.

Pine arrived in Philadelphia during the summer of 1784, amid a stir of interest; he brought 27 paintings to exhibit. His family did not join him until a year and a half later.

Portrait of Aaron Levy, 29⅛ x 23⅝ in.
The Historical Society of Pennsylvania.

The public display of his art at Independence Hall in 1784 is considered America's first one-man show and it had what was probably the first published exhibition catalogue. Two years later, Pine opened a large studio and exhibition hall in his own home.

Of the historical scenes painted there and in Independence Hall, none remain. Pine's unfinished *Congress Voting Independence* is known only through an uninspired copy and engraving by Edward Savage. It is notable for its accuracy; Pine painted the original directly from life. John Trumbull's idealized, less accurate treatment of the subject is better known.

Supporting himself by teaching, Pine continued to paint leading patriots. His portraits of George Washington, painted from life during a three-week stay at Mount Vernon, and of Francis Hopkinson and Samuel Vaughn are among his best known.

Pine sometimes used a common English timesaving device, painting the sitter's head from life on a small canvas but pencil-sketching the body, to be finished later, often by others. An X-ray of Pine's portrait of General William Smallwood (date unknown, National Gallery) reveals a separately painted face pieced into place.

This technique sometimes created problems. According to Charles Willson Peale, Pine asked Peale to correct details on Smallwood's uniform, as well as to alter unflattering aspects of the figure to satisfy the general's vanity.

Some believe that Pine, had he lived, might have matched or surpassed Gilbert Stuart. Others see in his American paintings a decline from his best English work.

All agree he was a superb colorist. Pine's paintings went on display two years after his death in Bowen's Colombian Museum in Boston, where artist Washington Allston, noted for his artful use of pigment, called them "my first masters."

SEASON	75-76	76-77	77-78	78-79	79-80	80-81	81-82	82-83	83-84	84-85
Paintings								1	1	2
Dollars								$1,400	$4,726	$5,912

Record Sale: $4,726, C, 5/21/84, "Portrait of Lord Amherst," 49 × 38 in.

MEMBERSHIPS
Royal Academy

PUBLIC COLLECTIONS
Independence Hall, Philadelphia
National Portrait Gallery, Washington, D.C.

WILLIAM WILLIAMS
(1727-1791)

William Williams is credited with two notable contributions to the development of portrait painting in America: the introduction of Benjamin West to painting as a boy of nine; and the popularization of "conversation piece" portraits—full-length group portraits in a landscape or room setting—which were common in England at the time.

Aside from a reference to him in West's writings, little was known about Williams until the mid-1930s when, one by one, portraits painted by him began to be positively identified. They exhibit considerably more skill in composition and execution than most portraits of that period.

He was born in Bristol, England, in 1727, the son of a sailor, and shipped out as an apprentice seaman as a teenager. Whether he was self-taught as a painter or where he might have received some training is unknown. At age 20 he was painting portraits in Philadelphia. One of his clients, Samuel Shoemaker, asked him to show a work he had just finished to young Benjamin West. It was the first painting the boy had ever seen.

Williams took an interest in the lad and lent him some of his own books on art. He also showed him other paintings and gave him some instruction. Most important, he advised West's family to encourage the boy's interest in painting. In later years West wrote, "Had it not been for him I should never have become a painter."

Some accounts report that in 1759 Williams was one of the builders of the first theater in Philadelphia and that he painted scenery for it. Other accounts, however, put him in New York City from 1757 to 1760. He also spent several years painting in Jamaica.

In the late 1760s, Williams painted several highly stylized allegorical works. One of them, *Woman with a Book* (1767, Deerfield Academy), depicts an Old Testament sibyl in oriental dress

The Denning Family, 1772, 35½ x 52 in., signed l.r. Courtesy of Hirschl & Adler Galleries, Inc., New York, New York.

against a rocky landscape with a synagogue in the background.

His most important works, however, were his full-length portraits, such as *Conversation Piece* (1775, Winterthur Museum), which shows a gentleman and lady in a park setting that seems almost theatrical. His portraits were unsophisticated, yet showed imagination. He liked to use strong colors and elegant accesso-

ries, with landscape backgrounds that reflected his English heritage.

Along with writing an autobiographical novel, *The Journal of Llewellyn Penrose, a Seaman,* Williams continued to paint in the colonies through 1775. It is believed that he returned to his native Bristol in 1776 and spent the last years before his death in 1791 at the Merchants' and Sailors' Almshouse. While there he painted a revealing *Self-Portrait* (date unknown, Winterthur Museum).

PUBLIC COLLECTIONS
Brooklyn Museum
Newark Museum, New Jersey
Winterthur Museum, Delaware
Yale University Art Gallery, New Haven, Connecticut

SEASON	75-76	76-77	77-78	78-79	79-80	80-81	81-82	82-83	83-84	84-85
Paintings									1	3
Dollars									$1,050	$5,358

Record Sale: $2,940, S, 10/24/84, "Portraits of J. Jiffard and His Wife," 50 × 39 in.

JOHN GREENWOOD
(1727-1792)

To the modern eye, it may seem surprising that John Greenwood was one of the most important portrait painters in Boston during the brief time he painted there. Greenwood came by his profession like most American painters of his time, through the trades, rather than through the academic route of the European painter. Born in Boston in 1727, he was apprenticed to a sign painter and engraver in the 1740s and started painting portraits in 1745. Greenwood's pictures from that period show the technique of the sign painter, with flat space, bright colors, and awkward poses.

One reason for Greenwood's success was that he had little competition; but during the decades before the American Revolution, colonial Americans wanted very much to emulate their cosmopolitan English counterparts. The only information about current art to which they had access came from engraved copies of the more popular oil paintings in England. Greenwood had access to these engravings, borrowing his sophisticated poses and opulent settings from them and thus satisfying his sitters' social aspirations.

Despite his success in Boston, Greenwood seemed to share his compatriots' perception of America as a second-rate place to be. In 1752, he shipped to Surinam as a clerk, where he continued to paint more than 100 portraits and one genre piece. In 1758 he went to Holland, where he mastered the then-important technique of mezzotint engraving. Finally he landed in England and stayed there, making a good living as an art dealer and occasional painter of portraits and landscapes, until his death in Margate in 1792.

Greenwood's painting style became considerably more polished and subtle during these later years, and doubtless he considered himself to have achieved the pinnacle of success. Yet it is for his early, awkward, raw paintings that he is

Mrs. Welshman, 1749, 36 x 28 in., signed c.l. Courtesy of National Gallery of Art, Washington, D.C., Gift of Edgar William and Bernice Chrysler Garbisch.

remembered; they have a provincial charm that his later pictures lack.

PUBLIC COLLECTIONS
St. Louis Museum, Missouri
New-York Historical Society, New York City

SEASON	75-76	76-77	77-78	78-79	79-80	80-81	81-82	82-83	83-84	84-85
Paintings										1
Dollars										$850

Record Sale: $850, SPB, 12/8/84, "Portrait of Judge Robert Brown," 36 × 28 in.

JOHN HESSELIUS
(1728-1778)

John Hesselius, one of the last baroque colonial painters, was born in 1728. He became a leading portrait painter in the Mid-Atlantic colonies.

He first studied under his father, Gustavus, a Swedish-born painter of portraits and religious and mythological subjects. The Hesselius family lived for a while in Philadelphia, where John Hesselius was exposed to the work of Robert Feke, which influenced Hesselius's early work.

His later work may have been influenced by British painter John Wollaston. Some portraits show Wollaston-like facial styling, particularly in the complacent expression, almond-shaped eyes and curious diagonal tilt of the head.

During his most active period, from 1750 to 1763, Hesselius produced portraits for patrons from Pennsylvania, Delaware, Maryland and Virginia.

Charles Calvert (1761, Baltimore Museum of Art) is Hesselius's most famous portrait. The artist posed his five-year-old subject as if he were a general in command of his troops, although he is attended only by his black slave. Traces of Wollaston's influence are again seen in Hesselius's choice of warm tones, and in the diagonal tilt of the heads. Yet the portrait shows the artist's individual style in form and presentation.

In later works, mannerism gives way to strong, honest realism. Like his father, Hesselius is thought to have painted religious and classical subjects. However, only his portraits have been authenticated. Nearly 100 of them survive.

Hesselius traveled infrequently after his 1763 marriage to a wealthy Annapolis woman. Instead, he lived like a country gentleman on his estate, "Bellefield." It was there, in 1763, that Hesselius gave instruction to Charles Willson Peale.

Hesselius died and was buried at "Bellefield" in 1778.

Mrs. Richard Brown, ca. 1760, 30⅛ x 25⅛ in. Courtesy of National Museum of American Art, Smithsonian Institution, Purchased in memory of Ralph Cross Johnson.

PUBLIC COLLECTIONS
Baltimore Museum of Art
National Portrait Gallery, Washington, D.C.
Pennsylvania Academy of the Fine Arts,
    Philadelphia
Philadelphia Museum of Art
Winterthur Museum, Delaware

SEASON	75-76	76-77	77-78	78-79	79-80	80-81	81-82	82-83	83-84	84-85
Paintings					1					
Dollars					$32,000					

Record Sale: $32,000, S.W, 9/23/79, "Portraits of William & S.F. Knox," 30 × 25 in.

JOHN WOLLASTON
(Active 1733-1767)

The work and success of British painter John Wollaston, who completed more than 300 portraits during a mid-eighteenth-century decade, are said to have greatly influenced many American painters—Benjamin West, Matthew Pratt, and John Hesselius among them.

Wollaston's place and date of birth are not known; it is speculated because of his evident training that he was the son of a portraitist, or possibly of a professional "drapery painter" who specialized in doing the costumes and details of portraits by other painters.

Wollaston is known to have been painting in London by 1733 (series at Bodleian Library, Oxford). In 1749, he came to America and lived until 1752 in New York City, one of the first painters of significance to work there.

He worked in Maryland (1753 to 1754), in Virginia (1755 to 1757) and in Philadelphia (1758 to 1759), before interrupting his career to travel with the British East India Company to Bengal. He returned in January 1767, to Charleston, where he made about 20 portraits. In May of that year, he left for England; little more is known of him.

Wollaston was an accomplished practitioner of the British mode: large canvases displaying the subject with appropriate formality for flattering result, rather than capturing individual character.

He endowed all of his sitters with a fashionable almond-eyed look, and their dress and expressions seldom varied in style. These mannerisms did not affect his popularity. Wollaston's great skill in rendering the richness of silks, velvets, lace and other details of dress, the elegance of his chosen set of poses, the impressiveness of the whole—all must have appealed to the status-consciousness of the new gentry.

Wollaston left an invaluable record of colonial aristocracy, with surviving portraits of members of virtually every leading family of the day. His portrait of

Mary Walton Morris, 1749-1752, 30⅛ x 25⅛ in. Courtesy of National Gallery of Art, Washington, D.C., Andrew W. Mellon Collection.

Martha Washington was engraved, and Francis Hopkinson wrote a complimentary verse about the artist in *American Magazine* in the fall of 1758.

Wollaston had great success in attracting commissions. This, as well as his unquestioned ability as a painter, won the admiration of his fellow portraitists.

PUBLIC COLLECTION
Bodleian Library, Oxford, England
National Gallery, Washington, D.C.
New-York Historical Society, New York City

SEASON	75-76	76-77	77-78	78-79	79-80	80-81	81-82	82-83	83-84	84-85
Paintings								1		
Dollars								$12,000		

Record Sale: $12,000, CH, 6/3/83, "Mr. & Mrs. Brandt Schuyer," 28 x 22 in.

MATTHEW PRATT
(1734-1805)

Matthew Pratt, a significant painter of the Revolutionary period, enjoyed considerable success as a portraitist. He is even better known as a painter of artistically distinguished signs.

Born in Philadelphia in 1734, Pratt was apprenticed to his uncle, James Claypoole, Sr., a journeyman artist and dealer in colors. When Pratt began his professional career in the mid-1750s, his aptitude gained him a fairly steady flow of commissions.

It happened that a relation of Pratt's—a Miss Shewell—was engaged to Benjamin West, the young expatriate painter who had become a favorite of the English court. In 1764, Pratt accompanied his relative to her wedding in London, gave the bride away, and stayed on to become West's first American pupil.

Although experienced and four years older than West, Pratt eagerly learned West's popular neoclassical techniques. Living in West's household for two and a half years, Pratt became so adept as a studio assistant that it was difficult to tell his work from West's.

In this period, Pratt produced his most famous painting, *The American School* (1765, Metropolitan Museum of Art). The group portrait depicts West critiquing work by Pratt and three other students, including Pratt's fellow American, Abraham Delanoy.

Beyond its historical interest, the picture displays elements of Pratt's intrinsic style. West's influence is seen in the static precision of the figures, and his Colonial training in the sharp definition of line. However, the subtle use of color, the intelligent organization of space and authentic skill in design, the subordination of the figures to a compositional whole, are Pratt's own.

After 18 months as an independent portraitist in Bristol, England, Pratt came back to America for two years' work in New York City and Philadel-

The Duke of Portland, ca. 1774, 30 x 25 in. Courtesy of National Gallery of Art, Washington, D.C., Gift of Clarence Van Dyke Tiers.

phia. After another two years in England and Ireland, he returned finally in 1768, working in New York and Virginia.

The *Virginia Gazette* of March 4, 1773, advertised a show of Pratt's work in the King's Arms Tavern at Williamsburg. Listed is a copy of Correggio's *St. Jerome,* one of Pratt's exercises in West's studio.

Settled in Philadelphia by 1785, Pratt continued to do well at portraiture, but the painters who were to dominate the Federalist period—Charles Willson Peale, Gilbert Stuart, John Trumbull—were also active.

Though well known, Pratt may not have been inclined to join the newly fierce battle for portrait commissions. Contemporaries described Pratt as mod-

est, friendly and likeable, with an unaffected dignity.

It was the heyday of sign-painting in the bustling post-war capital. Pratt began to paint them with the skill in composition and color that he brought to his portraits, raising the signs to the level of art and gaining a new public prominence. Painter John Neagle (1796 to 1865) wrote that Pratt's signs—"broad in effect and loaded with color"— made him want to become an artist.

Most notable was Pratt's *Federal Convention of 1788.* The large sign, at the corner of Fourth and Chestnut Streets, included likenesses of the conventioners; it attracted crowds of passersby and remained on display until 1814.

Pratt, who continued to paint well into the 1790s, died in 1805 in his native Philadelphia.

SEASON	75-76	76-77	77-78	78-79	79-80	80-81	81-82	82-83	83-84	84-85
Paintings								1		
Dollars								$22,000		

Record Sale: $22,000, 6/3/83, CH, "Portrait of Abigail Willing," 29 x 25 in.

PUBLIC COLLECTIONS
Metropolitan Museum of Art, New York City
National Gallery of Art, Washington, D.C.
New York Chamber of Commerce
Pennsylvania Academy of the Fine Arts,
  Philadelphia

JOHN SINGLETON COPLEY
(1738-1815)

John Singleton Copley was significant on three different levels: as the preeminent artist in Colonial America; as one of the most distinguished portrait painters in England, along with Sir Joshua Reynolds and Thomas Gainsborough; and as a history painter who influenced the work of Eugene Delacroix and Theodore Gericault.

His portraits from the 1760s and early 1770s are among the finest examples of early American art. Usually of prominent men and women, they are solid, insightful and full of sharp detail, as in *Paul Revere* (1765, Museum of Fine Arts, Boston). Copley's talent for rendering textures was remarkable, and reached its full development as his style became more ornate.

Copley was born in 1738. His father died shortly after his birth. His mother ran a tobacco shop at Long Wharf on Boston Harbor. In 1748, she married Peter Pelham, a portrait painter and mezzotint engraver. Copley learned from his stepfather.

He also observed the methods of other artists of the time—John Greenwood, Robert Feke and Joseph Blackburn. By age 19, Copley was already established.

Benjamin West saw *Boy with a Squirrel* (1765, location unknown), which Copley had sent to London in 1766 for exhibition, and encouraged Copley to study in Europe. But Copley married in 1769, moving into a mansion on Boston's Beacon Hill.

John Gardiner, 48 x 38¾ in. Photograph courtesy of Hirschl & Adler Galleries, Inc., New York, New York.

By 1774, the American Revolution was in the offing; Copley's clients were sometimes Whig and sometimes Tory. It seemed a good time to fulfill his dream of going to Europe.

He started with a Grand Tour of Italy, France, Germany and the Netherlands, studying and copying the old masters.

When his family arrived in London he demonstrated the results of his studies by painting *The Copley Family* (date and location unknown), which was sent to the Royal Academy exhibition of 1777. It was executed in the elaborate, artificial "Grand Manner" prevalent in London at that time. Copley was highly successful as a portraitist in London.

Yet, he most wanted to be a history painter; his *Watson and the Shark* (1778, National Gallery of Art) has a rich history of its own. Copley painted an incident from the youth of a local merchant who was attacked by a shark, and lost his leg while swimming in Havana Harbor. Watson became a successful politician, and Copley's painting made a sensation in 1778 at the Royal Academy.

Another masterwork, *The Death of the Earl of Chatham* (1779, Tate Gallery), depicted the stroke that felled William Pitt in the House of Lords in 1778. Copley exhibited the painting and charged admission. Likenesses of nearly 50 peers appeared in the painting.

Copley continued to paint until about 1811, but his later paintings do not show the force of his earlier work. He died in London in 1815.

MEMBERSHIPS
Royal Academy

PUBLIC COLLECTIONS
Metropolitan Museum of Art, New York City
Museum of Fine Arts, Boston
National Academy of Design, New York City
National Gallery of Art, Washington, D.C.
Tate Gallery, London

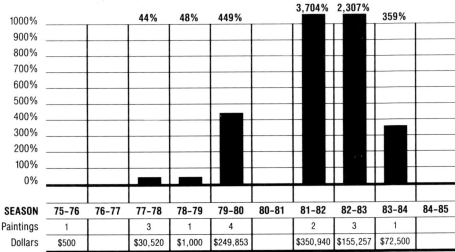

10-Year Average Change From Base Years '75-'76: 987%

SEASON	75-76	76-77	77-78	78-79	79-80	80-81	81-82	82-83	83-84	84-85
			44%	48%	449%		3,704%	2,307%	359%	
Paintings	1		3	1	4		2	3	1	
Dollars	$500		$30,520	$1,000	$249,853		$350,940	$155,257	$72,500	

Record Sale: $350,000, CH, 11/12/81, "Portraits of Mr. J. Henshaw and Wife," 30 x 26 in.

BENJAMIN WEST
(1738-1820)

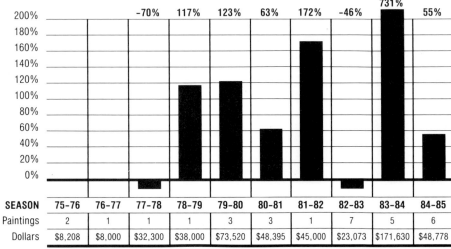

10-Year Average Change From Base Years '75-'76: 115%

SEASON	75-76	76-77	77-78	78-79	79-80	80-81	81-82	82-83	83-84	84-85
			-70%	117%	123%	63%	172%	-46%	731%	55%
Paintings	2	1	1	1	3	3	1	7	5	6
Dollars	$8,208	$8,000	$32,300	$38,000	$73,520	$48,395	$45,000	$23,073	$171,630	$48,778

Record Sale: $150,000, SPB, 5/30/84, "Study for the Death of General Wolfe," 17 x 24 in.

Helen Brought to Paris, 1776, 56½ x 75⅜ in., signed l.r. Courtesy of National Museum of American Art, Smithsonian Institution, Museum Purchase.

Despite the fact that he spent almost all his adult life in London and painted for the British crown, Benjamin West is generally acknowledged as the "father of American painting" because of his influence on his contemporaries and on later generations of American painters. Even as an expatriate, West was largely responsible for transforming the comparatively primitive American portraiture into artistic achievement with true sophistication. Even more, he revolutionized historical painting by daring to depict his subjects in the uniforms and dress of their day, rather than in the classical robes of antiquity.

West was born near Philadelphia in 1738, the son of a stagecoach innkeeper. Even as a child he showed an interest in sketching people. He saw his first portrait when the self-taught, English-born portraitist William Williams showed him a painting he had recently finished. Williams took an interest in the boy and lent him books on art, the first West had ever seen. Perhaps most important, Williams encouraged West's parents to nurture his talent. West later declared that he would not have become a painter had it not been for Williams.

By his mid-teens, West was already painting portraits in Lancaster, Pennsylvania, showing a mature instinct for modeling, form and pattern. Before age 20 he had completed his first history painting, *The Death of Socrates* (ca. 1756, private collection), the only such signed work he painted in America. Within a few years a group of Philadelphia merchants had raised a subscription fund to send young West to Europe to study, hoping to make him America's first truly professionally trained painter.

When he arrived in Rome West caused a stir immediately; the aristocrats and princes of the Church had expected some sort of noble savage from the wilderness and discovered instead a composed, intelligent and highly articulate young man. After three years of study in Italy, he traveled through France to London, arriving there in 1763.

The biblical and classical scenes he had painted in Italy brought West instant attention in London. When the Royal Academy was founded in 1768, he was a charter member. That same year he painted *Agrippina with the Ashes of Germanicus* (1768, Yale University) for the Archbishop of York. This impressive work brought him both the patronage and the friendship of the king, George III, which lasted for 40 years.

His *Death of Wolfe* (1771, National Gallery of Canada) created a sensation when it was exhibited because of its realism. Showing the death of a British general in the French and Indian War, it was the first history painting on the grand scale that was not transformed into a classical allegory.

West was known for his tact and civility, which enabled him to retain his close relationship with the king even during the American Revolution. West made no secret of his support for the cause of independence and at times counseled the monarch on the rebel viewpoint, but never lost royal favor.

When Sir Joshua Reynolds died in 1792, West was elected president of the Royal Academy and, except for one term, from 1805 to 1807, held the prestigious post until his death in 1820.

West was prodigiously generous with his time and in the course of his long life instructed and guided a legion of young American painters who flocked to London to study. Among them were Gilbert Stuart, John Trumbull, Charles Willson Peale, Rembrandt Peale, Thomas Sully and Samuel F.B. Morse. Through them, West set the course of American painting for the first half of the nineteenth century.

MEMBERSHIPS
Royal Academy

PUBLIC COLLECTIONS
Kensington Palace, London
Museum of Fine Arts, Boston
National Gallery, Washington, D.C.
National Gallery of Canada
Pennsylvania Academy of the Fine Arts,
    Philadelphia
Swarthmore College, Pennsylvania
Wadsworth Atheneum, Hartford, Connecticut
Yale University Art Gallery, New Haven,
    Connecticut

CHARLES WILLSON PEALE
(1741-1827)

Charles Willson Peale was a master of many arts and trades—soldier, inventor, curator, naturalist and entrepreneur, as well as painter.

Peale's museum of art and natural history was world-famous for more than 40 years. Its picture gallery contained more than 250 Peale portraits of celebrated Americans, of which 120 survive in the Independence Hall collection in Philadelphia.

A schoolmaster's eldest son, Peale was born in 1741 in Chester, Maryland. He grew up in Annapolis as the main support of his widowed mother.

Apprenticed in 1762 to a saddler, Peale became a saddler, chaise-maker, clock repairman, silversmith, sign-painter and portraitist, having traded a saddle for instruction from Philadelphia artist John Hesselius.

Peale also was an outspoken anti-Royalist. To allow Tory tempers to cool, in 1765 he went to Boston, where John Singleton Copley encouraged him and gave him an oil portrait to copy.

When he returned to Maryland, Peale's talent was recognized. A subscription was raised to pay for his study with Benjamin West in London. For 26 months, Peale absorbed West's polished neoclassicism and acquired skill in miniature painting, mezzotint and sculpture.

Peale returned to America in late 1769, and became the established portraitist of the middle colonies. Peale's portrait from life of George Washington (1772, Washington and Lee University) is treasured as the first authentic likeness of Washington.

In 1775, Peale moved to Philadelphia. During the War of Independence, he saw action as captain of the Pennsylvania militia.

During and after the war, Peale made seven portraits from life of Washington (14 in all). At Valley Forge, using bed

The Artist in His Museum, 103½ x 80 in. Courtesy of The Pennsylvania Academy of the Fine Arts, Philadelphia.

ticking for canvas, he painted dozens of other leaders, including Lafayette and Nathaniel Green.

Near the war's end, Peale's vociferous Whig "radicalism" outraged many of his wealthy-merchant patrons. He kept quiet until Cornwallis's surrender. Then his house blossomed with illuminated victory scenes painted on paper, candle-lit from behind.

Peale's family grew faster than his income. (He eventually fathered 17 children, many of whom became artists and artisans.) In 1782, he began charging the public admission to his home gallery of American heroes.

He organized his collection of natural history items, and Peale's Museum, "a school of Nature," opened in 1788, in Independence Hall. Eventually it held more than 100,000 objects, including his own splendid paintings, stuffed animals, birds, insects, reptiles, minerals, fossils and the mastodon skeleton he himself exhumed, the first ever assembled.

Peale painted in an assured, finished and accurate style. He tended to experiment with pigments, sometimes unluckily, but often with innovative effect. His portraits, as his son Rembrandt wrote, were "strong, but never flattered; his execution spirited and natural," in a fine balance of sophistication and simplicity.

Peale established a short-lived art academy in 1795, and in 1805 was a founder of the Pennsylvania Academy of the Fine Arts.

He embodied the new American humanism and practical creativity. He experimented with gunpowder and invented an improved chimney, a steam bath, a telescopic gun-sight and new farming methods.

An artist to the end, Peale completed his last self-portrait two years before his death at age 86 in 1827.

MEMBERSHIPS
American Philosophical Society
Columbianum
American Academy of Fine Arts
Pennsylvania Academy of the Fine Arts

PUBLIC COLLECTIONS
Brooklyn Museum
Detroit Institute of Arts
Metropolitan Museum of Art, New York City
National Institute of Arts and Letters,
   New York City
New-York Historical Society, New York City
Peale Museum, Baltimore
Pennsylvania Academy of the Fine Arts,
   Philadelphia
State House, Annapolis, Maryland

SEASON	75-76	76-77	77-78	78-79	79-80	80-81	81-82	82-83	83-84	84-85
Paintings	1		2		1		1			1
Dollars	$1,260		$181,000		$67,500		$30,000			$17,000

Record Sale: $165,000, S.W, 10/9/77, "Mrs. Charles Carroll of Carrollton," 30 × 25 in.

HENRY BENBRIDGE
(1743-1812)

An early portrait painter who worked chiefly in Charleston, South Carolina, Henry Benbridge produced a body of paintings which are extremely uneven in quality. He was capable of painting likenesses of the utmost sensitivity and grace, but he also did figures with heads grossly out of proportion with the bodies. He painted some large group portraits that were ponderously serious and stiff. Yet, when it came to groups on a smaller scale, he was exceedingly adept, and he was one of the finest American miniaturists of his day.

Benbridge was born in Philadelphia in 1743. When John Wollaston came to the city to paint a portrait of Benbridge's stepfather in 1758, the boy was allowed to leave school to study with him. After Wollaston left, Benbridge continued to study, painting members of his family and decorating the family house with allegorical murals based on prints after Rubens and Raphael.

Coming into a substantial inheritance when he was 21, he sailed for Italy and studied for five years with Battoni and Mengs. A commission to do a portrait of Corsican hero Pascal Paoli assured Benbridge's recognition in England. When he arrived in London in 1769, he called on Benjamin West, exhibited at the Royal Academy, and requested Benjamin Franklin, who was representing the colonies there at the time, to sit for a portrait.

Returning to Philadelphia with glowing letters of recommendation from both West and Franklin, Benbridge soon married miniaturist Letitia Sage. The couple settled in Charleston, where Benbridge had no difficulty in getting commissions for portraits of the local gentry. When the British captured Charleston in 1780, however, he refused to swear allegiance to the king and spent two and a half years on a British prison ship.

The best of Benbridge's work has a naturalism which is unusual for its time

Portrait of the Hartley Family, 76¼ x 59¼ in. Photograph courtesy of Hirschl & Adler Galleries, Inc., New York, New York.

and akin to the colonial portraits of John Singleton Copley. The shadow in his modeling tends to be dark and opaque in flesh-tones, but he excelled in the representation of rich fabrics.

Towards 1800, Benbridge retired from painting because of ill health and a devo-tion to agricultural pursuits. At the turn of the century, however, he gave lessons to the young Thomas Sully in Norfolk. Eventually he returned to Philadelphia, where he died in 1812.

PUBLIC COLLECTIONS
Anderson House Museum, Washington, D.C.
Carnegie Institute, Pittsburgh
Charleston Museum, South Carolina
Detroit Institute of Arts
National Portrait Gallery, Washington, D.C.
National Gallery of Art, Washington, D.C.
Philadelphia Museum of Art
Winterthur Museum, Delaware

SEASON	75-76	76-77	77-78	78-79	79-80	80-81	81-82	82-83	83-84	84-85
Paintings			1	1						1
Dollars			$1,300	$6,750						$7,500

Record Sale: $7,500, CH, 12/7/84, "Portrait of Jonathan Potts," 19 × 24 in.

WINTHROP CHANDLER
(1747-1790)

Captain Samuel Chandler, ca. 1780, 54⅞ x 47⅞ in. Courtesy of National Gallery of Art, Washington, D.C., Gift of Edgar William and Bernice Chrysler Garbisch.

Winthrop Chandler was an itinerant and impecunious painter who today is regarded as an important artist of the Revolutionary period. He was born in 1747 at "Chandler Hill" in Woodstock, Connecticut, near where he lived and worked most of his life. He may have studied in Boston and is thought to have been apprenticed to a house and sign painter.

This seems confirmed by his strong, clear style, which also captured details of architecture and clothing. His simplicity and self-confidence anticipated what may be called a Connecticut school of painters, including Ralph Earl, Reuben Moulthrop, John Brewster, Jr., Joseph Seward and William Jennys in the late eighteenth and early nineteenth centuries.

Chandler painted a number of overmantel landscapes and decorations in homes, including an oil on wood of a shelf of books in 1761 for the home of General Samuel McClellan in South Woodstock, Connecticut; it is now in the Shelburne Museum, Vermont. He was related to the McClellans, and also painted their family portraits.

Indeed, it is for portraits that Chandler is chiefly remembered. He painted about 50 of them, all limning family, friends and neighbors, in order to augment his meager earnings as a house painter and decorator.

Chandler painted seven portraits of members of the Devotion family of Scotland, Connecticut before 1791; they are enumerated in the will of Ebenezer Devotion, Jr. in 1829, and are considered key in determining the attribution of other Chandler works. Two of these, *Mrs. Ebenezer Devotion* and *Rev. Ebenezer Devotion* (both Brookline Historical Society), are representative of his best work for their stark realism and fine structural design.

Portraits of his elder brother and sister-in-law—*Captain Samuel Chandler* and *Mrs. Samuel Chandler* (1780, National Gallery of Art)—represent the same high standards. For both portraits, the artist received the sum of six pounds. This was considerably better than *Homestead of General Timothy Ruggles* (private collection), for which there is a record probably referring to this painting: "1 large landscape, 33 cents." Most of his other known landscapes are on wooden chimney breasts.

Chandler worked mostly in and around Woodstock and Thompson, Connecticut. He spent the last five years of his life in Worcester, Massachusetts, where he gilded the courthouse weathervane, " . . . laying on 8 books of gold leaf at 2 shillings per book."

Eight weeks before his death in 1790, in Thompson, Chandler signed a quitclaim deeding all his property to the local selectmen as full payment in advance for expenses incurred during his last illness and burial. This was the final irony for a man who, in historical perspective, is now considered to have been one of the finest provincial artists in early America.

PUBLIC COLLECTIONS
Brookline Historical Society, Massachusetts
National Gallery of Art, Washington, D.C.
Ohio State Archaeological Society
Shelburne Museum, Vermont

SEASON	75-76	76-77	77-78	78-79	79-80	80-81	81-82	82-83	83-84	84-85
Paintings						1			1	
Dollars						$50,000			$1,100	

Record Sale: $50,000, SPB, 4/30/81, "Portrait of the Rev. Ebenezer Gay, Sr.," 38 × 29 in.

GEORGE BECK
(1748?-1812)

George Beck was one of the first generation of English-trained landscape artists to emigrate to the United States in the 1790s. Working primarily in Baltimore and Philadelphia, Beck received critical praise and some enthusiastic patronage. Two of his best known paintings, views of the Potomac Falls, were purchased by George Washington, and continue to hang in the Washington home at Mt. Vernon.

Beck was born in Ellford, England and served as a draftsman in the British Corps of Engineers for 10 years before turning to a career in art. He is thought to have taken up art seriously after his marriage to painter and teacher Mary Renessier in 1786.

Beck exhibited his landscapes with some success at the Royal Academy in London from 1790 to 1794. Around 1794, the Becks emigrated to the United States, residing primarily in Baltimore from 1795 to 1797, and in Philadelphia from 1797 to 1806.

In Baltimore and Philadelphia, Beck's work earned critical praise and the patronage of collectors such as Robert Gilmor and George Washington. Beck's dramatic landscapes, recalling the seventeenth-century Dutch tradition, were considered some of the best among the work of his contemporaries, including William Groombridge and Francis Guy.

In 1804, George and Mary Beck traveled throughout the Western regions of New York, Pennsylvania, and the Ohio Valley, and Beck gained a reputation as the first professional artist to paint west of the Allegheny Mountains. Among his known subjects of this period are views of Niagara Falls, of the Monongahela Valley around Pittsburgh, and of the Ohio River Valley around Cincinnati.

By 1806, George and Mary Beck had settled in Lexington, Kentucky, where—despite continued critical praise—Beck's

Great Falls of the Potomac, ca. 1797, 38⅞ x 50¹/₁₆ in. Courtesy of The Mount Vernon Ladies' Association, Virginia.

career languished. Although his paintings were exhibited annually from 1811 to 1814 at the Philadelphia Society of Artists, the Becks became increasingly dependent on Mary Beck's activities as a teacher and founder of girl's schools in Baltimore, Philadelphia, Cincinnati and Lexington.

George Beck died of tuberculosis in 1812 in Lexington, Kentucky.

PUBLIC COLLECTIONS
Maryland Historical Society, Baltimore
George Washington Estate,
    Mount Vernon, Virginia

(No sales information available.)

JAMES PEALE
(1749-1831)

The youngest brother of Charles Willson Peale, James Peale was born in Chestertown, Maryland in 1749. He grew up in Annapolis, where he was trained in and practiced the craft of cabinetmaking. Influenced by his brother, Peale became a professional painter and produced miniatures and still lifes until his death in 1831.

While a cabinetmaker, Peale built frames for his brother's paintings. Simultaneously, Charles shared with James the techniques of watercolor and oil painting.

When the American Revolution came, both served in the Continental Army. James Peale had a distinguished military record, rising from ensign to captain between 1776 and 1779. He resigned after the Battle of Monmouth, but was present at the siege of Yorktown. This battle experience he incorporated into two full-length portraits of George Washington, one of which hangs in the National Portrait Gallery at Independence Hall. Other notable historical paintings followed, such as *The Battle of Princeton* (1781, Princeton University).

After the war, Peale settled in Philadelphia, doing portraits, painting watercolor miniatures on ivory, and assisting with the family museum. James began his independent painting career in 1782 and, that same year, married artist James Claypoole's daughter Mary. They had seven children, five of whom are known to have become painters.

In 1786, James and Charles formally agreed to divide the portrait market, with James specializing in miniatures. James's early miniatures are difficult to distinguish from his brother's, as the two often copied and touched up each other's work. Their style was one of sharp outlines, dense shadows, and opaque backgrounds.

James's miniature painting changed slightly, as miniature painting in general

Paul Ambrose Oliver and Mary Ann, 36 x 26 in. Courtesy of Vose Galleries of Boston, Inc., Massachusetts.

changed, and he eventually developed his own style. *Rembrandt Peale* (1795, location unknown), a miniature of the artist's nephew, showed a looser technique and a departure from monochromatic backgrounds.

Peale produced several miniatures, as well as large-scale portraits and landscapes, until the early 1800s. Eventually, failing health and eyesight precluded the

exacting process of miniature painting, and he began doing still lifes. The first showing of his work was at the Peale Museum in Baltimore in 1823.

He showed many more for a number of years thereafter at the annual Pennsylvania Academy of the Fine Arts exhibits. These still lifes were highly realistic, often very detailed, and immensely popular with the art-buying public. Peale continued to paint until his death in 1831.

SEASON	75-76	76-77	77-78	78-79	79-80	80-81	81-82	82-83	83-84	84-85
Paintings	1		1	3	2	2	1	1	3	
Dollars	$318,600		$18,000	$59,000	$12,100	$282,400	$50,000	$2,600	$58,000	

Record Sale: $318,600, C, 6/18/76, "Washington and Generals at Yorktown," 25 × 33 in.

PUBLIC COLLECTIONS
Corcoran Gallery of Art, Washington, D.C.
Museum of Modern Art, New York City
National Portrait Gallery, Independence Hall, Philadelphia
New-York Historical Society, New York City
Princeton University

RALPH EARL
(1751-1801)

The late-eighteenth-century portraits by New Englander Ralph Earl, combining elements of his early, native talent with refinements acquired in seven years of work and study in England, are counted among the most distinctive of the Federalist period.

Born in 1751, in Worcester County, Massachusetts, the artist married a cousin, Sarah Gates. He had become a painter in New Haven, Connecticut by 1774. In 1775, directly after the battles of Lexington and Concord, Earl visited their sites with engraver Amos Doolittle to create what were among America's first historical pictures. Of Earl's four scenes of the Battle of Lexington (later engraved by Doolittle), only one is known: *View of the Town of Concord.*

Openly a Loyalist sympathizer, Earl decamped to London in 1778, leaving behind his wife and children. There are various versions of the circumstances. One is that Earl, disinherited when he refused to join his father's American regiment, hid from imprisonment and later escaped to England.

Before his journey, Earl had completed what is considered one of his masterpieces—his portrait of Roger Sherman of New Haven, signer of the Articles of Association, the Declaration of Independence, the Articles of Confederation, and the Constitution. Sherman's rough-hewn personality and steadfastness are fully revealed by the uncompromising pose, the use of severe light, and his direct gaze. The Sherman portrait has a primitive force and revelation that modern critics find wanting in Earl's post-English work, despite their more polished technique.

In England, Earl was a sometime pupil of Benjamin West and was strongly influenced by Sir Joshua Reynolds, from whose paintings he is said to have copied many of his poses. His portraits frequently incorporated the landscape backgrounds typical of Reynolds's

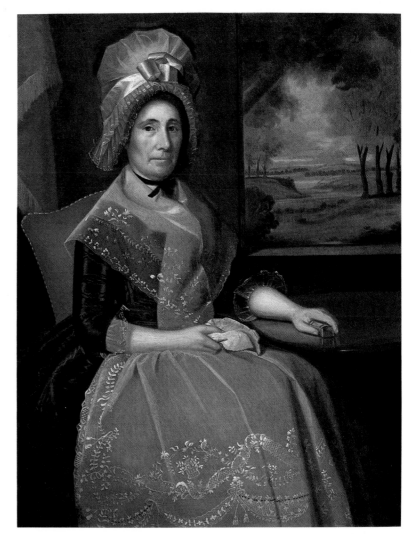

Mrs. Richard Alsop, 1792, 45⅝ x 36⅛ in. Courtesy of National Museum of American Art, Smithsonian Institution, Museum Purchase and Gift of Joseph Alsop.

later work. They were exhibited from 1783 to 1785 at the Royal Academy.

With his second wife, Earl moved in 1785 to Boston and then to New York. Profligate and a drinker, he spent more than a year in debtor's prison, emerging in 1788.

Earl prospered in his art; during the 1790s he became a sought-after portraitist for leading families in New York, Connecticut, Vermont and Massachusetts. His portraits departed from the "set" formula then common. Instead, they typically included background scenes (often seen through a window) that were related to the sitter—a landscape or an estate.

Earl's work of this period incorporates an appealing mix of his own American informality and literalness, overlaid with the compositional massing, touches of elegance and technical polish of English academics. Some critics believe Earl's works were strengthened as the artist's early directness of approach gradually reasserted itself.

After two final downhill years, Earl died "of intemperance" in 1801 at Bolton, Connecticut.

PUBLIC COLLECTIONS
Amherst College, Massachusetts
Corcoran Gallery of Art, Washington, D.C.
Litchfield Historical Society, Connecticut
Metropolitan Museum of Art, New York City
National Gallery of Art, Washington, D.C.
Museum of Fine Arts, Boston
Museum of Fine Arts, Springfield, Massachusetts
Wadsworth Antheneum, Hartford, Connecticut
Worcester Art Museum, Massachusetts
Yale University

SEASON	75-76	76-77	77-78	78-79	79-80	80-81	81-82	82-83	83-84	84-85
Paintings	1		1	3	1		1			2
Dollars	$1,743		$2,100	$8,750	$4,000		$19,000			$4,200

Record Sale: $19,000, S.W, 2/7/82, ''Andrew Jackson,'' 30 × 25 in.

JOSEPH BLACKBURN

(Active 1752-1763)

Joseph Blackburn, an English rococo portraitist noted for his fine draperies and backdrops, was active in Bermuda in 1752 and 1753. He then moved to New England, where he became popular with the colonial elite and quickly monopolized portrait painting. Eighty signed portraits by him exist in the United States.

Little is known of Blackburn's life. He came to Bermuda from London, where he was most likely an assistant in the studio of a master like Joseph Highmore or Thomas Hudson. After leaving Bermuda, he brought his knowledge and talents to New England, working in Rhode Island, New Hampshire and Boston before returning to England in 1763.

Blackburn replaced the heavy, baroque style of artists such as John Smibert with the delicate, elegant style of English conversation pieces and portraits. Using a bright palette and invisible brushstrokes, he painted hands, faces and fabrics with unmatched richness. He added jewels and finery to flatter his patrons, who wanted to be part of the aristocratic society he portrayed. Backgrounds and poses were often borrowed from well-known English portraits, such as Kneller's *Princess Anne,* from which Blackburn derived his *Susan Apthorp* (1757, Museum of Fine Arts, Boston).

Although highly polished and smart, Blackburn's glossy daintiness makes his subjects smaller than life. His compositional sense and the posing of his sitters is often awkward, as in the ambitious *Winslow Family* (1755, Museum of Fine Arts, Boston). He does, however, achieve immediacy and vivacity by having his subjects relate to one another, or to the viewer, with their gazes and hands.

The timing was right for Joseph Blackburn in Boston, for there was no serious competition during the years of his activity there. His work influenced the young John Singleton Copley, who soon provided stiff competition for Blackburn. It may have been this that drove Blackburn back to England, where he continued his work in small provincial areas.

Col. Henry Babcock, 50 x 40 in. Photograph courtesy of Hirschl & Adler Galleries, Inc., New York, New York.

SEASON	75-76	76-77	77-78	78-79	79-80	80-81	81-82	82-83	83-84	84-85
Paintings			1	1		1			1	2
Dollars			$2,534	$1,880		$5,000			$1,008	$9,600

Record Sale: $7,000, CH, 12/07/84, "Portrait of Mrs. John Harvey," 40 × 33 in.

PUBLIC COLLECTIONS
Metropolitan Museum of Art, New York City
Museum of Fine Arts, Boston
Rhode Island School of Design, Providence
Warner House, Portsmouth, New Hampshire
Worcester Art Museum, Massachusetts

WILLIAM BIRCH
(1755-1834)

Born in England in 1755 and trained in the art of enameling, William Birch was a master craftsman and copyist, and an accomplished painter in his own right. Although perhaps best known for his fine enamels after Gilbert Stuart's portraits of Washington, Birch also painted a series of exquisite portraits from life which establish him as an artist of the first rank.

Born into an old Warwickshire family, Birch attended Latin School as a youngster, but showed no interest in formal education. Sent to the London shop of jeweler Thomas Jeffreys, a family friend, he applied himself wholeheartedly to learning the jeweler's art.

Birch's enameled miniatures were first exhibited at the Society of Artists in 1775, when he was 20. Ten years later he was awarded a medal by the Society in recognition of his contributions to the art of enameling.

Birch enjoyed aristocratic patronage and a warm friendship with Sir Joshua Reynolds, who engaged the young painter to copy many of his portraits. With such a promising career well underway, it is difficult to understand what prompted Birch to pack up his family and move to the United States, yet this is what he did in 1794.

Arriving in Philadelphia with a letter of introduction from Benjamin West to William Bingham, a patron and friend of the arts, Birch set about building a clientele in America. Soon commissions began pouring in, some for miniature copies of large paintings done by other artists, but many for portraits from life with originals done by Birch.

George Washington offered to sit for the English artist, but Birch preferred to paint Washington from the Stuart portraits. In all, he made about 65 copies of the Stuart works.

Birch was an accomplished engraver. Shortly after arriving in Philadelphia, he began documenting the city's buildings and urban activities in an album of

Portrait of Arthur Lee, 1795, signed l.r. The Historical Society of Pennsylvania.

engravings copied from designs by his son Thomas. The work was published in 1800 under the title *City of Philadelphia.* Later he published another group titled *Country Seats of America,* in which he illustrated rural scenes in Delaware, Maryland and Pennsylvania.

Birch died in 1834 at age 79, leaving a remarkable unpublished autobiography, *Recollections,* which is still in the possession of the Birch family in Philadelphia.

PUBLIC COLLECTIONS
Historical Society of Pennsylvania, Philadelphia
Metropolitan Museum of Art, New York City
Mount Vernon Association, Mt. Vernon, Virginia

SEASON	75-76	76-77	77-78	78-79	79-80	80-81	81-82	82-83	83-84	84-85
Paintings					21	1		1		
Dollars					$22,375	$1,673		$2,240		

Record Sale: $2,700, S.W, 6/8/80, "The Natural Bridge, Virginia," 5 × 5 in.

GILBERT STUART
(1755-1828)

Gilbert Stuart was the supreme portraitist of his day both in England and in the United States. Seldom has his extraordinary ability to capture essential personality in a subject's face been surpassed. Few have matched his "breathing" flesh tones, lively surfaces and brilliant handling of paint.

Stuart was born in 1755 in North Kensington, Rhode Island, where his father ran a snuff mill. By 1761, Stuart had studied with local portraitist Samuel King in Newport.

In 1769, the talented 14-year-old was apprenticed to itinerant Scottish painter Cosmo Alexander. The pair arrived at Edinburgh, Scotland in 1771. When Alexander died the next year, the penniless, 17-year-old Stuart earned passage home to Newport as a sailor.

As the impending war dried up commissions in Newport, Stuart sailed for England in 1775. He found London already full of society portraitists. He subsisted as a church organist, but had not a farthing by Easter of 1777.

Stuart appealed for help from the prominent expatriate artist, Benjamin West. For five years, until 1782, Stuart was a member of West's London household, his avid student and, finally, partner of the master painter.

West concentrated on historic painting, leaving much of the portrait work to Stuart. This suited Stuart, whose fascination and skill centered on his subject's faces.

John Adams, 1826, 30 x 25⅛ in. Courtesy of National Museum of American Art, Smithsonian Institution, Adams-Clement Collection, Gift of Mary Louisa Adams Clement in memory of her mother, Louisa Catherine Adams Clement.

His first full-length portrait was of Scotsman William Grant of Congalton. Arriving at the studio on a cold morning, Grant remarked to Stuart that the day was better for skating than for sitting. They promptly went skating instead.

The impromptu outing fueled Stuart's ingenious mind. He portrayed Grant skating in Hyde Park, borrowing the dynamic pose from the studio cast of the Apollo Belvedere. The complete novelty of *The Skater* (1782, National Gallery of Art) attracted crowds at the 1782 Royal Academy show. It lifted Stuart into fame.

Fees poured in, but the extravagant Stuart lived far beyond his means. He ducked London creditors by moving to Dublin in 1787. He avoided his Dublin creditors by returning in 1793 to the United States, where his work was soon in demand.

In late 1794, Stuart painted his first portrait from life of George Washington, then 63. Stuart tried, as usual, to amuse

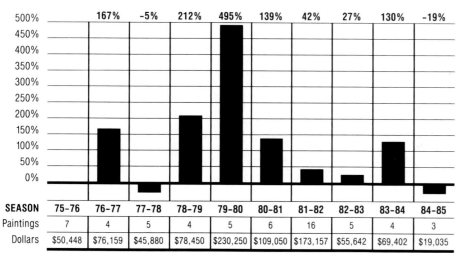

10-Year Average Change From Base Years '75-'76: 119%

	167%	-5%	212%	495%	139%	42%	27%	130%	-19%
SEASON	75-76	76-77	77-78	78-79	79-80	80-81	81-82	82-83	83-84	84-85
Paintings	7	4	5	4	5	6	16	5	4	3
Dollars	$50,448	$76,159	$45,880	$78,450	$230,250	$109,050	$173,157	$55,642	$69,402	$19,035

Record Sale: $150,000, CH, 5/22/80, "George Washington," 29 x 24 in.

Ama Powell Mason, 32¼ x 26¼ in. Courtesy of Vose Galleries of Boston, Inc., Massachusetts.

his subject, but Washington grew more severe. Stuart's quick, intuitive technique gave such life to the picture, dour look and all, that it was acclaimed. It is the portrait on the American dollar bill.

Stuart painted 104 known likenesses of Washington, copied from three portraits from life, and portrayed practically every notable of the Federal period.

His best work was done in unconventional methods which reflected his spontaneity and confidence. Painting from life, he sketched directly on the canvas instead of working from preliminary drawings, and he chatted with his sub-jects to animate their expressions. Instead of pre-blending, he applied clear, separate tints to achieve luminous skin tones. The resulting immediacy of his portraits is captivating.

The Stuarts lived in Philadelphia from 1794 to 1803, moved to Washington, D.C., and then settled in Boston in 1805.

Stuart's continued carelessness in obligation and finances was forgiven in light of his genius, his status as the foremost painter of his time and his personal charm.

He died in 1828 in Boston.

MEMBERSHIPS
American Academy
National Academy of Design

PUBLIC COLLECTIONS
Athenaeum, Newport, Rhode Island
Metropolitan Museum of Art, New York City
Museum of Fine Arts, Boston
National Gallery of Art, Washington, D.C.
National Portrait Gallery, Washington, D.C.
National Portrait Gallery, London, England
Pennsylvania Academy of the Fine Arts, Philadelphia

JOHN TRUMBULL
(1756-1843)

John Trumbull's historical pictures are among the most famous and familiar artistic records of the American Revolution and the early days of independence. The "Patriot Artist" succeeded in his four-decade mission to record and immortalize the events and leaders of the nation's birth.

School children in the United States grow up with reproductions of Trumbull's tour de force, *Declaration of Independence* (1799, Yale University). It is among his four paintings chosen in 1817 as large-scale murals to decorate the Capitol rotunda in Washington, D.C.

Trumbull was born in Lebanon, Connecticut, the second son of the governor, in 1756. He showed early interest in art, which was not encouraged. Precocious, Trumbull was graduated from Harvard University in 1773 at age 17, the youngest in his class.

After 18 months in the Continental Army, Trumbull was in Boston by 1777, turning out portraits in a fairly fresh, albeit provincial manner. He received encouragement from John Singleton Copley, and adopted Copley's frank realism of style.

In 1780, Trumbull went to London to study with famed American-born artist Benjamin West. Only months later, Trumbull was imprisoned in reprisal for the American hanging of Major John Andre. West obtained the king's pledge of safety, and Trumbull, jailed for seven months, was allowed to paint in his cell. In his five years with West, Trumbull's straightforward technique had acquired his master's polish.

Trumbull's work is meticulously accurate, formal and very skillful, though neither intuitive nor particularly insightful. A childhood accident blinded Trumbull in one eye, limiting his depth perception. It affected the spatial management of his large canvases, but his small-scale work surpassed that of the best European painters in excellence,

Alexander Hamilton, ca. 1792, 30¼ x 24⅛ in., signed l.r. Courtesy of National Gallery of Art, Washington, D.C., Gift of the Avalon Foundation.

especially his miniature oil portraits.

His *Independence* painting, only 30 inches wide, contains 48 figures of the signers. A careful researcher, Trumbull created 36 miniature portraits from life for the work.

To begin his life's work on the Revolution's events and heroes, Trumbull returned to New York City in 1785. Beginning in 1789, Trumbull lived alternately in the United States and England, until his final return to New York City in 1816.

In 1817, the Capitol murals were commissioned, and Trumbull was elected president of the revived American Academy of Fine Arts. A Federalist, but no egalitarian, Trumbull snubbed aspiring plebian artists in favor of "gentleman" patrons. The rejected artists founded the National Academy of Design in 1826.

Trumbull died at age 88 in 1843. The remains of the artist and his wife rest beneath the present Yale University Art Gallery, reinterred there after the Trumbull Gallery was demolished in 1901.

MEMBERSHIPS
American Academy of Fine Arts

PUBLIC COLLECTIONS
Harvard University
National Gallery of Art, Washington, D.C.
New-York Historical Society, New York City
Yale University

SEASON	75-76	76-77	77-78	78-79	79-80	80-81	81-82	82-83	83-84	84-85
Paintings			2		1		1	1		
Dollars			$8,486		$3,100		$37,500	$2,500		

Record Sale: $37,500, SPB, 4/23/82, "Portrait of John M. Trumbull," 29 × 25 in.

FRANCIS GUY
(1760-1820)

Landscape and estate painter Francis Guy was born in the small town of Lorton, in the Lake District of England. He spent the first part of his life as a silk dyer in London. Emigrating to New York in 1795, he established a silk dyeing plant in Brooklyn. The failure of this project led Guy to experiment with a variety of trades, including dentistry, tailoring and art.

He painted a large genre scene entitled *The Tontine Coffee House* (New-York Historical Society) in New York in 1797. He moved to Baltimore in 1798, and turned to painting as a full-time profession in 1800.

Although he had no formal training in painting, Guy achieved great detail and proper perspective; he invented a tent-like device with a glass opening, over which he would stretch the canvas to mark the shapes within the picture frame.

In 1804, he executed a series of murals for the "Painted Room" of Bryden's Fountain Inn in Baltimore. The bulk of his work, however, came from the local gentry, who commissioned him to do "portraits" of their country estates. These portraits, such as John Taggart's *Prospect* and George Grundy's *Bolton* (locations unknown), were executed between 1804 and 1817. They usually included a tiny pair of figures in a great open space, to indicate the scale of the houses.

In 1811, Guy was represented by 23 landscape paintings and drawings at the first exhibition of the Society of Artists, at the Academy of the Fine Arts in Philadelphia. His work sold very well there, despite the indifference of the critics.

Guy was commissioned to paint a view of the newly constructed Baltimore Cathedral in 1812. He claimed to have painted naval conflicts during the War of 1812, and Perry's victory at Lake Erie, but none of these works have been located.

Winter Scene in Brooklyn, ca. 1817-1820, 58¾ x 75 in. Courtesy of The Brooklyn Museum, Gift of the Brooklyn Institute of Arts and Sciences, Brooklyn, New York.

He returned to Brooklyn in 1817, where he lived for the remainder of his life. In 1819, he made a brief trip to Baltimore for an exhibition of 100 paintings at an auction sale. Later that year he held a New York opening, which included special light effects and a musical accompaniment. The popular event was praised by fellow artist Charles Willson Peale, among others.

Guy's famous *Winter Scene in Brooklyn* (ca. 1817, Brooklyn Museum) was his last major work. A large genre painting, it depicts an everyday moment in the life of the American city with much detail and humor.

Guy died in 1820. More than 400 paintings have been attributed to him, of which 25 (including 12 of the Baltimore-estate portraits) have been verified as his work.

(No sales information available.)

EDWARD SAVAGE
(1761-1817)

Edward Savage's huge life-size group portrait of *The Washington Family* (1796) highlighted his career as a portrait painter, engraver, and director of galleries in Philadelphia, New York and Boston, where the popular painting was exhibited.

Born in Princeton, Massachusetts in 1761, Savage, a self-taught artist, may have copied John Singleton Copley's works to learn portraiture. After beginning his career in Boston in the mid-1770s, he went to New York to paint George Washington's portrait, a commission in 1789 from Harvard University. John Adams commissioned him in 1790 to do companion portraits of George and Martha Washington.

Documentation reveals that the unique concept for his masterpiece of Washington's family existed before Savage's sojourn abroad from 1791 to 1793, when he learned the art of engraving and possibly studied under Benjamin West in London.

On his return to the United States in 1794, he was married in Boston. He settled in Philadelphia in 1795 and exhibited a panorama of London and Westminster, the first ever shown in that city. His Columbian Gallery opened in Philadelphia in 1796, showing ancient and modern paintings and prints. *The Washington Family,* then completed, was over nine feet long, and the first and only work of its kind to be executed in the Federal period. He charged "one quarter of a dollar" admission to view the life-size painting.

In 1798, engravings of the masterwork were published, presumably with the assistance of David Erwin and John Wesley Jarvis, talented English engravers.

The gallery was moved to New York City in 1802; a natural-history display, following the example of Charles Willson Peale, was added. Eventually P.T. Barnum became its owner. Savage

The Washington Family, ca. 1796, 84⅜ x 111⅞ in. Courtesy of National Gallery of Art, Washington, D.C., Andrew W. Mellon Collection.

worked in New York until 1810, then from 1811 or 1812 operated the gallery in Boston.

Savage painted many other prominent figures in addition to his portraits of Washington. He died at his birthplace in 1817.

PUBLIC COLLECTIONS
National Gallery of Art, Washington, D.C.

(No sales information available.)

MATHER BROWN
(1761-1831)

A moderately successful portraitist, Mather Brown painted many distinguished Americans of the Revolutionary era. He was a student of Benjamin West and competed with Gilbert Stuart for highly lucrative portrait commissions in London. An expatriate American born in Boston, the son of a clock-maker and a descendant of Cotton Mather, Brown went abroad in 1780. He worked in London and later in the provincial cities of Manchester and Liverpool.

Brown was only 12 when he had his first art lessons, taught by the teenaged Gilbert Stuart. Four years later, in the midst of America's war for independence, Brown toured Massachusetts and New York, selling wine and painting miniatures to earn enough money to sail for Europe. He arrived in London in 1881 and spent the rest of his life abroad.

Brown's portraits are looser and more lively than those of Stuart. He liked vivid colors, and would occasionally outline eyelids in bright red paint. As an historical painter, he had a softer and more colorful style than West, and never achieved the same distinction.

Like his teachers, Brown painted in the aristocratic manner characteristic of the eighteenth century, such as the idealized portraits of Abigail and John Adams, Thomas Jefferson, Dolley Madison and George III, among others. At the height of his career, Brown became portrait painter to the Duke of York and historical painter to the Prince of Wales.

Thomas Dawson, Viscount Cremorne, 1788, 29⅞ x 25 in., signed l.c. Courtesy of National Gallery of Art, Washington, D.C., Andrew W. Mellon Collection.

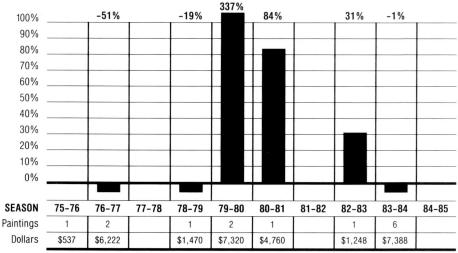

10-Year Average Change From Base Years '75-'76: 54%

SEASON	75-76	76-77	77-78	78-79	79-80	80-81	81-82	82-83	83-84	84-85
		-51%		-19%	337%	84%		31%	-1%	
Paintings	1	2		1	2	1		1	6	
Dollars	$537	$6,222		$1,470	$7,320	$4,760		$1,248	$7,388	

Record Sale: $5,160, CH, 6/24/77, "King Louis XVI of France," 84 x 110 in.

PUBLIC COLLECTIONS
Boston Athenaeum
National Portrait Gallery, London

REUBEN MOULTHROP
(1763-1814)

Reuben Moulthrop was one of the finest self-taught New England portrait painters of the eighteenth century. Approximately 45 of his portraits and miniatures are known today.

Moulthrop's primary occupation was modeling in wax; he depicted many notable figures, including George Washington and John Adams. None of these wax figures survive. His waxworks were exhibited in Massachusetts, New York and Pennsylvania, while his paintings seem to have appeared only in Connecticut.

Born in East Haven, Connecticut in 1763, Moulthrop was active in New Haven as early as 1793, and in New York City in 1794.

His earliest portraits were done around 1788. They were probably influenced by the work of Winthrop Chandler. Both Chandler and Moulthrop used heavy dark outlines around subjects placed in shallow space. The solidity of Moulthrop's figures may have been an effect of his sculptural works in wax. Around 1790, Moulthrop's portraits became somewhat more sophisticated in style, probably influenced by the work of John Durand. All of Moulthrop's portraits were insightful character studies.

It has been difficult to attribute paintings to Moulthrop for a variety of reasons: first, he rarely signed his portraits; second, his technical ability ranged from amateurish to accomplished; and third, he did not work in a single recognizable style.

Moulthrop died in East Haven, Connecticut in 1814.

The Reverend Ammi Ruhamah Robbins, 1812, 59⅛ x 59⅛ in. Yale University Art Museum, Gift of the Trustees of the Ellen Battell Stoeckel Foundation.

JACOB MAENTEL
(1763-1863)

The story of Jacob Maentel, like that of many American folk artists of the early nineteenth century, has many gaps. Tantalizing questions about his life remain unanswered.

According to Maentel's descendants, he was born in Kassel, Germany in 1763, although if this is so he was almost one hundred years old when he died and nowhere was any mention made of this remarkable longevity.

In Germany he was trained as a physician, and he is said to have served as Napoleon's secretary before coming to America. The exact date of his arrival is not known, but it seems certain that he settled in Lancaster or Lebanon County in Pennsylvania.

However, there is solid evidence he had moved to New Harmony, Indiana by 1841. In June of that year he painted, signed and dated a pair of watercolors depicting a New Harmony resident, Jonathan Jacques, and his wife, Rebecca (Abby Aldrich Rockefeller Center, Williamsburg, Virginia). Other signed portraits of New Harmony families survive; with these pictures as a guide, many unsigned canvases, painted in Pennsylvania and previously attributed to Samuel Stettinious, have now been assigned to Maentel.

Although no specific records have been found to place Maentel and his family in Pennsylvania, careful detective work has shown that he was active there in the years between 1800 and 1840. A signed picture, *Johannes Zartmann,* now in a private collection, is the key that links the Pennsylvania portraits with those done in Indiana. But why was Jacob Maentel never mentioned in Lancaster and Lebanon County court records? There are no tax records, no wills, deeds, births or baptisms listed for a family that evidently was very much a part of the scene for at least 40 years. This is but one of the unanswered questions about the life of Jacob Maentel.

Joseph Gardner and Son Tempest Tucker Gardner, ca. 1815, 12⅛ x 10 in. Courtesy of Abby Aldrich Rockefeller Folk Art Center, Williamsburg, Virginia.

Pennsylvania Gentleman and His Wife, 1810, (man) 11 x 4½ in., (woman) 11 x 5 in. Courtesy of New York State Historical Association, Cooperstown, New York.

SEASON	75-76	76-77	77-78	78-79	79-80	80-81	81-82	82-83	83-84	84-85
Paintings				1		1				
Dollars				$1,100		$14,000				

Record Sale: $14,000, SPB, 4/30/81, ''Boy with Parrot,'' 6 × 7 in.

PUBLIC COLLECTIONS
Abby Aldrich Rockefeller Folk Art Center, Williamsburg, Virginia
Henry Francis du Pont Winterthur Museum, Winterthur, Delaware

JOHN BREWSTER, JR.

(1766-1854)

Although John Brewster, Jr. was a deaf-mute from birth, he worked successfully as an itinerant portrait painter along the New England coast. Born in Hampton, Connecticut, he was taught to communicate through writing at an early age. In 1771, he received art instruction from Reverend Joseph Steward, although his style does not reflect that of his teacher.

The artist inserted advertisements in local papers, such as this one partially quoted from a *Newburyport Herald* of 1802: "John Brewster Portrait and Miniature Painter Respectfully informs the Ladies and Gentlemen of Newburyport, that if they wish to employ him in the line of his profession, he is at Mr. James Prince's where a Specimen of his Paintings may be seen. He flatters himself, if any will be pleased to call, they will be pleased with the striking likeness of his, and with the resonableness of his prices."

By 1809, Brewster's prices were $15 for portraits and $10 for miniatures.

From Maine to Connecticut, scores of the best parlors were adorned with this artist's work, which he rarely signed in the beginning. Perhaps because of his handicap, Brewster's paintings reveal an extraordinary sensitivity and concentration upon his subjects, who are portrayed with clearness, tranquility and precision; an aura of stopped time pervades his work. By the first decade of the nineteenth century, he began moving away from large, full-length compositions to the more conventional bust, or half-length figures.

In 1817, Brewster enrolled as a member of the opening class of the Connecticut Asylum for the Deaf and Dumb in Hartford. He remained there for three years, apparently studying lipreading and speech.

After he left school, his paintings showed a renewed enthusiasm and vigor, with greater depth and strength of char-

Captain Samuel Lewis, ca. 1800, 30½ x 25¾ in. Courtesy of Wunderlich and Company, Inc., New York, New York.

Mrs. Abigal Lewis (Mrs. Samuel Lewis), ca. 1800, 30¾ x 25¾ in. Courtesy of Wunderlich and Company, Inc., New York, New York.

acterization. While his clarity and precision never diminished, his facial expressions became increasingly somber and heavy, with more pronounced shadowing. He was always especially successful with small children.

This unusual artist, self-supporting despite his affliction, made his home in Buxton, Maine, where he died in 1854.

PUBLIC COLLECTIONS

Historical Society of Old Newbury, Newburyport, Massachusetts
Old Sturbridge Village, Massachusetts
Museum of Fine Arts, Boston

SEASON	75-76	76-77	77-78	78-79	79-80	80-81	81-82	82-83	83-84	84-85
Paintings			1	4	1		2	1		
Dollars			$2,500	$111,500	$110,000		$125,000	$26,000		

Record Sale: $120,000, D.NY, 11/18/81, "The Dow Twins," 20 x 22 in.

WILLIAM DUNLAP
(1766-1839)

Unhampered by the loss of one eye in a childhood accident, William Dunlap earned a permanent place in the history of American art and theater.

Dunlap was born in Perth Amboy, New Jersey in 1766, and by the time he was 17 he was already an enthusiastic portrait artist. Since he was an indefatigable historian of his own career, it is known that at that time he obtained a sitting from George Washington and drew his portrait in crayon.

When he was 18, in 1784, he set off for London. Like many other American artists of the time, he studied there with the famed American history painter Benjamin West; unlike most, he appears not to have acquired much from West by the time of his return in 1787, except some marketing techniques and several themes for pictures.

Undeterred, Dunlap embarked on a long and varied career. After attempting to make his living by painting portraits for a time, he entered his father's business. When this did not work out, he became manager of a theater and began writing plays. He was America's first professional playwright, though his 30-odd plays are not otherwise memorable. Throughout his life, he blended the arts of theater and painting, alternating between one and the other.

In 1817, Dunlap was appointed librarian of the American Academy. In 1821 he began producing—and touring with—large paintings of historical and religious themes, charging admission for their exhibition. And in 1826 he was instrumental, with a group of younger artists, in starting the National Academy of Design, becoming its treasurer and later its vice president.

In his later years, he wrote two books: *History of the American Theatre* (1832), and *History of the Rise and Progress of the Arts of Design in the United States* (1834). These opinionated, anecdotal, autobiographical works have since

Scene from The Spy, ca. 1822-1823, 22 x 27 in., signed l.r. Courtesy of New York State Historical Association, Cooperstown.

become invaluable sources; they provide information which would not otherwise be available to present-day scholars.

Dunlap died in 1839 in New York, in relative poverty.

MEMBERSHIPS
National Academy of Design

PUBLIC COLLECTIONS
Metropolitan Museum of Art, New York City
New York State Historical Association,
  Cooperstown
New-York Historical Society, New York City
Princeton University Art Museum, New Jersey

SEASON	75-76	76-77	77-78	78-79	79-80	80-81	81-82	82-83	83-84	84-85
Paintings					1	1			1	
Dollars					$1,700	$2,500			$2,070	

Record Sale: $2,500, W.W, 10/5/80, "Portrait of Mr. Perkins," 30 × 24 in.

CHARLES PEALE POLK
(1767-1822)

Born in Annapolis, Maryland, Charles Peale Polk was a folk painter of raw vigor. His father was killed on the quarterdeck of his privateer, *Black Joke,* in 1777, and the boy went to live with his uncle, painter Charles Willson Peale, in Philadelphia, where he learned his craft.

From 1787 until 1818, Polk attempted to earn a living as an artist, offering to paint houses, ships and signs, as well as portraits. Moving back and forth between Philadelphia and Baltimore between 1785 and 1793, he also worked in Richmond from 1799 to 1800.

Polk's specialty was executing portraits of revolutionary heroes, such as George Washington, Benjamin Franklin and Lafayette. He sold more than 50 portraits of Washington alone, all of them copied from his uncle's 1787 portrait.

Polk's most famous painting is his *Portrait of Thomas Jefferson* (private collection) painted at Monticello in November, 1799, upon the eve of the presidential campaign. The work was commissioned by Issac Hite, James Madison's brother-in-law, and shows the future president as youthful, plainly clad and determined. It is often called the "Republican" portrait.

Polk was unable to support himself by painting and, in 1818, he accepted a government clerkship in Washington, D.C. He believed his failure was a result of his political opinions, often at odds with those of his potential patrons. However, his work has been characterized as stiff and unimaginative, his coloring harsh.

After 1818, Polk no longer painted in oils, but did draw portraits in the medium of verre eglomise, a method of painting on glass that first became popular in late-eighteenth-century France.

Man in Yellow Waistcoat, 34½ x 26½ in. Courtesy of Kennedy Galleries, New York, New York.

PUBLIC COLLECTIONS
Abby Aldrich Rockefeller Folk Art
  Collection, Williamsburg, Virginia
American Antiquarian Society
Corcoran Gallery of Art,
  Washington, D.C.
Maryland Historical Society, Baltimore

SEASON	75-76	76-77	77-78	78-79	79-80	80-81	81-82	82-83	83-84	84-85
Paintings						1				2
Dollars						$2,500				$57,000

Record Sale: $45,000, SPB, 1/31/85, "Portraits of Richard and Diana Lawson," 37 × 33 in.

EZRA AMES
(1768-1836)

Portraitist Ezra Ames specialized in painting the political and social elite of New York State in the early nineteenth century. His 450 portraits of New York State leaders constitute an important record of Albany in the last century; his work is prized more for its historical value than for its artistic quality—a simplified and rather provincial imitation of Gilbert Stuart.

Little is known of Ames's life. Born in Framingham, Massachusetts, he began as a carriage painter, working later as a miniaturist, engraver and decorator. A self-taught painter, he settled in 1793 in Albany where he remained for the rest of his life and became a leading portraitist. He was a prolific artist, with a long and successful career that included some banking interests.

In 1812, Ames exhibited his masterpiece, a portrait of Vice President George Clinton, at the Pennsylvania Academy of the Fine Arts, winning a place in the annals of American art. The painting now hangs in the New York State · Capitol, along with portraits of Governor Clinton and Herman Bleecker. Other Ames portraits, many of New York legislators, are scattered around the state.

Ames drew his inspiration from Stuart, the premier portraitist of the late eighteenth and early nineteenth centuries. His subject's pose, gazing directly out from the canvas, was modeled after Stuart, as were the pearly tones of the flesh and the thickly painted highlights. Ames did vigorous, solid work, leaving portraits on ivory as well as on canvas, and a variety of miniatures.

PUBLIC COLLECTIONS
Albany Capitol Building, New York
Metropolitan Museum of Art, New York City

Theodore Sedgwick, 35 x 31 in. Courtesy of National Portrait Gallery, Washington, D.C., Gift of Lillian Swann Saarinen.

SEASON	75-76	76-77	77-78	78-79	79-80	80-81	81-82	82-83	83-84	84-85
Paintings			1				1	2		1
Dollars			$2,000				$900	$7,550		$900

Record Sale: $7,000, SPB, 1/27/83, "Mr. and Mrs. John Meads," 30 x 24 in.

RUFUS HATHAWAY
(1770-1822)

Rufus Hathaway was a self-taught, itinerant portraitist-turned-physician. The strength and naive charm of his paintings have made him one of the most highly regarded of the New England provincial artists.

Hathaway's known and attributed paintings, most executed in the 1790s, are few: about 20 portraits, including watercolor miniatures; a landscape; a still life.

Rufus Hathaway is believed to have been born in Freetown, Rhode Island in 1770, descended from one of the original purchasers of Taunton, Massachusetts. The artist's parents frequently moved about in several towns in Rhode Island and in Massachusetts.

Hathaway may have left home in his teens to seek portrait commissions; the earliest portraits attributed to him were completed at Taunton in 1790 to 1791, as he was entering his twenties.

An oil painting of Taunton pastor Reverend Caleb Turner—there is a companion portrait of Turner's wife—is the only picture ascribed to Hathaway which is signed and dated (1791) by the artist. These were the first documented paintings. Another early work, *Lady with Her Pets* (1790), exhibits Hathaway's affinity for decorative patterning, an element always present in his work.

Soon after, Hathaway arrived in the small coastal town of Duxbury, Massachusetts, where he began to paint portraits of members of the town's leading families. Reportedly, he fell in love with Judith Winsor when her father, Joshua Winsor, a well-to-do merchant, commissioned Hathaway to make portraits of the 17-year-old girl and her older sister.

Married in 1795, Hathaway decided—or was convinced—that, in his new circumstances, medicine was perhaps a more seemly and lucrative vocation than painting. He studied under Dr. Isaac Winslow in Marshfield, and became Duxbury's sole practicing physician until his death in 1822.

Sylvanus Sampson, 38½ x 25 in. Courtesy of Vose Galleries of Boston, Inc., Massachusetts.

Hathaway continued to paint as a pastime, including portraits of members of his wife's family. He portrayed members of three generations of the prominent Ezra Weston family. His portraits have forceful presence, conveying the character and circumstances of his subjects.

That Hathaway was largely unschooled in art is evidenced by his mistakes and naivete in drawing and perspective, in anatomy, and in mixing paint. He also employed the wooden postures and generally flat effect typical of primitive or folk art. But his portraits are not rude, nor do they show hasty ineptitude.

Hathaway's astute sense of design in composition; his ability to unify the whole, through conservative detail and brushwork; his presentation of the subject plainly and exactly, without artifice—all serve to subordinate the errors in draftsmanship.

Hathaway is said to be the artist of an overmantel decoration of two peacocks for the John Peterson House in Duxbury, and he is known to have carved in wood a large spread eagle for an archway on a bridge built in 1803 over the nearby Bluefish River.

Hathaway died in 1822, at age 52.

SEASON	75-76	76-77	77-78	78-79	79-80	80-81	81-82	82-83	83-84	84-85
Paintings									1	
Dollars									$6,000	

Record Sale: $6,000, D.NY, 11/9/83, "Portrait of Jerusha Weston," 18 × 16 in.

HENRY SARGENT
(1770-1845)

Although the bulk of his work was portraiture, Boston painter Henry Sargent is best remembered for his anecdotal genre paintings, which were among the first of their kind in the United States. He also painted historical subjects.

Sargent was born in Gloucester, Massachusetts in 1770; the family moved to Boston after the departure of British troops from that city. The young Sargent sketched copies of works by John Singleton Copley and other artists, and received encouragement toward an artistic career. In 1793, he left for London to study with Benjamin West.

Upon returning to the United States in 1799, Sargent settled in Boston and took up a career as a painter. He did not apply himself single-mindedly to art, however; he had a military career, during which he rose to the rank of colonel, and he also occupied himself with mechanical invention. In 1806, he studied for a time in the studio of his friend, portraitist Gilbert Stuart. Examples of his portraits are a self-portrait (ca. 1795, Museum of Fine Arts, Boston) and *John Turner Welles Sargent* (ca. 1819, Museum of Fine Arts, Boston).

The influence of West is discernible in Sargent's *The Landing of the Pilgrims* (ca. 1813, Pilgrim Hall, Plymouth), an essay in historical documentation. Of greater interest are *The Dinner Party* (ca. 1821, Museum of Fine Arts, Boston) and *The Tea Party* (ca. 1821-1825, Museum of Fine Arts, Boston). Both offer valuable insight into upper-class Boston social life and both demonstrate striking use of back-lighting and perspective. In the former, Sargent applied the romantic compositional structure of Francois Granet's *The Choir of the Capuchins* to a domestic genre scene.

Sargent became an honorary member of the National Academy of Design in 1840. In 1845, he was elected first president of the Artists' Association of Boston. He died later that year in Boston.

The Tea Party, ca. 1821-1825, 64¼ x 52¼ in. Courtesy of the Museum of Fine Arts, Boston, Massachusetts. Gift of Mrs. Horatio A. Lamb in memory of Mr. and Mrs. Winthrop Sargent.

MEMBERSHIPS
Artists' Association of Boston
National Academy of Design

PUBLIC COLLECTIONS
Pilgrim Hall, Plymouth, Massachusetts
Museum of Fine Arts, Boston

(No sales information available.)

SARAH PERKINS
(1771-1831)

A long-standing mystery in American art history was solved in 1984, when two art scholars identified an important early portraitist, who had only been known as "the Beardsley Limner," as Sarah Perkins, who lived in Plainfield, Connecticut in the late eighteenth century.

A group of 14 oil portraits of prominent New Englanders had been attributed to the Beardsley Limner, so called for the portraits of *Dr. Hezekiah Beardsley* and *Elizabeth Davis Beardsley* (both 1789, Yale University Art Gallery). These oils have now been attributed to Perkins, who executed several paintings and made many pastel portraits of her friends and relatives.

Perkins was born in Plainfield in 1771, the daughter of a physician and teacher. Although she appears not to have received any formal training in art, she was part of a social and intellectual circle linked by the medical profession and by various families' connections with Yale University. Most of her work seems to have been done between the late 1780s and 1793. She married in 1795, had three children, and died in 1831 at age 59.

Perkins used a set formula to depict facial features: almond-shaped eyes, under slightly puffy lids, gazing directly out of the picture from an obliquely angled head; thin, contoured lips; and distinctively modeled noses. Good examples of these are the pastel of *Mehitable Jones Hatch* (ca. 1791, Chrysler Museum) and the oil of *Harmony Child Wright* (ca. 1792, Abby Aldrich Rockefeller Folk Art Center).

Even Perkins's early work—such as the Beardsley portraits—show her high level of skill in handling fabrics and texture, and her attention to detail. Elizabeth Beardsley's lace bonnet, for example, is rendered with delicacy and almost photographic precision. But Perkins's latest known works, including

Mrs. Hezekiah Beardsley, 1788-1790, 45 x 43 in. Courtesy of Yale University Art Gallery, New Haven, Connecticut. Gift of Mrs. E.A. Giddings.

portraits of *Clarendon Dix* and *Alexander Dix* (both ca. 1793, private collections) show that she was moving toward a more painterly style, with looser brushwork, greater abstraction of clothing and objects, and better handling of perspective and background.

PUBLIC COLLECTIONS
Abby Aldrich Rockefeller Folk Art Center,
    Williamsburg, Virginia
Chrysler Museum, Norfolk, Virginia
Connecticut Historical Society, Hartford
Montclair Art Museum, New Jersey
National Gallery of Art, Washington, D.C.
Princeton University Art Gallery, New Jersey
Rhode Island Historical Society, Providence
Yale University Art Gallery, Connecticut

SEASON	75-76	76-77	77-78	78-79	79-80	80-81	81-82	82-83	83-84	84-85
Paintings						1				
Dollars						$20,000				

Record Sale: $20,000, SPB, 4/30/81, "Portrait of Major Billings," 30 × 25 in.

RAPHAELLE PEALE
(1774-1825)

Raphaelle Peale was skilled as a portraitist and a master of still life. His depiction of judiciously chosen subject matter, each form carefully painted, became the prototype for American still-life painting in the nineteenth century.

Born in Annapolis, Maryland in 1774, Peale was the first son of Charles Willson Peale, whom many consider the most significant painter and naturalist in American history. Charles had 17 children; many became artists, and all contributed to what could be called the Peale dynasty in American art and science.

Named after an artist (as were his younger brothers Rembrandt, Rubens and Titian Ramsay Peale), Raphaelle grew up surrounded by art, poetry and music. He studied painting with his father and was highly influenced by the still lifes of his uncle, James Peale. In the early 1790s, he helped his father run the Peale Museum in Philadelphia, which synthesized the wonders of art and nature, and exhibited a gallery of portraits of great men.

Peale painted portraits and miniatures from 1796 to 1797 in Baltimore, with his brother Rembrandt. Thereafter, his sensitive and cheerful wit began to unveil itself to the public, as he traveled a great deal and advertised his work in local newspapers by offering discounts and guarantees.

In 1812, he began exhibiting his still-life compositions. His sparing and robust selection of fruits, dishes and other objects, carefully placed on a table, was a significant deviation from the standard opulent display of foliage and objects. He became a master of trompe l'oeil. His most remarkable "deception" is *After the Bath* (1823, Nelson Gallery).

In addition to being an artist, Peale was known as a jokester, punster and ventriloquist who was prone to drink a bit too much. At the time of his death in

Rubens Peale-Mascot of the "Macpherson Blues", 26 x 22 in. Photograph courtesy of Kennedy Galleries, New York, New York.

1825, caused by intemperance, he was employed by a Philadelphia baker, writing love poems for cake decorations.

PUBLIC COLLECTIONS
Nelson Gallery, Kansas City, Missouri
Pennsylvania Academy of the Fine Arts,
  Philadelphia

SEASON	75-76	76-77	77-78	78-79	79-80	80-81	81-82	82-83	83-84	84-85
Paintings		1	1	1						
Dollars		$45,000	$170,000	$1,664						

Record Sale: $170,000, PB, 4/21/78, "Strawberries and Cream," 13 × 19 in.

ROBERT SALMON
(1775-1843?)

Robert Salmon, a prolific painter of ships and marine scenes, was born and died in England, or possibly Scotland—details of his life are sketchy. Nevertheless, he lived and worked in Boston for years, and produced an astonishing number of paintings depicting Boston Harbor. His work had a strong influence on the development of a number of important later American marine painters.

Salmon spent half his working life in England and Scotland, painting the British coast. His light-filled compositions are representative of the best English marine paintings, and reflect the influence of seventeenth-century Dutch painting on that genre. But Salmon's work was marked by precise detailing and a scrupulous clarity not always present in the works of other marine painters. He delighted in peopling his ships and harbor scenes with tiny, remarkably well-drawn figures. Why he left an apparently successful career in his native land to embark on a new life in America is not known, but he did so in 1828.

For the next 13 years, Salmon was a familiar sight in the busy milieu of Boston Harbor. He became known as something of an eccentric, living as he did in a little hut among the wharves. Still, he enjoyed enormous popularity, and his works were eagerly sought after by Bostonians and others interested in ships and sailing.

The Barque "Marblehead" Coming in to Port, 15⅞ x 23¾ in. Photograph courtesy of Hirschl & Adler Galleries, Inc., New York, New York.

Salmon was fortunate in that he arrived in Boston at a time when a vigorous building program was being pursued along the waterfront. The added activity provided an aura of excitement and industry that must have been highly invigorating to the artist, for he produced about 300 paintings in the years he lived in his little waterfront hut.

Mostly, he painted on small panels, but he also made a large drop curtain for a Boston theater. He was equally adept at creating both hazy and marvelously clear atmospheric effects, and is credited with being a founder of luminism in American painting. He died sometime after returning to England in 1843.

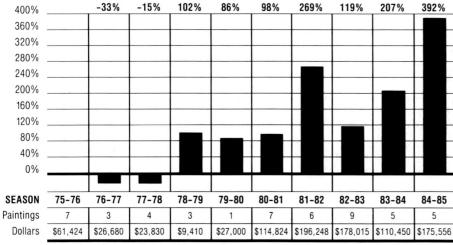

10-Year Average Change From Base Years '75-'76: 123%

SEASON	75-76	76-77	77-78	78-79	79-80	80-81	81-82	82-83	83-84	84-85
		-33%	-15%	102%	86%	98%	269%	119%	207%	392%
Paintings	7	3	4	3	1	7	6	9	5	5
Dollars	$61,424	$26,680	$23,830	$9,410	$27,000	$114,824	$196,248	$178,015	$110,450	$175,556

Record Sale: $92,500, D.NY, 10/24/84, "Schooner with View of Boston," 16 x 24 in.

PUBLIC COLLECTIONS
Boston Public Library
Corcoran Gallery of Art, Washington, D.C.
Mariner's Museum, Newport News, Virginia
Museum of Fine Arts, Boston
U.S. Naval Academy Museum,
 Annapolis, Maryland
Virginia Museum, Richmond

JOHN VANDERLYN
(1775-1852)

John Vanderlyn, the first American painter to study in Paris, was a leading exponent of both the French neo-classical style and romantic subject matter. Although he painted a number of portraits, as well as panoramas and still lifes, his most noted works are three paintings on historical subjects.

Vanderlyn was born in Kingston, New York in 1775, the grandson of Pieter Vanderlyn, an early Manhattan painter. He showed an early interest in art and was sent to New York City to study under Archibald and Alexander Robertson at the Columbian Academy of Painting. While working for an art dealer, Vanderlyn copied Gilbert Stuart's portrait of Aaron Burr. Burr saw the copy and became Vanderlyn's patron, sending him first to Philadelphia to study under Stuart and then to Paris, where he was the pupil of Francois Andre Vincent at the Ecole des Beaux-Arts.

Vanderlyn remained in Europe from 1796 until 1815, except for a trip to New York in 1802, when he sketched Niagara Falls. While in Europe, he absorbed the tenets of French neoclassicism as practiced by Jacques-Louis David and Jean-Auguste Ingres: strong line, especially in the molding of figures, somber coloration, and an adherence to antique and mythological subjects or poses.

The first of Vanderlyn's great paintings, *The Death of Jane McCrea* (1804, Wadsworth Atheneum), attempts to apply these principles to an incident in American history, the scalping of a white girl by Indians, described in Joel Barlow's poem "Columbiad." The three central figures are reminiscent of classical sculpture. Even more classical is *Marius Amid the Ruins of Carthage* (1807, M.H. de Young Memorial Museum), which won a gold medal from Napoleon and established Vanderlyn's reputation in Europe. The romantic, melancholy subject of the painting has

Henry Vanderlyn, 26¼ x 21¼ in. Courtesy of Vose Galleries of Boston, Inc., Massachusetts.

been interpreted as an allusion to Vanderlyn's patron, Burr.

Vanderlyn's third great painting was a nude based on Renaissance masterpieces, *Ariadne Asleep on the Island of Naxos* (1812-1814, Pennsylvania Academy of the Fine Arts). Exhibited upon his return to the United States, however, it created only a scandal. At this time he also painted a *Portrait of the Artist* (1814, Metropolitan Museum of Art).

Although he had hoped to prosper in his native land, Vanderlyn found his polished European style to be out of touch with American tastes. A special rotunda was built in New York City's Central Park for the exhibition of his panoramic paintings of Versailles and other sites, but the venture proved to be a financial failure; the city eventually cancelled Vanderlyn's lease.

His connection with Burr made it difficult for him to obtain political commissions, although he did execute *The Landing of Columbus* in 1837 for the rotunda of the Capitol Building. Discouraged and impoverished, he died in 1852 in his native Kingston.

MEMBERSHIPS
National Academy of Design

PUBLIC COLLECTIONS
Corcoran Gallery of Art, Washington, D.C.
M.H. de Young Memorial Museum, San Francisco
Metropolitan Museum of Art, New York City
Pennsylvania Academy of the Fine Arts, Philadelphia
United States Capitol Building, Washington, D.C.
Senate House, Kingston, New York
Wadsworth Atheneum, Hartford, Connecticut

(No sales information available.)

JACOB EICHHOLTZ
(1776-1842)

Although he did not embark on a full-time art career until age 35, Jacob Eichholtz became one of Pennsylvania's leading portraitists in the early nineteenth century.

Eichholtz was born in Lancaster, Pennsylvania in 1776. He was trained as a coppersmith. Between 1810 and his death in Lancaster in 1842, he painted more than 850 portraits and several landscapes and history paintings.

Eichholtz was aided in his early development by Thomas Sully, one of Philadelphia's leading portrait painters. Sully directed Eichholtz to Gilbert Stuart of Boston, who gave Eichholtz further advice and encouragement.

The eager Eichholtz absorbed all the information he could from other artists, while painting constantly. Although he lacked formal training, his mature style was direct and strong, exhibiting the flat texture of the ornamental painter and capturing the character of his subjects.

These traits were evident in portraits such as his *Self Portrait* (ca. 1810, Pennsylvania Academy of the Fine Arts). His full charm is present also in his 1838 companion portraits of *Judge and Mrs. Thomas Emlen Franklin* (Franklin and Marshall College).

Eichholtz specialized in strong, brightly-colored linear portraits of well-known people living near Philadelphia and Baltimore. Among his many subjects were chief justice John Marshall; the attorneys general of Pennsylvania Thomas Elder, Thomas Emlen Franklin and Benjamin Champneys; and president of the Bank of the United States Nicholas Biddle.

Eichholtz's love of history contributed to the careful detail that characterized his portraits. He possessed a solid understanding of the tradition of historical painting which he admired, although he painted few such works.

The artistic respect Eichholtz commanded from his contemporaries enabled him to attain financial success in a time of keen competition. At a testimonial dinner given on his return from Philadelphia to Lancaster, he received the toast: "The skill of the artist is equalled only by the moral excellence of the man."

Portrait of a Man, ca, 1809, 10 x 7⅞ in., Courtesy of National Museum of American Art, Smithsonian Institution, Gift of Mary L. Schaff.

PUBLIC COLLECTIONS
Franklin and Marshall College, Lancaster, Pennsylvania
Historical Society of Pennsylvania, Philadelphia
Metropolitan Museum of Art, New York City
National Gallery of Art, Washington, D.C.
Philadelphia Museum of Art

SEASON	75-76	76-77	77-78	78-79	79-80	80-81	81-82	82-83	83-84	84-85
Paintings									1	3
Dollars									$2,500	$9,155

Record Sale: $4,250, SPB, 1/31/85, "Portraits of Members of the Clyde Family," 9 x 7 in.

JOSHUA SHAW
(1777-1860)

Landscape artist Joshua Shaw was born in Bellingborough, Lincolnshire, England. An orphan, he was apprenticed at an early age to a country sign painter. Shaw practiced this trade in Manchester, where he also started painting portraits, landscapes and genre pieces. His talent was soon recognized, and at age 22 he exhibited at the Royal Academy. His success grew rapidly, and his paintings were shown in several London galleries before he emigrated to Philadelphia in 1817.

In Philadelphia, Shaw was active in artistic circles; he was a founder of both the Artists' Fund Society and the Artists and Amateur Association. In 1819, Shaw published *A New and Original Drawing Book,* a manual for artists, and began a journey along the Eastern seaboard making sketches for a second book. This work, entitled *Picturesque Views of American Scenery,* was published in 1820 and 1821 with Shaw's sketches, engraved by John Hill.

Shaw was also an active inventor. His improvements on the design of firearms earned him several awards from the United States and Russian governments.

Shaw is best known for his landscape paintings. Although these works have been criticized as being dry and rather listless, they were among the first depictions of American topographical views to be reproduced and widely distributed.

About 1843, Shaw moved to Bordentown, New Jersey, where he continued to paint landscapes and Indian subjects. He exhibited in Philadelphia, Boston, New York and Baltimore, and painted until 1853, when he was stricken with paralysis. He died in Burlington, New Jersey, seven years later.

Fantasy with Classical Ruins, 1851, 33 x 48 in., signed l.r. Courtesy of Kennedy Galleries, New York, New York.

PUBLIC COLLECTIONS
Museum of Fine Arts, Boston
Metropolitan Museum of Art, New York City
Victoria and Albert Museum, London

SEASON	75-76	76-77	77-78	78-79	79-80	80-81	81-82	82-83	83-84	84-85
Paintings						1		5	2	
Dollars						$32,000		$59,812	$5,780	

Record Sale: $40,000, CH, 12/3/82, "The First Ship," 25 × 36 in.

REMBRANDT PEALE
(1778-1860)

Rembrandt Peale was the most prominent of several artist sons of Charles Willson Peale. Like his father, he painted portraits, was interested in natural history, tried his hand 'at running museums and was one of the founders of the Pennsylvania Academy of the Fine Arts. In addition, he painted large historical scenes and was a founding member of the National Academy of Design.

Peale painted his first portrait at age 13; when he was 17, George Washington sat for him as a courtesy to his father, who had painted Washington many times. Years later, Rembrandt Peale used this likeness as the basis for an idealized official portrait of Washington for the United States Senate.

Peale was born in Bucks County, Pennsylvania in 1778, while his father was with Washington at Valley Forge. Close to his father, he became his favorite pupil.

In 1797, Rembrandt helped his brother Raphaelle open a museum of art and natural history in Baltimore. It was to be a smaller version of their father's museum in Philadelphia, but it did not succeed.

Four years later he assisted in unearthing and assembling the first complete skeleton of a mastodon ever found and, in 1802, took it to London to be exhibited. While there, he painted portraits and studied at the Royal Academy, assisted by the American president of the Academy, Benjamin West.

On trips to Paris in 1808 and from 1809 to 1810, Peale was impressed by neoclassicism and by the grandiose paintings on historical themes in the galleries. He decided that he, too, should paint historical scenes on a similar scale. During his stay, he was invited to become one of Napoleon's court painters, but declined. He did, however, paint an equestrian portrait of the emperor.

George Washington, 1860, 35½ x 29¼ in., signed l.l. Courtesy of Vose Galleries of Boston, Inc., Massachusetts.

When his first attempt at painting a classical subject, *The Roman Daughter* (1811, National Museum of American Art), was exhibited, it was criticized as tasteless and unsuitable. This so disheartened Peale that he gave up painting altogether for several years.

His next effort, however, *The Court of Death* (1820, Detroit Institute of Arts), was a resounding success. Enormous both in size (24 feet wide) and scope, it was a masterful composition. Never one to miss a chance to publicize his work, Peale took it on tour, making $9,000 in the first year.

In 1823, he went back to work on what he vowed would be the "definitive" portrait of Washington. After three months of frenzied concentration,

he finished the "porthole" portrait (ca. 1823, White House), so named because it is centered in an oval of simulated stone. In all, Peale painted 78 copies of it, changing Washington's garb in many.

While this portrait is Peale's best-known, it is generally agreed that the finest of all his portraits was that of Thomas Jefferson (1805, New-York Historical Society).

During his long life, Peale lived and worked in many cities and traveled to Europe five times. In 1831, however, he settled in Philadelphia for good and died there in 1860.

MEMBERSHIPS
National Academy of Design

PUBLIC COLLECTIONS
Detroit Institute of Arts
Metropolitan Museum of Art, New York City
Municipal Museum of Baltimore
National Portrait Gallery, Washington, D.C.
New-York Historical Society, New York City
Pennsylvania Academy of the Fine Arts, Philadelphia
United States Capitol, Washington, D.C.
United States Supreme Court, Washington, D.C.
White House, Washington, D.C.

SEASON	75-76	76-77	77-78	78-79	79-80	80-81	81-82	82-83	83-84	84-85
Paintings	4	3	4	3	5	3	4	8	6	4
Dollars	$58,900	$12,000	$102,600	$30,500	$35,500	$9,000	$26,950	$113,500	$46,750	$72,500

Record Sale: $57,500, SPB, 12/6/84, "Portrait of George Washington," 36 × 29 in.

WASHINGTON ALLSTON
(1779-1843)

Painter, poet and inspiration of the American romantic tradition, Washington Allston was born in Georgetown, South Carolina in 1779. He graduated from Harvard College in 1800.

Already a painter of religious subjects and friend of the noted miniaturist Edward Greene Malbone, Allston determined to go to Europe to study art, in spite of family opposition. Like many American artists, he sought in Europe the history, mystery and tradition he thought lacking in his home country. What he acquired in Europe, during the period of 18 years that he spent alternately there and in the United States, was a romantic classicism and a power of expression that exerted a tremendous influence on many painters who followed him.

Allston studied for several years at the Royal Academy in London under the expatriate American history painter Benjamin West, who was his most important influence; he was impressed as well by the Swiss artist Henry Fuseli, then a professor at the Academy. In England Allston also met the painter John Vanderlyn, a traveling companion with whom he shared a kinship of ideals. In Paris, where he studied at the Louvre for a time, he created his first major work, the dark and dramatic painting *The Rising of a Thunderstorm at Sea* (1804).

Allston soon moved on to Rome, and there garnered a considerable reputation for his classical landscapes. However, it was from his paintings with religious, historical and allegorical themes that his reputation was made, exemplified by *The Dead Man Restored to Life by the Touch of the Bones of the Prophet Elijah* (1813-1814). Allston's mastery of color theory gave him the appellation "the American Titian," though to present-day eyes his admiration for Michelangelo is more apparent in the massiveness of his figures.

Hermia and Helena, 29¾ x 25 in. Photograph courtesy of Hirschl & Adler Galleries, Inc., New York, New York.

In 1818, Allston returned permanently to America, staying mainly in Boston and Cambridge, Massachusetts. He was less productive from this point on, though he remained influential on such artists as painter Samuel F.B. Morse and sculptors Horatio Greenough and Thomas Crawford.

The major impediment to Allston's work, ironically, was an important commission to complete his large painting *Belshazzar's Feast* (begun 1817), which he struggled unsuccessfully to finish for the rest of his life. His style had evolved into a more poetic and intimate mode which was antithetical to this grand and Gothic composition, though even unfinished it retains great drama. He died in Cambridgeport, Massachusetts in 1843.

Allston, with his poetry-writing, his dark, wild, and mystical painting style, and his lofty ideals, was largely responsible for changing the image of the artist in the United States from that of a slightly disreputable artisan to that of the romantic, poetic idealist.

MEMBERSHIPS
Royal Academy

PUBLIC COLLECTIONS
Addison Gallery of American Art, Andover, Massachusetts
Amherst College, Massachusetts
Columbia Museum of Art, South Carolina
Detroit Institute of Arts
Harvard University
Metropolitan Museum of Art, New York City
Munich Museum, Germany
Museum of Fine Arts, Boston
National Gallery, Washington, D.C.
Pennsylvania Academy of the Fine Arts, Philadelphia
Yale University

SEASON	75-76	76-77	77-78	78-79	79-80	80-81	81-82	82-83	83-84	84-85
Paintings							1	1		
Dollars							$200,600	$9,000		

Record Sale: $200,600, S, 12/9/81, "Hermia and Helena," 29 × 25 in.

BARONESS HYDE de NEUVILLE
(1779?-1849)

French artistocrat Anne-Marguerite-Henriette Hyde de Neuville was married to such an outspoken supporter of the deposed Bourbon monarchy that Napoleon put a price on his head. They spent 13 years in the United States. Wherever they lived and traveled, she sketched and painted in watercolors. Nature, houses, Indians and servants all were her subjects. She had a good eye, recording candidly whatever she saw, and the sketches and watercolors she left form a valuable historical picture of life in the early decades of the nineteenth century.

Some sources set her birth in either 1776 or 1779 in Sancerre, France. In his memoirs, however, her husband mentions that she was considerably older than he, and that she was a centenarian when she died in 1849.

In any event, as a genteel young lady she was taught to sketch. In 1794, she married Jean-Guillaume Hyde de Neuville, who was then 18 and enmeshed in plots to restore the Bourbons to power. In 1797, the government ordered his arrest, and he went into hiding. In 1805, Napoleon seized his estates. Madame Hyde de Neuville followed Napoleon to Vienna and pleaded for their return. Napoleon agreed on the condition that Hyde de Neuville take an oath of loyalty, which he refused to do. The couple went into exile.

On their arrival in America in 1807, they traveled from New York City up the Hudson, westward to Niagara Falls and south into Tennessee. They eventually settled on a farm in New Brunswick, New Jersey, but when Napoleon was overthrown in 1814 they returned to France.

Two years later Hyde de Neuville was appointed French minister to the United States, and they returned to Washington, where they stayed for six years. Along with her official duties, Madame Hyde de Neuville again found time to make many sketches of American life.

An Indian and His Squaw, 1807, 6½ x 13¼ in. Courtesy of The New-York Historical Society, New York, New York.

PUBLIC COLLECTIONS
Abby Aldrich Rockefeller Folk Art Center,
  Williamsburg, Virginia
New-York Historical Society,
  New York City
New York Public Library, New York City

SEASON	75-76	76-77	77-78	78-79	79-80	80-81	81-82	82-83	83-84	84-85
Paintings							1			
Dollars							$900			

Record Sale: $900, SPB, 4/29/82, "Self Portrait," 6 × 5 in.

THOMAS BIRCH
(1779-1851)

Thomas Birch was one of America's foremost marine painters, and possibly the best landscape painter of his generation. From England, he brought a new emphasis on nature and landscape; many of his pictures contrast man's insignificance to the power of natural forces. He had a profound influence on Hudson River School artist Thomas Cole.

Birch was born in London in 1779, the son of William Russell Birch, an engraver and painter of enamel miniatures. They emigrated to the United States in 1894. In 1795, at the Columbianum Exhibition in Philadelphia, William showed engravings and miniatures on enamel (an art form he introduced into America), and Thomas showed drawings, scenes of London environs and of the Pennsylvania countryside.

From 1799 to 1800, father and son worked together as the firm of W. Birch & Son, designing, engraving and publishing views of Philadelphia and the surrounding area. Thomas's topographical scenes are valuable documentations of the city; they are considered some of the finest cityscapes done in America in the late eighteenth century.

In 1806, Thomas Birch was doing miniatures on ivory. His interest in marine subjects may have originated around this time, during trips to the mouth of the Delaware River. It was not long before he had made a reputation for himself as a marine painter. Characteris-

Coastal View with Ships, 1847, 20 x 30 in., signed l.r. Courtesy of Wunderlich and Company, Inc., New York, New York.

tic of his work are a clear atmosphere and well-delineated waves. His ship portraits are scarce and much sought-after. He also painted many fine winter landscapes.

Birch's most famous works were done during the War of 1812, depicting American naval victories. *The Engagement of the Constitution and the Guerriere* (1812, Historical Society of Pennsylvania), *The United States and the Macedonian* (1813, Historical Society of

Pennsylvania) and *The Wasp and The Frolic* (New-York Historical Society) are among the best known. Many of these works were exhibited at the Pennsylvania Academy of the Fine Arts and were engraved.

Birch designed coins for the United States Mint, and in 1816 he contributed designs for the historical pictures on the Naval Monument in Boston.

He painted many harbor and river views, usually of Philadelphia, but also of New York City; *Point Breeze on the Delaware* (1818, private collection) is an example. Some of Birch's most moving paintings, such as *Shipwreck* (1829, Brooklyn Museum), are romantic and imaginary.

Birch was active in Philadelphia art circles and was an influential figure at the Pennsylvania Academy of the Fine Arts.

He died in 1851.

MEMBERSHIPS
National Academy of Design

PUBLIC COLLECTIONS
Brooklyn Museum
Historical Society of Pennsylvania, Philadelphia
New-York Historical Society, New York City
Pennsylvania Academy of the Fine Arts, Philadelphia

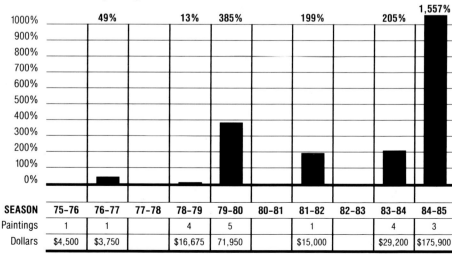

10-Year Average Change From Base Years '75-'76: 344%

	75-76	76-77	77-78	78-79	79-80	80-81	81-82	82-83	83-84	84-85
%		49%		13%	385%		199%		205%	1,557%
SEASON	75-76	76-77	77-78	78-79	79-80	80-81	81-82	82-83	83-84	84-85
Paintings	1	1		4	5		1		4	3
Dollars	$4,500	$3,750		$16,675	71,950		$15,000		$29,200	$175,900

Record Sale: $165,000, SPB, 12/6/84, "The Battery and Harbour, New York," 29 x 41 in.

JOHN WESLEY JARVIS
(1780-1840)

For a brief period between 1808 and 1820, John Wesley Jarvis was one of New York City's leading portrait and miniature painters. A flamboyant lifestyle, however, caused the undoing of his successful but short career.

Born in England in 1780, Jarvis was brought to Philadelphia at age five. Despite Gilbert Stuart's discouragement, he pursued an art career, at which he prospered. He was apprenticed to engraver Edward Savage, with whom he moved to New York City in 1801. David Edwin, an employee of Savage, taught the novice Jarvis how to draw.

In 1802, Jarvis began a five-year partnership with Joseph Wood, a specialist in small, cabinet-size portraits. During this association, Jarvis invented a machine for drawing profiles on glass. At his peak he earned $100 daily, charging $5 for each gilded silhouette.

As Jarvis's work became well known, he established a close relationship with writer Washington Irving, whose portrait he painted in 1809.

During the next few years, Jarvis earned a fortune doing miltary portraits. His geniality was the main reason he was able to secure so many commissions.

In 1815, Jarvis was commissioned to do five full-length depictions of war heroes of 1812, for New York's City Hall. These historical portraits are considered some of his best works. Among his famous sitters were John Randolph of Virginia, De Witt Clinton, Commodore Oliver Hazard Perry and Andrew Jackson.

Typical of the period, Jarvis's paintings possess a limited grasp of form and a stiffness of manner. His work was close to Charles Willson Peale's, in that he emphasized virtue and self-restraint.

Jarvis was described as an inimitable raconteur and practical joker. His high living led to his eventual illness and the subsequent decline from his pinnacle as

Thomas Paine, ca. 1806-1807, 25¾ x 20½ in., signed l.r. Courtesy of National Gallery of Art, Washington, D.C., Gift of Marian B. Maurice.

New York City's leading portraitist. By the late 1820s, he was supplanted by Henry Inman. Jarvis died in 1840, penniless and separated from his wife and children.

PUBLIC COLLECTIONS
City Hall, New York City
Detroit Institute of Arts
New-York Historical Society, New York City

SEASON	75-76	76-77	77-78	78-79	79-80	80-81	81-82	82-83	83-84	84-85
Paintings				2	1	2	1		1	1
Dollars				$11,200	$1,418	$30,200	$5,000		$3,000	$1,300

Record Sale: $27,500, CH, 4/24/81, "Port. of Commodore Oliver Hazard Perry," 29 x 21 in.

EDWARD HICKS
(1780-1849)

Entirely self-taught, and employing a primitive style of painting, Edward Hicks matured from a sign painter into one of the most significant American folk artists.

He was born in 1780 in what is now Langhorne, Pennsylvania. Orphaned at age three, Hicks was raised by a kind Quaker family, the Twinings. At age 13, Hicks was apprenticed to a carriage maker and began to paint. He decorated coaches, tavern signs, tables, chairs, firebacks, fire buckets and chests.

After suffering a tremendous hangover and illness at age 20, Hicks joined the sober Society of Friends and soon became an active Quaker preacher. He was deeply affected by the Quaker Separatist Movement, as he was both an admirer and a relative of its founder, the Reverend Elias Hicks.

While he was most famous as a Quaker preacher during his lifetime, today Hicks is primarily remembered as a painter. His subjects were portraits of family farms, and historical and religious scenes.

His favorite subject, and the one he is most famous for, is *The Peaceable Kingdom*. He painted more than 100 versions of this theme, illustrating the passage from chapter 11 of the Book of Isaiah: "The wolf also shall dwell with the lamb, and the leopard shall lie down with the kid; and the calf and the young lion and the fatling together; and a little child shall lead them."

Hicks based the composition of *The Peaceable Kingdom* on an engraved illustration of a painting by English academician Richard Westall. In a number of Hicks's depictions of *The Peaceable Kingdom,* he included a scene from an engraving by John Hall of Benjamin West's famous painting, *William Penn's Treaty with the Indians.* To Hicks, this modern historical event embodied Isaiah's prophecy of peace between opposing groups. Like many others,

The Declaration of Independence, 26 x 30 in. Photograph courtesy of Hirschl & Adler Galleries, Inc., New York, New York.

Washington Crossing the Delaware, ca. 1825, 16¼ x 21½ in. Courtesy of Wunderlich and Company, Inc., New York, New York.

Hicks believed that America was the realization of the promised land of the Bible.

When Hicks died in 1849, the thousands of people at his funeral came to mourn the preacher, not the artist. Like the pious Quakers, Hicks did not value

his artistic talent. He wrote in his diary: "I have nothing to depend on but the mercy and forgiveness of God, for I have no works of righteousness of my own. I am nothing but a poor old worthless insignificant painter."

SEASON	75-76	76-77	77-78	78-79	79-80	80-81	81-82	82-83	83-84	84-85
Paintings			1		2	3				
Dollars			$125,000		$480,000	$510,000				

Record Sale: $270,000, SPB, 4/30/80, "The Peaceable Kingdom," 24 × 31 in.

JOHN ARCHIBALD WOODSIDE, SR.
(1781-1852)

Buffalo Hunt, 18 x 24 in., signed l.l. Photograph courtesy of The Gerald Peters Gallery, Santa Fe, New Mexico.

Philadelphia-born artisan-painter John Archibald Woodside, Sr. became the most celebrated painter of signs in the Federal era.

Credited in his lifetime with "talent beyond many who paint in higher branches," Woodside also created precise, colorful easel paintings—genre, still lifes, animals, and peopled landscapes—which were shown from 1817 to 1835 at the Pennsylvania Academy of the Fine Arts.

Before Woodside, Matthew Pratt was the preeminent artist-sign painter; Woodside may have studied with Pratt. Pratt died in 1805, the year that 24-year-old Woodside opened his Philadelphia studio.

At that time, signs and decorative painting, no longer restricted to taverns, were noteworthy street art, generating lively critical interest and, of course, business. Almost every trade depended on the art.

By 1810, Woodside was "that justly celebrated artist," the recognized leader in the field. Though most in the sign trade were itinerants, Woodside stayed put and prospered. His designs are extraordinary for bright, lucid color and precise "finished to perfection" technique.

Woodside also created many allegorical or quasi-classical scenes for the side panels of fire engines and hose carriers. Fire companies were privately operated on subscriptions. Attention-getting quality decoration was a necessary advertisement.

An outstanding Woodside example is *Lady With Guitar* (1840-1850, Philadelphia Museum of Art), which was painted for a fire company.

In 1820, Woodside earned praise for his sign for Philadelphia's new Union Hotel, an adaptation of an engraving of the Declaration of Independence. He is said also to have painted the first locomotive decoration.

Woodside's early paintings, like the landscape *Laurel Hill* (1802, Pennsylvania Historical Society), exhibit "beginner's faults" in draftsmanship and tentative use of color. By contrast, the 1824 *Country Fair* (Metropolitan Museum of Art) is appealing for its confident, sunlit clarity, frankness of line and visual immediacy.

Like Pratt's, much of Woodside's best work remained in use long after his death in 1852. His son Abraham was a painter; another son, John, Jr., was a wood engraver.

MEMBERSHIPS
Artists Fund Society

PUBLIC COLLECTIONS
Insurance Company of North America, Philadelphia
Metropolitan Museum of Art, New York City
Pennsylvania Historical Society, Philadelphia
Philadelphia Museum of Art

SEASON	75-76	76-77	77-78	78-79	79-80	80-81	81-82	82-83	83-84	84-85
Paintings							2		1	
Dollars							$265,000		$2,000	

Record Sale: $260,000, CH, 6/3/82, "A Pennsylvania Country Fair," 20 × 26 in.

ZEDEKIAH BELKNAP
(1781-1858)

Portrait painter Zedekiah Belknap was born in Auburn, Massachusetts in 1781. He studied at Dartmouth College and was graduated in 1807. There is no evidence that Belknap had any formal art training.

By 1810, Belknap was working as an itinerant limner, traveling to Vermont, New Hampshire, Massachusetts and New York City. Some of his early portraits show attempts to imitate academic painting. But Belknap soon developed a stylized formula that allowed him to paint rapidly and produce portraits that pleased his customers.

Like many primitive painters, Belknap used bright color and paid particular attention to the details of a sitter's clothing, hairstyle and accessories. He used bold outline and very little modeling. Belknap used a formula for painting faces, usually outlining the nose in profile, and accentuating it with a reddish shadow. He painted sharply outlined round eyes, full mouths, and red, flattened ears.

Mrs. Thomas Harrison (ca. 1815, Abby Aldrich Rockefeller Folk Art Center) provides an early example of Belknap's technique. He used a minimum of brushwork, yet the portrait is alive in its detail of the sitter's exaggerated hairstyle, feather headpiece, ruffled dress and bountiful jewelry.

Belknap's specialty was full-sized portraits. He painted on wood panels scored with diagonal lines to imitate canvas. This texture also provided a better surface for painting. Occasionally, he painted on heavy twill canvas.

In his later work, Belknap used a more realistic style, perhaps in reaction to the growing popularity of daguerreotypes. More than 170 portraits have been attributed to Belknap; they date from 1807 to 1848. Belknap died in Weathersfield, Vermont in 1858.

Young Lady with Lace Shawl and *Young Man with Red Hair: A Pair of Portraits,* ca. 1810, 26 x 21½ in., Courtesy of Sotheby's, Inc.

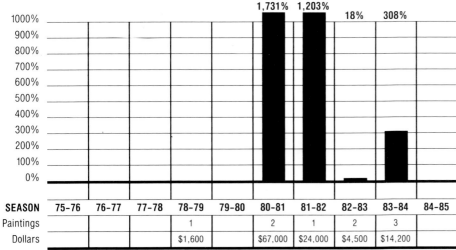

10-Year Average Change From Base Years '78-'79: 652%

SEASON	75-76	76-77	77-78	78-79	79-80	80-81	81-82	82-83	83-84	84-85
						1,731%	1,203%	18%	308%	
Paintings				1		2	1	2	3	
Dollars				$1,600		$67,000	$24,000	$4,500	$14,200	

Record Sale: $45,000, SPB, 4/30/81, "Portrait of Dorman Warren," 27 x 22 in.

PUBLIC COLLECTIONS
Abby Aldrich Rockefeller Folk Art Center,
Williamsburg, Virginia

MICAH WILLIAMS
(1782-1837)

For many years, a large collection of excellent American folk portraits—all in pastel and almost certainly all by the same artist—were catalogued as by "artist unknown" in their repository, the Monmouth County Historical Association in Northern New Jersey. Painstaking research and cross-checking over a period of years, however, finally identified the portraitist as Micah Williams, who worked primarily in the area surrounding New Brunswick, New Jersey in the early nineteenth century. A few oil portraits by Williams also have now been authenticated.

It is not known exactly where Williams was born, but old papers refer to him as a native of Essex County. His tombstone in North Brunswick Township gives the date of his birth as 1782 and of his death as 1837. Records of the First Presbyterian Church in New Brunswick show that he and his wife were married there in 1806, and that in time they had six children. Aside from that, little is known of his life.

Most of his known pastels were done in or near Monmouth County between 1818 and 1830. He was entirely self-taught and, according to one of his descendants, made his own pastels. One of his clients noted admiringly in his diary in March, 1823, that Williams had completed his likeness in a single day, starting in the morning and finishing by sundown.

Williams's work was noted for its rich, harmonious colors and its realistic effects. Like many primitive painters, he had problems with hands. In many portraits, they are stylized and folded stiffly across the lap or chest; in some of his depictions of men, one hand is conveniently tucked inside the coat between the buttons.

He tended to use standard poses and costumes. Women usually were portrayed in either a bright blue Empire dress with white ruffles at the neck or a black dress with rounded neckline and a kerchief. His portraits of men were keyed to the color of the sitter's eyes. A man with blue eyes, for instance, often was shown in a dark blue coat against a brilliant blue-green background.

From about 1829 until 1833, Williams worked in New York City. It is possible that he may have taken some instruction from "masters" in the city during that period. His last work shows more graceful poses for his sitters and a more realistic treatment of their hands.

A hallmark of Williams's work was the newspaper he always applied to the back of the paper used for his pastels, and additional newspaper glued to the back after the portrait had been framed.

Solomon Avery, 1820-1825, 26 x 22 in., signed verso. Courtesy of Abby Aldrich Rockefeller Folk Art Center, Williamsburg, Virginia.

SEASON	75-76	76-77	77-78	78-79	79-80	80-81	81-82	82-83	83-84	84-85
Paintings				1			2			
Dollars				$6,000			$13,500			

Record Sale: $9,000, SPB, 4/29/82, "Portrait of Lady and Gentleman," 33 × 28 in.

PUBLIC COLLECTIONS
Abby Aldrich Rockefeller Folk Art Center,
    Williamsburg, Virginia
Monmouth County Historical Association,
    New Jersey
Rutgers University, New Brunswick, New Jersey

Robert King, ca. 1830, 31 x 27 in.
Courtesy of The Passaic County Historical Society,
Paterson, New Jersey.

Jane Griffeth King, ca. 1830, 31 x 27 in.
Courtesy of The Passaic County Historical Society,
Paterson, New Jersey.

JOHN RITTO PENNIMAN
(1782-1841)

John Ritto Penniman was a very productive ornamental painter in the Boston area, as well as a talented academic portrait painter. He also did landscapes and paintings of historical and religious subjects.

In *Antiques* magazine, July, 1981, Carol Damon Andrews called Penniman "perhaps the most skilled, inventive and versatile ornamental artist and draftsman of his time in America." He was acquainted with Gilbert Stuart, and Stuart's influence can be seen in his portraits.

There is uncertainty about the year of Penniman's birth. Current conjecture is that he was born in Milford, Massachusetts in 1782 and baptized in January, 1783.

Whatever the correct date, he was a precocious boy and was apprenticed at 10, probably to a local ornamental painter. A painted clock dial with Penniman's signature is dated 1793; a *Self-Portrait in Miniature* (private collection) was done in 1796; and *The Family Group* (Museum of Fine Arts, Boston), an oil on canvas, was painted in 1798, when he was only 16.

In 1803, he opened his first shop in Roxbury, Massachusetts. While doing ornamental work on looking-glasses, frames and clocks, he was also trying to establish himself as an easel painter. He showed an early talent for portraiture, catching both the vitality and the individuality of his subjects.

He became a Mason in 1810, and over the next decade painted many commissions for the order. Eleven years later, however, he was expelled, probably because of a drinking problem. On at least two occasions, he also was committed to the House of Correction for non-payment of debts.

In 1819, Penniman completed what was considered the crowning achievement of his middle years—a 15-foot-square painting on glass of the

Henry Nolan (1782-1860), 1828-1830, 19⅞ x 16½ in.
Courtesy of Worcester Art Museum, Massachusetts.

spectacular fire which destroyed the Exchange Coffee House in Boston the previous year. Five years later, he painted the same scene on canvas.

When the Pendleton Lithographic Press was established in Boston in 1825, Penniman was one of the first artists to work for them. An inscription on one of his lithographs in 1826, in fact, indicates that it was the first drawing on stone ever done in the United States.

Plagued by drink and debts in later life, Penniman first moved to West Brookfield, near Worcester, Massachusetts, then, in 1837, to Baltimore, where he died four years later.

MEMBERSHIPS
Massachusetts Charitable Mechanics Association

PUBLIC COLLECTIONS
American Antiquarian Society,
  Worcester, Massachusetts
Christ Church, Boston
Essex Institute, Salem, Massachusetts
Fruitlands Museum, Harvard, Massachusetts
Hardwick Historical Society, Massachusetts
Museum of American China Trade,
  Milton, Massachusetts
Museum of Fine Arts, Boston
National Museum of American Art, Washington, D.C.

(No sales information available.)

SAMUEL L. WALDO
(1783-1861)

Recognized as a good, and sometimes even as an outstanding, portrait painter in his own right, Samuel Waldo is also known today as a partner in the longest-lived partnership in the annals of American art. For more than 30 years he and William Jewett, who began as his apprentice and then became his partner, collaborated successfully on portraits. It is generally believed that Waldo planned the overall design and painted the heads and hands, while Jewett did the figures, backgrounds and accessories.

Waldo was born in Windham, Connecticut in 1783. When he was 16 he went to Hartford to study with Joseph Steward, a retired minister who was also a self-taught artist and silhouettist. In 1803, he opened his own studio in Hartford, but then moved it to Litchfield, Connecticut.

Invited by John Rutledge, Waldo traveled South to Charleston, South Carolina, and spent three years there, busily painting portraits. This work, plus aid from patrons in New York, enabled him to go to London in 1806 to study with Benjamin West and John Singleton Copley, both of whom were prospering as painters in the British capital.

In 1809, Waldo returned to New York City and opened a studio there. Three years later he took on Jewett, first to grind paints and then as a pupil. The portraits that Waldo painted himself in these early days were both professional and proficient. One of the best examples is his *Self-Portrait* (1817, Metropolitan Museum of Art).

One critic has written that, when he painted portraits alone, Waldo could be both brilliant and solid, but that when he worked with Jewett the brilliance vanished and only the solidity remained. Be that as it may, the partnership flourished until Waldo retired in 1854.

The portraits bore the names of both men and, in general, they are considered among the strongest and the most three-

Robert G.L. De Peyster, 1828, 33 x 25¼ in., signed l.r. Courtesy of National Gallery of Art, Washington, D.C., Andrew W. Mellon Collection.

dimensional likenesses painted at that time.

Waldo painted landscapes and a few portraits independently, even during the years of his association with Jewett. He died in New York City in 1861.

MEMBERSHIPS
National Academy of Design

PUBLIC COLLECTIONS
Boston Athenaeum
Corcoran Gallery of Art, Washington, D.C.
Metropolitan Museum of Art, New York City
New-York Historical Society, New York City

SEASON	75-76	76-77	77-78	78-79	79-80	80-81	81-82	82-83	83-84	84-85
Paintings				3	4		1	1	1	
Dollars				$36,300	$7,000		$4,250	$2,500	$3,000	

Record Sale: $33,000, SPB, 10/27/78, "Major General Andrew Jackson," 33 × 26 in.

THOMAS SULLY
(1783-1872)

Thomas Sully, the leading American portrait painter of his generation, was born in Horncastle, England in 1783. He helped promote the romantic expression of mood in the more than 2,000 portraits he executed. Sully also painted nearly 500 landscapes, historic compositions and copies of old masters.

When Sully was nine, his actor parents brought the family to Charleston, South Carolina, where Sully grew up. He received early instruction from his brother-in-law, Jean Belzons, his older brother, Lawrence, a miniaturist, and Henry Benbridge.

At the beginning of his career, Sully worked as a miniaturist in Richmond and Norfolk, Virginia, living with his brother and family. After marrying Lawrence's widow in 1805, Sully moved to New York City, where he may have worked briefly with John Wesley Jarvis.

Sully visited Boston in 1807, and received criticism from Gilbert Stuart. He settled in Philadelphia in 1808, but continued to travel for study and commissions. He lived in London from 1809 to 1810, studying with Benjamin West and Thomas Lawrence. The latter's flowing, aristocratic style had a more lasting effect on Sully.

The artist combined his own theatrical tendencies with Lawrence's idealization and smoothly flowing oils. The resulting new-found flair for conveying personality is evident in paintings made after 1810. *Dr. Samuel Coates* (1811, Pennsylvania Hospital, Philadelphia) is an intimate portrait of a wealthy physician, whose casual pose and earnest expression provide insights to the man's character. This engaging realism is a marked departure from the conventional formal portraits of West, Copley and Stuart.

Yet Sully was no slave to realism. His faces are uniformly "pretty." Even a grizzled, 78-year-old Andrew Jackson resembled a matinee idol when painted

Daniel Lamotte, 1812-1813, 36⅜ x 29 in. Courtesy of National Museum of American Art, Smithsonian Institution, Gift of Mr. and Mrs. Ferdinand Lamotte III.

by Sully in 1845. As advice to others Sully wrote, "From long experience I know that resemblance in a portrait is essential; but no fault will be found with the artist (at least by the sitter) if he improve the appearance."

From his base in Philadelphia, Sully produced portraits of some of the most prominent figures of the nineteenth century, including *Thomas Jefferson* (1821, American Philosophical Society) and Andrew Jackson, as well as members of Philadelphia society. At the death of Charles Willson Peale in 1827, Sully was unquestionably Philadelphia's leading portrait painter.

He returned to England in 1838 to paint his most famous portrait, of young Queen Victoria, on a commission from the society of the Sons of St. George in Philadelphia (the original oil study is in the Metropolitan Museum of Art).

Sully was named an academician at the Pennsylvania Academy of the Fine Arts in 1812, and remained an active member of the organization. A book of advice for young artists, written in 1851, was published posthumously.

Sully died in Philadelphia in 1872.

PUBLIC COLLECTIONS
American Philosophical Society, Philadelphia
Corcoran Gallery of Art, Washington, D.C.
Detroit Institute of the Arts
Metropolitan Museum of Art, New York City
Museum of Fine Arts, Boston
National Gallery of Art, Washington, D.C.
National Portrait Gallery, Washington, D.C.
Pennsylvania Academy of the Fine Arts, Philadelphia
Philadelphia Museum of Art
Yale University Art Gallery, New Haven, Connecticut

SEASON	75-76	76-77	77-78	78-79	79-80	80-81	81-82	82-83	83-84	84-85
Paintings				1		10	7	8	15	8
Dollars				$7,000		$39,450	$56,900	$55,150	$65,300	$41,100

Record Sale: $22,000, CH, 12/11/81, "The McIlvaine Sisters," 25 × 30 in.

BASS OTIS
(1784-1861)

Bass Otis was a prolific painter of portraits during the first part of the nineteenth century. His work owes much to the influence of John Wesley Jarvis, with whom he studied, as well as to that of Gilbert Stuart and Thomas Sully. Otis received particular acclaim during his lifetime as a painter of the deceased. He was also known as the first lithographer in America.

Otis was born in 1784 in Bridgewater, Massachusetts, where he was apprenticed to a scythe-maker. After finishing his apprenticeship in 1805, he spent time learning painting from a coach painter. He may have worked as a limner, painting flat, folk-art portraits of residents of Massachusetts and Connecticut.

In 1808, Otis moved to New York City, working in the studio of John Wesley Jarvis, where he refined his technique. In 1812, he moved to Philadelphia.

His professional reputation grew following a July 1812 review in *The Port Folio,* one of the country's leading literary publications, which led to commissions for portraits for a national biography published by Joseph Delaphaine. *Dolly Madison* (1816, New York State Historical Association) is one of the few surviving original paintings from the collection of 14. Otis made many copies of a portrait of Thomas Jefferson that was considered the best of the series.

Although Otis was known to produce as many as 200 portraits in a single year, he painted few subject pictures. *Interior of a Smithy* (ca. 1815, Pennsylvania Academy of the Fine Arts), Otis's only major genre scene, reveals his fascination with the mechanical process. The painting has an overall romantic feel, yet it is painted with an eye to careful detail.

As an inventor, Otis created the perspective protractor. His experiments with lithography included the publica-

Interior of a Smithy, 1815, 51 x 81 in. Courtesy of The Pennsylvania Academy of the Fine Arts, Philadelphia.

tion of "House and Trees at Waterside" in the July, 1819 issue of *Analectic Magazine.*

Otis traveled extensively during his lifetime. He lived briefly in Wilmington, Delaware and Baltimore, Maryland, while pursuing commissions. He also resided in New York City and Boston before returning to Philadelphia, where he died in 1861.

MEMBERSHIPS
Columbian Society of Artists

PUBLIC COLLECTIONS
Museum of Fine Arts, Boston
New York State Historical Association, Cooperstown
Pennsylvania Academy of the Fine Arts, Philadelphia
Virginia Historical Society, Richmond

SEASON	75-76	76-77	77-78	78-79	79-80	80-81	81-82	82-83	83-84	84-85
Paintings				1	1	1			1	
Dollars				$3,000	$1,400	$1,500			$1,500	

Record Sale: $3,000, F.P., 10/31/78, "Napoleon Crossing the Alps," 32 × 26 in.

RUBENS PEALE
(1784-1865)

Rubens Peale, museum director and painter, was involved in the management of some of America's earliest museums, following the example of his father, artist-naturalist Charles Willson Peale.

Rubens Peale was born in 1784 in Philadelphia, where he grew up with weak eyes which prevented him from becoming a professional painter. Museum management became his chief activity. From 1810 to 1822, he was in charge of the Philadelphia Museum, founded by his father; from 1822 to 1825, he directed the Peale Museum in Baltimore; from 1825 to 1837, he managed the Peale Museum in New York City, where he had the enterprise to exhibit the first Egyptian mummy seen in America.

In 1837, Peale retired to his father-in-law's estate near Schuylkill Haven, Pennsylvania, spending his latter years as a country gentleman.

In 1855, Peale turned to creating art rather than exhibiting it, producing landscapes and, particularly, still-life paintings. Some of these were original compositions; many others were copies of works done by other members of the Peale family. Due in part to their varied sources, the still lifes vary greatly in quality. They display the general format used by the Peales, but often in a more primitive manner, due either to his limited artistic training or to his poor eyesight.

His best-known paintings are pictures of families of game birds in their natural settings. An example, *Ruffed Grouse in Underbrush* (1864), hangs in the Detroit Institute of Arts.

Peale died in 1865.

The Old Museum, 1858-1860, 14^{1}/$_{16}$ x 20 in. Courtesy of The Pennsylvania Academy of the Fine Arts, Philadelphia.

PUBLIC COLLECTIONS
Detroit Institute of Arts

SEASON	75-76	76-77	77-78	78-79	79-80	80-81	81-82	82-83	83-84	84-85
Paintings			1		1				1	
Dollars			$2,000		$1,900				$9,000	

Record Sale: $9,000, CH, 6/1/84, "Still Life," 15 × 19 in.

PHILIP TILYARD
(1785-1830)

A self-taught Baltimore portrait painter, Philip Tilyard once was described as an "honest and unfortunate man of genius." Critics now feel that, had he had the opportunity to fully develop his talents, his standing among the portraitists of the early nineteenth century would have been appreciably higher. As it is, his portraits were good likenesses, and reflected the influence of Thomas Sully in their moist skin tones.

Tilyard was born in Baltimore in 1785, the son of a glazier and sign-painter. He trained with his father to follow in his footsteps as a journeyman painter. Starting in 1814, however, he tried his hand at portrait painting and met with fair success. It is probable that he sought advice from Sully on how to develop his technique, during one of the latter's many visits to Baltimore.

When he won $20,000 in a lottery in 1816, Tilyard gave up painting altogether and bought a dry goods store, a venture which proved to be disastrous within a few years.

In 1882, he went back to painting portraits again. His work came to the attention of two of Baltimore's most important patrons of the arts, one of whom, John Pendleton Kennedy, sat for his portrait by Tilyard in 1827. Even Sully encouraged the now-promising painter.

One of Tilyard's most characteristic portraits is that of *Jonathan Granville* (1824, Baltimore Museum of Art), the first envoy from Santo Domingo to the United States. The silver earring in his left ear lends an interesting contrast to the otherwise straightforward depiction of the black envoy.

Tilyard died insane in 1830 before he had had the chance to realize his potential as a portraitist.

Jonathan Granville, 1824, 20 x 19 in. Courtesy of The Baltimore Museum of Art, Maryland, Purchase Fund.

PUBLIC COLLECTIONS
Baltimore Museum of Art

SEASON	75-76	76-77	77-78	78-79	79-80	80-81	81-82	82-83	83-84	84-85
Paintings					1		1			
Dollars					$1,000		$850			

Record Sale: $1,000, S.W, 12/2/79, "John Pillsbury Howard," 30 × 25 in.

JOHN JAMES AUDUBON
(1785-1851)

A century and a half after the publication of his 1838 classic, *The Birds of America,* John James Audubon still ranks as America's leading naturalist-artist.

Self-taught in both fields, Audubon captured the spirit of nature in hundreds of watercolors that record in accurate detail and vivid composition the rich variety of bird life in North America. The paintings of 489 species were based on expeditions Audubon made through the Ohio, Mississippi and Missouri river valleys, and up the Atlantic seaboard from Florida to Labrador, beginning in 1820.

Born in Haiti, the illegitimate son of a French sea captain and a Creole woman, Audubon struggled for years to find his professional niche. His mother died soon after his birth, and Audubon was taken by his father to France, where he was schooled for a naval career.

Audubon failed the officer-training tests, and in 1803 he fled to the United States to avoid military conscription. An unsuccessful attempt at farm management was followed by an equally unsuccessful attempt to run a general store in Kentucky.

In 1819, Audubon found himself in debtor's prison, bankrupt from having pursued his passion for art to the detriment of his business. "Nothing ... could ever answer my enthusiastic desires to present nature, except to copy her in her own way, alive and moving," he would say. Throughout his early years, Audubon hunted, captured and painted hundreds of birds.

Freed from jail in 1820, Audubon redoubled his efforts in ornithology, beginning the expeditions that would eventually establish his reputation as a naturalist of the first rank.

Philadelphia portraitist Thomas Sully encouraged Audubon, but publishers in New York and Philadelphia were less interested, and in 1826 Audubon sailed

Arctic Hare, ca. 1841, 24½ x 34¼ in. Courtesy of National Gallery of Art, Washington, D.C., Gift of E.J.L. Hallstrom.

Osprey with Weakfish, 40 x 26½ in. Courtesy of Vose Galleries of Boston, Inc., Massachusetts.

for England, gambling everything on a positive reception there. He was richly rewarded. England loved the charismatic frontiersman. A handsome, engaging 35-year-old, clothed in buckskins, Audubon made a hit in the drawing-rooms of London. His paintings, exhibited in Liverpool, in Manchester and at the Royal Academy, were well received.

Within a year, Audubon's watercolors were being engraved on copperplate for a four-volume classic by R. Havell and Son. The sets, completed in 1838, were sold by subscription for $1,000 each.

They are valued not only for Audubon's work, but also for the beautiful engravings by artist Robert Havell, Jr.

Successful at last, Audubon returned to his wife and two sons in the United States, settling on a 30-acre estate at Washington Heights on the Hudson River.

Audubon made his last trip into the wilderness in 1843. With the collaboration of his sons, Victor and John, both painters, he published his final major work—150 paintings of animals in *The Viviparous Quadrupeds of North America.* His other works, published before Audubon left England, are *Ornithological Biography* and *Synopsis of the Birds of America.*

MEMBERSHIPS
National Academy of Design
Linnean Society
Royal Society

SEASON	75-76	76-77	77-78	78-79	79-80	80-81	81-82	82-83	83-84	84-85
Paintings									2	
Dollars									$4,100	

Record Sale: $2,800, CH, 6/1/84, "Blue Feather," 9 × 7 in.

CHARLES BIRD KING
(1785-1862)

Charles Bird King was one of the most significant American still-life painters of his era, but it is for his portraits of American Indian leaders that he is best known.

King was born in 1785 in Newport, Rhode Island. After studying under painter Samuel King, the young artist ran away at 15 to work for five years in Edward Savage's New York City studio. From 1805 to 1812, King lived in London. There, he was a pupil of Benjamin West and shared a studio with Thomas Sully.

Again in America, King worked in Baltimore, Richmond and Philadelphia before permanently settling in Washington, D.C. in 1816. By the time the artist was 30, he had become the first significant resident artist in the nation's capital. He painted the leading political figures of the day, including John C. Calhoun, John Quincy Adams and Henry Clay.

As a portraitist, however, King is best known for his paintings of American Indian chiefs. Commissioned to paint members of a five-tribe Indian delegation which visited the capital city in 1821, King worked on the series for the next 16 years. These paintings were the foundation for the Smithsonian Institution's National Indian Portrait Gallery.

In 1832, Secretary of War James Barbour commented that King painted "the most exact resemblances, including the costume of each." Some critics, however, claimed that King's Indians were glorified white men, betraying the fact that the artist had never been West of the Mississippi and was painting his subjects largely from memory.

In 1865, a fire at the Smithsonian Institution destroyed most of King's Indian portraits; before the disaster, however, almost all of them had been lithographically preserved in the book *The Indian Tribes of North America*.

Young Omahaw, War Eagle, Little Missouri, and Pawness, 1821, 28 x 36⅛ in. Courtesy of National Museum of American Art, Smithsonian Institution, Lent by Smithsonian Institution, National Museum of Natural History, Department of Anthropology.

Important, though less well-known, are King's still lifes. Though the artist painted several tabletop arrangements, he often departed from tradition. Working in the trompe l'oeil tradition, he assembled objects to tell a story.

In *Vanity of An Artist's Dream* (1830, Fogg Art Museum, Cambridge), for example, King showed a cupboard filled with books, palette and the notice of a sheriff's sale—to symbolize the often difficult economic realities of an artist's life.

King died in Washington, D.C. in 1862.

SEASON	75-76	76-77	77-78	78-79	79-80	80-81	81-82	82-83	83-84	84-85
Paintings	3			2				5		1
Dollars	$34,700			$46,100				$14,950		$825

Record Sale: $45,000, CH, 5/23/79, "John Quincy Adams, James Madison," 24 × 19 in.

JOHN LEWIS KRIMMEL

(1787-1821)

Country Wedding: Bishop White Officiating, 1814, 16 x 22 in. Courtesy of The Pennsylvania Academy of the Fine Arts, Philadelphia, Pennsylvania.

John Lewis Krimmel was known as "the American Hogarth" for his genial scenes of everyday life in the early nineteenth century. He is considered the first professional genre painter in the United States and an important influence on the later development of this type of painting.

Krimmel's American career was only 11 years long. He came to Philadelphia from Wurtenberg, Germany in 1810 and drowned in 1821, at age 34.

When Krimmel arrived in America, Europe and England were enamored of genre painting, a style with roots in seventeenth-century Holland. Krimmel's fine brushstrokes, careful detail, crowded eventful scenes and humorous elements indicate that he was a student of the mode and certainly had training, perhaps in the painting of miniatures.

His scenes of country weddings, dances and other frolics appealed to both popular and critical taste. The originals were exhibited often, and purchased by leading museums and serious collectors.

Hundreds of engravings and lithographs of his pictures raised Krimmel to the height of popularity. They became a much-imitated source of ideas and style for the next generation of genre painters.

His *View of Central Square, on the 4th of July* (date and location unknown), shown at the 1812 Pennsylvania Academy exhibition in Philadelphia, assured his continuing success.

Krimmel sensibly resisted suggestions that he paint traditional historical works, apparently recognizing that the limitations and virtues of his talent were precisely attuned to his subject, and thus provided works of unique historical importance. Beyond their stylistic qualities, Krimmel's pictures give an authentic, if romanticized, glimpse into bygone folkways. He often made his own versions of continental "best-selling" genre art, sometimes borrowing from the well-known English engraver, David Wilkie.

PUBLIC COLLECTIONS
National Gallery of Art, Washington, D.C.
Pennsylvania Academy of the Fine Arts,
Philadelphia

SEASON	75-76	76-77	77-78	78-79	79-80	80-81	81-82	82-83	83-84	84-85
Paintings								1	2	
Dollars								$659	$287,000	

Record Sale: $280,000, CH, 12/9/83, "Blind Man's Bluff; Blind Fiddler," 17 × 22 in.

JAMES FULTON PRINGLE
(1788-1847)

Smith & Dimon Shipyard, 1833, 32 x 50¾ in., signed l.r. Courtesy of New York State Historical Association, Cooperstown, New York.

James Fulton Pringle was an important American painter of ship portraits during the early nineteenth century, but he also painted portraits and landscapes.

Born in 1788 in Sydenham, England, Pringle came to the United States around 1830. He settled in Brooklyn and became an active member of the National Academy of Design. He frequently exhibited at the Academy between 1832 and 1844.

Pringle's paintings of ships and shipbuilding form an important part of the American genre painting that flourished in the nineteenth century. New York City was a center of the shipbuilding industry during Pringle's lifetime, and his detailed paintings serve as valuable documents of the beginning of the clipper-ship era, as in *The Eagle* (1833, location unknown). In addition to the numerous ships in action which Pringle depicted,

he painted a few dramatic marine disasters, some landscapes and portraits. Paintings such as *The Smith and Dimon Shipyard, East River, New York* (1833, New York State Historical Society) document city life.

Pringle's work is detailed and carefully executed. Every tree, person, animal, flag or building is sharply defined. His style is charming in its naivety.

Pringle died in 1847 in Brooklyn.

SEASON	75-76	76-77	77-78	78-79	79-80	80-81	81-82	82-83	83-84	84-85
Paintings									1	
Dollars									$9,000	

Record Sale: $9,000, S.W, 4/29/84, "Sailing Ships, Louisville," 28 × 36 in.

MEMBERSHIPS
National Academy of Design

PUBLIC COLLECTIONS
New York State Historical Association,
Cooperstown

AMMI PHILLIPS
(1788-1865)

Itinerant portraitist Ammi Phillips, known as the Border Limner and Kent Limner, stands out among America's folk artists. He was a prolific painter whose career spanned about 55 years.

Phillips was born in Colebrook, Connecticut in 1788. His earliest known work is dated 1811, but it was not until about 1958 that researchers uncovered facts revealing Phillips to be the Kent-Border Limner, solving a long-standing puzzle of identity.

A self-taught artist, Phillips traveled in Massachusetts and the area claimed by New York and Connecticut as Border Country—thus the name Border Limner. It is believed that works by Reuben Moulthrop influenced his formative years.

His Border portraits, from 1812 to 1819, tend to be primitive in style; characteristic is a full-length portrait of *Harriet Leavens* (1815), where the flat outlined figure, in soft hues, is naively simple. Light pearly tones of this period create an ethereal charm.

Phillips married in 1813 and made Troy, New York his home base, covering the nearby territory and working on neighborhood commissions. He generally moved on after exhausting prospects in the area. After the death of his young wife, he remarried and subsequently lived in Poughkeepsie, Amenia, and Northeast in Dutchess County.

The Kent portrait period, when he painted prominent members of Kent,

Dr. Benjamin Brewster Darrance, ca. 1817-1818, 30 x 24 in. Courtesy of Wunderlich and Company, Inc., New York, New York.

Connecticut families from the late 1820s to the 1840s, was his most productive. He journeyed down the Hudson River to Phillipsburgh in Orange County, away from his farm and family on painting trips. Sharply defined expressions and an often poster-like appearance typified his subjects, and his stylized and decorative compositions exhibited certain abstract qualities.

Phillips lived and worked in the Massachusetts Berkshires in later years, until his death at age 77. By the 1860s, the advent of the daguerreotype, coupled with the changing tastes of the public, caused his work to become more realistic than his several earlier styles.

PUBLIC COLLECTIONS
Abby Aldrich Rockefeller Folk Art Collection, Williamsburg
Albany Institute of History and Art
Art Institute of Chicago
Berkshire Museum, Pittsfield, Massachusetts
Connecticut Historical Society, Hartford
Harvard University
Metropolitan Museum of Art, New York City
National Gallery of Art, Washington, D.C.
Princeton University
Senate House, Kingston, New York

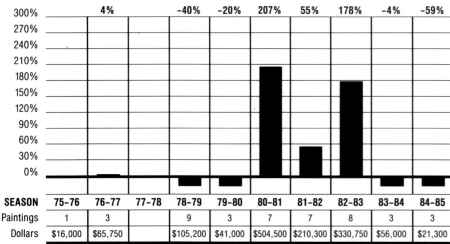

10-Year Average Change From Base Years '75-'76: 36%

	75-76	76-77	77-78	78-79	79-80	80-81	81-82	82-83	83-84	84-85
	4%			-40%	-20%	207%	55%	178%	-4%	-59%
SEASON	75-76	76-77	77-78	78-79	79-80	80-81	81-82	82-83	83-84	84-85
Paintings	1	3		9	3	7	7	8	3	3
Dollars	$16,000	$65,750		$105,200	$41,000	$504,500	$210,300	$330,750	$56,000	$21,300

Record Sale: $185,000, SPB, 11/21/80, "The Ten Broeck Twins," 30 × 50 in.

JOSHUA JOHNSON
(Active 1789-1832)

Reputed to be America's first professional black artist, Joshua Johnson (or Johnston) practiced portrait painting in Baltimore from 1796 until 1824. There is conjecture regarding his early life and artistic training; his style is believed to have been influenced by Charles Peale Polk, a Baltimore painter during the 1790s.

In 1948, the Peale Museum in Baltimore exhibited a comprehensive group of Johnson's portraits, some owned by descendants of the prominent Baltimoreans who were his subjects. There is conflicting information from these families as to whether the painter was a slave owned by the forebears.

A Baltimore directory for 1796 first listed Johnson as a portrait painter, continuing until 1824. Listings never included slaves; at least twice he was named as a freeman. Therefore, it is believed that though he may have been a slave, in all probability he was able to purchase freedom through his endeavors. During the 28-year period of his activity, directory records describe him as a limner or portrait painter. It is likely, if he had a legal or artistic "master," it would have been a member of the Peale family.

Characteristic of Johnson's style are stiff, doll-like figures, with eyes staring forward from expressionless faces. Tight-lipped and prim, his thinly painted figures of flat appearance, often posed individually or in family groups, possess a certain charm. Sheraton chairs or settees, on which they were often seated, show detailed brass nailheads. Women wore Empire gowns and children often appeared in high-waisted white dresses and red slippers. Attention was given to bright gold buttons, jewelry, lace collars, cords and tassels; sitters often held objects such as gloves, letters, fruit or flower baskets.

Johnson's painting *The Westwood Children* (1807, National Gallery of Art)

Letitia Grace McCurdy, 41 x 34½ in. Photograph courtesy of Hirschl & Adler Galleries, Inc., New York, New York.

portrays three young sons of John Westwood wearing dark-green suits with lace collars. Two of the boys hold a flower while the older boy holds a basket of flowers. As in many of his paintings, there is a dark background and a glimpse of trees through a window. Strange-looking dogs appear in several of his paintings of children, and this one depicts a dog in profile clenching a retrieved bird.

After Johnson's time, it was many years before another member of his race even attempted portraiture; Johnson's contribution to American history and the American Negro's cultural development was therefore important.

SEASON	75-76	76-77	77-78	78-79	79-80	80-81	81-82	82-83	83-84	84-85
Paintings										1
Dollars										$4,000

Record Sale: $4,000, SPB, 1/31/85, "Portrait of Mr. & Mrs. Hilmar Schumacher," 22 × 18 in.

PUBLIC COLLECTIONS
Baltimore Museum of Art
Frick Museum, New York City
Maryland Historical Society, Baltimore
National Gallery of Art, Washington, D.C.

SAMUEL F.B. MORSE
(1791-1872)

Samuel Finley Breese Morse, figure and portrait painter, sculptor and inventor, was born in Charlestown, Massachusetts in 1791. Though perhaps remembered best as the inventor of the telegraph, Morse was a major influence on the development of American art in the first half of the nineteenth century.

Morse is known for his portraits, miniatures and history paintings, as well as for his role in founding the National Academy of Design in 1826. He served as the organization's first president from 1826 to 1845.

Upon graduation from Yale College in 1810, where he had painted miniatures on ivory, Morse accompanied Washington Allston to London. There, he studied with both Allston and Benjamin West. In 1813, he received a gold medal from the Society of Arts for his clay model for the painting, *The Dying Hercules* (ca. 1812, Yale University).

While in London, Morse came to believe that history painting was an artist's highest calling. But upon his return to the United States in 1815, he found no commissions for this genre, and resorted to portraiture to make a living. For the next nine years, Morse seasonally migrated from Massachusetts to New Hampshire to South Carolina seeking portrait commissions.

He painted *The Old House of Representatives* (1822, Corcoran Gallery of Art) and sought to display it throughout the country, but was forced to work for seven more years as a portraitist to get out of debt.

After settling in New York City in 1823, Morse achieved the height of his fame. In 1824, the City of New York commissioned him to paint a full-length portrait of the Marquis de Lafayette for its City Hall. The work is one of the finest Romantic portraits of the period. It is both symbolic and historic, with its rich sunset silhouetting the majestically elongated Lafayette.

William Whitlock, Jr. (One of a Pair), 36 x 29 in. Courtesy of Kennedy Galleries, New York, New York.

Soon after this work was completed, Morse led a disgruntled group away from the American Academy of Fine Arts to found the National Academy of Design. In 1829, seeking a different intellectual climate, he traveled to Europe. Upon his return, he completed *The Exhibition Gallery of the Louvre* (1833, Syracuse University), a tribute to the old masters he tried to emulate.

Morse's next few years were frustrating. He taught at New York University, and also privately instructed some students in painting and photography, including Matthew Brady. But when he failed to win a commission for the historic paintings on the Capitol Rotunda, Morse abandoned painting altogether.

His last two major paintings, however, are noteworthy. *Allegorical Landscape* (1836, New-York Historical Society) was a history picture done in accordance with a color theory which Morse attributed to Veronese. *The Muse* (1836, Metropolitan Museum of Art) was a chromatically brilliant painting of Morse's daughter.

From 1837, when he invented the telegraph, until his death in 1872, Morse's artistic activity was limited to management of the National Academy and his interest in the daguerreotype.

MEMBERSHIPS
National Academy of Design

PUBLIC COLLECTIONS
Chrysler Museum, Norfolk, Virginia
City Hall, New York City
Corcoran Gallery of Art, Washington, D.C.
Metropolitan Museum of Art, New York City
National Gallery of Art, Washington, D.C.
Yale University

SEASON	75-76	76-77	77-78	78-79	79-80	80-81	81-82	82-83	83-84	84-85
Paintings			1	1	1		2	1		
Dollars			$19,000	$451	$2,000		$11,270	$2,600		

Record Sale: $19,000, SPB, 3/22/78, "Portrait of Robert Young Hayne," 30 × 25 in.

ALVAN FISHER
(1792-1863)

A pioneer in American genre, landscape, and animal painting, Alvan Fisher was born in Dedham, Massachusetts in 1792. He studied his craft in Boston under ornamental painter John Ritto Penniman.

Although Fisher's first rural landscapes, painted in 1811, were harshly dramatic, by 1821 his style had become softer and more delicate.

After a trip to Europe in 1825, Fisher's work was more refined. He set up his own studio in Boston. Although he was an unsophisticated painter, he was also successful; his notebooks record sales of nearly 1,000 paintings between 1826 and his death in 1863.

Fisher traveled throughout the Eastern United States, recording his observations in his notebook. He painted a number of views of Niagara Falls, emphasizing the grandeur of the natural scene as contrasted with insignificant figures along the shore. While his interpretation does not approach in scope or vitality the definitive treatment of Frederic Edwin Church, it has a certain charm of its own.

Sugar Loaf Mountain (1821, location unknown) contains the "water, rising ground, and woodbanks" prescribed by eighteenth-century landscape theorist William Gilpin as ingredients of the picturesque. This painting demonstrates how Fisher combined and rearranged observed details to conform to the existing conventions of romantic landscape.

Indians Crossing a Frozen Lake, 1841, 24 x 30 in., signed l.l. Courtesy of Vose Galleries of Boston, Inc., Massachusetts.

Like all his paintings, it has a pleasantly idyllic quality enhanced by his lyrical use of color.

Fisher also painted anecdotal rural scenes (in the tradition of eighteenth-century British painter George Morland) and was the first American to paint race horses. Like the work of his contemporaries and associates, Thomas Doughty and Joshua Shaw, his art was a modest prelude to the paintings of the Hudson River School, to the heroic compositions of Cole and Church, and to the quieter panoramas of Kensett and Lane.

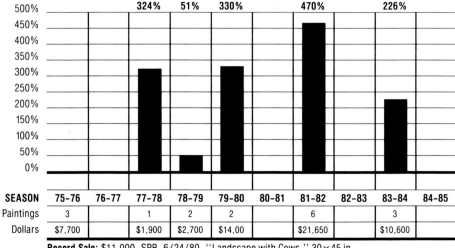

10-Year Average Change From Base Years '75-'76: 234%

	75-76	76-77	77-78	78-79	79-80	80-81	81-82	82-83	83-84	84-85
			324%	51%	330%		470%		226%	
SEASON	75-76	76-77	77-78	78-79	79-80	80-81	81-82	82-83	83-84	84-85
Paintings	3		1	2	2		6		3	
Dollars	$7,700		$1,900	$2,700	$14,00		$21,650		$10,600	

Record Sale: $11,000, SPB, 6/24/80, "Landscape with Cows," 30 × 45 in.

MEMBERSHIPS
National Academy of Design

PUBLIC COLLECTIONS
National Collection of Fine Arts, Washington, D.C.
Wadsworth Atheneum, Hartford, Connecticut

WILLIAM GUY WALL

(1792-1864?)

Covered Bridge across the Sacandaga River, Hadley, New York, ca. 1820, 19 1/8 x 27 in. Courtesy of the New-York Historical Society, New York, New York.

Although he was born and died in Ireland, William Guy Wall was a prominent figure in the early history of American landscape painting.

Born in Dublin in 1792 and married there in 1812, he came to New York City already an accomplished artist. Much of his importance was due to his sophisticated training, which was superior to that which most native-born American artists acquired. Wall's skillful handling of atmospheric perspective and his understanding of the effects of light were highly impressive to eyes used to more naive and literal renderings.

His delicate and subtle watercolors were first published in an edition of engravings, the *Hudson River Portfolio,* which enjoyed great success and ensured a brisk business for Wall as a painter of Hudson River and New York scenes.

After his son, William Archibald Wall (also later to become a landscape painter), was born in New York City in 1828, Wall moved to Newport, Rhode Island. From there he moved to New Haven, Connecticut and then to Brooklyn, New York.

During this first stay in America, Wall assisted in the' founding of the

influential National Academy of Design. He exhibited his paintings there and in other such important institutions as the Pennsylvania Academy of the Fine Arts in Philadelphia and the Apollo Association.

After 1835, Wall returned to Ireland for about 20 years, continuing to exhibit in England and the United States as well as in Ireland. Although he returned to the United States in 1856, to live in Newburgh, New York for four years, he came home finally to Ireland and died some time after 1864.

SEASON	75-76	76-77	77-78	78-79	79-80	80-81	81-82	82-83	83-84	84-85
Paintings	1						1			
Dollars	$3,100						$700			

Record Sale: $3,100, PB, 12/12/75, "The Coroner's Letter," 7 × 12 in.

MEMBERSHIPS
National Academy of Design

PUBLIC COLLECTIONS
Metropolitan Museum of Art, New York City

CHESTER HARDING
(1792-1866)

Chester Harding's career took him from the American backwoods to the salons of Boston and London. Self-taught, he was one of the mid-nineteenth century's most successful portraitists, matching the popularity of his exemplar, Gilbert Stuart. He was also a woodworker, army drummer in the War of 1812, peddler, tavernkeeper and sign painter.

Harding was born in 1792 in Conway, Massachusetts. The family later moved to New York State.

In Pittsburgh in 1817, influenced by an itinerant painter, Harding tried a portrait of his wife in sign colors. He wrote, "The moment I saw the likeness, I became frantic with delight; it was like the dawning of a new sense."

Pursuing his new calling in Paris, Kentucky, Harding prospered, commanding $25 a likeness. He had astonishing natural talent and no conceit. Seeking improvement, he enrolled at the Pennsylvania Academy of the Fine Arts in Philadelphia in 1820. He left after two months, intimidated by Stuart's work: "It was a good while before I could get into my former free style of painting," he said.

He returned to Kentucky, where he painted the only life portrait of Daniel Boone, then 90. He went on to great success in lower Ohio and St. Louis.

Harding went to Boston in 1822. Academicians there disparaged his work as unschooled, overlooking its virtues. Other Bostonians rushed to sit for "an untutored backwoodsman newly caught" who could paint "a tolerable portrait," as Harding wrote. Stuart, who lost many commissions to his admiring rival, would inquire wryly, "How goes the 'Harding fever'?"

Unaffected by adulation, Harding sought instruction in England in 1823. There he was lionized. To have time for study, he had to refuse commissions from all but the royal family.

Daniel Webster, ca. 1828, 36¼ x 28¼ in. Courtesy of National Portrait Gallery, Washington, D.C., Gift of Mrs. Gerard B. Lambert.

Harding returned to Boston in 1826, settling in Springfield, Massachusetts in 1830. For more than two decades he painted American statesmen, leading citizens and their families.

He painted Charles Carroll at age 91, the last surviving signer of the Declaration of Independence, as well as fine portraits of Daniel Webster, John C. Calhoun, Henry Clay and William T. Sherman.

The technical polish Harding had acquired in England did not obscure the original honesty and vitality of his art. Not innovative, Harding's work resembles that of other competent artists of his day.

Harding died in Boston in 1866.

MEMBERSHIPS
Harding's Hall, Boston
National Academy of Design

PUBLIC COLLECTIONS
Bar Association of New York
Corcoran Gallery, Washington, D.C.
Metropolitan Museum of Art, New York City
Museum of Fine Arts, Boston
National Gallery, Washington, D.C.

SEASON	75-76	76-77	77-78	78-79	79-80	80-81	81-82	82-83	83-84	84-85
Paintings		2	1		1	2			1	1
Dollars		$3,335	$1,320		$950	$6,071			$882	$2,442

Record Sale: $5,000, CH, 4/24/81, "Portrait of Mrs. Humphrey Devereux," 27 x 21 in.

RUFUS PORTER
(1792-1884)

An inventor, scientist and journalist, Rufus Porter is best known today for his work as an itinerant artist. His murals, landscapes and inexpensive portraits and silhouettes have secured his place as one of America's outstanding native artists.

Porter was born a farmer's son in Massachusetts in 1792. When the family moved to Maine eight years later, the young Porter attended school for only six months before taking up fiddling, farming and shoemaking.

In 1816, Porter became a portrait painter. For the next eight years, he traveled through New England and the mid-Atlantic states executing silhouettes and portraits. According to his advertising handbills dating from the early 1800s, the artist painted "correct likenesses" in full-color or ivory miniature.

By 1861, Porter had constructed a camera obscura, a device which enabled him to make silhouette portraits in less than 15 minutes. These portraits cost 20 cents and were in great demand.

But it is for his work as an itinerant muralist that Porter is best known. With the same ingenious dispatch that characterized his portraits and silhouettes, Porter basically established a one-man factory for interior design and decoration.

Porter's murals, naturalistic and reminiscent of the Hudson River School, were painted over mantelpieces; occasionally they covered entire walls. To expedite his painting, he used outline drawings, stencils and a limited (albeit bright) range of colors. The resulting landscapes are large-scale and bold, evoking a unique amiability, despite the fact that they are highly stylized.

From 1824 to 1845, Porter is credited with having painted more than 150 such murals.

His work as a muralist came to an abrupt end in 1845, when he moved to New York City to become a journalist.

Profile of a Lady with a Ruff, ca. 1820, 4⅝ x 3⁹/₁₆ in. Courtesy of Abby Aldrich Rockefeller Folk Art Center, Williamsburg, Virginia.

Porter published and edited *New York Mechanic, American Mechanic* and *Scientific American.* He published several books and, during the last few years of his life, concentrated on creating new inventions.

Porter was visiting one of his 16 children in New Haven, Connecticut when he died in 1884.

PUBLIC COLLECTIONS
Maine State Museum, Augusta

(No sales information available.)

WILLIAM JENNYS
(Active 1793-1807)

William Jennys was an early itinerant portrait painter. A good number of his works survive, but very little is known about his life. Most of his figures are shown in three-quarter view within an oval format. His sitters are distinctive for the intensity of their expressions; they all tend to stare directly at the viewer.

Jennys was painting in the New Milford, Connecticut area in the mid-1790s, and then moved to New York City for two years. After 1800, he traveled the Connecticut River valley into Massachusetts and then moved into Vermont, painting portraits as he went. Finally he turned East to Newburyport and Portsmouth, New Hampshire.

A Richard Jennys also painted portraits in a similar style, and there is considerable speculation that the two may have been related, perhaps even brothers who may have emigrated from England together. What is known is that both were painting portraits in the New Milford area around the same time. William Jennys's earliest work bore a strong resemblance to Richard's, but after 1795 his portraits became considerably more realistic.

In his later work, William Jennys allowed direct light to throw strong shadows across the features of his sitters. The results were well-modeled faces unique at the time. It seems likely that William Jennys influenced other Connecticut Valley artists with his strong, pictorial style. It is reflected in the work of such men as Simon Fitch and Reuben Moulthrop.

Like other primitive painters, Jennys had difficulty with arms and hands, and in many instances avoided showing them. Where limbs do show, the arms tend to appear tube-like.

There was some confusion at one time over portraits that appeared to have been signed "J. William Jennys." This now appears to have resulted from a misreading of the signature, however, and those works that were once in doubt are now included in the modest body of work known to have been painted by William Jennys.

Gentleman of the Brewer Family of Hartford, Connecticut, ca. 1800, 29 x 24½ in. Courtesy of The Shelburne Museum, Shelburne, Virginia.

Young Lady, 20 x 16 in., signed l.r. Courtesy of William A. Farnsworth Library and Art Museum, Rockland, Maine.

SEASON	75-76	76-77	77-78	78-79	79-80	80-81	81-82	82-83	83-84	84-85
Paintings				1	2	3				1
Dollars				$20,000	$19,000	$28,750				$6,000

Record Sale: $20,000, SPB, 1/27/79, "Portrait of a Young Woman," 30 × 25 in.

PUBLIC COLLECTIONS
Abby Aldrich Rockefeller Folk Art Center, Williamsburg, Virginia
Corcoran Gallery of Art, Washington, D.C.
Lyman Allyn Museum, New London, Connecticut
Museum of Fine Arts, Boston
Westfield Athenaeum, Massachusetts

THOMAS DOUGHTY
(1793-1856)

A trailblazer for the Hudson River School, Thomas Doughty was one of the first American painters to turn exclusively to landscape.

Born in Philadelphia in 1793, Doughty turned to art as a leisure activity; his apprenticeship and business were in the manufacture of leather. For art instruction, he received a scant three months' training in India-ink drawing. Yet the pull of his creativity was strong; against the urgings of family and friends, he began in 1814 to alternate between the professions of painter and leather currier. In 1820, he cut ties to his former profession completely.

The decision was a good one. By 1822, the prolific artist was exhibiting frequently at the Pennsylvania Academy of the Fine Arts, and was elected an academician two years later. In 1827, he was named an honorary member of the National Academy of Design.

Although he was immersed in the creative Pennsylvania Academy milieu, which included his friends, the noted portraitists Chester Harding and Thomas Sully, Doughty worked exclusively as a landscape artist at a time when no other American painter was doing so. He appealed to the nation's awakening interest in its own landscape, and thereby achieved a substantial success.

He was also an innovator in lithography. With his brother John, he published the monthly journal *Cabinet of Natural*

Cottage by a Lake, 25 x 30 in. Private Collection, Photograph courtesy of Vose Galleries of Boston, Inc., Massachusetts.

History and American Rural Sports from 1830 to 1834. In it, animals and birds were drawn carefully from stuffed specimens, but landscape backgrounds were added by Thomas Doughty.

Doughty classified his works into three categories: "from nature," "from recollection" and "composition." One chief complaint of his later detractors was that even those works he placed in the first category tended to belong to the last. There was often more of Doughty in his landscapes than there was of the location he painted.

In ·1832, Doughty left Philadelphia, settling primarily in Boston for the next five years, although he lived in Baltimore and Washington as well. In 1837,

he went to England for two years, where his tendency to idealize his landscapes was accentuated. He returned to the United States and settled semi-permanently in New York City, except for two short stays in other parts of New York State and another long trip to Europe. He died in New York City in 1856.

The factors which had ensured Doughty's first success contained the seeds of his downfall. His lyrical views of the Hudson River Valley and of other East Coast scenes (both real and imagined) were acceptable to his early, wary American public. Tranquil and gossamer-like, they paved the way for but were surpassed by the less ingratiating, monumental works of Thomas Cole and the other artists of the later Hudson River School. By the end of his life, Doughty's work was seen as over-mannered and too unspecific compared to that of his successors.

MEMBERSHIPS
Pennsylvania Academy of the Fine Arts
National Academy of Design

PUBLIC COLLECTIONS
Brooklyn Museum
California Palace of the Legion of Honor
Corcoran Gallery of Art, Washington, D.C.
Detroit Institute of Arts
Metropolitan Museum of Art, New York City
New York State Historical Society, Cooperstown
Newark Museum, New Jersey
Harvard University
Pennsylvania Academy of the Fine Arts, Philadelphia

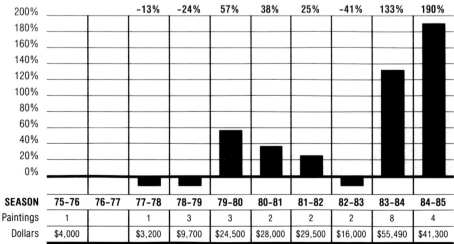

10-Year Average Change From Base Years '75-'76: 41%

		-13%	-24%	57%	38%	25%	-41%	133%	190%

SEASON	75-76	76-77	77-78	78-79	79-80	80-81	81-82	82-83	83-84	84-85
Paintings	1		1	3	3	2	2	2	8	4
Dollars	$4,000		$3,200	$9,700	$24,500	$28,000	$29,500	$16,000	$55,490	$41,300

Record Sale: $25,000, BB.SF, 10/3/81, "Fisherman by a Mountain Stream," 22 × 28 in.

ROBERT HAVELL, JR.
(1793-1878)

Fortunate, coincidental and unplanned events moved Robert Havell, Jr., through a successful art career.

Born in Reading, England in 1793, the son of an engraver, his vocation awaited him. He is chiefly remembered for engraving all but the first 10 plates for John James Audubon's *Birds of America.* Aquatint was enjoying its heyday; the skills of Audubon and Havell were complementary, mutually advancing their fame.

In 1839, Havell visited Audubon in New York City, and resided in Brooklyn until 1841. He traveled and sketched in the countryside with his family in a homemade horse-drawn trailer. The travel-weary Mrs. Havell acquired a house for the family in Ossining, on the Hudson River, in 1842. He later moved to Tarrytown, New York in 1857, residing there until his death in 1878.

His published engraving, *West Point from Fort Putnam* (1848), received public acclaim. Among his engravings were views of American cities.

While competent in oils and watercolors, Havell thought of himself basically as an engraver, during a period when many artists tailored their efforts toward volumes of engraved views.

He frequently traveled the countryside making sketches, supplemented with copious notes. Returning home, he would translate his sketches into oil paintings, only a few of which were sold during his lifetime. Most are Hudson River scenes.

PUBLIC COLLECTIONS
Metropolitan Museum of Art, New York City
New-York Historical Society, New York City

View of the Hudson River from Tarrytown Heights, 22 x 30 in. Photograph Courtesy of Kennedy Galleries, New York, New York.

Niagara Falls, 36 x 48 in. Courtesy of Vose Galleries of Boston, Inc., Massachusetts.

SEASON	75-76	76-77	77-78	78-79	79-80	80-81	81-82	82-83	83-84	84-85
Paintings						1		2		
Dollars						$21,000		$5,828		

Record Sale: $21,000, SPB, 10/17/80, "View from Tarrytown of the Hudson River," 36 × 50 in.

JOHN NEAGLE
(1796-1865)

John Neagle had a successful career painting the portraits of affluent Philadelphians who wanted it known that they were successful and secure. His most famous painting, however, considered a masterpiece of nineteenth-century portraiture, flaunted convention and showed its subject not as a gentleman, but as a rugged, defiant blacksmith working in his smithy.

His *Pat Lyon at the Forge* (1826-1827, Museum of Fine Arts, Boston) was painted as it was because Lyon requested it that way. Although a wealthy engineer when the portrait was done, in his younger days the subject had been a blacksmith and a locksmith, and had been falsely accused and imprisoned for a bank theft. Even after he was completely exonerated, Lyon wanted no part of a genteel portrait that would make him appear a member of the class he resented.

Neagle was born while his parents were visiting in Boston in 1796, but spent nearly all his life in Philadelphia. He attended drawing school as a boy and, in 1813, was apprenticed to Thomas Wilson, a coach painter who was himself taking lessons from Bass Otis, the portrait painter and lithographer.

Neagle, too, began studying with Otis, who in turn introduced him to Thomas Sully, then the reigning portrait painter in Philadelphia. Eventually Neagle would marry Sully's stepdaugh-

Adam Eckfeldt, 24 x 20 in. Courtesy of The Pennsylvania Academy of the Fine Arts, Philadelphia.

ter. Sully's influence, his vivid coloring and his tendency to idealize his subjects, can be seen in Neagle's work.

In 1818, Neagle set out for Lexington, Kentucky and New Orleans in search of portrait commissions. Both cities had established portraitists, however, and he returned to Philadelphia. In time, he found plenty of sitters to paint there.

In 1825, now with a growing reputation, Neagle traveled to Boston to get advice from Gilbert Stuart, the most influential portrait painter of the day. Not only did Stuart give advice, but he also allowed Neagle to paint his portrait (1825, Museum of Fine Arts, Boston). Today it is looked upon as one of the finest portraits of Stuart that exists. Stuart's influence, as well as Sully's, can be seen in Neagle's later portraits, particularly in his remarkable brushwork.

Aside from two trips to Kentucky to paint portraits, Neagle remained in Philadelphia until he was immobilized by a stroke and died in 1865.

MEMBERSHIPS
Artists' Fund Society
National Academy of Design

PUBLIC COLLECTIONS
Baltimore Museum of Art
Corcoran Gallery of Art, Washington, D.C.
Detroit Institute of Arts
Metropolitan Museum of Art, New York City
Newark Museum, New Jersey
Pennsylvania Academy of the Fine Arts, Philadelphia
Pennsylvania Historical Society, Philadelphia

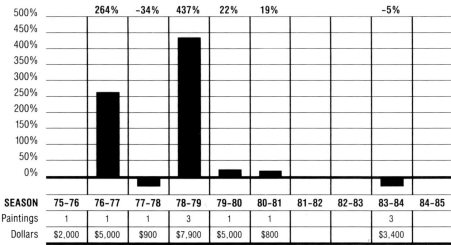

10-Year Average Change From Base Years '75-'76: 100%

	264%	-34%	437%	22%	19%			-5%	

SEASON	75-76	76-77	77-78	78-79	79-80	80-81	81-82	82-83	83-84	84-85
Paintings	1	1	1	3	1	1			3	
Dollars	$2,000	$5,000	$900	$7,900	$5,000	$800			$3,400	

Record Sale: $5,000, PB, 10/28/76, "Portrait of Rev. Henry B. Bascom," 29 × 24 in.

ROBERT STREET
(1796-1865)

Robert Street was a successful and popular artist. He is known to have painted historical and biblical compositions (none of the latter seem to have survived), and was highly noted as a portraitist. His ability to dignify his subjects on canvas with a firm visual honesty made him a sought-after and unique portrait painter.

Nothing is known of Street before 1815, except that he was born in the Germantown section of Philadelphia in 1796. It was in 1815 that he first exhibited at the Pennsylvania Academy of the Fine Arts in Philadelphia, which he would continue to do on occasion until 1861. By 1824 his fame had risen; he had exhibited for the first time in Washington, D.C., and painted a portrait of Andrew Jackson. (He painted Jackson again in 1840 in Philadelphia.)

In 1834, Street painted Joseph Bonaparte, the eldest brother of Napoleon, who was living on an estate in Bordentown, New Jersey.

Street exhibited more than 200 paintings at the Artist's Fund Hall in Philadelphia in November of 1840. The exhibition consisted of landscapes and historical compositions as well as portraits. Street was also a collector of art; he showed the works of artists such as Annibale, Carracci, Rubens and Van Dyke in the same exhibition.

Street's portraits show restraint in color. He painted with a kind of clarity that only a dedicated draftsman could

Portrait of Robert Case Clark, 1840, 29½ x 24½ in.
Courtesy of Montclair Art Museum, New Jersey.

employ; the men are depicted in dark coats with healthy reddish complexions, and the women wear brightly colored clothing, painted in abstract form, so as to effectively personify their facial images.

Four of Street's six children, by three wives, became artists: Austin, Rubens, Claude and Theopolis.

Street is something of a forgotten artist, many of his works having been lost after his death in 1865. But many of his portraits have survived to carve him a niche in the history of American art.

PUBLIC COLLECTIONS
Delaware Art Museum, Wilmington

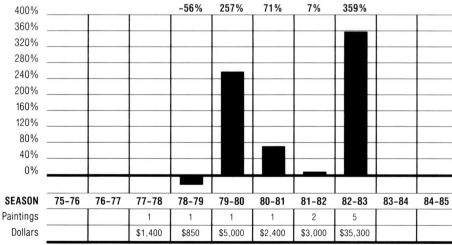

10-Year Average Change From Base Years '77-'78: 106%

| | | -56% | 257% | 71% | 7% | 359% | | |

SEASON	75-76	76-77	77-78	78-79	79-80	80-81	81-82	82-83	83-84	84-85
Paintings			1	1	1	1	2	5		
Dollars			$1,400	$850	$5,000	$2,400	$3,000	$35,300		

Record Sale: $24,000, SPB, 10/22/82, "Village in Winter," 30 x 36 in.

ASHER BROWN DURAND
(1796-1886)

Known as "the father of American landscape painting," Asher Brown Durand was the principal exponent of the aesthetics and style associated with the Hudson River School. Yet Durand was almost 40 before he began his landscape painting, after attaining fame as the early nineteenth century's outstanding engraver.

The artist was born in 1796 in Jefferson Village (now Maplewood), New Jersey, the son of a watchmaker. Apprenticed in 1812 to engraver Peter Maverick, Durand became his partner in New York City by 1817.

Durand became so accomplished that in 1820 John Trumbull engaged him to engrave Trumbull's famous painting, *Declaration of Independence* (1786-1787, Yale University). The three-year project made Durand's reputation as the country's best engraver. Now in his own studio, Durand was in demand for banknotes, landscapes and portraits.

Among his commissions were an engraving for *The American Landscape,* illustrating a poem by William Cullen Bryant, and a fine engraving of John Vanderlyn's renowned nude, *Ariadne* (1812, Pennsylvania Academy of the Fine Arts), said to be more artistically effective than the original. But by the 1830s, Durand had turned to painting— portraits, genre and history pictures, and some landscapes.

In 1840, Durand toured Europe with three engraving pupils who would later

Dover Plain, Dutchess County, New York, 1848, 42½ x 60½ in. Courtesy of National Museum of American Art, Smithsonian Institution, Museum Purchase and Gift of Thomas W. Evans.

become well-known landscape painters: John F. Kensett, John W. Casilear and Thomas P. Rossiter. He had previously been influenced by seventeenth-century landscapist Claude Lorrain's pastoral scenes, and by contemporary English painter John Constable. On his return, Durand began to paint landscapes almost exclusively.

Typically, these landscapes are serene, full of atmospheric effect, precise in detail, with a finished surface and invisible brushwork. His colors are natural and clear, faithfully expressing the season, time of day and conditions of light. Botanists can identify species of plants and trees in his foregrounds.

Durand's famous series of "Letters on Landscape Painting," for *The Crayon* magazine (1855) outlines principles that characterized the Hudson River School. In them, he urged American landscapists to pursue an independent style. He led a generation of artists away from the contrived drama, allegorical content and studio manipulation of natural scenes.

The accepted convention was to use nature as scenery, the virtuoso techniques of the artist controlling mood and effect. Thomas Cole, Durand's friend and predecessor as premier American landscapist, was its foremost practitioner.

In Durand's view, nature was not the

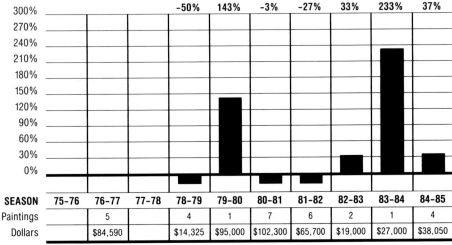

10-Year Average Change From Base Years '76-'77: 46%

				-50%	143%	-3%	-27%	33%	233%	37%
SEASON	75-76	76-77	77-78	78-79	79-80	80-81	81-82	82-83	83-84	84-85
Paintings		5		4	1	7	6	2	1	4
Dollars		$84,590		$14,325	$95,000	$102,300	$65,700	$19,000	$27,000	$38,050

Record Sale: $95,000, SPB, 4/25/80, "Pastoral Landscape," 39 x 49 in.

Landscape, 1838, 32¼ x 48¼ in. Courtesy of Vose Galleries of Boston, Inc., Massachusetts.

setting but the exalted subject. He viewed nature reverentially, as the visible manifestation of Deity, and the artist as its humble instrument. As such, he believed natural scenes must be painted from direct observation, realistically but not slavishly, caught at their moments of ideal beauty, in order to spiritually elevate the viewer. Ideally, the artist must efface his technique and capture the scene as found, in natural composition, light, atmosphere and textures.

Durand taught, wrote, painted and exhibited. As an acclaimed artist, master of the new theory and its practice, and president of the National Academy of Design from 1845 to 1861, his unconventionalities became new conventions.

MEMBERSHIPS
National Academy of Design

PUBLIC COLLECTIONS
Metropolitan Museum of Art, New York City
Museum of the City of New York
National Academy of Design, New York City
New-York Historical Society, New York City
New York Public Library, New York City
Pennsylvania Academy of the Fine Arts,
    Philadelphia
Walters Art Gallery, Baltimore
Worcester Museum, Massachusetts
Yale University

Dance of the Haymakers, 36 x 54½ in. Courtesy of Vose Galleries of Boston, Inc., Massachusetts.

GEORGE CATLIN
(1796-1872)

Buffalo Bull's Back Fat, head chief, Blood tribe, 1832, 29 x 24 in. Courtesy of National Museum of American Art, Smithsonian Institution, Gift of Mrs. Joseph Harrison, Jr.

Much of what is known of American Indian life comes from the work of George Catlin, who spent about eight years traveling among 48 North American tribes. His understanding of the Indians is reflected in the nearly 600 paintings and drawings he produced, a major portion of which was preserved in the Smithsonian Institution. Accounts of his travels in the wilderness, first published in 1841, demonstrate his eloquence as a writer.

Born in Wilkes-Barre, Pennsylvania in 1796, the son of a lawyer, Catlin attended law school in Litchfield, Connecticut, and practiced law for a few years in Luzerne County, Pennsylvania. He moved to Philadelphia in 1823. By then, a self-taught artist, he was painting portraits and miniatures successfully, and gave up the practice of law. In 1824, he was elected to the Pennsylvania Academy of the Fine Arts; he received membership in the National Academy of Design in 1826.

One day in Philadelphia a delegation of Plains Indians en route to Washington so impressed him that he adopted the goal of becoming pictorial historian of the Indians. As a prelude to his great Western travels, Catlin visited Indian reservations in Western New York State. He joined General William Clark, regional commissioner of Indian affairs, in St. Louis in 1830. By 1832 his mission to "snatch from hasty oblivion . . . a truly lofty and noble race" was under way.

Catlin roamed the world of the Crow, Blackfoot, Comanche and Mandan fearlessly—often alone in a canoe or with his horse—sketching, painting and collecting implements and costumes, which later became his "Indian Gallery." His diplomacy enabled him to capture Indian ceremonies, games and village scenes faithfully.

Though at times criticized for lack of technical sophistication in anatomy and perspective, his Indian portraits, rendered as busts or full-length figures, exhibit remarkable ability. His work was done rapidly, but was accurate, showed great detail and was often thinly painted. Motion was emphasized in his genre scenes, where hundreds of freely sketched figures performed tribal rituals.

Turning entrepreneur in 1837, Catlin exhibited his "Indian Gallery" in the Eastern United States; in 1839 it toured England, Holland and France. By 1851, expenses soared and the gallery closed in London. The collection, to Catlin's great disappointment, was eventually sold to a Philadelphian who stored it for many years in a boilerworks' cellar.

The American Museum of Natural History in New York City holds Indian paintings produced during Catlin's extensive travels in the 1850s, when he visited Latin America and the Pacific Coast of North America.

Catlin's paintings are an important contribution to American art, not only for their ethnological significance but also for their artistic strength.

MEMBERSHIPS
National Academy of Design
Pennsylvania Academy of the Fine Arts

PUBLIC COLLECTIONS
American Museum of Natural History,
  New York City
Chicago Natural History Museum
Thomas Gilcrease Institute of American History
  and Art, Tulsa
National Museum of American Art,
  Washington, D.C.
National Gallery of Art, Washington, D.C.
New-York Historical Society, New York City
Newberry Library, Chicago
University of Pennsylvania, Philadelphia

SEASON	75-76	76-77	77-78	78-79	79-80	80-81	81-82	82-83	83-84	84-85
Paintings					2	3		1	1	1
Dollars					$28,000	$298,000		$25,000	$15,000	$47,500

Record Sale: $280,000, SPB, 10/17/80, "Battle Between Sioux and Sauk and Fox," 26 × 32 in.

118

SHELDON PECK
(1797-1868)

Mother and Son, ca. 1820, 31½ x 25¼ in. Courtesy of Munson-Williams-Proctor Institute, Utica, New York.

Born in Cornwall, Vermont, the ninth of 11 children, Sheldon Peck was a traveling painter of portraits in oil. Although this self-taught artist did not sign his work, a study of the works attributed to him and those still held by his descendants has made his distinctive style recognizable.

His earliest works, family portraits painted in Vermont, are brushed directly onto wood panels. In those years, the artist developed a decorative motif that would later appear in all his work—a long brushstroke flanked by two shorter ones, similar to the print of a rabbit's foot.

Peck's use of somber colors and dark backgrounds accentuates the immobility of his subjects, who were portrayed from the waist up. Great attention was paid to their coiffures and costumes.

In 1828, Peck moved to a farm in Jordan, Onandaga County, New York. There he continued to paint half- and three-quarter-length portraits on wood panels, but he began to use brighter colors and more detailed settings. He added furniture and other accoutrements, such as a family Bible or other books, and occasionally a landscape in the background.

In approximately 1845, the artist moved to Babcock's Grove (now known as Lombard), 20 miles west of Chicago. He built a home, became a farmer and community leader, and opened a school in his home for the benefit of his and neighboring children. His descendants, who still live in this house, believe that he was an abolitionist, hiding runaway slaves there.

After the summer farming season, Peck traveled and painted. Utilizing canvas instead of wood panels, his later work is characterized by yet brighter colors, larger sizes, and trompe l'oeil frames made by the artist himself.

Peck adapted his style to the tastes of his clientele—simplifying his earlier technique. His clients repaid him in kind. One entry in a family Bible states that he painted on a linen sheet owned by the family, made his own stretchers, and received a cow in exchange for his services. Peck also advertised himself as a decorative painter, embellishing chairs and other furniture.

He died in 1868.

MEMBERSHIPS
Chicago Academy of Design

SEASON	75-76	76-77	77-78	78-79	79-80	80-81	81-82	82-83	83-84	84-85
Paintings				1		1				
Dollars				$27,000		$65,000				

Record Sale: $65,000, SPB, 4/30/81, "Portraits of Miss Dodge," 30 × 27 in.

ISAAC SHEFFIELD
(1798-1845)

Only five portraits of adults (including three miniatures) and two pictures of children constitute the known works of Isaac Sheffield, an itinerant Connecticut painter in the 1830s and early 1840s.

Four of his five adult portraits are of sea captains—half-length, three-quarter-face views—posed stiffly in dark coats, starched white shirts and wide silk stocks.

Typically, a telescope is held in one hand, and a red background drape is looped back to show the captain's principal ship under full sail on a middle-distance seascape.

Like those of other underschooled portraitists of his time, Sheffield's pictures are linear, with limited technique and faults in modeling.

Sheffield, however, captures some individuality. Though the facial expressions are not animated, the eyes of his subjects are sentient, aware, and reveal a certain introspection. These qualities, along with a refinement of color, raise Sheffield's work a step above more primitive American portraitists, whose best efforts have a cardboard effect.

Little is known of the artist. He was born in Guilford, Connecticut, probably in 1798.

His earliest known portrait is of a captain, dated April, 1833. It is a companion to a picture of the captain's wife, the only known Sheffield portrait of a woman.

Another captain's picture was completed in May, 1833, and a full-length portrait of a little girl is also dated 1833.

Two miniatures, now untraceable, are dated 1836 and 1837. Sheffield's other known portrait of a child, the young son of a whaling captain, is dated 1837.

Sheffield's work placed him in Guilford, Stoningham and New London, though he may have visited other Connecticut towns.

His known New London portraits, including the third miniature (private collection) are dated 1840, the year he probably settled in the whaling center, most likely at age 38.

Sheffield died in 1845 in New London.

Connecticut Sea Captain, 1833, 30 x 24½ in. Courtesy of National Gallery of Art, Washington, D.C. Gift of Edgar William and Bernice Chrysler Garbisch.

PUBLIC COLLECTIONS
Lyman Allyn Museum, New London, Connecticut
National Gallery of Art, Washington, D.C.

SEASON	75-76	76-77	77-78	78-79	79-80	80-81	81-82	82-83	83-84	84-85
Paintings						1				
Dollars						$12,000				

Record Sale: $12,000, SPB, 4/30/81, "Portrait of Mary Wheeler," 30 × 24 in.

TITIAN RAMSAY PEALE
(1799-1885)

Titian Ramsay Peale was one of a fascinating family of painters which spanned several generations of American art. The youngest son of 17 children of famed portraitist Charles Willson Peale, he was born in 1799 in Philadelphia, where his father had founded a museum.

Related to numerous Peales of varying artistic talent, Titian achieved distinction as an artist-naturalist. After training in his father's museum and at the University of Pennsylvania, he joined Major Stephen H. Long's expedition to the Rocky Mountains. Of the 122 sketches he made on the trip, 50 are held by the American Philosophical Society in Philadelphia.

In the 1800s, public interest in science resulted in many illustrated publications on plants, insects and birds. Peale combined his scientific schooling and artistic ability in a career as an illustrator of natural life. Trips to the Georgia and Florida coasts, to South America and to the Pacific provided material. He is noted for his illustrations for *American Ornithology* and *Lepidoptera Americana*.

Primarily an illustrator, Peale also painted oils and watercolors in a muted, elegant style. Animal and bird watercolors from field sketches were exhibited at the Pennsylvania Academy of the Fine Arts in Philadelphia.

Between expeditions, Peale worked in his father's museum; he became manager in 1833. When it failed, he became an examiner in the United States Patent Office.

In his later years, he took up photography as a hobby and helped develop the new craft. Upon retirement, Peale returned to Philadelphia, where he died in 1885.

Bright House, Rehoboth Beach, Delaware, 1882, 8½ x 12 in., signed l.l. Photograph courtesy of Kennedy Galleries, New York, New York.

PUBLIC COLLECTIONS
American Philosophical Society, Philadelphia
Pennsylvania Academy of the Fine Arts,
  Philadelphia

SEASON	75-76	76-77	77-78	78-79	79-80	80-81	81-82	82-83	83-84	84-85
Paintings	1		2				1	1		
Dollars	$2,800		$5,750				$1,700	$5,250		

Record Sale: $5,250, SPB, 10/22/82, "Morpho Cypris," 12 × 10 in.

CHARLES CODMAN

(1800-1842)

Entertainment of the Boston Rifle Club in Portland Harbor, August 12, 1829, 1830, 24⅜ x 32½ in., signed l.l.
Courtesy of The Brooklyn Museum, New York, Dick S. Ramsey Fund.

Charles Codman, a landscape, marine and sign painter, was born in Portland, Maine in 1800. He was self-taught, and was painting signs and crude portraits by 1823.

Codman achieved recognition as a landscape painter after art critic John Neal discovered his work while visiting Portland in 1828. Almost overnight the artist catapulted from a local painter to one worthy of prestigious gallery shows. He exhibited at the Boston Athenaeum, the National Academy of Design and the Apollo Gallery.

Both Codman's literal and his imaginary landscapes were painted with a romantic touch. Man and his endeavors always appear in small scale, as if to emphasize the grandeur of nature. Codman manipulated the effects of light and clouds to heighten the drama in his paintings. He excelled at producing extremely detailed renderings of vegetation, and also was adept in his use of perspective.

While his work most closely resembles that of Thomas Cole, Codman at times shows his provincial origins and lack of

formal training. For example, some of his imaginary scenes have a forced, artificial feel.

Typical of his realistic style is *Old State House, Augusta* (1836, State of Maine), which shows the original design of the building before it was remodeled in the early twentieth century. *Entertainment of the Boston Rifle Club* (1830, Brooklyn Museum) offers a recording of a local event, while providing a contemporary view of early Portland's Eastern Promenade.

Codman also painted occasional still lifes. He died in Portland in 1842.

SEASON	75-76	76-77	77-78	78-79	79-80	80-81	81-82	82-83	83-84	84-85
Paintings				1			2	1		
Dollars				$11,000			$9,250	$4,000		

Record Sale: $11,000, B.P, 4/7/79, "Diamond Cove, Hog Island," 21 × 32 in.

PUBLIC COLLECTIONS
Brooklyn Museum
Portland Museum of Art, Maine
State Library, Augusta, Maine

GEORGE HARVEY

(1800-1878)

Born in Tottenham, England, George Harvey was a versatile painter who executed miniatures, large landscapes and flower paintings. Many consider him the earliest flower specialist in America.

In 1820, the artist visited America. He wrote in his journal that "he found himself in the remote wilds of the New World, hunting and trapping, scribbling poetry and prose, drawing and sketching." After two years in the West—probably Ohio, Michigan and Canada—he returned to New York City and Boston. By 1829, he had completed approximately 400 portrait miniatures. He also did delicate watercolor studies revealing precisely delineated expanses of landscape.

Harvey traveled between England and America from that time forward, living in both places. In 1835, he bought land along the Hudson River, where he built a home and continued to record the American landscape, predominantly in watercolor. He also helped his friend Washington Irving in the design and decoration of his home "Sunnyside" in Tarrytown.

As Harvey continued to paint in America, he consciously increased his use of light, in deference to the clarity of hue he found in this country. His technique remained English. Most of his still lifes are floral pieces—beautiful, large blooms in vases or pitchers resting on marble tabletops. His selection of blossoms demonstrated his knowledge of the symbolic language of flowers.

In 1838, Harvey hoped to publish 40 of his delicate and charming landscapes by subscription, accompanied by a text he had written, edited by Washington Irving. The cost of the engravings was enormous and only 250 copies with four scenes were published in 1841. Nearly 20 watercolors for an unpublished series of phases of the day and year are in the New-York Historical Society.

Landscape View of Farm, 33 x 48 in., signed l.c. Courtesy of Jeffrey Alan Gallery, New York, New York.

Later, in 1848, he used some original watercolors to illustrate a series of London lectures he gave on the wonders of the frontier.

PUBLIC COLLECTIONS
Museum of Fine Arts, Boston
New-York Historical Society, New York City

SEASON	75-76	76-77	77-78	78-79	79-80	80-81	81-82	82-83	83-84	84-85
Paintings							2	1	5	2
Dollars							$3,900	$9,000	$18,094	$4,500

Record Sale: $9,000, SPB, 6/2/83, "Sunset in Rural Landscape," 44 × 60 in.

SARAH MIRIAM PEALE
(1800-1885)

A member of the Peale dynasty of artists, Sarah Miriam Peale is one of America's early professional female artists. In an era when few women pursued careers, she supported herself for 60 years, successfully competing with male painters of the day, including Thomas Sully. She never married.

Born in 1800 in Philadelphia, "Sally" Peale grew up painting in her father James's studio. She specialized in portraits and also painted still lifes. She worked at her uncle Charles W. Peale's studio in Washington briefly. Charles championed equality of the sexes and sponsored Sarah into society, where she made important career contacts.

From 1816 to 1831, Peale worked between Philadelphia and Baltimore. After 1831, she moved to Baltimore, working with her cousin Rembrandt in a studio in the Peale Museum. She became the leading portraitist of the city, painting more than 100 of its leading citizens.

Ill health forced Peale to move to St. Louis, Missouri in 1845. She lived there until 1877, when she returned to Philadelphia to live with two sisters until her death in 1885.

Examination of the evolution of Peale's painting reveals the influence of her family and of the change in American taste during the 60 years she painted. Her portraits show a strength of design that almost contradicts the realism of her approach. From her father and uncle came firm drawing and attention to the details of fur, lace and fabric. From her cousin Rembrandt came her rich color and glazing technique. Her early portraits, elegant and precise, reflect the influence of his French neoclassical training.

Peale's early still lifes are formal fruit arrangements. Some are simple and clear in form, like her cousin Raphaelle's; others show her father's

Little Old Lady with Lace Cap, 30 x 25 in. Courtesy of Kennedy Galleries, New York, New York.

concern with immediacy. Responding to the prevailing. romanticism, she later worked more loosely. Fruit was painted outdoors, often on the ground or hanging from a tree.

Peale's many portraits include those of Thomas Hart Benton, Caleb Cushing and Daniel Webster. The Marquis de Lafayette sat four times for a portrait that has unfortunately been lost.

MEMBERSHIPS
Pennsylvania Academy of the Fine Arts

SEASON	75-76	76-77	77-78	78-79	79-80	80-81	81-82	82-83	83-84	84-85
Paintings					3		1		1	
Dollars					$3,400		$2,600		$2,200	

Record Sale: $2,600, S.W, 2/7/82, "Portrait of Bond Martin," 30 × 25 in.

HENRY INMAN
(1801-1846)

Versatile, American-trained Henry Inman painted portraits, miniatures, idyllic landscapes and popular genre scenes.

Inman was born in 1801 in Utica, New York; his family moved to New York City when he was 13. There he was apprenticed for seven years to portraitist John Wesley Jarvis, an expert likeness-maker. They worked in tandem—Jarvis would paint the likeness and Inman would finish the canvas. On a visit to New Orleans in 1820 and 1821, the two completed six portraits, grossing $6,000.

From Jarvis, Inman developed a technique that passed for romantic inspiration, and he was able to create elaborate likenesses with little effort. He borrowed from Thomas Sully and Gilbert Stuart in the development of his flesh tones. His life-size oil portraits emphasized the beauty of women, the dash and dignity of gentlemen, and the innocence of children.

Inman opened his own studio in New York City in 1824, and two years later was a founder of the National Academy of Design. He spent a three-year period in Philadelphia as a partner in the lithographic firm of Childs and Inman. He served as a director of the Pennsylvania Academy of the Fine Arts in 1834. His income from portrait painting was so good that he spent little time on landscapes or genre paintings by age 30. By 1838, Inman was one of the highest-paid painters in America.

One of his most interesting paintings is *Self-Portrait* (1834, Pennsylvania Academy of the Fine Arts); realism prevails and sentimentalism is withheld. Sometimes considered an uneven painter, Inman was caught in a transitional period between eighteenth-century classicism and the more realistic styles of the succeeding generation of artists.

Inman won a commission for a large historical painting for the rotunda of the United States Capitol in Washington, D.C. He died in 1846, before the work was finished. The following month, the National Academy of Design exhibited Inman's work in one of the earliest one-man memorial shows in the United States.

Mrs. Robert Charles Wetmore, ca. 1830, 37⅝ x 29 in. Courtesy of National Museum of American Art, Smithsonian Institution, Bequest of Florence Adele Wetmore.

Moanahonga, 30½ x 25 in. Photograph courtesy of The Gerald Peters Gallery, Santa Fe, New Mexico.

MEMBERSHIPS
National Academy of Design
Pennsylvania Academy of the Fine Arts

PUBLIC COLLECTIONS
Boston Athenaeum
Capitol Building, Albany, New York
Essex Institute, Salem, Massachusetts
Harvard University
Independence Hall, Philadelphia
Museum of Fine Arts, Boston
New York City Hall
New-York Historical Society, New York City
Pennsylvania Academy of the Fine Arts, Philadelphia
University of Pennsylvania, Philadelphia
Worcester Art Museum, Massachusetts

SEASON	75-76	76-77	77-78	78-79	79-80	80-81	81-82	82-83	83-84	84-85
Paintings					2		3		3	1
Dollars					$3,200		$5,500		$13,800	$500

Record Sale: $10,000, SPB, 12/8/83, ''Long Island Landscape,'' 13 × 9 in.

THOMAS
COLE
(1801-1848)

The Subsiding of the Waters of the Deluge, 1829, 36 x 48 in., Gift of Mrs. Katie Dean in Memory of Minnibel S. and James Wallace Dean, and Museum Purchase through the major acquisitions fund, Smithsonian Institution.

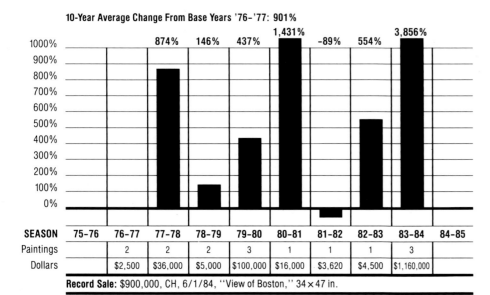

10-Year Average Change From Base Years '76–'77: 901%

	75–76	76–77	77–78	78–79	79–80	80–81	81–82	82–83	83–84	84–85
			874%	146%	437%	1,431%	–89%	554%	3,856%	
SEASON	75–76	76–77	77–78	78–79	79–80	80–81	81–82	82–83	83–84	84–85
Paintings		2	2	2	3	1	1	1	3	
Dollars		$2,500	$36,000	$5,000	$100,000	$16,000	$3,620	$4,500	$1,160,000	

Record Sale: $900,000, CH, 6/1/84, "View of Boston," 34 x 47 in.

A Snow Squall, 31¼ x 41¼ in. Courtesy of Vose Galleries of Boston, Inc., Massachusetts.

Recognized not only as the influential founder of the Hudson River School of landscape painting, Thomas Cole also is credited with making landscapes, which had been lightly regarded in England, acceptable subjects for serious painters.

Cole was a master of the detailed view of nature, but he also was a romantic at heart and revealed this in his work. "To walk with nature as a poet is the necessary condition of the perfect artist," he wrote to a friend. He was, in fact, a poet, writer and philosopher as well as a painter. In his later years he became a religious moralist, too, and painted series of panels on allegorical themes.

Born in Lancashire, England in 1801, he was apprenticed as a teenager to an engraver of textile designs for calico. When his family emigrated to America in 1818 he came with them, worked briefly for an engraver in Philadelphia, traveled to the West Indies and then joined his family in Steubenville, Ohio in 1819.

Cole learned the rudiments of painting from an itinerant painter in Steubenville and then tried his own hand at portrait painting in the area. He also began sketching along the Monongahela River. In 1823, he returned to Philadelphia to study at the Pennsylvania Academy of the Fine Arts and, two years later, he moved to New York City.

Almost immediately he started taking sketching trips up the Hudson River and into the Catskill Mountains. When three of his earliest Hudson River landscapes were hung in a picture-framer's window they were seen and purchased by the current deans of American art: John Trumbull, William Dunlap and Asher Durand. Cole's reputation was made. In 1826, he was one of the founding members of the National Academy of Design.

By the mid-1820s, Cole's awe for the American wilderness, which his patrons clamored to see, was tempered by his desire to paint allegorical scenes. The first was *Expulsion from the Garden of Eden* (1827, Museum of Fine Arts, Boston), a magnificent visualization of the biblical story.

By 1829, his fame and finances were secure and he went to Europe for three years. He painted many landscapes and classical ruins abroad, but never let the sophistication of European art spoil his own style. Even so, he rarely depicted nature as it actually was. "A scene is rather an index to feelings and associations," he wrote.

While still in Europe, Cole planned a monumental series of large paintings which would follow the evolution of civilization from its initial savagery to its apex and thence to its destruction. When he returned to America the series was

commissioned by collector Luman Reed and, in 1835 and 1836, Cole painted *The Course of Empire* (New-York Historical Society).

During the 1830s, Cole was at the height of his powers, alternating between his allegories and the hugely profitable landscapes which, ironically, he looked upon as hack work. In 1841 and 1842 he made another trip to Europe, and came back more interested than ever in religious subjects.

It was Cole's majestic landscapes that the public longed to see, however, and during the mid-1840s he painted some of his finest. When he died of pneumonia in 1848 it was regarded as a national tragedy.

MEMBERSHIPS
National Academy of Design

PUBLIC COLLECTIONS
Cincinnati Art Museum
Cleveland Museum of Art
Corcoran Gallery of Art, Washington, D.C.
Detroit Institute of Arts
Metropolitan Museum of Art, New York City
Museum of Fine Arts, Boston
New-York Historical Society, New York City
Rhode Island School of Design, Providence
Wadsworth Atheneum, Hartford, Connecticut

JOHN QUIDOR

(1801-1881)

Although his reputation faded after the middle of the nineteenth century, John Quidor was a highly original painter of romantic and literary subjects, often drawn from the works of Washington Irving. Appreciation for his work rose following a major exhibition in 1942.

Quidor was born in 1801 in Tappan, New York, in the Hudson River country Irving was to chronicle. He was raised in New York City. Apprenticed sometime between 1814 and 1822 to portraitist John Wesley Jarvis, Quidor is listed in an 1827 directory as a portrait painter, although no portraits by him are known. He supported himself primarily by painting side panels for fire engines.

Quidor's acrimonious relationship with Jarvis ended in a lawsuit, and he was to remain on poor terms with the art community. His relationships with his own pupils, including Charles Loring Elliott and Thomas Bangs Thorpe, were no better.

His earliest known work, a scene from *Don Quixote,* is dated 1823. During the late 1820s and the 1830s, he produced most of his greatest paintings: *Ichabod Crane Pursued by the Headless Horseman* (1828, Yale); *The Return of Rip Van Winkle* (1829, National Gallery); *The Money Diggers* (1832, Brooklyn Museum); *Rip Van Winkle at Nicholas Vedder's Tavern* (1839, Museum of Fine Arts, Boston), and others. It has been suggested that Quidor identified with the figure of Rip Van Winkle, whom he depicts as alienated and misunderstood.

From 1837 to 1850, Quidor lived in Quincy, Illinois. In 1847, he exhibited three large religious paintings at the National Academy of Design, but the show was unsuccessful. He eventually retired to his daughter's home in New Jersey, and when he died in 1881 his children noted that he had not painted for 10 years.

Leatherstocking's Rescue, 27 x 34¼ in. Courtesy of Vose Galleries of Boston, Inc., Massachusetts.

Quidor was a visionary, not an illustrator; he infused a literary setting with the power of his own imagination, evoking terror or a grotesque humor like that of Rowlandson or Hogarth. He used vibrant brushwork and a dark golden palette reminiscent of the Dutch School, although the transparent glazes he invented have browned with age. His later paintings reveal a calmer, almost nostalgic mood, as in *The Embarkation from Communipaw* (1861, Detroit Institute of Arts), which parodies Watteau.

PUBLIC COLLECTIONS
Brooklyn Museum
Detroit Institute of Arts
Munson-Williams-Proctor Institute, Utica, New York
Museum of Fine Arts, Boston
National Gallery, Washington, D.C.
Yale University Art Gallery

SEASON	75-76	76-77	77-78	78-79	79-80	80-81	81-82	82-83	83-84	84-85
Paintings	1				1					
Dollars	$30,000				$120,000					

Record Sale: $120,000, P.NY, 5/2/80, "The Money Diggers," 27 × 34 in.

RUTH WHITTIER SHUTE
(1803-1882)

SAMUEL A. SHUTE
(1803-1836)

It was not until 1978 that painstaking research, published by art scholar Helen Kellogg, established that R.W. Shute and S.A. Shute were indeed a husband-and-wife team of primitive portrait painters working in New England and upper New York State in the 1820s and early 1830s. Both worked independently at first, but their finest work was done when they worked together, with Ruth drawing the face and hands and Samuel doing the painting. Eventually their styles melded together so well that their individual contributions to a portrait became almost indistinguishable.

Ruth Whittier was born in Dover, New Hampshire in 1803, the eighth of nine children. Samuel Addison Shute was born the same year in Byfield, Massachusetts. He was a doctor, as well as a portrait painter. They were married in 1827, and settled initially in Weare, New Hampshire.

Kellogg's research indicates that they moved about considerably during the relatively few years that they painted together. They would arrive in a town, take a hotel room and advertise in the local newspaper that they were available for painting portraits. How long they stayed depended on the number of commissions they received. In Peterborough, New Hampshire in 1833, for example, they completed 18 portraits in just 31 remarkably productive days.

So far, some 25 portraits have been found from the Shutes' early period, from 1827 to 1831. Fifteen were by S.A. and 10 by R.W. All were watercolors and, even then, all have indications that both painters had a hand in one way or another in working on the portrait.

The earliest signed portraits on which they worked together were those of the

Portrait of a Young Woman in Blue, 20 x 16 in. Photograph courtesy of Kennedy Galleries, New York, New York.

Atkinson family in Lowell, Massachusetts in 1831. The next few years were their most prolific period.

The Shutes worked in a variety of media, often using several of them in a single portrait. The portraits of *Josiah C. and Abigail S. Burnham* (ca. 1832-1833, private collection), for instance, were done in watercolor, pencil, gouache and gilt-foil decoupage on paper. They also worked in oil and pastel. Their watercolors in particular were distinctive for their streaked backgrounds and the

careful pencil draftsmanship of the features of the face.

Kellogg's research indicates that Samuel Shute must have been ill for several years before his death in Champlain, New York in 1836. Ruth, however, continued to advertise for commissions during that period, and kept on painting portraits for three years after his death. In 1840, she remarried and moved to Kentucky, where she lived until her death in 1882. Her last known portrait was dated 1839.

SEASON	75-76	76-77	77-78	78-79	79-80	80-81	81-82	82-83	83-84	84-85
Paintings				4			1			
Dollars				$87,000			$2,750			

Record Sale: $32,000, SPB, 1/27/79, "Portrait of Miss Adeline Bartlett," 24 × 20 in.

ROBERT WALKER WEIR
(1803-1889)

Robert Walker Weir was recognized more for his 42 years of teaching than for his paintings. Yet the scope and diversity of his work—portraits, historical paintings, religious and genre scenes—establish him as one of the most representative figures of mid-nineteenth-century American art.

Born in New York City, Weir was only 10 years old when his father suffered a business setback in 1813 and lost nearly all of the family's money. As a boy, Weir was befriended by painter John Wesley Jarvis, and before going to work each day, Weir received artistic instruction from Robert Cooke, an English heraldic artist.

Weir's early paintings were so strikingly impressive that, in New York during the 1820s, they were sold as original works of the old masters.

Aspiring to be a historical painter, Weir traveled to Italy in 1824 and studied for three years in Florence under Pietro Benvenuti before returning to New York to set up a studio. In 1829, Weir became a member of the National Academy of Design, where he was regularly exhibited, and he numbered among his friends some of the leading artists of the time.

Weir began teaching at the U.S. Military Academy at West Point in 1834. During his 42-year tenure, his pupils included Ulysses S. Grant, Robert E. Lee and painter J.A.M. Whistler, as well as Weir's two sons, John F. and

St. Nicholas, ca. 1837, 29¾ x 24½ in. Courtesy of National Museum of American Art, Smithsonian Institution, Museum Purchase.

Julian A. Weir, who became successful painters.

For his subject matter, Weir often drew from the novels of James Fenimore Cooper and Washington Irving. He also continued to paint portraits and histori-

cal paintings. In the mid-1830s, he was one of four artists commissioned to paint canvases for the Rotunda of the United States Capitol in Washington, D.C. He received $10,000 for his *Embarkation of the Pilgrims* (completed 1840); though it is perhaps Weir's best-known work, it was received with little enthusiasm by Congress and critics alike.

After Weir retired from teaching at West Point in 1876, he returned to New York City, where he continued to paint until his death there in 1889. Though prolific, the artist never seemed to settle on either a style or a subject matter he could define and develop fully. His two sons ultimately achieved greater success.

MEMBERSHIPS
National Academy of Design

PUBLIC COLLECTIONS
Metropolitan Museum of Art, New York City
Rotunda, United States Capitol, Washington, D.C.

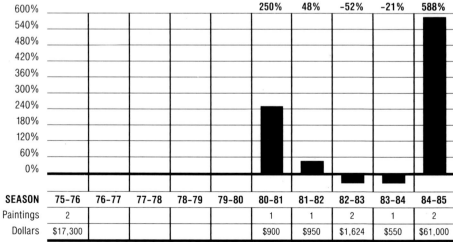

10-Year Average Change From Base Years '75-'76: 136%

						250%	48%	−52%	−21%	588%

SEASON	75-76	76-77	77-78	78-79	79-80	80-81	81-82	82-83	83-84	84-85
Paintings	2					1	1	2	1	2
Dollars	$17,300					$900	$950	$1,624	$550	$61,000

Record Sale: $60,000, SPB, 12/6/84, "Hudson River From West Point," 32 × 48 in.

130

FITZ HUGH LANE
(1804-1865)

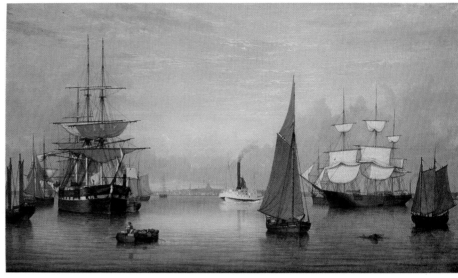

Boston Harbor, 25½ x 42 in. Courtesy of Vose Galleries of Boston, Inc., Massachusetts.

Fitz Hugh Lane's delicate, brilliant seascapes, famous in his lifetime, were rediscovered by critics after decades of neglect following his death.

Lane is now recognized as one of the preeminent luminists. He achieved sometimes spectacular effects of light and atmosphere, contained in serene, controlled pictures of ships and the coastal sea.

Lane was born in 1804 in Gloucester, Massachusetts, and christened Nathaniel Rogers Lane. At 18 months of age, he was crippled by a childhood disease; though he attained full stature, he had to walk with crutches.

Lane had no formal art training until he went to Boston in the early 1830s to work for lithographers William S. and John Pendleton. He drew topographical views of Boston and its harbor, and naval architectural drafts. He met and was greatly influenced by marine painter Robert Salmon.

In 1835, Lane began to produce his own lithographs, selling them by subscription, the first being a panorama of Gloucester. Alone, or sometimes with fellow artist John W.A. Scott, Lane continued to produce popular lithographs into the 1850s.

From 1840 on, however, Lane concentrated on his oil painting. In his 1844 *View of Gloucester from Dolliver's Neck* (location unknown), Lane showed for the first time the characteristic luminist use of light and air as dominant ele-

ments in the composition. Throughout the 1840s, he produced increasingly open poetic studies of natural beauty, turning away from his earlier detailed, depictive style.

Established artistically, with a fairly secure income, Lane eventually returned to Gloucester. Most of his best-known paintings are of that city and its harbor, ships and shorelines. He also did some landscapes and portraits. The limited

geographic range of his work was probably due to his physical handicap.

In the 1850s, Lane was among the first to try the new chemical-dye pigments in the red/yellow/orange spectrum. His unusual results encouraged the use of these pigments by other artists, among them Frederic E. Church. Lane was also an early user of photography and perspective devices as aids to finishing pictures.

All of Lane's mature luminist style is exhibited in *Lumber Schooners at Evening on Penobscot Bay* (1860, National Gallery of Art). It is a distillation of transitional light, warmth of color, harmony and an almost unworldly tranquility.

Lane's continuing popularity was enhanced by frequent exhibitions of his work, and through distribution by the American Art-Union. He died in 1865.

PUBLIC COLLECTIONS
Brooklyn Museum
Butler Institute of American Art, Youngstown, Ohio
Cape Ann Historical Association, Gloucester, Massachusetts
Museum of Fine Arts, Boston
National Gallery of Art, Washington, D.C.
Virginia Museum of Fine Arts, Richmond

10-Year Average Change From Base Years '76-'77: 14%

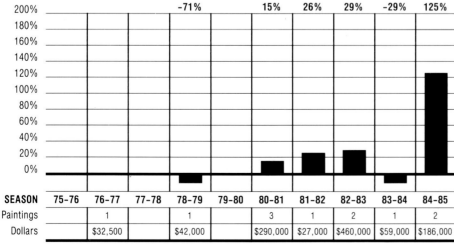

				−71%		15%	26%	29%	−29%	125%

SEASON	75-76	76-77	77-78	78-79	79-80	80-81	81-82	82-83	83-84	84-85
Paintings		1		1		3	1	2	1	2
Dollars		$32,500		$42,000		$290,000	$27,000	$460,000	$59,000	$186,000

Record Sale: $320,000, CH, 6/3/83, "Blue Hill Maine," 20 x 30 in.

131

SHEPARD ALONZO MOUNT
(1804-1868)

Rainbow Trout, 1842, 6¾ x 11 in. Private Collection, Photograph courtesy of Kennedy Galleries, New York, New York.

Shepard Alonzo Mount was a mid-nineteenth-century artist remembered chiefly as one of the three Mount brothers then active in the National Academy of Design, and as a portraitist·whose subjects included such prominent statesmen as President Martin Van Buren.

Shepard Mount was born in Setauket, Long Island, the second of three brothers who all had artistic careers. Henry Smith Mount was a distinguished sign painter, whose artisan-like work was much admired. William Sidney Mount supported himself as a portraitist, but is today more admired for his landscapes of rural life.

Shepard Mount was apprenticed as a carriage maker before entering the National Academy of Design in 1826. He exhibited his first work at the Academy in 1829, and was a regular exhibitor there for the rest of his career, having more than 100 works shown there during his lifetime.

He enjoyed a respectable career as a portraitist from the early 1830s on. In addition to his portraits, Mount also painted landscapes, genre paintings, and still lifes of flowers and small animals, such as squirrels, fish and birds.

Mount maintained his residence and studio in New York City until 1841, and afterwards in Stony Brook, Long Island. He was made an associate member of the National Academy in 1833, and a full academician in 1842. He remained active professionally until his death in 1868 in Setauket.

MEMBERSHIPS
National Academy of Design

PUBLIC COLLECTIONS
Suffolk Museum, Stony Brook, New York

SEASON	75-76	76-77	77-78	78-79	79-80	80-81	81-82	82-83	83-84	84-85
Paintings				1	1		1		3	
Dollars				$900	$2,400		$850		$23,500	

Record Sale: $15,000, SPB, 12/8/83, "Home of the Mounts," 12 × 16 in.

GEORGE R. BONFIELD
(1805-1898)

At the peak of his long career, George Robert Bonfield was one of America's most popular and acclaimed marine painters. Although his reputation waned in the years following the Civil War, his work is today recognized as being of high quality and historical interest.

Born in Portsmouth, England in 1805, Bonfield was brought to Philadelphia in 1816. There he learned the stone-carving trade, although he evidenced an early inclination to draw ships and seascapes.

While working with his master on the New Jersey estate of Joseph Bonaparte, Napoleon's brother, the young Bonfield was encouraged to study and copy European paintings. Bonfield exhibited one of his own paintings at the Pennsylvania Academy of the Fine Arts in 1820; he went on to study there under Thomas Vest.

It is not known whether Bonfield ever visited Europe. Many of his paintings, however, show European backgrounds and influences, possibly acquired through his study of eighteenth- and nineteenth-century prints and paintings. He was an active and productive artist who exhibited widely and was a prominent figure in Philadelphia's cultural life.

Although he executed some landscapes and nature scenes, Bonfield's primary subject was the sea and ships. Loose, flowing brushwork contributes to a feeling of motion in his paintings; his mature work is characterized by the use of light and shade to create drama, a technique reminiscent of the Dutch School, which Bonfield admired.

With the exception of brief sojourns in New Jersey during the 1850s, Bonfield spent the rest of his life in Philadelphia. The bulk of his work portrays the region: scenes along the Delaware River and the Atlantic coast.

Seascape with American Ships, 1865, 24 x 36 in., signed verso. Courtesy of Frank S. Schwarz & Son, Philadelphia, Pennsylvania.

Bonfield's subject matter—straightforward rather than allegorical or symbolic—appealed to popular taste during the 1840s and 1850s. Many of his patrons were industrialists whose fortunes were connected with the sea and shipping. After the Civil War, however, tastes in art turned first to the European masters and then to progressive trends, forerunners of impressionism, which Bonfield did not adopt. His popularity and productivity declined.

During the last decades of his life, while he continued to paint, Bonfield was also active as a collector and connoisseur. He compiled collections for such patrons as Philadelphia art-lover James L. Claghorn. Upon his death in 1898, Bonfield's own collection was found to contain hundreds of engravings and lithographs.

MEMBERSHIPS
National Academy of Design

PUBLIC COLLECTIONS
Mariners Museum, Newport News, Virginia
Museum of Fine Arts, Boston
Pennsylvania Academy of the Fine Arts, Philadelphia
Philadelphia Maritime Museum

SEASON	75-76	76-77	77-78	78-79	79-80	80-81	81-82	82-83	83-84	84-85
Paintings				1	1	3	7	1	4	
Dollars				$1,400	$2,000	$14,350	$10,350	$3,700	$11,950	

Record Sale: $5,750, D.NY, 9/24/80, "American Clipper in a Squall," 20 × 32 in.

ERASTUS SALISBURY FIELD
(1805-1900)

Erastus Salisbury Field was a self-taught folk painter whose life spanned most of the nineteenth century. He worked as an itinerant portrait artist in New England, although he also rendered depictions of historical, biblical and mythical scenes in his unique and primitive style.

Born in Leverett, Massachusetts in 1805, Field was to leave his native state only a few times during his life. He received little formal art training, although he did study with Samuel F.B. Morse in New York City in 1824.

From 1842 to 1848, Field lived in New York City. Although little is known about this period, it was probably then that he learned to make daguerreotypes and began to use them as aids in his work.

Field's style was occasionally criticized for its lack of modeling or other signs of academic expertise. Like other primitive or folk artists, such as Edward Hicks or "Grandma" Moses, Field created a flat effect with special use of color and simplified lines. Even among folk painters, however, his contribution stands out because of his inner vision and social idealism.

His early works were mostly portraits painted as he traveled through Massachusetts and Connecticut, looking for commissions. Contrary to a popular belief that folk artists filled in pre-painted bodies with their subjects'

Henry Carldon Hulbert, ca. 1835, 35 x 28 in. Courtesy of Henry B. Holt, Inc., Essex Fells, New Jersey.

heads, Field painted the faces first. His deliberate application of rich, flat color to the body often produced a decorative essay on the social standing or attitudes of his subject.

Around 1850, Field began to paint biblical and historical tributes. The most famous of these, *Historical Monument of the American Republic* (1876, Museum of Fine Arts, Springfield, Massachusetts), was painted in honor of the American Centennial. The centerpiece is a rambling structure with towers in many architectural styles; bas-reliefs on the towers represent events in American history. In his biblical paintings, such as *The Death of the First Born* (ca. 1870, Metropolitan Museum of Art) and *The Garden of Eden* (ca. 1860, Shelburne Museum), Field used original staging for his ideas, but drew some of his imagery from traditional Biblical illustration.

Field settled permanently in Sunderland, Massachusetts in 1859, the year his wife, who was also a painter, died. He continued to paint until his death in 1900.

PUBLIC COLLECTIONS
Abby Aldrich Rockefeller Folk Art Center, Williamsburg, Virginia
Metropolitan Museum of Art, New York City
Museum of Fine Arts, Boston
Museum of Fine Arts, Springfield, Massachusetts
National Gallery of Art, Washington, D.C.
Shelburne Museum, Shelburne, Vermont

10-Year Average Change From Base Years '75-'76: 481%

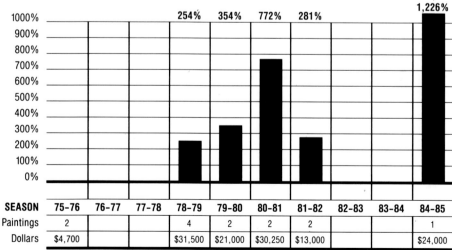

SEASON	75-76	76-77	77-78	78-79	79-80	80-81	81-82	82-83	83-84	84-85
Paintings	2			4	2	2	2			1
Dollars	$4,700			$31,500	$21,000	$30,250	$13,000			$24,000

Record Sale: $24,000, SPB, 1/31/85, "Portraits of Mr. & Mrs. William Leggett," 30 x 26 in.

WILLIAM MATTHEW PRIOR

(1806-1873)

William Matthew Prior, born in Bath, Maine in 1806, was a self-taught, itinerant portrait and landscape painter, and a painter on glass. His earliest work dates from 1824.

After a decade of traveling through New England and as far South as Baltimore, Prior settled in Boston in 1841. Here, along with his wife and his brothers-in-law, the Hamblins, he established a portrait studio.

The wide variation in technique shown in Prior's work does not represent development of the artist, but rather the price paid by the sitter. In 1831, he advertised in the *Maine Inquirer,* "Persons wishing for a flat picture can have a likeness without shadow or shade for one-quarter the price."

Prior is best known for primitive paintings, rather than his conventional academic images. These "flat" portraits, often of children, have vibrant colors. Subjects typically show high foreheads, wide-set eyes, sloping shoulders and stubby, massive legs. Little detail is given to hands, as exemplified by *Three Sisters of the Coplan Family* (1854, Museum of Fine Arts, Boston).

At times, Prior departed from the norm for nineteenth-century American folk art by placing his sitters against a background landscape of soft, atmospheric tones, rather than one of bright, flat color.

Girl with Rose and Toy Cat, 1855, 35½ x 29 in. Photograph courtesy of Kennedy Galleries, New York, New York.

Prior painted a number of copies on glass of Gilbert Stuart's portrait of George and Martha Washington. Some work attributed to Prior from his studio, "The Painting Garret," was actually executed by one of the Hamblin brothers. Prior usually signed and dated his paintings, while the others inscribed "Painted in Prior's Garret."

Prior died in East Boston in 1873.

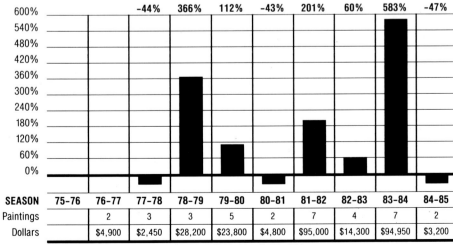

10-Year Average Change From Base Years '76-'77: 132%

		−44%	366%	112%	−43%	201%	60%	583%	−47%

SEASON	75-76	76-77	77-78	78-79	79-80	80-81	81-82	82-83	83-84	84-85
Paintings		2	3	3	5	2	7	4	7	2
Dollars		$4,900	$2,450	$28,200	$23,800	$4,800	$95,000	$14,300	$94,950	$3,200

Record Sale: $38,000, SPB, 1/28/82, "Girl in Pink," 27 x 22 in.

CLEMENT DREW
(1806-1889)

Homeward Bound, 20 x 30 in., signed l.r. Courtesy of Henry B. Holt, Inc., Essex Fells, New Jersey.

Like many painters of his day, Clement Drew worked at a variety of other jobs in addition to painting. Even after he was established as an artist, he sold art and art supplies, framed paintings and carved wooden figureheads as well. It is for his marine paintings, however, that he is now known. They were done between 1838 and 1886, a relatively long span of productive years for the nineteenth century.

Although he may well have been middle-aged before he saw the work of Fitz Hugh Lane, one of New England's leading marine painters, Drew painted in much the same style as Lane. His work, however, had neither the power nor the subtlety of mood that Lane was able to achieve.

Drew was born in Kingston, Massachusetts in 1806. By 1827, he was working in a dry goods store in Boston. In 1831, he switched to a job in a library, and 10 years later changed again to selling carpets. In 1846, he opened his own store to frame pictures and sell art and art supplies. During these years he had probably taught himself to paint.

Drew's earliest work dates from 1838; most of it consisted of views of Boston's south shore. Later he traveled extensively, and painted subjects ranging from Maine and the Grand Banks off Newfoundland to Cape Horn and San Francisco harbor. Whether he actually visited the more remote locations is unknown.

After 1860, many of his paintings were scenes of the coast near Gloucester on Cape Ann, north of Boston. He painted many vessels at sea as well. His last known work was in 1886, three years before he died in Roxbury, Massachusetts.

SEASON	75-76	76-77	77-78	78-79	79-80	80-81	81-82	82-83	83-84	84-85
Paintings						3	3	3	11	4
Dollars						$2,300	$2,675	$2,750	$19,150	$5,150

Record Sale: $4,500, RB.HM, 11/26/83, "The Ship James Crosby," 22 × 30 in.

WILLIAM JAMES HUBBARD
(1807-1862)

William James Hubbard was known more for his peculiar life than for the portraits he painted.

Hubbard was born in 1807, in Warwick, England. A man named Smith spotted Hubbard's early talent for cutting likenesses and exploited him as a child prodigy in England, before bringing him to the United States in 1824. After three years in Boston and New York City, Hubbard broke ties with his manager.

Portraitist Gilbert Stuart persuaded Hubbard to give up silhouettes for oil paints. With the help of portraitist Thomas Sully, Hubbard began a career as a portrait painter in 1829.

By the 1830s, Hubbard's modeling ability had so improved that his work showed no trace of his earlier awkardness in indicating proportions and three-dimensionality.

From 1838 to 1851, Hubbard enlarged his portraits and busts, while adding genre and historical themes to his repertoire. One of Hubbard's famous portraits of the period is *Horatio Greenough in His Studio in Florence* (1839, Valentine Museum, Virginia). But most of his paintings were considered ordinary and his subjects' appearances commonplace.

Bored with painting, Hubbard turned to sculpture in the 1850s. He spent seven years and all his savings working on a marble bust of George Washington, after the one by Jean Antoine Houdon. Hubbard felt the bust should have been cast in bronze, but was left penniless after six reproductions.

At the start of the Civil War, Hubbard tried to recoup his lost fortune by producing ammunition for the Confederacy. He was killed in an accident while experimenting with explosives in 1862.

John Marshall, ca. 1832, 24¼ x 15⅛ in. Courtesy of National Portrait Gallery, Washington, D.C.

PUBLIC COLLECTIONS
Corcoran Gallery of Art, Washington, D.C.
Valentine Museum, Richard, Virginia

SEASON	75-76	76-77	77-78	78-79	79-80	80-81	81-82	82-83	83-84	84-85
Paintings							1			
Dollars							$10,000			

Record Sale: $10,000, SPB, 10/22/81, "The Angler," 15 × 12 in.

WILLIAM SIDNEY MOUNT
(1807-1868)

The Painter's Triumph, 1838, 19½ x 23½ in., signed l.l. Courtesy of The Pennsylvania Academy of the Fine Arts, Philadelphia.

William Sidney Mount was the first American-born painter to devote most of his career to genre painting.

While he painted many portraits, some landscapes and a handful of still lifes, his depictions of ordinary life on rural Long Island brought Mount widespread recognition. Using meticulous draftsmanship, and planning compositions with mathematical accuracy rivaling that of Thomas Eakins, Mount painted scenes which he hoped would appeal to the many rather than the few.

Mount was born in Setauket, Long Island in 1807. Two older brothers also became painters, but neither approached William in ability. As a youth he spent long periods in New York City; in 1824, he was apprenticed to his brother Henry, a sign and ornamental painter there. He also studied briefly with portraitist Henry Inman, and was a member of the first class at the school of the National Academy of Design.

When Mount returned to Long Island, he first painted portraits and historical scenes which were stiffly composed and rather pompous. He soon abandoned the historical scenes, but continued the portraits. As a group, his portraits were uneven in quality, but the best displayed much the same clarity as his genre paintings.

While his first genre paintings, *The Rustic Dance after a Sleighride* (1830, Museum of Fine Arts, Boston), was immature in execution, its tremendous popularity when it was exhibited surprised even Mount. He painted his scenes with a dry objectivity, but his work was full of sun and air and had humorous touches that added to its enormous popularity.

Once established, Mount made an arrangement with William Schaus, a New York agent for a European dealer, to have lithographs made from a group of his genre paintings and circulated abroad. As a result, he became well known in Europe.

Before he met Schaus, Mount had included blacks in several of his paintings. Schaus, however, businessman that he was, knew what would sell to Europeans and encouraged Mount to include more of them, particularly black men playing musical instruments. *The Banjo Player* (1858, Suffolk County Museum) was one of the best of this type.

Although some critics contend that Mount portrayed blacks only in stereotypical roles, others argue that he was the first American painter to treat them with dignity.

Like many a self-reliant countryman, Mount was an inventor of sorts. Among his creations was a horse-drawn portable studio, complete with skylight and living quarters. It extended his trips into the countryside, protected him in inclement weather and, most important, permitted him to work almost unnoticed by his subjects.

Mount had many opportunities to travel to Europe, but always declined; he wanted to remain a thoroughly American painter. His output lessened after 1850, but he continued to paint the commonplace events near his Long Island birthplace until his death in 1868.

MEMBERSHIPS
National Academy of Design

PUBLIC COLLECTIONS
Art Institute of Chicago
Corcoran Gallery of Art, Washington, D.C.
Metropolitan Museum of Art, New York City
Museum of Fine Arts, Boston
National Collection of Fine Arts,
  Washington, D.C.
National Gallery of Art, Washington, D.C.
New York State Historical Association,
  Cooperstown
New York Public Library, New York City
Pennsylvania Academy of the Fine Arts,
  Philadelphia
Suffolk County Museum, Stony Brook,
  Long Island

SEASON	75-76	76-77	77-78	78-79	79-80	80-81	81-82	82-83	83-84	84-85
Paintings	1			1	4	4			7	
Dollars	$65,000			$17,000	$21,750	$16,650			2,010,550	

Record Sale: $800,000, CH, 12/9/83, "The Trap Sprung," 13 × 17 in.

JAMES REID LAMBDIN
(1807-1889)

Like other mid-nineteenth-century portrait painters, James Reid Lambdin moved about while establishing his reputation. Once recognized, he settled in Philadelphia. During his long career he painted many prominent political figures, among them Henry Clay, Daniel Webster, and Presidents Lincoln and Grant. He cannot be ranked with Thomas Sully, with whom he studied and whose influence was evident in all Lambdin's work, but he left a substantial body of very competent portraits and miniatures.

He was born in Pittsburgh, Pennsylvania in 1807. Oriented toward art as a child, at age 16 he went to Philadelphia and studied for six months with British-born miniaturist Edward Miles and for three years with Sully.

In 1826, Lambdin returned to Pittsburgh to paint portraits. Two years later he opened a museum and art gallery modeled after Charles Willson Peale's noted establishment in Philadelphia.

When the initial interest in the museum flagged and he saw his portrait commissions dwindling in Pittsburgh, Lambdin moved his museum and his family to Louisville, Kentucky. Over the next five years he traveled as far south as Mobile, Alabama in search of portrait commissions.

In 1837, he opened a studio in Philadelphia, where he worked until his death in 1889 as a portrait painter and in a number of art organizations. From 1845 to 1864, he was a director of the Pennsylvania Academy of the Fine Arts; from 1861 to 1865, he was professor of fine arts at the University of Pennsylvania.

In 1859, Lambdin was one of the organizers of a meeting of painters who protested the commissioning of a French artist, Horace Vernet, to paint the Battle of New Orleans in the Rotunda of the Capitol in Washington, D.C. As a con-

Delaware Water Gap, 1874, 28 x 44 in., signed l.l. Collection of La Salle University Art Museum, Philadelphia, Pennsylvania. Photograph courtesy of Kennedy Galleries, New York, New York.

sequence, President James Buchanan established the National Art Commission to supervise the commissioning of artwork for the federal government and appointed Lambdin as one of its members; the commission, however, soon became moribund.

MEMBERSHIPS
Artists' Fund Society
National Academy of Design

PUBLIC COLLECTIONS
Maryland Historical Society, Baltimore
Peabody Institute, Baltimore
Pennsylvania Academy of the Fine Arts,
  Philadelphia
University of Pennsylvania, Philadelphia

SEASON	75-76	76-77	77-78	78-79	79-80	80-81	81-82	82-83	83-84	84-85
Paintings			1	4	1	1			1	
Dollars			$15,000	$25,600	$4,750	$1,200			$550	

Record Sale: $15,000, PB, 2/3/78, "General Harrison," 30 × 25 in.

THOMAS CHAMBERS

(1808?-1866?)

Thomas Chambers was a naive landscape and marine painter about whose life the facts are sketchy at best. Some of his work was based on direct observation, but much of it, particularly the scenes of naval encounters for which he is best known, was derived from contemporary prints. His ability to translate them into lively oil paintings was considered exceptional. He used vivid, contrasting colors, laid on boldly, in a manner which conveyed a sense of movement and intensity.

Chambers was born in England, but there is uncertainty about the year of his birth. Some sources give it as 1808, while others put it in 1815. He came to America in 1832 and became a naturalized citizen shortly afterward. Presumably he had no formal art training.

From 1834 to 1843 he was listed in the official directory of the day as a resident of New York City; from 1843 to 1851 as a resident of Boston; from 1852 to 1857 of Albany, New York; and in 1858 and 1859 and again from 1861 to 1866 of New York City. No information has been found of his whereabouts after 1866 or, in fact, whether he was still living. Until 1838 he was listed as a landscape painter and thereafter as a marine painter.

Both in Albany and in New York City Chambers painted many views of the Hudson River, most of which were neither signed nor dated. One, *Villa on the Hudson near Weehawken* (date unknown, New York State Historical Association) is a colorful view of an elegant dwelling on a bluff overlooking the river, based on a Bartlett print published in 1838 in *American Scenery*. To achieve his bold composition, Chambers lowered the horizon line, omitted figures from the original and used strong outlines and bright colors.

Perhaps the most dramatic and best of Chambers's works were his paintings of naval battles during the American Revolution and the War of 1812. One of the

Destruction of Java by Constitution, 21¼ x 30 in. Courtesy of Wunderlich and Company, Inc. New York, New York.

finest, *The Constitution and the Guerriere* (ca. 1845, Metropolitan Museum of Art), was inspired by an engraving by Cornelius Tiebout which, in turn, was based on a painting by Thomas Birch. The encounter, in which the *Guerriere* was battered into such a wreck in half an hour that she had to be burned rather than towed, was a favorite subject for American painters of the time.

Chambers was unlike most primitive painters in that, instead of using flat forms unmodulated by light and shadow, he painted large, rhythmic shapes, frequently silhouetted against sky or water. His waves were crested with whitecaps to give the water motion. His paints, which he used lavishly, had an almost enamel-like finish.

PUBLIC COLLECTIONS

Brooklyn Museum
New York State Historical Association,
    Cooperstown
Smith College Museum of Art, Northampton,
    Massachusetts

SEASON	75-76	76-77	77-78	78-79	79-80	80-81	81-82	82-83	83-84	84-85
Paintings									3	4
Dollars									$7,572	$5,173

Record Sale: $4,000, D.NY, 4/18/84, "Mountain Landscape at Dusk," 18 × 24 in.

EDWARD TROYE
(1808-1874)

Edward Troye, one of the first artists in the United States to specialize in animal subjects, was the country's most esteemed painter of horses throughout his mid-nineteenth-century career.

He produced nearly 360 paintings and a dozen drawings of thoroughbreds from every leading American stud farm and racing stable. He also painted prize livestock and individual portraits; many of his pictures include figure portraits of trainers, grooms and jockeys.

His superb animal and sporting pictures possess vigor and animation of line, with a lustrous finish reflecting his sound academic training.

Born in 1808 to French sculptor Jean Baptiste de Troy at Lausanne, Switzerland, Edward Troye went to England at age 14 to study art under various masters.

His interest in animal subjects may have been awakened by Jacques Laurant Agasse, a friend of his father. In 1828, he went to the West Indies as a plantation bookkeeper. In 1831, he moved to Philadelphia, where he was a staff illustrator for *Sartain's Magazine.*

Troye traveled and painted in the early 1830s in New York, Virginia, South Carolina and Tennessee. He announced his decision to specialize in "the noblest of animals," the horse, in 1835, after a commission for Robert Alexander, owner of Woodburne Farms near Lexington, Kentucky.

Troye settled in Mobile, Alabama and taught art and French until 1855, when he traveled to the Middle East. He painted scenes of Syria and the Holy Land, exhibiting them in New Orleans, New York and Canada on his return in the late 1850s.

In 1866, Troye began to write an illustrated series, *The Race Horses of America.* The first and only volume was published in April of 1867.

Troye moved in 1869 to his final home at Owens Cross Roads, Alabama. He

Horse, Tatler, June 23, 1869, 25 x 30 in., signed l.c. Courtesy of Kennedy Galleries, New York, New York.

summered in Kentucky, and died there in 1874. A friend erected a heroic-sized monument to Troye in Georgetown, Kentucky.

PUBLIC COLLECTIONS
Bethany College, West Virginia
Historic Columbia Foundation, South Carolina
United States Capitol, Washington, D.C.
Yale University, New Haven, Connecticut

SEASON	75-76	76-77	77-78	78-79	79-80	80-81	81-82	82-83	83-84	84-85
Paintings							2	3		
Dollars							$100,000	$76,000		

Record Sale: $50,000, CH, 6/4/82, "Colonel Johnson's Fanny," 24 × 29 in.

SETH EASTMAN
(1808-1875)

Buffalo Hunt, 24 x 36 in. William J. Williams Family Collection, Photograph courtesy of Kennedy Galleries, New York, New York.

The military frontiers of mid-nineteenth-century America were the sources for Seth Eastman's paintings and drawings of landscapes and Indian life.

As a soldier-artist, the career Army officer served in several widely separated posts, but the greater part of his scenic and genre work reflects his assignments to the Upper Mississippi and the Southwest.

Born in 1808 in Brunswick, Maine, Eastman attended the Military Academy at West Point, New York from 1824 to 1828. The topographical drawing taught there was intended to give every young officer some skill in making accurate sketches of terrain, vital to military field tactics of the time. Eastman recognized his extraordinary affinity for this art and resolved to master it.

On graduation, the new second lieutenant spent almost four years at Crawford, Wisconsin and Fort Snelling, Minnesota; he then spent two years on topographical assignments in Louisiana and Connecticut.

His ability had so progressed that, only five years after graduating, Eastman returned to West Point as assistant drawing master. There, from 1833 to 1840, Eastman studied privately with Robert W. Weir, the Academy's drawing professor and an established artist. In 1837, Eastman wrote a treatise on topographical drawing.

He developed great competence in oil and watercolor landscapes in the Hudson River School manner, and exhibited in annual shows of the National Academy of Design.

After brief duty in the Florida war against the Seminoles, Eastman was again assigned to Fort Snelling in 1841, where he continued to paint, showing and selling his work in New York City and Cincinnati. He illustrated a book by his wife, *Dahcota, or Life and Legends of the Sioux Around Fort Snelling* (1849), said to have been a main source for Longfellow's poem, "Hiawatha."

In 1848, Eastman was transferred to Texas. It is from his years at Fort Snelling and from this reassignment trip down the Mississippi to the Delta, across the Gulf of Mexico to the Texas shore and overland to San Antonio and Comanche territory, that Eastman drew material for most of his best-known pictures of the West.

National recognition came in 1850, when Eastman was commissioned to illustrate Henry R. Schoolcraft's *History and Statistical Information Respecting the History, Condition, and Prospects of the Indian Tribes of the United States* (1851-1857). Between 1850 and 1855, he made drawings for more than 300 plates in the six-volume work.

During the Civil War, Eastman served in Maine and New Hampshire, was military governor of Cincinnati, and held commands in New York, Pennsylvania and Kentucky. He retired in 1866 as a brevet brigadier general.

By joint resolution of Congress in 1877, Eastman was commissioned to do a series of paintings of Western forts and Indian scenes for federal rooms—nine paintings for the House Committee on Indian Affairs and 17 for the House Committee on Military Affairs. Previously, European artists had also been employed in decorating federal buildings. After Eastman, only American artists were used.

Eastman's figures tend to be wooden in spite of his interest in depicting faithfully the daily life of the Indians, as he observed it. Though he was an Indian fighter, Eastman never drew a battle scene.

Eastman died in 1875, while working on his Congressional projects.

PUBLIC COLLECTIONS
Butler Institute of American Art,
  Youngstown, Ohio
Capitol Building, Washington, D.C.
Corcoran Gallery of Art, Washington, D.C.
Hill Reference Library,
  St. Paul, Minnesota
Joslyn Memorial Gallery, Omaha, Nebraska
Marion Koogler McNay Art Institute,
  San Antonio, Texas
Minneapolis Institute of the Arts,
  Minnesota
National Academy of Design, New York City
Harvard University
St. Louis Art Museum

SEASON	75-76	76-77	77-78	78-79	79-80	80-81	81-82	82-83	83-84	84-85
Paintings							1			
Dollars							$2,000			

Record Sale: $2,000, CH, 6/3/82, "Old Mill, Rhode Island," 10 × 14 in.

JOHN F. FRANCIS
(1808-1886)

John F. Francis played a significant role in the mid-nineteenth-century revitilization of the still life. His bright and radiant use of color, together with a visually intimate representation of his subject matter, enabled him to break away from the stern Peale mode, breathing new life and animation into the Philadelphia still-life tradition.

Born in Philadelphia in 1808 to French Catholic parents, Francis spent the early part of his career as a portraitist and silhouettist; he developed much of his craft in Schuylkill County, Pennsylvania. Armed with sufficient ability to execute portraiture in the romantic tradition, he returned to Philadelphia from 1840 to 1841. The Artists' Fund Society held his first exhibit during that year. Francis spent his next 25 years painting in many rural Pennsylvania communities, as well as in Delaware, Tennessee and Washington, D.C.

Around 1850, Francis began devoting most of his time to the still life, employing many of the mannerisms of seventeenth-century Dutch "luncheon piece" paintings. His travels, and his resultant isolation, apparently gave him the freedom to experiment. Though not recognized in his lifetime, he was to become the master of the "luncheon" or "dessert" type of still-life painting.

Francis favored food (primarily fruit) and glassware for his subject matter. A fine example, *Luncheon Piece* (date unknown, Newark Museum), is a well-

Luncheon Still Life, 1860, 25½ x 30⅜ in. Courtesy of National Museum of American Art, Smithsonian Institution, Museum Purchase.

defined exercise in appealing to the viewer's eye. A white tablecloth frames an abundance of richly adorned foodstuffs and glassware, before a typically irrelevant but compelling background.

Francis spent the last 20 years of his life in Jeffersonville, Pennsylvania, where he died in 1886.

PUBLIC COLLECTIONS
Newark Museum, New Jersey

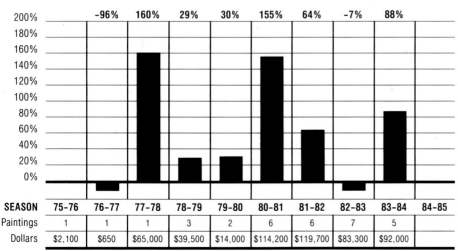

10-Year Average Change From Base Years '75-'76: 47%

	-96%	160%	29%	30%	155%	64%	-7%	88%	
SEASON	75-76	76-77	77-78	78-79	79-80	80-81	81-82	82-83	83-84	84-85
Paintings	1	1	1	3	2	6	6	7	5	
Dollars	$2,100	$650	$65,000	$39,500	$14,000	$114,200	$119,700	$83,300	$92,000	

Record Sale: $65,000, PB, 3/22/78, "Fruit and Wine," 25 × 30 in.

JOHN GADSBY CHAPMAN
(1808-1889)

John Gadsby Chapman was a prolific painter, illustrator, wood engraver and etcher who spent much of his working life as an expatriate in Italy. Early in his career he was known particularly as a figure painter; in his mature years, as a landscape painter. He was one of the first American artists to produce etchings, having started in 1843.

Born in Alexandria, Virginia in 1808, he studied under Charles Bird King and George Cooke. In 1827, he worked for a time as a professional artist in Winchester, Virginia. Later he enrolled briefly at the Pennsylvania Academy of the Fine Arts, but soon left for Europe, where he studied in Florence and Rome until 1831.

On his return to the United States he established his reputation as a portrait and historical painter, dividing his time between New York City and Washington, D.C. His most widely-recognized work of this period was a large mural, *The Baptism of Pocahontas at Jamestown, Virginia, 1613* (1837-1842) in the rotunda of the United States Capitol. Some contemporary critics considered it the most colorful of the rotunda paintings.

At the same time, Chapman was also much in demand as an illustrator for magazines and books. He executed some 1,400 illustrations for *Harper's Family Bible,* which was published in 1846 and gained a wide readership.

The Coronation of Powhatan, 22½ x 29 in. Photograph courtesy of The Gerald Peters Gallery, Santa Fe, New Mexico.

The following year Chapman's own *American Drawing Book,* which he wrote and illustrated, was published. Designed to simplify the teaching of drawing, it became probably the most popular American do-it-yourself art book of the century. It was followed by *Elements of Art* (1848) and the *Elementary Drawing Book* (1872).

In 1848, Chapman returned to Europe and remained there until shortly before his death in 1889. In this later period he was best known for landscapes and color etchings of the countryside surrounding Rome, although he also continued to paint historical and religious subjects.

Noted for their sensitivity and brilliant color, Chapman's landscapes were filled with gaily painted peasants and contadinas. They were highly esteemed by American and English tourists who frequented his studio in Rome.

The radiant luminosity of Chapman's work has been compared to the landscapes of seventeenth-century painter Claude Lorrain. In their breadth and sweep, Chapman's paintings are also reminiscent of the huge landscape panoramas that were popular during his lifetime.

MEMBERSHIPS
National Academy of Design

PUBLIC COLLECTIONS
Museum of Fine Arts, Boston
National Academy of Design, New York City
Virginia State Library, Richmond

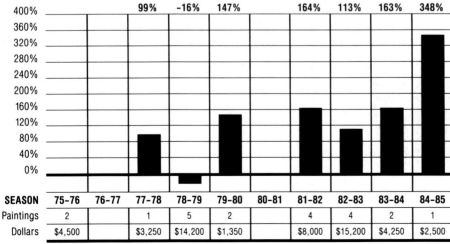

10-Year Average Change From Base Years '75-'76: 127%

	75-76	76-77	77-78	78-79	79-80	80-81	81-82	82-83	83-84	84-85
			99%	-16%	147%		164%	113%	163%	348%
SEASON	75-76	76-77	77-78	78-79	79-80	80-81	81-82	82-83	83-84	84-85
Paintings	2		1	5	2		4	4	2	1
Dollars	$4,500		$3,250	$14,200	$1,350		$8,000	$15,200	$4,250	$2,500

Record Sale: $7,500, S.W, 9/17/78, "Return From the Vineyard," 58 × 78 in.

NOAH NORTH
(1809-1880)

Noah North was an obscure portrait painter who was more accomplished in community affairs than in art. He was productive as an artist for only about a decade, never seeming to overcome financial difficulties for long enough to make more of a name for himself.

North was born in 1809 in Alexander, New York, one of eight children whose parents were always involved in civic matters. At what point his interest in art developed is not clear, but he may have studied with Van Rensselaer Hawkins, an art teacher who spent some time in Alexander.

The earliest portrait attributable to him is dated July 7, 1833, inscribed with the number 11. Apparently North used a numbering system as a means of identification, so it can be assumed numbers one through 10 existed at some point. Five numbered paintings have been discovered; but there are nine known North portraits dated 1833 and 1834.

North's characteristic portraits usually featured single figures, sometimes with babies or dogs. His subjects were richly detailed, with bright faces. They stood out in stark contrast against dark backgrounds.

North's paintings bear a similarity to the work of Ammi Phillips, a portraitist from Eastern New York and Connecticut. The two may have known each other and shared ideas, but the connection is sketchy: North's mother and Phillips's parents were from Colebrook, Connecticut, and Phillips's brother married North's aunt.

In the mid-1830s, North expanded his efforts beyond Alexander, to Holley and Rochester. His reputation had spread, or his original source of income was drying up.

He did travel to Cleveland and Cincinnati and into Kentucky during the remainder of the decade. He evidently found little success, because he returned to New York in 1841, settling in Mount

Boy Holding Dog, ca. 1835, 20¾ x 17½ in. Abby Aldrich Rockefeller Folk Art Center, Williamsburg, Virginia.

Morris. North married Ann Williams. They had two children.

No signed portraits have been found from the 1840s, but there are several attributions. No works from the 1850s to his death in 1880 are known. Apparently, he gave up painting.

Why he did so is not certain, but both the advent of photography and local competition probably cut deeply into his market. As his financial troubles mounted, he must have found it more difficult to produce the kind of portrait he accomplished early in his career.

SEASON	75-76	76-77	77-78	78-79	79-80	80-81	81-82	82-83	83-84	84-85
Paintings	1					1		1		
Dollars	$4,100					$5,000		$11,000		

Record Sale: $11,000, SPB, 1/27/83, "Portrait of Sally Fargo," 27 x 23 in.

JOHANN HERMANN CARMIENCKE
(1810-1867)

The Hudson River School included a range of artists who painted in many different parts of the world, not just in the namesake valley in New York State. These landscape painters were linked by their romantic reaction to the grand scale of nature, as epitomized by the boundless new republic of the United States. They tended to paint detailed, lush views of natural wonders, with a perspective that emphasized the smallness of the viewer.

Though Johann Hermann Carmiencke is considered a member of this school, he was actually German-born, and spent only the last 16 of his 57 years in the United States. He was born in Hamburg, Germany in 1810, and studied art in Dresden, Copenhagen and Leipzig in his twenties. After traveling in Sweden, Germany and Italy, he became painter to the court of the King of Denmark from 1846 to 1851.

It was only after this distinguished employment that Carmiencke came to the United States, settling in New York City. He was respectably successful, exhibiting at the National Academy of Design, the Pennsylvania Academy of the Fine Arts, and the Maryland Historical Society. He died in Brooklyn in 1867.

Carmiencke's work, influenced by his continental training, is darker and more mannered than that of his American-born counterparts. His landscapes, while emphasizing the contrast in scale between the viewer and the landscape, convey the countryside's rustic quality more than its sublimity.

MEMBERSHIPS
Brooklyn Academy
Artists' Fund Society of New York

PUBLIC COLLECTIONS
Yale University

Hyde Park, New York, 12 x 16 in., signed l.l. Private Collection, Photograph courtesy of Kennedy Galleries, New York, New York.

SEASON	75-76	76-77	77-78	78-79	79-80	80-81	81-82	82-83	83-84	84-85
Paintings					1	2	2	5	6	3
Dollars					$4,000	$2,182	$3,731	$13,889	$17,795	$4,429

Record Sale: $7,500, SPB, 7/1/82, "Deer by the River," 36 × 50 in.

ALFRED JACOB MILLER
(1810-1874)

Alfred Jacob Miller was an effective and important artist, highly respected for his landscapes and skilled as a portraitist. His romantic sketches and paintings gave the world its first salient glimpse of the American interior West.

Born in Baltimore, Maryland in 1810, Miller was encouraged to draw by his parents. After some early local training, he studied portraiture in Philadelphia from 1831 to 1832 with Thomas Sully. From 1833 to 1834, he studied art at the Ecole des Beaux-Arts in Paris, and at the English Life School in Rome. Upon his return to Baltimore in 1834, he opened up a portrait studio. Unfortunately, this venture proved unsuccessful.

In 1837, Miller made an important move to New Orleans. There he met wealthy British Army officer William Stewart, who wanted an artist to sketch his upcoming expedition to the Rocky Mountains. Intending those sketches to be transformed into oils for his castle in Scotland, he hired Miller, whom he thought capable of both tasks.

The expedition left from Missouri in May, traveling along what later became the Oregon trail. Miller did about 200 sketches in various media during the six-month journey, including his noted studies of the mountain men and Indian meetings in what is now Southwestern Wyoming. His spirited sociological depictions of the mountain men, whose heyday lasted from about 1820 to 1840, and those of everyday Indian life, gave him a niche in the history of American art.

Returning to New Orleans in 1838, Miller began developing the sketches into oils, and resumed his portraiture. He fulfilled his commitment to Stewart as artist-in-residence at Stewart's Murthly Castle in Perthshire, Scotland from 1840 to 1842, painting scenes from their journey in oils.

Plains Indians Pursuing, 10½ x 13 in., signed l.l. Photograph courtesy of The Gerald Peters Gallery, Santa Fe, New Mexico.

Returning to Baltimore, where he lived until his death in 1874, Miller painted hundreds of oils and watercolors from those Western sketches. And while the authenticity of his subject matter steadily declined, moving toward anecdote instead of documentation, he remained a popular and significant recorder of the early American West.

PUBLIC COLLECTIONS
Amon Carter Museum of Western Art,
  Fort Worth
Baltimore Museum of Fine Arts
Denver Art Museum
Joslyn Art Museum, Omaha,
  Nebraska
Museum of New Mexico Art Gallery,
  Santa Fe
University of Wyoming, Laramie
Walters Art Gallery, Baltimore

SEASON	75-76	76-77	77-78	78-79	79-80	80-81	81-82	82-83	83-84	84-85
Paintings	1		1		4	6	10	5	3	1
Dollars	$1,600		$30,000		$56,625	$318,200	$492,000	$152,000	$135,000	$18,000

Record Sale: $170,000, SPB, 10/17/80, ''The Thirsty Trapper,'' 24 × 20 in.

JUNIUS BRUTUS STEARNS
(1810-1885)

A Hat in the Pond, 1850, 28½ x 36 in., signed l.r. Courtesy of Vose Galleries of Boston, Inc., Massachusetts.

Portrait, genre and historical painter, Junius Brutus Stearns was born in Arlington, Virginia. He studied at the National Academy of Design in 1838; in 1849 he worked in Paris and London.

He used many techniques learned in Europe and was known as a fine draftsman. His modeling of form, observation of light, and liberal use of color were greatly admired during his lifetime. Stearns's sense of space was similar to that of many mid-century European genre painters.

While he painted many portraits, the artist was also known for his historical subjects. An excellent example is his treatment of George Washington: in five paintings, he represented Washington as a citizen, farmer, soldier, statesman and Christian. Stearns also included Indians in many of his historical paintings.

After 1850, Stearns painted a series of genre paintings illustrating the sport of fishing. His subjects included children fishing and group portraits of convivial fishermen, but only one of this series has been found. It is called *Still Life With Trout and Fishing Tackle* (1853, location unknown).

In this painting, the fisherman is seen indistinctly in the background at the edge of the stream, silhouetted against a broad landscape. The focus is on a still-life composition on the bank of the stream in the foreground: a fish, a tackle-box, a rod and reel. An autobiographical note is added by the artist's signature on a bottle half-submerged in the stream. It is possible that the fisherman represents a self-portrait.

Stearns died in 1885.

MEMBERSHIPS
National Academy of Design

PUBLIC COLLECTIONS
Butler Institute of American Art,
    Youngstown, Ohio
City Hall, New York
National Academy of Design, New York City

SEASON	75-76	76-77	77-78	78-79	79-80	80-81	81-82	82-83	83-84	84-85
Paintings				1	1	1	1	1		1
Dollars				$7,000	$2,600	$25,000	$20,000	$1,000		$3,000

Record Sale: $25,000, SPB, 1/29/81, "Trial of Major John Andre," 40 × 55 in.

GEORGE CALEB BINGHAM
(1811-1879)

George Caleb Bingham was a master of the Western genre. He immortalized the life of the Missouri River boatmen in elegantly structured, classical compositions that have an original and otherworldly quality. His early work, especially, has a crystalline light that is made even more luminous by a muting of brushwork. A sense of peace and lighthearted camaraderie pervades his most characteristic paintings.

Bingham's ordered groupings and pyramidal forms predate Cezanne's method of creating an organic flow, whether of figures, boats or objects. Bingham's *Raftsmen Playing Cards* (1847, City Art Museum of St. Louis) and Cezanne's *The Card Players* (ca. 1892, Courtauld Institute Galleries, London) have been compared. Their placing of forms in space, angled lines answering each other, and geometric structuring are similar.

Bingham was born in Augusta County, Virginia in 1811, but grew up in Franklin, Missouri. Whenever he could, he stole away from his rather restrictive environment to go down to the river and see what was going on. He did not know for 20 years or more how important that river would be to him.

His mother encouraged his artistic talent, but a later meeting with the painter Chester Harding probably had a greater effect. Harding gave Bingham a few pointers, and young Bingham began by executing simple portraits on trips along the Missouri and Mississippi Rivers.

The two friends both eventually painted portraits of Daniel Boone: Harding painted him from life in about 1820, when the famous pioneer was quite old; Bingham, in *Daniel Boone Escorting Settlers Through the Cumberland Gap* (1851 to 1852, Washington University Gallery of Art) painted him looking 40 years younger.

There are few women in Bingham's multi-figure scenes, due either to the subject matter or to the nineteenth-century notion of women's place.

In 1837, Bingham studied briefly at the Pennsylvania Academy of the Fine Arts. From 1840 to 1844, he painted portraits of officials in Washington, D.C.

He returned to Missouri in 1844 and began to paint his early genre pictures: *Fur Traders Descending the Missouri* (ca. 1845, Metropolitan Museum of Art) and *The Jolly Flatboatmen* (1846, private collection). Each of these paintings exists in more than one version.

The Jolly Flatboatmen helped Bingham financially when, about 1848, he sent it to the American Art-Union in New York City. The Art-Union was a combination of artist's cooperative, museum, dealer, publisher and mail-order art firm. They made an engraving of the painting and distributed it to their 10,000 members.

Bingham had a second career as a politician. He lost a disputed election in 1846, but was elected to the state legislature in 1848. His paintings of political subjects began to appear about this time; *Stump Speaking* (1854, The Boat-men's National Bank of St. Louis) is a well-known example.

From 1856 to 1859, Bingham traveled back and forth to Dusseldorf, Germany, where he studied the work of contemporary genre painters. Whether his studies there were beneficial is dubious, as his greatest painting is generally thought to be the original *Fur Trader,* and some of his celebrated luminist style was lost after about 1850.

With advancing years, Bingham became more involved with political life. From 1862 to 1865 he served as state treasurer, and in 1875 he was adjutant general. He once even dreamed of the Whig nomination for governor.

In 1877, Bingham was made professor of art at the University of Missouri at Columbia. Most of his works are still in that state, mostly in St. Louis.

Bingham died in Kansas City, Missouri in 1879.

Country Politician, 1849, 20 x 24 in., signed l.l. Courtesy of Vose Galleries of Boston, Inc., Massachusetts.

PUBLIC COLLECTIONS
The Boatmen's National Bank of St. Louis
Brooklyn Museum
Cincinnati Art Museum
City Art Museum of St. Louis
Detroit Institute of Arts
Museum of Fine Arts, Boston
National Academy of Design, New York City
Peabody Museum of Archaeology and Ethnology, Cambridge, Massachusetts
Pennsylvania Academy of the Fine Arts, Philadelphia
R.W. Norton Art Gallery, Shreveport, Louisiana
State Historical Society of Missouri
Washington Art Association
Washington University Gallery of Art, St. Louis

SEASON	75-76	76-77	77-78	78-79	79-80	80-81	81-82	82-83	83-84	84-85
Paintings			1				1	1		
Dollars			$980,000				$5,000	$175,000		

Record Sale: $980,000, SPB, 6/6/78, ''Jolly Flatboatmen No. 2,'' 26 × 36 in.

WILLIAM PAGE
(1811-1885)

William Page confounded and confused his contemporaries with his experimental and unsettling paintings. His use of color earned him the title "the American Titian," and the portraits with which he earned his keep were widely admired, but his paintings were as likely as not to turn black or peel off the canvas because of his experimental techniques.

Page tried to make his works of art independent realities in their own right, not merely copies of some other reality. The effect of this in his surviving pictures, such as *The Young Merchants* (1842, Pennsylvania Academy of the Fine Arts), is to produce in an otherwise normal picture an eerie "otherworldliness," a sensation of catching life itself off-guard.

Page was born in Albany, New York in 1811. His family moved to New York City when he was about nine. Though he was required to work for a law firm, he swiftly convinced everyone that his talent was in art, and began to study under portraitist James Herring in 1825. In 1827, he studied with the famed history-painter Samuel F.B. Morse and entered the drawing class at the National Academy of Design, where he received a silver medal.

He gained a reputation as a colorist and portraitist over the next two decades in Albany, New York City and Boston, also generating some controversy with his erotic *Cupid and Psyche* (1843, loca-

Shakespeare Reading, 1873-1874, 65 x 39 in. Courtesy of National Museum of American Art, Smithsonian Institution, Museum Purchase.

tion unknown). In 1850, he went to Italy, where he remained for 11 years. He became friendly with such luminaries as the poets Robert and Elizabeth Barrett Browning, and moved in an intellectually-elevated circle of American expatriates.

In Italy, he also became involved with spiritualism and with the Swedenborgian religion. Things spiritual and philosophical had always obsessed him; he briefly abandoned art and studied for the ministry.

Page returned to the United States in 1860. Though he was president of the National Academy of Design from 1871 to 1873, his work never received much acceptance from his fellow artists. His pictures were odd, disturbing and occasionally erotic. Had he been born a century later, his approach to art would not have seemed so unusual; as it was, he died in Staten Island, New York in 1885, appreciated by only a small group of admirers.

MEMBERSHIPS
National Academy of Design

PUBLIC COLLECTION
Boston Athenaeum
City Hall, New York City
Metropolitan Museum of Art, New York City
Museum of Fine Arts, Boston
Pennsylvania Academy of the Fine Arts,
 Philadelphia

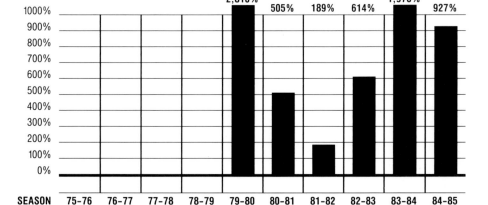

10-Year Average Change From Base Years '75-'76: 1,002%

SEASON	75-76	76-77	77-78	78-79	79-80	80-81	81-82	82-83	83-84	84-85
					2,810%	505%	189%	614%	1,970%	927%
Paintings	2				1	2	3	9	3	2
Dollars	$1,710				$550	$1,554	$2,708	$10,325	$1,813	$1,068

Record Sale: $3,750, D.NY, 4/20/83, "Evening Song," 27 x 20 in.

150

JOHN WILLIAM CASILEAR
(1811-1893)

Lake George, 12 x 20 in. Courtesy of Henry B. Holt, Inc., Essex Fells, New Jersey.

John William Casilear, like many leading landscape painters in the Hudson River School mode, was first a successful engraver. His tranquil, silvery landscapes reflect the engraver's habit of dealing strictly with form, in delicate detail.

Casilear was born in 1811 in New York City. In 1826, at 15, he began studies with master engraver Peter Maverick. On Maverick's death in 1831, Casilear became one of the few students of Asher B. Durand, the preeminent American landscapist, who had also been a pupil of Maverick.

Although landscape painting became Casilear's love, he continued to engrave for a livelihood. He worked for many years for the American Bank Note Company. He was also a partner in an independent engraving firm and later a co-proprietor of his own firm.

Casilear exhibited for years at the National Academy of Design, beginning in 1833. His landscapes were first shown there in 1835. His increasingly popular landscapes were also represented in exhibits of the Apollo Association, the American Art-Union, and the Pennsylvania Academy of the Fine Arts.

From 1840 to 1843, he traveled in Europe with Durand, John F. Kensett and Thomas P. Rossiter.

Not until 1854 did Casilear feel sufficiently secure financially to retire from engraving to paint. He opened a New York City studio; his career continued serene and successful.

Casilear was a leader in the group of Hudson River School practitioners called luminists (sometimes "air painters"), who strove for special effects of air, atmosphere, light and water. Many artists of this school gravitated towards scenic grandeur. Casilear's choices tended to be pastoral—gentle open spaces in subdued, sometimes misty tones, frequently with placid water.

He excelled in lake and mountain scenes and painted Lake George in upstate New York so often that he became identified with it. His most famous landscape is *View On Lake George* (1857, National Gallery of Art).

Casilear died in 1893 at Saratoga, New York.

10-Year Average Change From Base Years '75-'76: 222%

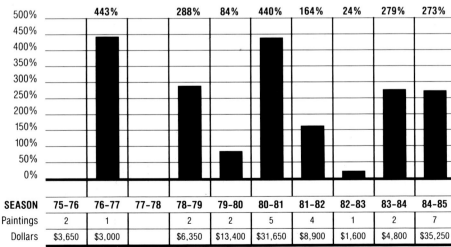

SEASON	75-76	76-77	77-78	78-79	79-80	80-81	81-82	82-83	83-84	84-85
		443%		288%	84%	440%	164%	24%	279%	273%
Paintings	2	1		2	2	5	4	1	2	7
Dollars	$3,650	$3,000		$6,350	$13,400	$31,650	$8,900	$1,600	$4,800	$35,250

Record Sale: $16,000, SPB, 10/26/84, "Mountain Lake," 19 × 30 in.

CHARLES LORING ELLIOTT
(1812-1868)

Charles Loring Elliott was one of the leading American portrait painters of the mid-nineteenth century, best known for his forceful and unembellished portrayals of prominent writers, artists, businessmen and politicians.

Elliott was born in Scipio, New York, the son of an architect. He began his art studies around 1829 or 1830, under John Trumbull and John Quidor in New York City. Failing to meet with success, he retreated to central New York State, where he sharpened his skills as an itinerant portrait painter.

During the following decade, Elliott refined his style, notable for its avoidance of flattery or decoration of any kind. Typically, he posed his subjects before a neutral background, in a traditional bust or full-length formula. Almost ruthlessly, the artist deleted any detail that might distract the viewer from an exclusive concentration on the character of the sitter.

Despite the severity of his technique, Elliott excelled in the portrayal of individual character, especially in the case of charismatic individuals. His method was ideally suited to the temperament of nineteenth-century America, with its emphasis on the personal achievement of the self-made man.

By 1839, Elliott had returned to New York City, where he quickly gained recognition, exhibiting regularly at the National Academy of Design, to which he was elected an associate in 1845. He was made a full academician the following year.

After the death of Henry Inman, Elliott came to be regarded as the premier portraitist of his time, despite the severe contrast between his own art and the more decorative styles of Inman and Thomas Sully. His subjects included many of the prominent writers, artists, businessmen and politicians of the time, such as William Cullen Bryant, James

William Sydney Mount, ca. 1850, 30⅜ x 25 in., signed l.r. Courtesy of National Gallery of Art, Washington, D.C. Andrew W. Mellon.

Fenimore Cooper, Erastus Corning and W.W. Corcoran.

Elliott died in Albany, New York in 1868.

MEMBERSHIPS
National Academy of Design

PUBLIC COLLECTIONS
Corcoran Gallery, Washington, D.C.
Metropolitan Museum of Art, New York City
National Academy of Design, New York City

SEASON	75-76	76-77	77-78	78-79	79-80	80-81	81-82	82-83	83-84	84-85
Paintings				2		1	1			2
Dollars				$3,600		$950	$1,600			$1,800

Record Sale: $1,900, SPB, 11/17/78, "Portrait Edwin Forrest," 30 × 25 in.

JOHN WILLIAM HILL
(1812-1879)

John William Hill, a city topographer turned landscape artist, was—in the second half of his career—the leading representative of pre-raphaelite painting in America. He is perhaps best known for his early lithographs of cities and buildings, created while he was employed by Smith Brothers of New York.

But that work ended in 1855, when the artist became entranced by the theories of John Ruskin and turned to nature as his subject. No artist followed the dictates of the pre-raphaelites more closely. His watercolor paintings of weedy banks, birds, masses of flowers and fruits portray the natural setting with extraordinary fidelity.

London-born, Hill came to the United States with his family when he was seven. His father, an engraver, taught his son the careful skills of his art.

In the 1830s, Hill went to work for the New York Geological Survey as a topographical painter, later moving to Smith Brothers, who published lithographs of his drawings. He produced several large commercial drawings of American cities, public buildings and private residences, the most famous of which is an aquatint of New York as seen from Brooklyn Heights.

When he was 43, Hill turned to pure landscape painting. Joining the pre-raphaelite movement, he became its leading spirit in the United States. His watercolors employ a detailed stipple

Study of Fruit, 1877, 6⅛ x 10⅝ in., signed l.r. M. and M. Karolik Collection of American Watercolors and Drawing, Courtesy of Museum of Fine Arts, Boston, Massachusetts.

technique that was developed for miniature art. It gives a microcosmic view that is highly exact and brilliant in color.

Hill's paintings were done primarily in New Jersey and along the Hudson River in New York. His son, John Henry, also a pre-raphaelite, made etchings of his father's landscape work.

PUBLIC COLLECTIONS
Field Museum, Chicago

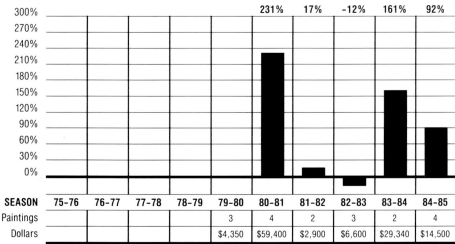

10-Year Average Change From Base Years '79-'80: 82%

SEASON	75-76	76-77	77-78	78-79	79-80	80-81	81-82	82-83	83-84	84-85
						231%	17%	-12%	161%	92%
Paintings					3	4	2	3	2	4
Dollars					$4,350	$59,400	$2,900	$6,600	$29,340	$14,500

Record Sale: $50,000, SPB, 11/21/80, "View of New York," 19 × 32 in.

153

RUSSELL SMITH
(1812-1896)

Russell Smith was a nineteenth-century artist who enjoyed a highly successful career as a scenic painter, landscape artist, panoramist and scientific illustrator. He is best known today as a panoramist, and as a painter of scenic drop curtains for major theaters in Philadelphia, Boston and other Eastern cities.

William Thompson Russell Smith was born in Glasgow, Scotland to parents who emigrated to Western Pennsylvania in 1819. Growing up in Pittsburgh, Smith taught himself to paint at an early age, painting commercial signs for money and life-size portraits of famous heroes for amusement, before studying formally under portraitist James Reid Lambdin from 1829 to 1832.

Smith first made his professional reputation around 1833 as scenic artist for the new Pittsburgh Theater. The following year, Smith moved to Philadelphia, where he spent six years at the Chestnut and Walnut Street Theaters as a scenic designer. He went on to design stage scenery and drop curtains for the Philadelphia Academy of Music and other major theaters in Boston, Baltimore and Washington, D.C.

In 1838, he married Mary Wilson, a painter of flowers, and settled in Glenside, near Philadelphia. He enjoyed success as a landscape painter, a painter of panoramas, and a scientific illustrator employed by such prestigious naturalists as Sir Charles Lyell, in addition to his

Chambersburg, PA., 1890, 7¾ x 11¾ in. Courtesy of Vose Galleries of Boston, Inc., Massachusetts.

already well-established career as a scenic artist.

Russell Smith had two children, Mary and Xanthus, who became artists. During his life, his paintings were exhibited at the Boston Museum of Fine Art, the Philadelphia Academy of Fine Art, and the Centennial Exposition of 1876 in Philadelphia. The artist died at his Glenside home in 1896.

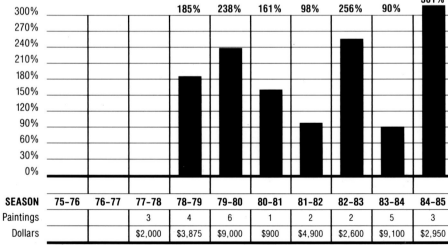

10-Year Average Change From Base Years '77-'78: 166%

SEASON	75-76	76-77	77-78	78-79	79-80	80-81	81-82	82-83	83-84	84-85
				185%	238%	161%	98%	256%	90%	301%
Paintings			3	4	6	1	2	2	5	3
Dollars			$2,000	$3,875	$9,000	$900	$4,900	$2,600	$9,100	$2,950

Record Sale: $3,200, CH, 1/29/82, "Mouth of the Wissahickon," 20 x 30 in.

JAMES HENRY BEARD
(1812-1893)

WILLIAM HOLBROOK BEARD
(1824-1900)

James Henry Beard was born in Buffalo, New York where he spent the first 11 years of his life, until his family moved West to Painesville, Ohio in 1823. It was in that little settlement that his brother, William, was born. Both began their careers as itinerant portrait painters, but later developed interests in genre painting and focused on animals as subjects.

James shared some of his expertise with William, but essentially both were self-taught; their work displayed naivete. Even William's extensive European trip did not alter their style.

During his European trip, from 1856 to 1858, William met fellow American artists Emanuel Gottlieb Leutze, Sanford Robinson Gifford, Worthington Whittredge, Albert Bierstadt and others. He returned to Buffalo, where he had established a studio in 1859, and married, but his wife died soon after their marriage. In 1863, he married the daughter of painter Thomas Le Clear.

James lived in the Cincinnati, Ohio area from about 1834 until 1870, when he moved back to New York State. During the Civil War, he saw active duty with the Union forces.

The Lost Balloon, 1882, 47¾ x 33¾ in., signed l.l. Courtesy of National Museum of American Art, Smithsonian Institution, Museum Purchase.

Humor is prevalent in the brothers' art, but one picture by James, *The North Carolina Emigrants* (ca. 1845, location unknown), departed from this mood by portraying poor people realistically. It was surprisingly successful and sold for $750, at that time a huge sum for a genre picture.

James was in demand for children's portraits. Sometimes he included pets, a popular touch, and later he turned to anthropomorphic animal subjects, treated with wry humor, social criticism and satire. Such paintings contrasted with the sentimental work typical of the period. Other paintings by James include *The Long Bill* (ca. 1830, Cincinnati Art Museum), and portraits of Henry Clay and presidents John Quincy Adams, William H. Harrison and Zachary Taylor.

While indoor animals interested James, William painted wild animals, but both used irony: they naturalistically depicted animals engaged in human activities. William is generally regarded as the better artist. He most frequently used bears as his satiric symbol for man, and they appeared in some of his most famous canvases: *The Bears of Wall Street Celebrating a Drop in the Market* (ca. 1880, New-York Historical Society); *Bears on a Bender, The Bulls and Bears of Wall Street* (ca. 1880, New-York Historical Society); and *The Bear's Temperance Question* (date unknown, Chicago Art Institute).

At the time of his death, James lived in New York City. William also died in New York City. The family's artistic bent showed up in James's children, including illustrators Daniel Carter Beard (1850-1941) and James Carter Beard (1837-1913); Frank Beard (1842-1905), illustrator and professor of fine arts; and Henry Beard (dates unknown), painter and publication designer.

MEMBERSHIPS
James:
National Academy of Design
Century Club
William:
National Academy of Design

PUBLIC COLLECTIONS
James:
Cincinnati Art Museum
William:
New-York Historical Society, New York City
Rhode Island School of Design, Providence
Art Institute of Chicago

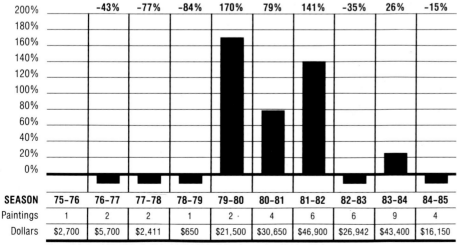

10-Year Average Change From Base Years '75-'76: 16%

	-43%	-77%	-84%	170%	79%	141%	-35%	26%	-15%

SEASON	75-76	76-77	77-78	78-79	79-80	80-81	81-82	82-83	83-84	84-85
Paintings	1	2	2	1	2	4	6	6	9	4
Dollars	$2,700	$5,700	$2,411	$650	$21,500	$30,650	$46,900	$26,942	$43,400	$16,150

Record Sale: $15,500, S.BM, 11/20/80, "Confrontation," 16 x 22 in.

ASAHEL LYNDE POWERS
(1813-1843)

Asahel Lynde Powers, an itinerant folk portraitist, was born in Springfield, Vermont in 1813. In his 10-year career, Powers traveled from Vermont to Illinois, leaving behind him portraits that evolved from crude but arresting composition that lacked modeling, to more mature works that retained a crisp and lively quality.

Very little is known about Powers's life and training. Apparently, he began to paint at age 18, and moved throughout Massachusetts, Vermont and New Hampshire accepting commissions. All of the artist's early works were executed on wood panels, a surface he abandoned for canvas as he traveled farther afield in the late 1830s and early 1840s.

Some of his earliest paintings are a group of nine portraits of the Cobb-Harris family of Windham, Vermont from 1831.

Typical of his early portraits is *Charles Mortimer French* (ca. 1832, New York State Historical Association) which shows Powers's strength in facial renderings, if also his unfamiliarity with anatomy and perspective, lack of modeling and highlighting, and drooping, awkward hands.

Powers never resorted to stereotyped images, but imparted individuality to each portrait through varied backgrounds and color effects, and the use of an assortment of props, such as a hearing trumpet, a stack of coins or a painted box. Like many other folk artists, Powers paid particular attention to the costumes of his sitters, with various styles of brushwork.

It is likely that Powers died in Olney, Illinois in 1843. On his migration Westward, he spent some time in and around Plattsburgh, New York, where he received an enthusiastic endorsement in the local newspaper. A group of 20 portraits date from this stay.

Portrait of Benjamin Clark, 1840, 36 x 30 in. Courtesy of the Fogg Art Museum, Harvard University. Gift of Mr. and Mrs. John F. Barss.

PUBLIC COLLECTIONS
Abby Aldrich Rockefeller Folk Art Collection,
  Williamsburg, Virginia
National Gallery of Art, Washington, D.C.
New York State Historical Association,
  Cooperstown

SEASON	75-76	76-77	77-78	78-79	79-80	80-81	81-82	82-83	83-84	84-85
Paintings			1						2	
Dollars			$2,500						$26,500	

Record Sale: $14,500, SPB, 1/28/84, "Double Portrait of Albert and Julius," 19 × 24 in.

WILLIAM TYLEE RANNEY
(1813-1857)

William Ranney, a genre, portrait and historical painter, is best known for his paintings of cowboys, hunters and trappers of the Southwest.

Born in Middletown, Connecticut in 1813, he was apprenticed as a tinsmith in Fayetteville, North Carolina, following the death of his sea-captain father. Ranney (who never used his middle name in adult life) had abandoned his trade to study art in New York City by 1833.

Seeking adventure, in 1836 Ranney enlisted with the Army of the Republic of Texas, and witnessed the struggle for independence from Mexico. Though he was in the Southwest for only several months, his experiences and observations there would influence Ranney's most successful work.

Upon his return, Ranney established a studio in New York City, later relocating to then-rural Hoboken, New Jersey. He produced portraits and romanticized history paintings of the Revolutionary War and the exploits of Daniel Boone for 10 years, before concentrating on scenes of Western and sporting life.

Ranney's Western paintings depict details of dress that reveal the origins of modern cowboy attire. One such painting was *Hunting Wild Horses* (1846, Joslyn Art Museum). He also produced a number of hunting scenes set against the New Jersey marshes outside his rustic studio, one of which was *Duck Shooting* (1850, Corcoran Gallery of Art).

Ranney was popular with his peers. After his untimely death in 1857, fellow members of the National Academy of Design organized a memorial show and benefit to establish a fund for his widow and family. Some of them, including William Sidney Mount, completed his unfinished paintings.

General Marion Crossing the Pedee River in South Carolina in 1778, 1850, 50 x 74¼ in. Courtesy of Vose Galleries of Boston, Inc., Massachusetts.

MEMBERSHIPS
National Academy of Design

PUBLIC COLLECTIONS
Corcoran Gallery of Art,
    Washington, D.C.
Joslyn Art Museum, Omaha, Nebraska
Museum of Fine Arts, Boston
Newark Museum, New Jersey
North Carolina Museum of Art, Raleigh

SEASON	75-76	76-77	77-78	78-79	79-80	80-81	81-82	82-83	83-84	84-85
Paintings						2			1	
Dollars						$950,000			$3,500	

Record Sale: $680,000, SPB, 10/17/80, "The Sleigh Ride," 30 × 40 in.

SAMUEL LANCASTER GERRY
(1813-1891)

In the 1840s, Samuel Lancaster Gerry was known as the leader of the White Mountain School. This area in New Hampshire is the setting for a large number of the landscapes for which he is most widely known, although he also painted portraits, genre pictures and animal studies.

Gerry was born in Boston in 1813. Although he had no formal instruction in art, he is believed to have been somewhat influenced by Asher Durand and Thomas Cole in the United States, and by Constant Troyon and Lambinet in Paris. He spent three years in England, France, Switzerland and Italy, studying and associating with some of America's most respected expatriate artists.

He sometimes copied others' works. Two copies of George Harvey pictures are reproduced in *The Old Print Shop Portfolio: A New Gallery of "Honest American" Paintings.* They are *Summer* (a scene of a road accident in which a cart has lost a wheel) and *Winter* (a scene of travelers in the Canadian woods stopped by a fallen pine).

Gerry's *West Point, Kosciusko Monument* (1838, private collection), is based on a composition by W.H. Bartlett. The tomb of the Lithuanian patriot rises tall in the upper left-hand corner, standing like a sentinel along the Hudson River and overlooking a view of ships and a holiday group of gentlemen and women with parasols. The color in Gerry's ver-

The Pemiqewasset River, 1857, 20 x 30 in., signed l.r. Courtesy of Vose Galleries of Boston, Inc., Massachusetts.

Hudson River, 8½ x 7 in., signed l.r. Courtesy of Henry B. Holt, Inc., Essex Fells, New Jersey.

sion of this scene is stronger than Bartlett's. Gerry's attention to detail and his expertise in bringing the work to a professional finish are apparent.

Franconia Mountains Near Thornton, New Hampshire (1857, location unknown), not a copy, is a serene composition of sky and hills in soft browns and lavenders; two horsemen water their horses in the shallow bend of a river.

Gerry was one of the founders of the Boston Art Club, organized in 1854. In 1858, he served as its president. He died in 1891 in Roxbury, Massachusetts.

MEMBERSHIPS
Boston Art Club

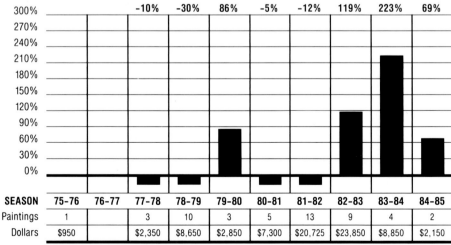

10-Year Average Change From Base Years '75-'76: 49%

| | -10% | -30% | 86% | -5% | -12% | 119% | 223% | 69% |

SEASON	75-76	76-77	77-78	78-79	79-80	80-81	81-82	82-83	83-84	84-85
Paintings	1		3	10	3	5	13	9	4	2
Dollars	$950		$2,350	$8,650	$2,850	$7,300	$20,725	$23,850	$8,850	$2,150

Record Sale: $15,000, SPB, 7/1/82, "Village Church," 23 x 31 in.

GEORGE PETER ALEXANDER HEALY
(1813-1894)

George Peter Alexander Healy achieved international recognition as a portrait painter in the nineteenth century. He was extremely prolific, completing approximately 100 portraits per year. He painted prominent statesmen, society figures, writers and religious leaders in America and Europe, making 34 transatlantic crossings during his lifetime.

Born in 1813 in Boston, Healy was the son of an impoverished Irish sea captain. With little training, Healy opened a studio at age 17 and began to paint portraits. With the patronage of Mrs. Harrison Gray Otis, and the encouragement of painter Thomas Sully, Healy went to Europe in 1834.

In France, Healy studied under Antoine-Jean Gros, and formed a friendship with painter Thomas Couture. After eight years in France and England, Healy had achieved an international reputation, and he spent his life traveling between Europe and America painting innumerable commissioned portraits. His subjects included Louis Philippe, Abraham Lincoln, John Quincy Adams, Andrew Jackson, Daniel Webster, Pope Pius IX, Franz Liszt, Henry Wadsworth Longfellow, Louisa May Alcott and hundreds of other notable figures. While his primary subject was portraiture, Healy also painted some genre and historical works.

Roxana Atwater Wentworth, 1876, 30¼ x 25 in., signed l.c. Courtesy of National Gallery of Art, Washington, D.C., Gift of Lady Vereker.

Healy's style was similar to the French school of painting; it was cool, hard-edged and strong. His unique ability to paint with a photographic eye for detail and still flatter his sitters gained him enormous popularity. He was fondly known as the "Yankee artist" and warmly received in high society both in America and abroad.

Healy lived in Chicago from 1854 to 1867; he returned to the United States and spent his last two years in Chicago, before his death in 1894.

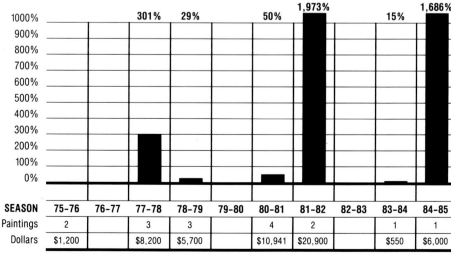

10-Year Average Change From Base Years '75-'76: 579%

SEASON	75-76	76-77	77-78	78-79	79-80	80-81	81-82	82-83	83-84	84-85
			301%	29%		50%	1,973%		15%	1,686%
Paintings	2		3	3		4	2		1	1
Dollars	$1,200		$8,200	$5,700		$10,941	$20,900		$550	$6,000

Record Sale: $20,000, D.NY, 9/23/81, "Portrait of George Inness," 23 × 18 in.

THOMAS H. HINCKLEY

(1813-1896)

Born in 1813 in Milton, Massachusetts, Thomas Hewes Hinckley had early artistic inclinations. His father frowned on such a career, apprenticing him to a Philadelphia merchant in 1829. Nevertheless, Hinckley soon began evening classes with William Mason, which were to be his only art instruction.

In 1833, he returned to Milton, where he first painted signs and then portraits, establishing a studio there.

Hinckley pioneered in painting cattle. His *Cattle Seeking Shelter from an Approaching Storm* and *Disputed Game* sold at high prices. In 1845, he executed drawings of Daniel Webster's famous Ayrshire dairy herd.

He was influenced by William Landseer's animal paintings and the Flemish masters while visiting Europe in 1851. The Royal Academy in London exhibited two of Hinckley's hunting scenes in 1858.

Returning home, he exhibited at the Pennsylvania Academy of the Fine Arts and the National Academy of Design. Gentlemen farmers readily purchased his works, reducing the occasions for exhibiting. Some of his paintings were engraved.

Living as a guest on the island of Naushon permitted detailed studies of deer; he produced many beautiful paintings of them. Traveling in California in 1870, Hinckley painted deer and elk on the rocky coastal promontories.

His genre works were skillfully composed. Street scenes are graphic and authentic. While capable of landscapes in the Hudson River School style, he used them mostly as backgrounds for his animals. In later years he painted landscapes more frequently, but refrained from exhibiting.

Bull, 1869, signed l.r. Photograph courtesy of the Brandywine River Museum, Chadds Ford, Pennsylvania, Anonymous Collection.

PUBLIC COLLECTIONS
Corcoran Gallery of Art, Washington, D.C.
Metropolitan Museum of Art, New York City
Museum of Fine Arts, Boston

SEASON	75-76	76-77	77-78	78-79	79-80	80-81	81-82	82-83	83-84	84-85
Paintings		1	2	3	2	2	2	1	1	
Dollars		$2,500	$2,700	$8,200	$5,920	$8,500	$9,700	$4,800	$600	

Record Sale: $6,000, CH, 12/11/81, "Majestic Stag and Family," 36 × 29 in.

JOHN MIX STANLEY
(1814-1872)

John Mix Stanley painted a chronicle of the American Indian and the early West that was massive in scope. Sadly, most of this important work was destroyed. Of those paintings which remain, some have been praised as skillful and accurate, while others have been denounced as tedious and cliched.

Stanley was born in Canandaigua, New York in 1814. Orphaned at age 14, he became a coachmaker's apprentice, an occupation which involved some decorative painting. He moved to Detroit in 1834 to become a sign painter, then studied with James Bowman in Philadelphia.

Bowman and Stanley became partners and opened a portrait studio in Chicago. Stanley started painting pictures of Indians encamped around Fort Snelling, then progressed to Indian portraits and scenes. In 1842, he set up a studio in Fort Gibson, Oklahoma, and the following year went with Indian agent Pierce Mason Butler to paint a council of Cherokee chiefs in Tahlequah, Oklahoma. In 1846, "Stanley and Dickerman's North American Indian Gallery" showed in Cincinnati and St. Louis.

Stanley did most of his painting while traveling, on his own or with expeditions as official artist. He was one of the first American artists to paint panoramic landscapes, a craft seen at its best in *Mountain Landscape with Indians* (date unknown, Detroit Institute). He also painted portraits, including two of Hawaii's royal family and several of notable Indian chiefs.

In 1852, Stanley took 152 paintings of 43 tribes to the Smithsonian Institution, hoping to sell them to the government for permanent display; the Smithsonian delayed making a decision. Stanley married and settled in Washington, traveling occasionally to work on special projects such as the ambitious *The Trial of Red Jacket* (1868, Buffalo Historical Society).

Osage Scalp Dance, 1845, 40¾ x 60½ in. Courtesy of National Museum of American Art, Smithsonian Institution, Washington, D.C. Gift of the Misses Henry, 1908.

The Buffalo Hunt, 1853, 29¾ x 39 in., signed l.l. Photograph courtesy of The Gerald Peters Gallery, Santa Fe, New Mexico.

In 1865, a fire at the Smithsonian destroyed all but five of the paintings the government had ultimately decided not to buy from Stanley. The very same year, a fire at P.T. Barnum's American Museum consumed the Stanley paintings held there. Stanley's seven remaining years were spent painting in his studio and ensuring the preservation of the five surviving images through chromolithography. He died in 1872.

(No sales information available.)

PUBLIC COLLECTIONS
Buffalo and Erie County Historical Society, New York
Detroit Institute of Arts
Honolulu Academy of Arts
Metropolitan Museum of Art, New York City
National Museum of American Art, Washington, D.C.

SAMUEL B. WAUGH
(1814-1885)

One of the foremost portrait painters in Philadelphia in the mid-nineteenth century, Samuel B. Waugh was known also for his landscapes, principally of Italy. He executed portraits of both President Lincoln and of Ulysses S. Grant, but whether they were painted from life or from the work of others is unknown; a portrait of Dr. Caspar Wistar, an early medical scientist in Philadelphia, which is in the collection of the American Philosophical Society there, was based on a portrait of Wistar by Bass Otis.

Waugh was born in Mercer, Pennsylvania in 1814. As a boy he received some instruction in painting from J.R. Smith in Philadelphia. He continued his training by studying the work of old masters in Italy, France and England when he lived abroad for eight years before 1841. He painted many portraits while in Europe.

On his return he settled in Philadelphia and remained there for most of the rest of his life. He lived in New York City in 1844 and 1845 and in Bordentown, New Jersey in 1853, probably while working on commissions. In 1847 he completed a large painting of the ships and bustle of activity around the wharves at the lower tip of Manhattan Island: *The Battery* (location unknown). He later did at least one other painting of New York harbor.

Robert J.C. Walker, 1873, 24 x 20 in., signed l.r. Courtesy of The Historical Society of Pennsylvania, Philadelphia.

It was for his panoramic paintings of Italy that he was first recognized. One was exhibited in Philadelphia from 1849 to 1855; another, *Italia* was exhibited from 1854 to 1858.

Waugh instilled his love of painting in other members of his family. His wife, son, daughter and nephew all became painters. Of the group only his son Frederick Judd Waugh established a reputation (he became a marine painter).

Waugh died in Wisconsin in 1885.

MEMBERSHIPS
Artists' Fund Society
National Academy of Design

PUBLIC COLLECTIONS
American Philosophical Society, Philadelphia
National Portrait Gallery, Washington, D.C.
University of Pennsylvania, Philadelphia

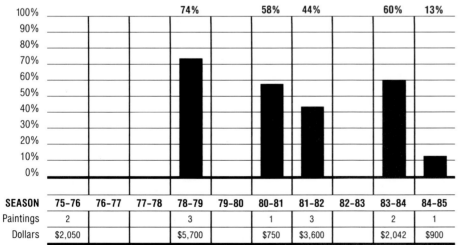

10-Year Average Change From Base Years '75-'76: 42%

SEASON	75-76	76-77	77-78	78-79	79-80	80-81	81-82	82-83	83-84	84-85
				74%		58%	44%		60%	13%
Paintings	2			3		1	3		2	1
Dollars	$2,050			$5,700		$750	$3,600		$2,042	$900

Record Sale: $2,800, W.W, 2/25/79, "Edward Phillips Mitchell," 24 x 19 in.

162

JEROME THOMPSON
(1814-1886)

Jerome Thompson's genre paintings on rustic themes, which were immensely popular in the late nineteenth century, have received new attention recently. This revived interest focuses on the unusual distinction of Thompson's landscape settings, which often dominate the pictures' simple foreground scenes of rural work, play or dalliance.

Thompson's natural elements—meadows, mountains, sky—have great luminosity and tonal subtlety. They show a high level of technical sophistication.

Thompson was born in 1814 to the Middleboro, Massachusetts portraitist, Cephas Thompson, who instructed only Jerome's older brother in art. His father wanted Jerome to farm, and destroyed Jerome's art work.

In his teens, Thompson moved with his sister to Barnstable, Massachusetts, where he painted signs, ornaments and portraits. Daniel Webster is said to have been one of Thompson's subjects, and in 1834 he painted the aging Abraham Quary, last of the Nantucket Indian tribe. In 1835, Thompson opened a New York City portrait studio.

His departure from portraiture came in 1850, when he exhibited *A Pic Nick, Camden, Maine* (date unknown, Museum of Fine Art, Boston) at the National Academy of Design, earning membership and creating a demand for his work.

Pike's Peak, 8¼ x 15 in. Courtesy of Kennedy Galleries, New York, New York.

In 1852, Thompson went to England for several years of independent study. He continued to paint the integrated genre-landscapes that made him famous, but by 1865 he ceased exhibiting the originals. Lithographic reproductions ensured his continuing prosperity. Works like *The Haymakers* (1859, private collection) and *Apple Gathering* (1856, Brooklyn Museum) earn modern praise as outstanding nineteenth-century landscapes.

On his return from England, Thompson lived at Mineola, Long Island, and Glen Gardner, New Jersey. He sketched in the Massachusetts Berkshires and in Vermont. He also painted some romantic Western subjects, including *Hiawatha's Homeward Journey with Minnehaha* (date and location unknown) and *Indian Prayer* (1884, location unknown).

Thompson died in 1886.

MEMBERSHIPS
National Academy of Design

PUBLIC COLLECTIONS
Brooklyn Museum
Museum of Fine Arts, Boston

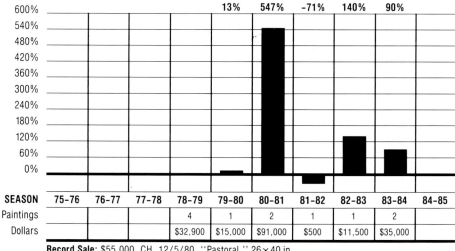

10-Year Average Change From Base Years '78-'79: 120%

					13%	547%	-71%	140%	90%	
SEASON	75-76	76-77	77-78	78-79	79-80	80-81	81-82	82-83	83-84	84-85
Paintings				4	1	2	1	1	2	
Dollars				$32,900	$15,000	$91,000	$500	$11,500	$35,000	

Record Sale: $55,000, CH, 12/5/80, "Pastoral," 26 × 40 in.

ALBERTUS DEL ORIENT BROWERE
(1814-1887)

Albertus Del Orient Browere was a genre, still-life and literary painter, as well as a landscapist of the Hudson River School. His subjects varied greatly; his landscapes included the Hudson River Valley, the steamy tropical scenery of Central America, and haunting California countrysides. He also did genre scenes based on the writings of Washington Irving and James Fenimore Cooper.

Born in Tarrytown, New York, Browere was the eldest son of John Henri Isaac Browere (1790-1834), a well-known sculptor, whose life masks included those of Thomas Jefferson and Gilbert Stuart. Although Browere inherited his father's sculpting talent, he turned his attention toward painting. At age 17 he exhibited his first painting at the National Academy of Design, where he was a student. One year later, he was awarded a medal by the American Institute in New York for the best original oil painting.

Between 1833 and 1848 Browere exhibited at the American Academy, the Apollo Association and the American Art-Union.

After the death of his father in 1834, Browere settled in Catskill, New York and earned his living as an apothecary. During his free time, he painted landscapes of the surrounding countryside.

Browere's quiet life changed drastically, however, when news of the California gold rush reached New York. He was suddenly smitten with gold fever and left Catskill in 1852 to sail via Cape Horn for California, where he remained for four years. He returned to New York in 1856.

In 1858, Browere made his second and final trip West, this time traveling by mule over the Isthmus of Panama to San Francisco. He remained there for three years, concentrating on depicting in his work the fervor of prospecting for gold. During this period, Browere painted

View of Stockton, California, 1838, signed l.l. Photograph courtesy of M. Knoedler & Co., Inc., New York, New York.

The Departure, 24 x 29 in., signed l.r. Photograph courtesy of M. Knoedler & Co. Inc., New York, New York.

some of his most remarkable scenes, using the beauty of California and Central America as subjects.

PUBLIC COLLECTIONS
Brooklyn Museum
Metropolitan Museum of Art, New York City
New York State Historical Association,
  Cooperstown

SEASON	75-76	76-77	77-78	78-79	79-80	80-81	81-82	82-83	83-84	84-85
Paintings			4			1			1	1
Dollars			$7,100			$1,600			$11,000	$3,750

Record Sale: $11,000, SPB, 1/27/84, ''Crossing the Isthmus,'' 33 × 48 in.

GEORGE LORING BROWN
(1814-1889)

One of the most prominent landscape painters of his time, George Loring Brown was born in Boston in 1814. He lived in Europe for 20 years, a well-known member of expatriate art colonies in Florence and Rome.

As a boy, Brown decided to make his living as an artist and apprenticed himself to a wood engraver; he then went on to illustrate children's books.

Encouraged by a portraitist friend to become a painter, he sold a landscape to an influential merchant who added a gift that enabled Brown to embark in 1832 on his first European venture.

Brown struggled in Antwerp and Paris until funds from sales of his paintings in Boston arrived. He studied in Paris with Eugene Isabey. Enthralled by Claude Lorrain's paintings, he copied them in the Louvre, along with those of Ruysdael and Constable. Because of his success in copying and interpreting the strong colors and formal composition of Claude's style, he was nicknamed "Claude" Brown.

On his return to Boston in 1834, he received encouragement from Washington Allston, who, influenced by Claude, had introduced romanticism to American art. Brown worked in New York State for a year, returned to the Boston area in 1838, and sailed for Europe in 1839, financed by commissions for copies of old masters. He remained there until 1859.

View of the Temple of Peace in the Roman Forum, 1864, 20⅛ x 36⅛ in., signed l.r. Courtesy of National Museum of American Art, Smithsonian Institution, Museum Purchase.

Brown captured atmospheric effects in many romantic scenes of Italy, such as *View at Amalfi* (1857, Metropolitan Museum of Art). *Castello dell'Ovo, Bay of Naples* (1844, location unknown) reflects the technique of Isabey, Brown's tutor, in its crusty impasto and precise brushstrokes.

After his return to the United States, Brown executed many American landscapes and continued to paint Italian scenery, though his use of color grew more subtle. He brought back to Boston a technique known as "Macchiorelli," based on a photo-impressionist point of view.

Brown frequently exhibited at the Boston Athenaeum, the National Academy of Design and the Pennsylvania Academy of the Fine Arts. He died in Malden, Massachusetts in 1889.

PUBLIC COLLECTIONS
Metropolitan Museum of Art, New York City
Museum of Fine Arts, Boston
National Museum of American Art,
  Washington, D.C.

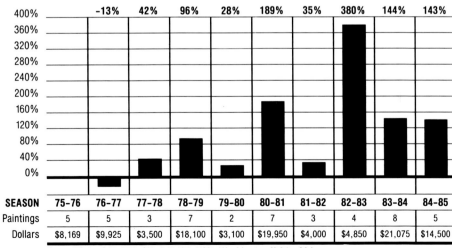

10-Year Average Change From Base Years '75–'76: 104%

	-13%	42%	96%	28%	189%	35%	380%	144%	143%
SEASON	75-76	76-77	77-78	78-79	79-80	80-81	81-82	82-83	83-84	84-85
Paintings	5	5	3	7	2	7	3	4	8	5
Dollars	$8,169	$9,925	$3,500	$18,100	$3,100	$19,950	$4,000	$4,850	$21,075	$14,500

Record Sale: $10,000, CH, 6/1/84, "Mt. Washington," 34 x 60 in.

JOSEPH WHITING STOCK
(1815-1855)

Joseph Whiting Stock, a painter in the folk art manner, produced more than 900 works during his brief artistic career. Most of them were portraits, although he also painted some landscapes, marine views, miniatures, anatomical illustrations and even windowshades.

Stock was born in 1815 in Springfield, Massachusetts. He was crippled in an accident at age 11, and took up painting at his doctor's suggestion when he was about 17 years old. Although he received some instruction from Francis White, who was in turn a pupil of Chester Harding, Stock was primarily self-taught.

Stock lived and worked for most of his life in Springfield, although he possessed a wheelchair which enabled him to travel to other cities in Massachusetts and Rhode Island. His diary, now owned by the Connecticut Valley Historical Museum, lists all his paintings and the fees he charged.

Although he began his career by copying popular depictions of historical figures, such as Napoleon, Stock is remembered for his portraits of his contemporaries, some painted from corpses after the fashion of the time. Many of his subjects were children, often portrayed with pets or toys, as in *William Howard Smith* and *Mary Jane Smith* (1838, Abby Aldrich Rockefeller Folk Art Collection, Williamsburg) and *Jane Henrietta Russell* (1844, Museum of Fine Arts, Boston).

Although Stock's figures were imperfectly modeled and his colors often raw, he captured qualities of expressiveness in his sitters. He occasionally shared a studio with photographer O.H. Cooley, and may have used photographic sources in some compositions.

Stock died in 1855 in Springfield.

Portrait of Jasper Raymond Rand, ca. 1845, 46 x 40½ in. Courtesy of The Newark Museum, New Jersey, Gift of Mrs. Henry Lang, 1935.

PUBLIC COLLECTIONS
Abby Aldrich Rockefeller Folk Art
  Collection, Williamsburg
Musuem of Fine Arts, Boston

SEASON	75-76	76-77	77-78	78-79	79-80	80-81	81-82	82-83	83-84	84-85
Paintings				1		2	2		1	
Dollars				$3,500		$35,500	$10,500		$1,628	

Record Sale: $28,000, SPB, 4/30/81, "Captain Gardner's Son, Samuel," 45 × 36 in.

DAVID GILMOUR BLYTHE

(1815-1865)

David Gilmour Blythe was the leading satiric genre painter of his generation in the United States. Like his contemporary in France, Honore Daumier, he exposed vice, corruption and poverty. He was not a great painter, but in nineteenth-century America, at a time when artists were encouraged to paint idealized images of the country, Blythe was one of the very few who dealt with its realities: the environmental and human costs of industrialization, violence and slavery.

Blythe was born in 1815 to immigrant Irish and Scottish parents in East Liverpool, Ohio. At age 16, he was apprenticed to Joseph Woodwell, a Pittsburgh wood-carver. He had little formal art training, but an interest in art was encouraged by his proximity to the studio shop of J. J. Gillespie. The store was a meeting place for artists and traveling portrait painters.

From 1837 to 1840, Blythe served in the navy as a ship's carpenter, traveling to Boston and the West Indies. He was an itinerant portrait painter in Western Pennsylvania and Eastern Ohio from 1841 to 1845. It was at about this time that he began to paint city scenes. This was a departure in style as well as subject—although his portraits had been stiff and primitive, his genre paintings were humorous and realistic.

Blythe settled in Uniontown, Pennsylvania in 1846. He nicknamed his studio "the rat's nest," wrote doggerel for the newspaper and met and married a lovely young woman. Unfortunately, she died after only one year of marriage. Blythe had already been prone to depression and this started his descent into alcoholism.

He immersed himself in his work, creating a 300-foot panorama of the Western Pennsylvania mountains with which he toured Maryland, Virginia and Pennsylvania in 1851. Also at this time, he created a heroic eight-foot statue of Lafayette for the Fayette County Court-

Boy Playing Marbles, ca. 1858, 22 x 26½ in. Courtesy of National Museum of American Art, Smithsonian Institution, Museum Purchase.

house in Pennsylvania; this was his major work of sculpture.

Blythe painted many pictures of young street urchins—they are dated mostly between 1854 and 1860. An excellent example is *Street Urchin* (1856-1858, Butler Institute of American Art). *Art versus Law* (date unknown, Brooklyn Museum) records Blythe's own struggles to keep a roof over his head. *Trial Scene* (date unknown, Rochester Memorial Art Gallery) is typical of his attacks on the legal system. *The Pittsburgh Horse Market* (date unknown, Carnegie Institute) is another example of his preoccupation with oppression, in this case extending to the animal kingdom.

Most outstanding of Blythe's Pittsburgh paintings are *The Post Office* (ca. 1860, Carnegie Institute) and *The Hideout* (ca. 1850-1860, private collection).

The Civil War affected Blythe deeply. His largest body of work stems from this period. He followed the 13th Regiment of Pennsylvania Volunteers in the field and made many sketches of army life, as well as some important paintings. A masterpiece is *The Battle of Gettysburg* (ca. 1863-1865, location unknown). It powerfully depicts the tumult of battle. Others were *General Abner Doubleday Watching His Troops Cross the Potomac* (ca. 1863, National Baseball Hall of Fame and Museum), and *Libby Prison* (1863, Museum of Fine Arts, Boston), a realistic rendering of the inhuman conditions at that Confederate jail. Blythe also illustrated his Union sympathies in a series glorifying Lincoln (an example is in the Museum of Fine Arts, Boston).

Blythe's last years were spent in Pittsburgh; he died in 1865.

PUBLIC COLLECTIONS
Brooklyn Museum
Carnegie Institute, Pittsburgh
Museum of Fine Arts, Boston
National Baseball Hall of Fame and Museum,
   Cooperstown, New York
Rochester Museum, New York
University of Rochester, New York

SEASON	75-76	76-77	77-78	78-79	79-80	80-81	81-82	82-83	83-84	84-85
Paintings		1					1	3	1	
Dollars		$5,500					$48,000	$66,500	$60,000	

Record Sale: $60,000, CH, 6/1/84, "On The Sly, Schoolboy Studying," 26 × 21 in.

JAMES BARD
(1815-1897)

JOHN BARD
(1815-1856)

James Bard and his twin brother, John, were born in the Chelsea section of New York City in 1815. Both self-taught, they collaborated on more than 350 portraits of steamboats and sailboats operating around New York, Long Island Sound and the Hudson River.

Because the boats are accurately observed and drawn to scale, the Bards' paintings are important to historians of navigation. It is believed that James provided the outline sketches, while John filled in the color and the backgrounds. James stopped working with his brother after 1849 (John died in 1856), but continued alone to produce at a tremendous rate, executing nearly 4,000 paintings during his lifetime.

The Sidewheeler "Oliver M. Petit" (1857, location unknown) is a good example of Bard's style. The ship is viewed broadside, parallel to the picture plane; its movement is indicated by the spray of water. Like much of Bard's work, the painting is primitive in its careful drawing, flatness and use of very bright colors.

The monumentally conceived ship is silhouetted against an unlocalized landscape background. The tiny figures of sailors and passengers are stiff and anonymous, serving to indicate the scale of the steamship. Bard's name and address appear in the lower right-hand corner of the painting, as an invitation to prospective buyers who might want to visit the artist's studio on Washington Street in New York City.

James Bard left a record of almost every steamship operating on the Hudson River during the second half of the nineteenth century. His last work was completed the year of his death in White Plains, New York in 1897.

Lewis R. Mackey, 31 x 52 in., signed l.r. Courtesy of Henry B. Holt, Inc., Essex Fells, New Jersey.

Reindeer, 1822, 30 x 60 in., signed l.r. Courtesy of Smith Gallery, New York, New York.

PUBLIC COLLECTIONS
Albany Institute of History and Art, New York
Brooklyn Museum
Mariners Museum, Newport News, Virginia
New York State Historical Association,
    Cooperstown
Peabody Museum, Salem, Massachusetts
Shelburne Museum, Vermont
Smithsonian Institution, Washington, D.C.
Wadsworth Athenaeum, Hartford, Connecticut

SEASON	75-76	76-77	77-78	78-79	79-80	80-81	81-82	82-83	83-84	84-85
Paintings	1				1	2	2	1	1	1
Dollars	$11,000				$38,000	$67,000	$36,000	$6,500	$2,800	$20,000

Record Sale: $38,000, P.NY, 5/2/80, "Neversink," 30 x 50 in.

EMANUEL LEUTZE
(1816-1868)

Claimed by America as an American painter and by Germans as a German painter, Emanuel Gottlieb Leutze was some of both. Because he lived for nearly 20 years in Dusseldorf as student and painter, and hosted dozens of young American painters who came there to study, he represents the link between the Dusseldorf School of historical painting and the American school.

He is best known for two enormous depictions of significant events in American history—*Washington Crossing the Delaware* (1851, Metropolitan Museum of Art), and *Westward the Course of Empire Takes Its Way* (1862, United States Capitol). The latter dramatizes the trek of pioneers into the West. Both were done in the somewhat dry, but heroic, German style.

Leutze was born in Germany in 1816. When he was nine, his family came to America for political reasons and settled in Philadelphia. He studied portrait painting, and at 20 started painting in Lancaster County, Pennsylvania and in the South.

He returned to Philadelphia in 1839, and the next year, thanks to financial support from local patrons, went to Dusseldorf to study at the academy there. When he became dissatisfied there, he set up his own studio. He sold one of his first historical works to the Dusseldorf Art Union. In 1843, he set off on a two-year trip through Germany and Italy. He spent some time in Munich, where he was influenced by the historical paintings of the artists there.

Ironically, *Washington Crossing the Delaware* was painted while he was in Germany, not as a patriotic tribute to the great American, but rather to rally the spirits of German liberals whose Revolution of 1848 had failed. However, he used many of his American friends in Dusseldorf as models.

The original painting was damaged by fire, repaired and exhibited in Bremen,

Lady Schuyler Burning her Wheat Fields on the Approach of the British, 1852, 32 x 40 in., signed l.l. Courtesy of Vose Galleries of Boston, Inc., Massachusetts.

where it was destroyed by bombs during World War II. Leutze, however, painted a second version in 1851, and brought it to the United States for exhibition and eventual sale. It is this second version that is known to millions of Americans.

Largely on the strength of his Washington painting, Leutze received the commission for the huge mural in the Capitol. Before starting it, however, he returned to Germany to learn stereochromy, a process of applying watercolor directly to plaster without losing color intensity. He used the process with great success. Most critics consider the murals in the Capitol mediocre at best, but agree that Leutze's work, while not great art, is the best of the lot.

In 1863, Leutze finally brought his wife and children from Germany to Washington, D.C., where they lived until his death five years later.

MEMBERSHIPS
National Academy of Design

PUBLIC COLLECTIONS
Corcoran Gallery of Art, Washington, D.C.
Metropolitan Museum of Art, New York City
National Portrait Gallery, Washington, D.C.
New-York Historical Society, New York City
Smithsonian Institution, Washington, D.C.
United States Capitol, Washington, D.C.

SEASON	75-76	76-77	77-78	78-79	79-80	80-81	81-82	82-83	83-84	84-85
Paintings								1		1
Dollars								$1,300		$650

Record Sale: $1,300, SPB, 1/27/83, "Portrait of Albert George Emerick," 24 × 19 in.

JOHN FREDERICK KENSETT
(1816-1872)

The paintings of John Frederick Kensett are among the finest and most sought-after work produced by the second generation of Hudson River School artists. With an engraver's eye for sharp detail and a sensitivity to atmospheric variation, Kensett created powerful portraits of rocks, water and sky, reflecting infinite depth, power and peace. A wave breaking on the shore, as in *Eagle Rock, Manchester, Massachusetts* (1859, private collection), has weight behind it.

He was considered a luminist painter, one of a group that was especially interested in weather effects. Stanford Gifford, a follower of Kensett, referred to luminism as "air-painting."

Kensett was more a follower of Asher B. Durand than he was of Thomas Cole. He attempted to concentrate on compositions that were realistic and detailed, rather than contrived and dramatic. His work falls into four major categories: shorelines; mountain and water views from above; mountain lake scenes from a lower point of view; and woodland interiors.

Kensett was born in Cheshire, Connecticut in 1816. His father was Thomas Kensett, an immigrant English engraver. At his father's firm in New Haven, Connecticut, he learned how to draw.

In New York City, Kensett found work as an engraver of labels, maps and banknotes. John W. Casilear, a fellow artist, encouraged him to turn to painting.

Newport Harbor, 13½ x 24 in. Courtesy of Taggart, Jorgensen, & Putman Galleries, Washington, D.C.

In 1840, Kensett went to Europe with Casilear, Thomas Rossiter and Asher Durand. He stayed for seven years, helping to support himself by doing engravings for American companies.

When he returned to America in 1847, he had no trouble selling his work. His timing was good: in 1846 he had sent several Italian landscapes home, two of which were purchased by the American Art-Union.

By 1849, he had been elected to full membership in the National Academy of Design in New York City. Having a gift for friendship, Kensett was often asked to join clubs, participate in art politics and help with artists' charities. In 1859, he served on the short-lived art commission to oversee the decoration of the United States Capitol in Washington, D.C. In 1870, he became a founder, later a trustee, of the Metropolitan Museum in New York.

His studio became a magnet for the art world. Travelers delighted in identifying precise locations in the Catskills or Newport or New England in the oil sketches and drawings that covered his walls.

Kensett died in his studio in 1872.

MEMBERSHIPS
National Academy of Design

PUBLIC COLLECTIONS
Art Institute of Chicago
Brooklyn Museum
Cummer Gallery of Art, Jacksonville, Florida
Metropolitan Museum of Art, New York City
New York Historical Society, New York City

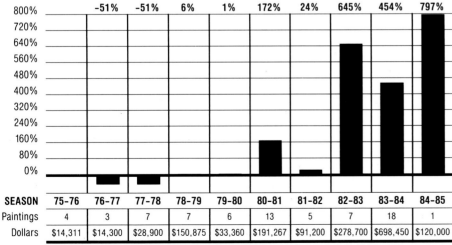

10-Year Average Change From Base Years '75-'76: 200%

	-51%	-51%	6%	1%	172%	24%	645%	454%	797%

SEASON	75-76	76-77	77-78	78-79	79-80	80-81	81-82	82-83	83-84	84-85
Paintings	4	3	7	7	6	13	5	7	18	1
Dollars	$14,311	$14,300	$28,900	$150,875	$33,360	$191,267	$91,200	$278,700	$698,450	$120,000

Record Sale: $540,000, SPB, 12/8/83, "Eagle Cliff, Coast of Massachusetts," 28 x 46 in.

170

WILLIAM RIMMER
(1816-1879)

Although William Rimmer was not notably successful in his artistic career, he is today recognized as a gifted and imaginative sculptor and painter who worked outside the mainstream of contemporary tradition.

Rimmer was born in England in 1816. His father was an expatriate Frenchman who believed that he was the lost heir to the throne of France; his delusions of persecution and exile were, to some extent, shared by his sons.

The family emigrated to the United States when Rimmer was two, and settled in Boston in 1826. By age 15, Rimmer had begun a series of jobs, including signpainting and lithography. Beginning around 1840, he taught himself medicine, which he practiced in East Milford, Massachusetts from 1855 until 1863.

During the 1860s, Rimmer began sculpting, first in granite and then in bronze. Due to his aloofness and his disregard for the popular neoclassical conventions of sculpture, he secured only one public commission: a granite head of Alexander Hamilton on Boston's Commonwealth Avenue (1864), one of his less successful works.

His original, expressive and anatomically-sophisticated bronzes— *Falling Gladiator* (1861, Museum of Fine Arts, Boston), *Fighting Lions* (1871, Metropolitan Museum of Art), and *Dying Centaur* (1871, Museum of Fine Arts, Boston)—have been likened to the naturalism of Rodin.

Rimmer continued to paint and draw, although he showed these works so seldom that most people were unaware of them. His work shows a powerful anatomical sense. He drew poignant, emotional Civil War scenes and painted exotic and romantic canvases, distinguished by a precise—even academic— style and almost invisible brushwork. His best-known painting, *Flight and Pursuit* (1872, Museum of Fine Arts, Boston), evokes a surreal aura of mystery and menace.

At the Window, ca. 1870, 20¼ x 14⅛ in., signed l.r. Courtesy of National Museum of American Art, Smithsonian Institution, Museum Purchase.

Rimmer wrote several books on anatomy and art, and taught artistic anatomy in Boston and in New York City, where he directed the School of Design for Women at the Cooper Union from 1866 until 1870. He died in South Milford, Massachusetts in 1879.

PUBLIC COLLECTIONS
Metropolitan Museum of Art, New York City
Museum of Fine Arts, Boston

SEASON	75-76	76-77	77-78	78-79	79-80	80-81	81-82	82-83	83-84	84-85
Paintings						2		1	1	
Dollars						$71,500		$3,500	$10,000	

Record Sale: $52,500, S.BM, 5/21/81, "Interior," 12 × 9 in.

FRANCOIS-REGIS GIGNOUX
(1816-1882)

View of Peekskill, 1844, 45 x 72½ in., signed l.c. Photograph courtesy of Hirschl & Adler Galleries, Inc., New York, New York.

Francois-Regis Gignoux was born in Lyons, France. He studied at the Ecole des Beaux-Arts under Paul Delaroche.

In 1840, he visited America in pursuit of an American lady, whom he later married. Impressed with the magnificent variety of scenic beauty to be found in America, he decided to stay. His precise academic style and technique suited the tastes of the time. He soon found that he was given more commissions than he could execute.

In 1843, for a brief period, George Inness was one of his pupils, although Inness soon pursued his own vision.

Gignoux settled in Brooklyn. He remained in America until 1869, when he returned to France. He died in Paris in 1882.

Although Henry T. Tuckerman in his *Book of the Artists* praises Gignoux highly, saying that he "catches nature's pleasantest language," modern critics are less enthusiastic. Unlike those of the Hudson River School, his crisply detailed landscapes are today considered sentimental.

The artist specialized in snow scenes or "snowscapes." This was primarily because his competitors, the Hudson River School of painters, rarely painted winter scenes. Well-known for his views of Niagara Falls, New England and Virginia, the artist painted the natural landscape in all seasons, although his "snowscapes" were the most in demand.

MEMBERSHIPS
Brooklyn Art Association
Century Association
National Academy of Design

PUBLIC COLLECTIONS
Corcoran Gallery of Art, Washington, D.C.
New-York Historical Society, New York City
William Rockhill Nelson Gallery of Art,
  Kansas City, Missouri

SEASON	75-76	76-77	77-78	78-79	79-80	80-81	81-82	82-83	83-84	84-85
Paintings						2	3	1	3	1
Dollars						$23,000	$18,500	$3,400	$29,100	$5,388

Record Sale: $24,000, S.BM, 11/17/83, "American Scenery," 20 × 36 in.

SAMUEL MARSDEN BROOKES

(1816-1892)

British-born Samuel Marsden Brookes was a successful portrait, miniature and landscape painter. He is best known for his minutely detailed, highly finished still lifes of fish, executed on the West coast after 1862.

Brookes was born in Middlesex, England in 1816, and emigrated with his parents to Chicago in 1832. He began painting in 1841, and a year later traveled to Milwaukee. Selling his paintings by lottery, the young artist returned to England for further artistic training.

Upon his return to the United States in 1847, Brookes visited Chicago, where his works were well-received. According to biographical sources, he painted his first portrait in 1858, and continued to work in portraiture for the next four years.

In 1862, Brookes traveled to California and settled in San Francisco. Although he continued to paint portraits, he began to experiment with elaborate still lifes. His studies of peaches and grapes, often silhouetted against a wall or shallow niche, were greatly admired. Despite his accomplishment with these earlier still lifes, the artist did not find a true creative outlet until he included fish in his arrangements.

Brookes's first great success was his *Still Life* (1862, location unknown), a vividly baroque composition of many types of fish, fowl and vegetables arranged on a ledge and hanging against a wall. The exuberant colors and dynamic composition of cascading fruit, fish and game are reminiscent of seventeenth-century still lifes.

As the artist began to focus on fish, he depicted them in a variety of situations. Sometimes they are shown alive, as in *Trout in a Tank* (date unknown, California Historical Society). More often, however, they are depicted in a traditional still-life setting, hanging against a wall or lying on a surface. Characteristic conventional arrangements are *California Smelts* (date unknown, Brooklyn Museum) and *String of Fish* (date unknown, de Young Museum).

Highly skilled in rendering the silvery sheen of fish scales, the artist was admired for his ability to depict close detail. Brookes's remarkable expertise in producing illusionistic images inspired a number of minor myths, anecdotes and poems. One poem hailed the artist's talent in capturing the essence of a quivering smelt or salmon, freshly pulled from the river or bay.

Involved in the art community of San Francisco, Brookes helped organize the California Art Union in 1865. This short-lived organization was an important forerunner of the San Francisco Art Association, in which Brookes was also very active. He was patronized by such prominent citizens as Judge Edwin Bryant Crocker and Mrs. Mark Hopkins. Before his death in 1892, Samuel Marsden Brookes had gained a great measure of popular and financial success.

California Mission Grapes, 23 x 19 in., signed l.l. Courtesy of John H. Garzoli Gallery, San Francisco, California.

Still life of Apples, 20 x 16 in., signed l.l. Courtesy of John H. Garzoli Gallery, San Francisco, California.

SEASON	75-76	76-77	77-78	78-79	79-80	80-81	81-82	82-83	83-84	84-85
Paintings							3			2
Dollars							$13,600			$21,500

Record Sale: $14,000, BB.SF, 2/28/85, "Still Life of Grapes," 24 × 20 in.

MEMBERSHIPS
San Francisco Art Association

PUBLIC COLLECTIONS
Brooklyn Museum
California Historical Society, San Francisco
E.B. Crocker Art Gallery, Sacramento, California
Lyman Allyn Museum, New London, Connecticut
M.H. de Young Memorial Museum, San Francisco

DANIEL HUNTINGTON
(1816-1906)

Although he was one of the most popular painters of his day, Daniel Huntington's prestige collapsed after his death. His pious, sentimental paintings and idealized portraits failed to capture the attention of twentieth-century audiences. During his lifetime, however, Huntington was one of the leading portraitists of New York City. Many of the public buildings there have one or more Huntington portraits, recognized today for their intricate costumes rather than for the character of the sitters.

Born in 1816 in New York City, Huntington studied at Hamilton College with portraitist Charles Loring Elliott, and later in New York with Samuel F.B. Morse and Henry Inman. He went abroad for three years in 1839 to study in Rome, where he was influenced by Titian.

Huntington's early ambition—to bring historical and allegorical art to America—resulted in one of the most popular paintings of the 1840s: *Mercy's Dream* (1842, Pennsylvania Academy of the Fine Arts), a quasi-religious figure painting taken from *Pilgrim's Progress*.

In 1850, Huntington began a highly productive career in portraiture, turning out more than 1,000 canvases in his lifetime. The paintings tend to be stiffly posed and marked by romanticism.

Huntington served twice as president of the National Academy of Design, from 1862 to 1870 and from 1877 to 1890. He died in 1906.

Italia, 1843, 38⅝ x 29⅛ in., signed l.r. Courtesy of National Museum of American Art, Smithsonian Institution, Washington, D.C. Museum Purchase.

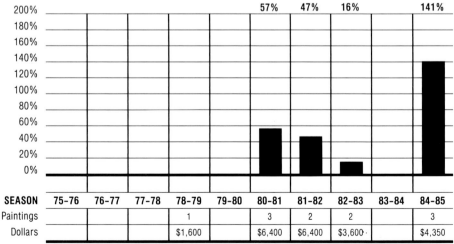

10-Year Average Change From Base Years '78-'79: 52%

SEASON	75-76	76-77	77-78	78-79	79-80	80-81	81-82	82-83	83-84	84-85
						57%	47%	16%		141%
Paintings				1		3	2	2		3
Dollars				$1,600		$6,400	$6,400	$3,600·		$4,350

Record Sale: $5,700, S.W, 12/6/81, "Portrait of Hubert Welles," 50×40 in.

MEMBERSHIPS
American Academy and American Art-Union
National Academy of Design

PUBLIC COLLECTIONS
Brooklyn Museum
Corcoran Gallery of Art, Washington, D.C.
Metropolitan Museum of Art, New York City
Montclair Art Museum, New Jersey
National Gallery of Art, Washington, D.C.
New York Historical Society, New York City
Pennsylvania Academy of the Fine Arts, Philadelphia

ROBERT SCOTT DUNCANSON

(1817-1872)

Robert Scott Duncanson's reputation as a painter rests largely on the many landscapes he produced during his later years in the style of the Hudson River School, but his floral still lifes first brought him recognition. He was also a portraitist and did some undistinguished genre painting.

Most significant, however, is that he is thought to be the first black painter in America to earn his living by painting and to become known internationally. He was also the first black muralist.

There is considerable confusion over Duncanson's date of birth. He was probably born between 1817 and 1822 in New York State, the son of a Scottish-Canadian father and a black or mulatto mother.

Slavery was still widespread at the time and his father took Duncanson to Canada, hoping that he could grow up in an atmosphere less poisoned by prejudice. Duncanson was self-taught as an artist, but presumably in his youth he studied reproductions of work by Hudson River and other painters.

In 1841, he rejoined his mother near Cincinnati, Ohio. He may have studied in Scotland the previous year, but this cannot be confirmed. In any event, he was already skilled enough to have three paintings accepted for exhibition in 1842.

Cincinnati at the time, known as "the Athens of the West," was dedicated to fostering the arts. Nicholas Longworth, one of its wealthiest citizens, was an early patron of Duncanson and, in 1848, commissioned him to paint murals in his home, "Belmont," now the Taft Museum.

Duncanson made his home in Cincinnati, but traveled widely. He also worked for a time as a daguerreotypist, and some of his compositions may have stemmed from photographic prints that he made. His landscape of this period, *Blue Hole, Flood Waters, Little Miami*

Mount Healthy, Ohio, 1844, 28 x 36¼ in. Courtesy of National Museum of American Art, Smithsonian Institution, Washington, D.C. Gift of Leonard Granoff.

River (1851, Cincinnati Art Museum), reveals for the first time his fully-developed mature style. It also acknowledges his debt to the Hudson River painters.

In 1853, Duncanson traveled to Italy, France and England with two painter friends, quite probably with his expenses paid by the Anti-Slavery League. Back home, he began to incorporate classical motifs and literary allusions into his work.

Duncanson spent the Civil War years painting in England and Scotland. In 1872, in Detroit, he suffered a mental breakdown and died three months later.

SEASON	75-76	76-77	77-78	78-79	79-80	80-81	81-82	82-83	83-84	84-85
Paintings				1	1	1		1	1	2
Dollars				$1,100	$1,400	$7,000		$15,000	$7,500	$27,000

Record Sale: $17,000, CH, 12/7/84, "Landscape with Waterfall," 41 × 56 in.

WILLIAM GAY YORKE
(1817-?)

William Gay Yorke left a considerable legacy of excellent ship portraits, but there is a dearth of information about many aspects of his life and work. There is even uncertainty about the correct spelling of his name. From 1861 to 1870, he spelled it without the "e." After 1870, however, he always signed it with the "e." From the signature information on his paintings, however, it is known definitely that he worked in Liverpool and New York City.

Yorke was born in St. John's, New Brunswick in 1817. He became a shipwright by trade and, as he had artistic talents, painted portraits of ships in his spare time. A son, William Howard York, was born in 1848, and two years later father and son sailed for Liverpool, England.

Yorke prospered well enough there as a ship portraitist to be able to give up manual work on ships altogether. In time he also taught his son to paint, and the two worked together until 1870. Their styles were very similar, but while both were good at accuracy and detail, no indication exists of who did what in the collaboration.

The father and son had a falling-out in 1870 and the father sailed for America. He lived and painted in Brooklyn, moving often from one address to another. His last known location was noted in 1882. A painting of the Statue of Liberty, done around 1888, is his last known work. There is no record that he ever returned to England, nor of the date of his death. His son continued as a ship portraitist in Liverpool and died there in 1921.

Most of Yorke's paintings were of sailing ships, but he also did some of steam vessels, private yachts and even tugboats. Liverpool was a center of international commerce at the time he lived there, and many of his early paintings were of British, or at least non-

Richard Washburn, 29 x 36 in. Courtesy of Smith Gallery, New York, New York.

American, vessels. As one observer put it, the elder Yorke's paintings were never typically American, just as his son's were never typically British. The most appropriate label for both probably would be painters of the Atlantic.

PUBLIC COLLECTIONS
Mystic Seaport Museum, Connecticut

SEASON	75-76	76-77	77-78	78-79	79-80	80-81	81-82	82-83	83-84	84-85
Paintings						1			2	
Dollars						$5,500			$22,500	

Record Sale: $14,500, P, 12/12/83, "An Incident During the Am. Civil War," 26 × 36 in.

JAMES EDWARD BUTTERSWORTH
(1817-1894)

James Edward Buttersworth was born in Middlesex County in England in 1817. Little is known of him before he arrived in America about 1850 and settled in West Hoboken, New Jersey. There his long career as a marine, landscape and portrait painter flourished; many of his paintings were translated into popular prints by Currier and Ives.

It is presumed that Thomas Buttersworth (1768-1842), an English marine painter who exhibited in London galleries, was his father. Given his background, it is likely that James Buttersworth first learned to paint ships from his father.

New York Harbor became the background for many vessels that he depicted faithfully. With an eye for precise detail, he delighted in painting clipper ships and had an excellent reputation for portraying the great sailing yachts. Scenes of yachting races and of warships in historic actions are included in his works.

Typically, Buttersworth accented the length of a yacht by painting full sails on a diagonal, lending a feeling of swift motion against a low horizon. Dramatically stormy skies and churning waves romanticized the settings.

From 1850 to 1852, a number of his landscapes and marine paintings were exhibited at the American Art-Union. Buttersworth lived until 1894, having painted many great vessels from the sailing era, as well as some of those from the new age of steam.

Yacht Race, 8 x 12 in., signed l.r. Courtesy of Smith Gallery, New York, New York.

5 Yachts, 18 x 24 in. Courtesy of Vose Galleries of Boston, Inc., Massachusetts.

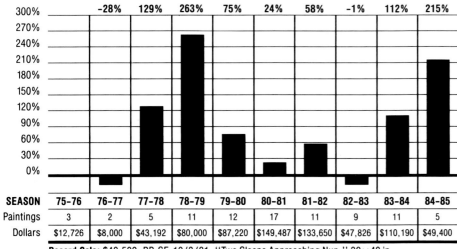

10-Year Average Change From Base Years '75-'76: 85%

		-28%	129%	263%	75%	24%	58%	-1%	112%	215%
SEASON	75-76	76-77	77-78	78-79	79-80	80-81	81-82	82-83	83-84	84-85
Paintings	3	2	5	11	12	17	11	9	11	5
Dollars	$12,726	$8,000	$43,192	$80,000	$87,220	$149,487	$133,650	$47,826	$110,190	$49,400

Record Sale: $42,500, BB.SF, 10/3/81, "Two Sloops Approaching Nun," 30 x 40 in.

PETER FREDERICK ROTHERMEL
(1817-1895)

Venezia, 1863, 11 x 19 in., signed l.r. Courtesy of Raydon Gallery, New York, New York.

Although he was one of the best-known American history painters of his day, Peter Frederick Rothermel's reputation dwindled as the public's appetite for depictions of emotionally charged events, both real and allegorical, ebbed.

Rothermel was noted both for his use of color and for the complexity of his vast compositions, in which he combined sharply defined figures in the foreground with hazy forms in the distance. Some compared him to Delacroix in the way he used color, but at the same time conceded that he fell short of the French artist in achievement.

Rothermel was born in Nescopeck, Pennsylvania, probably in 1817, although the year of his birth is occasionally given as 1814 or 1812. Initially he was trained as a surveyor, then worked as a sign painter. He studied briefly with John R. Smith and Bass Otis. Later he said that it took him six months to get rid of the bad habits Otis taught him in three months. He also studied the collections of the Pennsylvania Academy of the Fine Arts.

He began painting portraits in Philadelphia, but soon turned to history, considered then to be the highest form of painting to which an artist could aspire. He soon became active in the administration of the Pennsylvania Academy, and was a benevolent influence on several generations of aspiring artists.

In 1851, he painted *Patrick Henry in the House of Burgesses of Virginia, Delivering His Celebrated Speech against the Stamp Act* (Patrick Henry Memorial Foundation), one of his best-known paintings. Some critics of the day hailed it as "perhaps the best historical painting executed in America"; others thought it looked unfinished.

Rothermel went to Europe in 1856 and lived in Rome until 1859, painting religious and historical works. After the Civil War he was commissioned by the Pennsylvania Legislature to paint a colossal work on the Battle of Gettysburg. It took him three years to complete the painting, now in the William Penn Memorial Museum in Harrisburg, and when it was finished it was too large for its intended location.

He continued to paint his grandiose scenes, some of them taken from popular literature, until the mid-1880s, when poor health forced him to abandon painting altogether. He died in 1895.

MEMBERSHIPS
Artists' Fund Society
Graphics Club of Philadelphia
National Academy of Design
Sketch Club of Philadelphia

PUBLIC COLLECTIONS
Patrick Henry Memorial Foundation,
  Brookneal, Virginia
Pennsylvania Academy of the Fine Arts,
  Philadelphia
William Penn Memorial Museum,
  Harrisburg, Pennsylvania

SEASON	75-76	76-77	77-78	78-79	79-80	80-81	81-82	82-83	83-84	84-85
Paintings				1	2	3	1			
Dollars				$1,500	$3,000	$4,800	$2,400			

Record Sale: $2,400, SPB, 10/6/81, "Allegorical Study," 37 × 29 in.

BENJAMIN CHAMPNEY
(1817-1907)

Mount Chocorua, 16 x 24 in., signed l.l. Courtesy of Raydon Gallery, New York, New York.

Landscape, flower and portrait painter Benjamin Champney was active in New England. He also became well known for his guidance of young artists.

Born in New Hampshire in 1817, Champney began his career as an apprentice to a lithographer in Boston. By 1830, he was receiving encouragement for his developing talent from Washington Allston, one of Boston's most admired artists, who persuaded Champney to study European artists.

In 1841, Champney took the first of many European trips, which led him to Italy and Paris. His European experience sparked Champney's interest in landscape painting.

Champney's landscapes dealt chiefly with the North Conway region of New Hampshire. They combined tightly controlled detail with panoramic monochromes of White Mountain scenery.

The White Mountains became Champney's summer sketching retreat, beginning around 1849. Each winter he would paint pictures based on his studies from the previous summer.

Champney, who was also a noted flower painter, painted many oil sketches directly from nature. These were considered among his best works.

Champney's interest in the development of young artists was evident when he taught at North Conway; his open hospitality attracted many of New England's budding artists of the 1850s. He instilled the Hudson River School's landscape techniques into the White Mountain painters.

When he died in 1907, Champney's credits included the founding of the Boston Arts Club, exhibits in Boston and New York City, and an autobiography entitled *Sixty Years' Memories of Art and Artists.*

Although many other artists' works are more noted than Champney's, his influence in developing young American artists during the second half of the nineteenth century was of major importance.

MEMBERSHIPS
Boston Arts Club

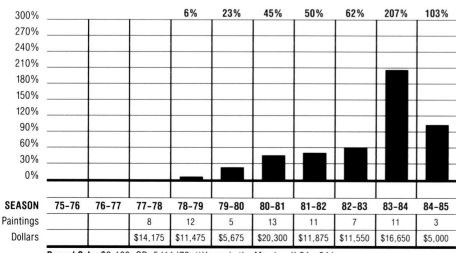

10-Year Average Change From Base Years '77-'78: 62%

			6%	23%	45%	50%	62%	207%	103%
300%									
270%									
240%									
210%									
180%									
150%									
120%									
90%									
60%									
30%									
0%									

SEASON	75–76	76–77	77–78	78–79	79–80	80–81	81–82	82–83	83–84	84–85
Paintings			8	12	5	13	11	7	11	3
Dollars			$14,175	$11,475	$5,675	$20,300	$11,875	$11,550	$16,650	$5,000

Record Sale: $3,100, SB, 5/11/78, ''House in the Meadow,'' 24 x 34 in.

CHARLES DEAS

(1818-1867)

Charles Deas was an early painter of romantic Western scenes, who had a prolific career in the 1840s, unfortunately cut short by insanity in the 1850s. Deas's paintings are best known for their full-blown melodrama, characterized by idealized paintings of American Indians, and scenes of danger, struggle or imminent death.

Charles Deas was born in Philadelphia, the grandson of revolutionary war leader Ralph Izard. Groomed for a military career, Deas was exposed to art early in his youth, and preferred painting trips around the Hudson River Valley to a career at West Point.

Deas studied briefly at the National Academy of Design in the mid-1830s, and gained a reputation as a painter of sporting pictures and humorous domestic genre scenes. He first exhibited at the National Academy in 1838, and was elected an associate in 1839.

Inspired by an exhibition of George Catlin's paintings of Indians, in 1840 Deas traveled West to visit his brother, a military officer, at Fort Crawford in Prairie du Chien, Wisconsin. He explored the regions around the upper Mississippi, the Missouri and the Platte Rivers in the company of hunters, trappers and army expeditions, making sketches that he turned into paintings after settling in St. Louis in the early 1840s.

Throughout most of the 1840s, Deas worked in St. Louis, where he is said to have made many friends and patrons. His paintings generated considerable interest back East. He exhibited regularly at the National Academy of Design, the Artists Fund Society, the Boston Athenaeum and the Pennsylvania Academy of the Fine Arts. In addition, his work was widely disseminated by popular engravings.

Despite his considerable successes, Deas's career was cut short by insanity

Death Struggle, 1845, 30 x 25 in., signed l.r. Courtesy of The Shelburne Museum, Vermont.

in the 1850s, and the artist spent his last 16 years in a mental institution. His final paintings, executed in confinement, included purely fantastic scenes of death and despair.

MEMBERSHIPS
National Academy of Design

PUBLIC COLLECTIONS
Brooklyn Museum
Museum of Fine Arts, Boston
Webb Gallery of Art, Shelburne, Vermont

(No sales information available.)

WILLIAM W. KENNEDY
(1818-1870?)

Few facts are known about the life of painter William W. Kennedy. Although he was not directly linked with a specific group of painters, he is considered to be a lesser-known "Prior-Hamblin" portrait artist.

Kennedy was born in New Hampshire in 1818, and census data combined with family history indicate that the artist was living and painting in New Bedford, Massachusetts when he was 37 years old. Records also imply that Kennedy and his family lived in subsequent years in Connecticut and Maine, before settling in Baltimore during the winter of 1849 to 1850.

It is likely that Kennedy was exposed to the work of artist William Matthew Prior in Baltimore. Prior's signed paintings bear an address several doors away from Kennedy's studio.

To date, there are 14 paintings extant by Kennedy; they are signed and occasionally dated. Peculiarities of anatomical description and artistic style in these works provide reference points which allow 39 additional portraits to be attributed to the artist.

As seen in the attributed *Boy with Eton Collar* (ca. 1845-1850, private collection), Kennedy's portraits are often marked by exaggerated shading around the nose, a dark line between the lips, and hands rendered simplistically with gentle curvature.

Occasionally, Kennedy would pull the outside world into his portraits, in a background landscape, window view or flower basket. More often, however, the artist depicted his subjects at half-body length, either seated on a chair or against a dark backdrop. He placed roses in the hands of his female subjects and books in those of the males.

The artist either used a standard-sized canvas for his portraits or worked on a small academy board—another characteristic link to the "Prior-Hamblin" group.

Brother and Sister Sharing a Book, 1845, 19⅞ x 23⅞ in. Courtesy of New York State Historical Association, Cooperstown.

Kennedy is thought to have lived and painted in Baltimore for at least 20 years. He died sometime after 1870.

SEASON	75-76	76-77	77-78	78-79	79-80	80-81	81-82	82-83	83-84	84-85
Paintings									3	6
Dollars									$56,500	$2,768

Record Sale: $35,000, SPB, 1/28/84, "Young Girl with Basket of Flowers," 30 × 25 in.

CHARLES CHRISTIAN NAHL

(1818-1878)

Charles Christian Nahl was a German-born and European-trained painter, photographer and illustrator, who has been described as California's first significant artist. Nahl is best known for his depictions of the mining camps of the California gold rush, and for his design of the bear on the California state flag.

Nahl was born in Kassel, Germany to an established artistic family. Together with his brother and lifelong partner, Hugo Wilhelm Arthur Nahl, the young Charles Christian attended the art academy of Kassel, before going to study in Paris under Horace Vernet and Paul Delaroche.

Following the 1848 revolution in France, the Nahl family emigrated to New York, where the Nahl brothers painted and exhibited. In 1851, the two traveled to California in search of gold. They worked for a brief time in the mines, where they are said to have accumulated more sketches than gold. In 1852, they moved to Sacramento, where they painted portraits in exchange for gold dust. They also illustrated books and magazines, until a fire destroyed their studio, together with most of their work.

By the end of 1852, the Nahl brothers had moved to San Francisco and established a commercial art and photography studio, which provided most of their income for the next 15 years. During this period, the brothers turned out a steady stream of illustrations for books, magazines and newspapers. Among the more enduring of these were Charles's illustrations for two books by writer Alonzo Delano, *Penn-Knife Sketches* (1853) and *Old Block's Sketch Book* (1856).

By 1867, Nahl had secured the patronage of Judge E.B. Crocker, for whom he executed a number of large paintings. Of these, perhaps the best

The Fandango, 1873, 73¼ x 109¾ in., signed l.c. Courtesy of Crocker Art Museum, Sacramento, California.

known is *Sunday Morning in the Mines* (1872, Crocker Gallery), which, in keeping with the artist's fashion, is crowded with picturesque and humorous detail.

During the 1870s, Nahl's paintings enjoyed a heady following along the West coast. Upon his death in 1878 in San Francisco, he was eulogized as one of the leading painters of pioneer life in California.

PUBLIC COLLECTIONS
Amon Carter Museum of Western Art,
   Fort Worth
Brooklyn Museum
E.B. Crocker Art Gallery, Sacramento,
   California
Museum of Fine Arts, Boston
Stanford University Museum and Art Gallery,
   California

SEASON	75-76	76-77	77-78	78-79	79-80	80-81	81-82	82-83	83-84	84-85
Paintings							2	3		
Dollars							$27,500	$9,850		

Record Sale: $23,000, SPB, 10/5/81, "Boaters Rowing to Shore at Chagres," 9 × 12 in.

182

WILLIAM RICKARBY MILLER

(1818-1893)

Still Life: Two Peaches on a Branch, 1863, 8 x 12 in., signed l.l. Private Collection, Photograph courtesy of Kennedy Galleries, New York, New York.

William Rickarby Miller was a fine young watercolorist in his native England who emigrated to the United States in search of fame.

Born in County Durham in 1818, he was first trained by his artist-father and then attended schools in Newcastle. Upon his arrival in the United States, he settled briefly in Buffalo, where he painted his first known American view, *Mountain Landscape, Buffalo* (1845, location unknown). He soon moved to New York City, but upper New York State remained a favorite setting for his art.

Miller earned his living by portraiture, but he preferred the outdoors. In 1849 he sketched in the Catskill Mountains. His nature sketches were executed with a draftsman's keen eye for detail and later rendered into full-scale oil paintings, such as *On the Roundout Canal Near Rosendale, New York* (undated, Hirschl and Adler Galleries).

Although Miller painted in the same region as his contemporaries of the Hudson River School, he was neither impressed nor influenced by their immense paintings. Rather, his landscapes were more intimate and narrative, using figures in scale, as in *Erie Canal at Little Falls, New York* (1884, New-York Historical Society).

Miller was especially proficient at watercolor and sold his work through the American-Art Union. By 1853, he was enjoying a lucrative period, in which he illustrated books and magazines. *Homes of American Authors,* by Putnam Company, was his first illustration assignment. He also illustrated popular weeklies.

A disciplined man and a prolific painter, he produced hundreds of watercolors, oils and pen-and-ink sketches. As late as 1885, he painted a striking still life, *Two Pineapples* (private collection). Much earlier, still lifes had been exhibited at annual shows of the National Academy of Design.

Sadly, Miller's planned volume of landscape paintings, *A Thousand Gems,* was never published, although he spent years on the project.

Separated from his wife and children, Miller died alone in the Bronx in 1893, while on one of his sketching trips.

PUBLIC COLLECTIONS
New-York Historical Society, New York City

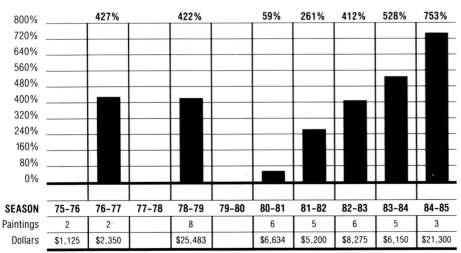

10-Year Average Change From Base Years '75–'76: 358%

	75-76	76-77	77-78	78-79	79-80	80-81	81-82	82-83	83-84	84-85
		427%		422%		59%	261%	412%	528%	753%
SEASON	75-76	76-77	77-78	78-79	79-80	80-81	81-82	82-83	83-84	84-85
Paintings	2	2		8		6	5	6	5	3
Dollars	$1,125	$2,350		$25,483		$6,634	$5,200	$8,275	$6,150	$21,300

Record Sale: $18,000, SPB, 12/6/84, "Mother and Child," 39 x 29 in.

JAMES AUGUSTUS SUYDAM

(1819-1865)

Paradise Rocks, Newport, 1865, 25 x 45 in., signed l.r. Courtesy of National Academy of Design, New York, New York.

A second-generation Hudson River School painter, James Suydam is appreciated today for the subtlety of his peaceful compositions. John I.H. Baur, writing in 1950 in *The Art Quarterly,* said that Suydam belonged "to that mid-century group of tonal realists who achieved through their intensity of observation and feeling a poetic interpretation of nature which was rooted in the genuine pantheism of the time." *Paradise Rocks, Newport* (date unknown, National Academy of Design) is a typical example.

Suydam was a follower of John F. Kensett, and a contemporary of Martin Johnson Heade and Fitz Hugh Lane. Considered a luminist, he explored the infinite variations of aerial perspective, and usually preferred noon light on clear days. The effects of water meeting land were of particular interest to the second generation of Hudson River School painters.

Suydam was born in New York City in 1819. In the mid-1850s he began to paint, after 10 years in business with his brother. He studied with portraitist

Minor C. Kellogg and accompanied him on a tour of Greece and Turkey.

Suydam's character seems to have been as innocuous as his paintings. He was a bachelor and, according to his eulogist, was not a publicity-seeker.

His painting career was pitifully short. In 1856, he first exhibited his work at the National Academy of Design. When he died in 1865, he left $50,000, his own finished paintings, and his collection of nineteenth-century American and European paintings to that institution.

SEASON	75-76	76-77	77-78	78-79	79-80	80-81	81-82	82-83	83-84	84-85
Paintings				2				1		
Dollars				$9,000				$6,000		

Record Sale: $6,250, SPB, 6/21/79, "River Scene," 6 × 10 in.

MEMBERSHIPS
Century Association
National Academy of Design

PUBLIC COLLECTIONS
Century Association, New York City
National Academy of Design, New York City

JAMES HAMILTON
(1819-1878)

Seascape painter James Hamilton was born in Ireland in 1819 of Scottish parentage. At age 15, he came to the United States and trained as an illustrator for books and magazines, including *Blackwood's Magazine* in Philadelphia. He attended drawing school and later studied at the Pennsylvania Academy of the Fine Arts, where he gained additional skill in engraving and etching.

Hamilton particularly admired the work of J.M.W. Turner and Samuel Prout. Hamilton was often called "the American Turner" because of his vivid lighting effects in coastal scenes and seascapes. His favorite subjects were scenes of storm or bombardment.

What Are the Wild Waves Saying? (1859, Brooklyn Museum) shows the loose brushwork often associated with Turner. Because this painting was inspired by a chapter heading in Charles Dickens's *Dombey and Son,* Hamilton presented Dickens with the painting when the author visited the United States in 1868—the only gift, Dickens said, that he accepted while in America.

Hamilton's seascapes, many painted along the New Jersey coast, sometimes showed the passions of nature, sometimes those of men. *The Bombardment of Fort Mifflin* (date and location unknown) contrasts a level sea with leaping flames around ships and straining men in a boat.

Hamilton was perhaps best known for his illustrations in *Arctic Explorations,* a book by Elisha Kent Kane. Other well-known paintings include *An Egyptian Sunset, The Capture of the Serapis* and *A Moonlight Scene near Venice* (dates and locations unknown). Perhaps looking for a real-life adventure to match his paintings, Hamilton embarked on a trip around the world—but died in San Francisco in 1878 without completing it.

Scene on the Hudson (Rip Van Winkle), 1845, 38⅛ x 57⅛ in. Courtesy of National Museum of American Art, Smithsonian Institution, Museum Purchase.

PUBLIC COLLECTIONS
Atwater Kent Museum, Philadelphia
Free Library of Philadelphia
Pennsylvania Academy of the Fine Arts,
    Philadelphia
Philadelphia Maritime Museum
Pennsylvania Historical Society, Philadelphia

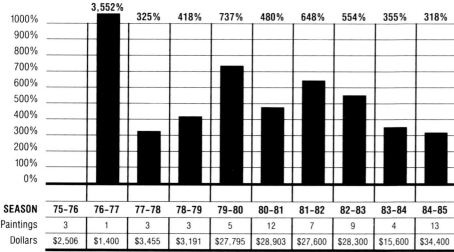

10-Year Average Change From Base Years '75-'76: 739%

	3,552%	325%	418%	737%	480%	648%	554%	355%	318%

SEASON	75-76	76-77	77-78	78-79	79-80	80-81	81-82	82-83	83-84	84-85
Paintings	3	1	3	3	5	12	7	9	4	13
Dollars	$2,506	$1,400	$3,455	$3,191	$27,795	$28,903	$27,600	$28,300	$15,600	$34,400

Record Sale: $21,500, S.W, 12/2/79, "Baltimore Harbor," 40×60 in.

185

MARTIN JOHNSON HEADE
(1819-1904)

Martin Johnson Heade's career was longer and more varied than that of most American artists. He began as a portraitist but switched in mid-career to landscape painting.

Heade was born in rural Pennsylvania in 1819 and first studied portrait painting under Quaker painters Edward and Thomas Hicks.

While in his twenties, Heade refined his skills as a professional portrait artist. His occasional landscapes were roughly imitative of the then-popular Hudson River School style.

Heade, an incessant traveler throughout his life, spent two years in Italy and visited France and England in the 1840s. Over the next 15 years, he lived in several American cities, still working primarily as a portrait painter. By age 40, he had not yet produced a work of enduring artistic merit.

Heade's turning point came in the late 1850s, when he moved to New York City. He gave up portrait painting and focused instead on landscapes and shore scenes, topographically inspired by the salt marshes around the Narragansett Bay region of Rhode Island. His later landscapes—and the still lifes he painted near the end of his career—are lush and rich in color, reflecting his luminist style.

As exemplified by his *Approaching Storm: Beach Near Newport* (1860, Museum of Fine Arts, Boston), Heade's luminist landscapes are eerie and com-

Sunset on the Marsh, ca. 1875, 13 x 26 in., signed l.r. Courtesy of Wunderlich and Company, Inc., New York, New York.

pelling. Intent primarily on conveying mood, Heade sacrificed realistic representation, while elongating form, distorting perspective and exaggerating color contrast. More than 100 of his seascapes and marsh paintings survive.

Heade had an avowed lifelong obsession with hummingbirds. In 1863, he made the first of three trips to South America. He first went to Brazil to prepare illustrations for a book on hummingbirds. When the book project was ultimately rejected by a London publisher, Heade began a series of paintings in the 1870s which dramatically combined orchids and hummingbirds in lush tropical settings.

The combination of the tiny birds and the large overwhelming flowers in these paintings was unprecedented. The pictures were startling—not just because of the uniqueness of subject and intensity of color, but also because of the underlying sensual evocativeness of the flowers. *Two Fighting Hummingbirds with Two Orchids* (1875, location unknown) is one of the best examples of this period.

Heade finally settled in St. Augustine, Florida, about 19 years before his death there in 1904. He continued to paint seascapes and birds. He also painted a number of still lifes, frequently incorporating flowers, more for evocative effect than for decorative addition.

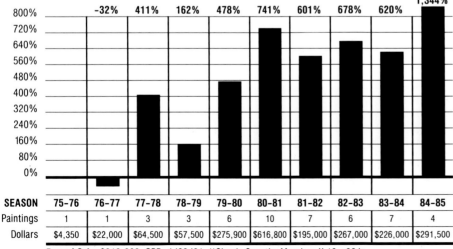

10-Year Average Change From Base Years '75-'76: 500%

SEASON	75-76	76-77	77-78	78-79	79-80	80-81	81-82	82-83	83-84	84-85
		-32%	411%	162%	478%	741%	601%	678%	620%	1,344%
Paintings	1	1	3	3	6	10	7	6	7	4
Dollars	$4,350	$22,000	$64,500	$57,500	$275,900	$616,800	$195,000	$267,000	$226,000	$291,500

Record Sale: $310,000, SPB, 4/23/81, "Clouds Over the Marshes," 13 × 26 in.

PUBLIC COLLECTIONS
Metropolitan Museum of Art, New York City
Museum of Fine Arts, Boston

ARTHUR FITZWILLIAM TAIT

(1819-1905)

Arthur Fitzwilliam Tait, a British-born landscape artist, was one of the nineteenth century's most popular painters. A good story-teller on canvas, Tait was able to instill in his genre paintings a strong sense of drama and conflict.

Although he never traveled further West than Chicago, he acquired a reputation as a frontier artist, painting scenes of hunters and wildlife, mainly from his experiences in upstate New York. *The Quail and Young* (date unknown, Corcoran Gallery of Art), is a typical example.

Tait was born in 1819 in Liverpool, and schooled in Lancaster. By his mid-teens, he was working at Agnews, an art dealer in Manchester. In his spare time, he taught himself how to paint by copying works at the Royal Institute.

During these years, he was able to assist George Catlin with his traveling Indian gallery in England and Paris. Tait was impressed with Catlin's interpretation of the American West; it provided the impetus for his own immigration to the United States in 1850.

Tait worked out of New York City, but spent considerable time in the Adirondack Mountains, becoming a proficient marksman and woodsman. Using this rugged setting as a background, Tait focused much of his art on capturing the drama of man against

A Good Chance, 1883, 20 x 30 in., signed l.l. Courtesy of Vose Galleries of Boston, Inc., Massachusetts.

nature. His style, which combined misty, atmospheric landscape settings with detailed renderings of human figures, reminds one of that of George Caleb Bingham.

The period 1850 to 1860 was a prolific time for Tait. His paintings were accepted by Easterners as definitive views of life on the frontier. Currier and Ives reproduced much of his work, mak-

ing him one of the most popular artists of the period.

These genre paintings were not his only source of success. Tait mastered still lifes of dead game, influencing a whole generation of artists, beginning with William Michael Harnett 25 years later. He also did barnyard landscapes, a pastoral departure from his frontier scenes.

Tait's style did not change from 1860 until his death in 1905; he continued to work in the style which he had found successful.

MEMBERSHIPS
National Academy of Design

PUBLIC COLLECTIONS
Addison Gallery of American Art, Andover, Massachusetts
Adirondack Museum, Blue Mountain Lake, New York
Amon Carter Museum of Western Art, Fort Worth, Texas
Corcoran Gallery of Art, Washington, D.C.
Denver Art Museum
Metropolitan Museum of Art, New York City
Museum of the City of New York
R.W. Norton Art Gallery, Shreveport, Louisiana
Philadelphia Museum of Art
Yale University Art Gallery, New Haven, Connecticut

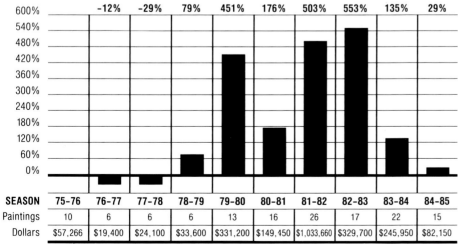

10-Year Average Change From Base Years '75-'76: 189%

	-12%	-29%	79%	451%	176%	503%	553%	135%	29%
SEASON	75-76	76-77	77-78	78-79	79-80	80-81	81-82	82-83	83-84	84-85
Paintings	10	6	6	6	13	16	26	17	22	15
Dollars	$57,266	$19,400	$24,100	$33,600	$331,200	$149,450	$1,033,660	$329,700	$245,950	$82,150

Record Sale: $250,000, CH, 6/4/82, "Duck Shooting," 38 x 50 in.

GEORGE HENRY DURRIE
(1820-1863)

Born in Hartford, Connecticut in 1820, George Henry Durrie commenced studies in 1839 with New Haven portraitist Nathaniel Jocelyn. In the early 1840s he traveled about the Connecticut and New Jersey countryside painting portraits. During this period he also painted still lifes, genre and Shakespearean scenes. He then settled in New Haven, where he lived most of his life.

In the mid-1840s, Durrie turned to landscapes and scenes of rural life. The American public was showing increasing interest in landscapes at that time; his fame and fortune accordingly improved somewhat. Durrie's landscapes usually included human activity, animals and artifacts.

Detractors called Durrie and his work prosaic, unimaginative, countrified and repetitious. The outlines of his forms were muffled in thick pigment, and his scenes were rustic. Those who liked his work found an unsophisticated charm and a semi-primitive originality.

An undeniable contribution to the art of the period was Durrie's discovery that farm scenes and landscapes, when blanketed with snow, had a unique charm. The style with which he brought these subjects to his canvas was key to Durrie's success. His pictures emphasize the cold whites of the snow and the bleak, wintry skies of New England. His *Home for Thanksgiving* (date and location unknown) ranks highly as a nostalgic memento of rural American contentment.

Winter Scene (with Old Mill), 10¾ x 18, signed l.r. Private Collection, Photograph courtesy of Kennedy Galleries, New York, New York.

Durrie's career coincided with the success of Currier and Ives in merchandising hand-colored lithographs in the 1860s. His winter scenes lent themselves excellently to their formula, and the resulting widespread public exposure of his work contributed significantly to Durrie's success in his later years.

Following his death in 1863, Durrie's work remained in the public eye through further adaptations by Currier and Ives.

PUBLIC COLLECTIONS
New-York Historical Society, New York City
Wadsworth Athenaeum, Hartford, Connecticut
Yale University Art School

10-Year Average Change From Base Years '76-'77: 85%

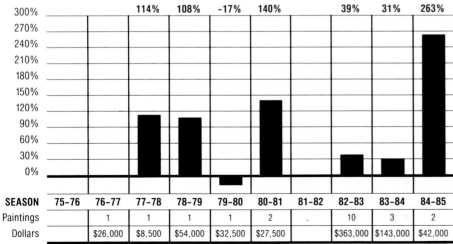

SEASON	75-76	76-77	77-78	78-79	79-80	80-81	81-82	82-83	83-84	84-85
			114%	108%	-17%	140%		39%	31%	263%
Paintings		1	1	1	1	2	.	10	3	2
Dollars		$26,000	$8,500	$54,000	$32,500	$27,500		$363,000	$143,000	$42,000

Record Sale: $90,000, SPB, 10/22/82, ''The Jones Inn Near Farmington in Winter,'' 26 x 36 in.

THOMAS ADDISON RICHARDS
(1820-1900)

Thomas Addison Richards had a deep affection for the natural beauties of the Southern United States. He was one of the first artists to bring them to the eye of the American public, through his many paintings, illustrated travel guides and magazine articles.

Yet Richards preferred to maintain a studio in New York City for convenience, ease of travel and proximity to his fellow artists. He is generally regarded as a member of the loose confederation known as the Hudson River School.

Richards was born in London in 1820, but came to the United States at age 11 and grew up in Hudson, New York and in Penfield, Georgia.

At age 18, he published a book on flower painting, following it with an illustrated book on Georgia in 1842. This second book was remarked upon the following year in Charleston, South Carolina, as containing some of the earliest pictures of the state of Georgia.

In 1844, he went from the Carolinas to New York City to study at the National Academy of Design for two years, and eight years later he became corresponding secretary of that institution, a position he was to hold for 40 years.

Richards was also a professor of art at New York University from 1867 to 1887. He painted landscapes in the area of Lake George, New York, traveled widely in the United States and Europe, wrote and illustrated books and articles and painted portraits. He died in 1900 in Maryland, but was buried in Rhode Island.

MEMBERSHIPS
National Academy of Design

Hudson River - Landscape, 1853, 48 x 48 in., signed l.l. Courtesy of Henry B. Holt, Inc., Essex Fells, New Jersey.

SEASON	75-76	76-77	77-78	78-79	79-80	80-81	81-82	82-83	83-84	84-85
Paintings		1	2	2	1		1		4	
Dollars		$650	$4,000	$2,400	$2,600		$1,700		$25,800	

Record Sale: $18,000, D.NY, 4/4/84, "Meditation in the Catskills," 50 × 40 in.

189

THOMAS WORTHINGTON WHITTREDGE
(1820-1910)

In The Garden, 16¾ x 22 in., signed l.r. Courtesy of Vose Galleries of Boston, Inc., Massachusetts.

Thomas Worthington Whittredge, an important member of the later Hudson River School, specialized in landscapes, although he also painted some portraits and still lifes. His mature style incorporates both European and American influences, and celebrates the Catskill Mountains in New York and the American West, particularly the Great Plains.

Worthington Whittredge, as he called himself after about 1855, was born on a farm in Springfield, Ohio in 1820. He received little formal education. In 1837, he moved to Cincinnati, where he worked with his brother-in-law, a house- and sign-painter, while teaching himself to paint portraits and landscapes. He experimented with daguerreotypes in Indianapolis, and opened a portrait studio in Charlestown, West Virginia before returning to Cincinnati.

After about 1843, he devoted himself to landscapes. Works from this period, such as *The Hawk's Nest* (1848, Cincinnati Museum), reveal the romantic influence of Thomas Cole and Thomas Doughty.

Cincinnati at this time boasted a large and wealthy community of art lovers. A number of patrons, headed by Nicholas Longworth, sent Whittredge to Europe to study and paint in 1849. He spent five years in Dusseldorf, where he studied under Carl Lessing and Andreas Achenbach. For a time he adopted the hard, relatively monotone palette of the Dus-

seldorf School, as in *Landscape Near Minden, Germany* (1855, Christie's).

He also visited Switzerland and Paris, where he viewed—but was not impressed by—the naturalistic landscapes of the barbizon painters. He then spent five years in Rome, where he was part of an artists' colony that included Frederick Church and Nathaniel Hawthorne.

Upon returning to the United States in 1859, Whittredge settled in New York City. He opened a studio and began exhibiting at the National Academy of Design, to which he was elected in 1861; he served briefly as the Academy's president.

Gradually he abandoned the Dusseldorf manner, painting large, tonally harmonious canvases of woodlands and streams. He became particularly adept at rendering sunlight filtered through dense foliage, as in *Trout Brook in the Catskills* (date unknown, Corcoran Gallery). He also produced a few still lifes, such as *Apples* (1867, location unknown), showing richly colored living fruit on tree branches.

A series of trips to the West and Mexico, beginning in 1865, introduced Whittredge to the grandeur of frontier scenery, which he reflected in broad, spacious paintings such as *Crossing the Platte* (1870, Century Association) and *Camp Meeting* (1874, Metropolitan Museum of Art). His use of horizontal masses and golden, variegated light suggests vastness and serenity.

Whittredge died in 1910 in Summit, New Jersey.

MEMBERSHIPS
National Academy of Design

PUBLIC COLLECTIONS
Amon Carter Museum of Western Art,
Fort Worth, Texas
Century Association, New York City
Cincinnati Museum
Corcoran Gallery of Art, Washington, D.C.
Denver Art Museum
Joslyn Art Museum, Omaha
Metropolitan Museum of Art, New York City
Reynolda House, Winston-Salem,
North Carolina

10-Year Average Change From Base Years '75-'76: 139%

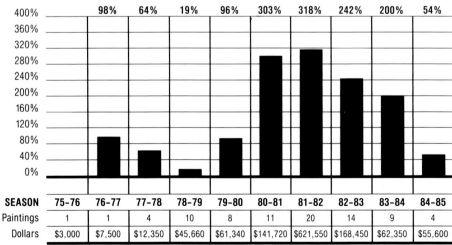

		98%	64%	19%	96%	303%	318%	242%	200%	54%
SEASON	75-76	76-77	77-78	78-79	79-80	80-81	81-82	82-83	83-84	84-85
Paintings	1	1	4	10	8	11	20	14	9	4
Dollars	$3,000	$7,500	$12,350	$45,660	$61,340	$141,720	$621,550	$168,450	$62,350	$55,600

Record Sale: $280,000, D.NY, 9/23/81, "Indian Encampment," 22 × 33 in.

CHARLES C. HOFMANN
(1821-1882)

Charles C. Hofmann was the first of three "Almshouse Painters" in Pennsylvania's Schuylkill River area. Poorhouses along the river were his only known homes, and the minutely-detailed views of these institutions which he painted for their administrators form the bulk of his surviving work.

Hofmann was born in Germany in 1821, and came to the United States in 1860. Certain paupers' registers contain the only record of his life. His occupation is given as "painter," and the cause of his pauperism as "intemperance." His skill in rendering detail and the appearance of the word "lithograph" in one painting suggest training in the graphic trade.

In 1865, Hofmann painted two watercolor views of the Berks County Almshouse in Reading, although his first commitment there did not occur until 1872. These early depictions, stylized and formal, set the pattern for at least eight subsequent paintings of the same scene, on canvas and on tin.

Between 1865 and 1872, Hofmann painted landscapes of businesses and farms for their owners. In two instances, periods of drunkenness followed payment for the pictures and were in turn followed by admissions to the almshouse. One view of the Benjamin Reber farm is in the National Gallery of Art in Washington, D.C.

Hofmann traveled the Schuylkill River and Canal during the next decade, staying at and painting the Berks County, Schuylkill County and Montgomery County almshouses. A bearded man drinking from a bottle appears in many of his compositions and is probably a self-portrait.

Despite the appalling conditions of public poorhouses, Hofmann portrayed them as sunlit and pristine; inmates, however, appear shadowy and anonymous. Although all his paintings are filled with action, the later ones are standardized and lack the earlier emphasis on individual incidents.

Hofmann died in the Berks County Almshouse in 1882 and was buried there in a pauper's grave.

Views of the Building and Surroundings of the Berks County Alms House, 1878, 32 x 38¾ in., signed l.r. Courtesy of National Gallery of Art, Washington, D.C., Gift of Edgar William and Bernice Chrysler Garbisch, 1953.

PUBLIC COLLECTIONS
National Gallery of Art, Washington, D.C.

SEASON	75-76	76-77	77-78	78-79	79-80	80-81	81-82	82-83	83-84	84-85
Paintings						1			1	
Dollars						$85,000			$8,000	

Record Sale: $85,000, SPB, 4/30/81, "View of Schuylkill County Almshouse," 30 × 42 in.

PLATT POWELL RYDER
(1821-1896)

Platt Powell Ryder was a genre and portrait painter, whose career lasted from around 1850 until his death in 1896. He was a respected member of the New York art community, a member of the National Academy of Design and a founder of the Brooklyn Academy of Design.

Ryder was born in Brooklyn, the son of a storekeeper. During his youth, Ryder's family moved to New Orleans, where the artist received his first formal instruction. In 1854, Ryder made his first trip to Europe, where he studied painting for three years before returning to the United States.

Upon his return from Europe, Ryder made his home in Brooklyn, and began exhibiting his work at the National Academy of Design, to which he was elected an associate member in 1868. During this time, Ryder also aided in the founding of the Brooklyn Academy of Design.

In 1869, Ryder made his second trip to Europe. He studied for a year under Bonnat in Paris, and traveled through Belgium, Holland and England. In 1871, Ryder returned to the United States and re-established his studio in New York City.

For the next 20 years, he enjoyed a successful career as a genre painter and portraitist. He is said to have had more commissions than he could execute in his later years.

Ryder died in Saratoga, New York in 1896.

MEMBERSHIPS
Brooklyn Academy of Design
Century Association
National Academy of Design

PUBLIC COLLECTIONS
Metropolitan Museum of Art, New York City

Mother and Boy with Picture Book, 17 x 13⅞ in., signed l.r. Courtesy of The Brooklyn Museum, Bequest of Caroline H. Polhemus.

SEASON	75-76	76-77	77-78	78-79	79-80	80-81	81-82	82-83	83-84	84-85
Paintings						2	1	1	1	
Dollars						$10,800	$10,000	$2,800	$4,750	

Record Sale: $10,000, BB.SF, 3/17/82, "The Reluctant Scholar," 17 × 14 in.

WINCKWORTH ALLAN GAY
(1821-1910)

Mount Washington, 1861, 141¾ x 201¼ in., signed l.r. Courtesy of The Boston Anthenaeum, Massachusetts.

Winckworth Allan Gay was a prolific landscape painter whose style represented a merging of the Hudson River School of landscape painters and the French barbizon style. Gay was a world traveler who painted scenes of New England, Paris, Egypt and the Orient.

He was born in West Hingham, Massachusetts, in 1821. In 1838, he traveled to West Point, New York to be tutored by Robert W. Weir.

Gay's earliest portait, *Ebenezer Gay* (1845, Hingham Historical Society), indicated that he was working near Boston during the early 1840s. In 1847, he embarked on a four-year tour of Europe that included brief stays in London and Dusseldorf. Gay was one of the first American artists of his generation to study in Paris. He was taught briefly by Constant Troyon, and was influenced by the barbizon movement and its emphasis on nature as the subject of and inspiration for art.

Gay returned to Boston in 1851, after making another tour of Europe. He often exhibited paintings based on his European sketches over the next decade. He also began visiting the White Mountains of New Hampshire, becoming a regular at the artists' colony in West Campton by the late 1850s.

At that time, Gay's work became popular with Boston collectors who understood and appreciated the French aesthetic. Yet these works show that Gay was as much influenced by the native school of landscape painting as he was by the barbizon artists. In *Farmhouse at Rye Beach* (ca. 1865, Museum of Fine Arts, Boston), Gay's tight brushwork and precise style show the influence of Kensett and Bricher. At the same time, his use of pale pinks and yellows in the sunset sky is similar to the style of the luminists.

Gay again traveled to Europe and Egypt in 1873. In 1877, he held a sale of 112 of his works to finance a journey to Japan and the Orient. He returned to Boston in 1881, where he continued to paint until 1890. Gay died in 1910.

SEASON	75-76	76-77	77-78	78-79	79-80	80-81	81-82	82-83	83-84	84-85
Paintings				2	1	3	2	2	3	5
Dollars				$1,050	$1,080	$3,134	$2,014	$1,850	$2,575	$5,005

Record Sale: $1,800, YG.P, 10/27/84, ''Edge of Forest,'' 36 × 24 in.

PUBLIC COLLECTIONS
Boston Athenaeum
Brooklyn Museum
Hingham Historical Society, Massachusetts
Museum of Fine Arts, Boston

GEORGE FULLER
(1822-1884)

Born in Deerfield, Massachusetts, George Fuller was a portraitist, landscapist and figure painter. He began his career by accompanying his deaf-mute half-brother, artist Augustus Fuller, on a painting tour. Upon his return, George Fuller moved to Boston, where he studied and worked until 1847 at the Boston Artists Association. He shared rooms for a time with sculptor Thomas Hall.

The artist then studied at the National Academy of Design until 1859. In 1860, he traveled to Europe, where he studied the masters and met such artists as preraphaelites Dante Gabriel Rossetti and William Holman Hunt. His work during these years was comparatively pedestrian and uninspired.

In 1861, the artist returned to Deerfield, where he worked the family farm for 15 years. He continued to paint in isolation, and developed a distinctive style and point of view.

In 1875, Fuller mounted a one-man show in Boston, inspired by the need to raise money for his farm. His paintings were highly acclaimed. Many of them were portraits of women taken from literature; they epitomized the spirit of the times—both nationalistic and romantic.

Although his work was compared to French barbizon painters Millet and Corot, it was actually closer in spirit to the more conservative French artists such as Jules Breton, Charles Jacque and Edouard Frere. Fuller's female fig-

Harvesting, 1879, 17 x 14 in. Courtesy of Vose Galleries of Boston, Inc., Massachusetts.

ures were tender, sentimental and romantic, without the political overtones of Millet's works.

Fuller said, "I have concluded to see nature for myself, through the eyes of no one else. . . ." He preferred a brown tonal scheme, which gave his work a sad, nostalgic quality. His style was blurred in outline, with light effects comparable to Corot's. Because of his lack of technical sureness, Fuller constantly reworked his paintings, painting and repainting to create a thick, crusty surface which critics believed added freshness to his pictures.

Fuller painted full-time after his successful show. Representative of his works is *The Dandelion Girl* (1877, location unknown), considered as the epitome of "womanly grace and child-like innocence."

MEMBERSHIPS
Society of American Artists

PUBLIC COLLECTIONS
Corcoran Gallery of Art, Washington, D.C.
Metropolitan Museum of Art, New York City
Worcester Art Museum, Massachusetts

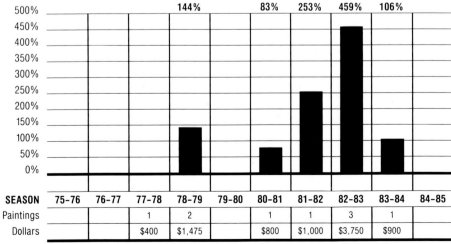

10-Year Average Change From Base Years '77-'78: 174%

SEASON	75-76	76-77	77-78	78-79	79-80	80-81	81-82	82-83	83-84	84-85
				144%		83%	253%	459%	106%	
Paintings			1	2		1	1	3	1	
Dollars			$400	$1,475		$800	$1,000	$3,750	$900	

Record Sale: $1,500, BB.SF, 12/8/82, "The Reaper," 8 x 6 in.

WILLIAM LOUIS SONNTAG

(1822-1900)

William Louis Sonntag was a nineteenth-century landscape painter associated with the Hudson River School. He is best remembered today for his romantic renditions of the American wilderness and his idealized visions of classical Italian ruins.

Born in East Liberty, Pennsylvania, near Pittsburgh, Sonntag pursued his career as an artist despite the objections of his parents. Sometime in the early 1840s, Sonntag moved to Cincinnati, where he is believed to have studied under Godfrey Frankenstein at the Cincinnati Academy of Fine Arts.

From the early 1840s to the mid-1850s, Sonntag maintained his studio in Cincinnati, making regular painting trips around the Ohio River Valley and into the mountains of West Virginia and Kentucky. His paintings of this period were technically accomplished scenes of grandeur, influenced by the works of painter Thomas Cole, and details from nature romantically composed.

Sonntag was encouraged in his early career by the popularity of his work exhibited in the Western Art Union shows. He first traveled to Europe in 1853, returning in 1855 for a year's study in Florence.

Upon his return to the United States, Sonntag established his studio in New York City. He became an associate member of the National Academy of Design in 1861, and he exhibited his work regularly at the Academy for almost 40 years.

(Mountain Landscape), 1854, 51¼ x 41⅛ in. Courtesy of National Museum of American Art, Smithsonian Institution, Museum Purchase.

In addition to his American landscapes, Sonntag is known for his highly idealized renditions of Italian ruins, inspired by his trip to Europe. Although painted with a naturalistic detail characteristic of the early Hudson River School realists, Sonntag's classical landscapes reflect the influence of the eighteenth-century neoclassical tradition of English literature and painting.

Sonntag died in New York City in 1900.

10-Year Average Change From Base Years '75-'76: 67%

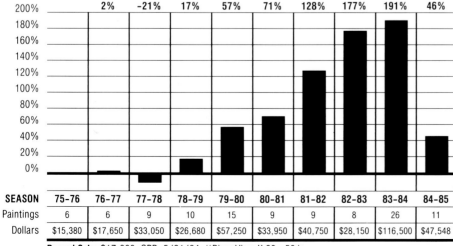

	2%	-21%	17%	57%	71%	128%	177%	191%	46%
SEASON	75-76	76-77	77-78	78-79	79-80	80-81	81-82	82-83	83-84	84-85
Paintings	6	6	9	10	15	9	9	8	26	11
Dollars	$15,380	$17,650	$33,050	$26,680	$57,250	$33,950	$40,750	$28,150	$116,500	$47,548

Record Sale: $17,000, SPB, 5/31/84, "River View," 30 x 50 in.

MEMBERSHIPS
American Water Color Society
National Academy of Design

PUBLIC COLLECTIONS
Corcoran Gallery of Art, Washington, D.C.
Peabody Institute, Baltimore

LILLY MARTIN SPENCER

(1822-1902)

Lilly Martin Spencer was a noted mid-nineteenth-century genre painter. Her sentimental scenes of family life were extremely popular and brought her international recognition.

Born in 1822 in Exeter, England to French parents, Lilly Martin was originally named Angelique Marie Martin. Her parents were intellectuals—active supporters of abolitionism, women's rights and the temperance movement. In 1830, her family emigrated to the United States, and in 1833 they settled in Marietta, Ohio. Martin was educated at home, where she read Shakespeare and the classics.

A childhood prodigy, Martin began painting in her teens. Her work soon attracted public notice. After viewing her first public exhibit of paintings in 1841, art patron Nicholas Longworth offered to pay for her education in Europe. She refused the offer, possibly because she objected to European training for American artists. Instead, Martin remained in America, where she studied with Charles Sullivan and Sala Bosworth, and made the acquaintance of animal and genre painter James Beard.

From 1841 to 1847, the artist painted in Cincinnati. She married in 1844, and in 1847 moved to New York with her husband. There, she took night classes at the National Academy of Design. She had 13 children, of whom only seven survived, and supported the children

We Both Must Fade (Mrs. Fithian), 1869, 71⅝ x 53¾ in. Courtesy of National Museum of American Art, Smithsonian Institution, Museum Purchase.

and her husband solely through the sales of her paintings.

Spencer was both prolific and popular. She created around 500 paintings during her lifetime. Some of the more sentimental scenes were reproduced in lithographs and etchings. Millions of copies of these prints were sold.

Spencer's early work was based on allegorical and Shakespearean subjects, while her later work focused on domestic life. She used members of her own family as models in works depicting the warmth, humor, and hustle and bustle of everyday life in a large household. Her subjects often included animals and small children.

Spencer's gift for instilling vitality in her subjects, combined with her close observation of details and textures, made her famous. She used bright colors, clear drawing in oils and dramatic lighting to enhance the domestic scenes she painted.

Spencer died in 1902 in New York.

MEMBERSHIPS
National Academy of Design

PUBLIC COLLECTIONS
National Museum of American Art, Washington, D.C.
Newark Museum, New Jersey

10-Year Average Change From Base Years '75-'76: 3,944%

	75-76	76-77	77-78	78-79	79-80	80-81	81-82	82-83	83-84	84-85
%		204%	264%	440%		4,394%	954%		11,290%	14,006%
SEASON	75-76	76-77	77-78	78-79	79-80	80-81	81-82	82-83	83-84	84-85
Paintings	1	1	3	2		1	2		2	1
Dollars	$1,000	$350	$5,450	$6,025		$11,000	$12,800		$103,000	$13,000

Record Sale: $90,000, CH, 12/9/83, "Young Husband—First Marketing," 30 x 25 in.

196

STURTEVANT J. HAMBLEN
(Active 1823?-1856?)

As with others of the lesser American primitive portrait painters, knowledge about the life and work of Sturtevant J. Hamblen is spotty at best. To date no record has been found of where or when he was born. His sister, Rosamond, who married William Matthew Prior, a better-documented New England portrait painter, was listed as a resident of Bath, Maine at the time of her marriage in 1828. Hamblen had three brothers, Eli, Joseph and Nathaniel. Like him, they probably began as ornamental painters and later painted portraits.

One source states that all of the Hamblen brothers worked in Portland, Maine from 1823 until 1839, the year in which Eli Hamblen died. A Portland Museum of Art *Bulletin,* however, states that Prior and his family, along with the Hamblen brothers, moved to Portland sometime between 1831 and 1834 and established themselves in business there. According to this source, the Portland City Register of 1834 listed Prior as living with his brother-in-law, Nathaniel. Two years later the Register listed Prior as owning his own house, and Joseph and Sturtevant Hamblen as living with him.

In any event, Prior and his brothers-in-law seemed to have functioned more or less as an artist-craftsman commune. Their production of portraits was considerable. While the other brothers were listed as "house, sign and fancy painters," Sturtevant Hamblen seems to have devoted himself chiefly to painting portraits. He may even have contributed to portraits bearing Prior's signature. Only a few of Sturtevant Hamblen's portraits have been positively identified to date, but the style in which they were painted is so close to Prior's that it is difficult to distinguish between the two. Both painted portraits of sea captains, and both introduced spyglasses and background sailing vessels into their compositions.

Baby Holding Rattle, ca. 1850, 24 x 20 in. Courtesy of Peter Tillou Gallery, Litchfield, Connecticut. Photograph courtesy of Sotheby's.

Prior actually had two styles, one well-drawn and modeled, and the other flat, without shade or shadow. While the quality of his likenesses was never compromised, he tailored his work to the pocketbook of his sitters, and charged only a quarter the price for his flat portraits. Sturtevant Hamblen may well have followed the same custom.

Two sources state that Hamblen continued to paint until 1856, when he went into the men's furnishings business in Portland with his brother, Joseph. Another source puts the date of his career switch in 1865. There is no indication of when Sturtevant Hamblen died.

SEASON	75-76	76-77	77-78	78-79	79-80	80-81	81-82	82-83	83-84	84-85
Paintings			1							
Dollars			$1,300							

Record Sale: $1,300, PB, 4/28/78, "Portrait of General Israel Putnam," 27 x 18 in.

PUBLIC COLLECTIONS
Colby College Museum of Art,
  Waterville, Maine
National Gallery of Art, Washington, D.C.

SANFORD ROBINSON GIFFORD
(1823-1880)

Tacoma Washington, 1875, 21 x 40¼ in., signed l.l. Photograph courtesy of The Gerald Peters Gallery, Santa Fe, New Mexico.

Landscape painter Sanford Robinson Gifford, who worked in the luminist style, was particularly interested in light and atmosphere. He strove to create landscapes free of allegorical, historical or literary allusions, which he regarded as affectations.

Born at Greenfield in Saratoga County, New York, Gifford was the son of a wealthy industrialist. He grew up in Hudson, New York, across the Hudson River from the home of a painter he would later idolize, Thomas Cole.

In 1842, Gifford entered the studio of

watercolorist John Rubens Smith, where he studied figure drawing. By the next year, however, he had discovered the irresistible lure of the landscape, which would inspire the rest of his career.

During the summer of 1846, Gifford made walking tours of the Catskill and

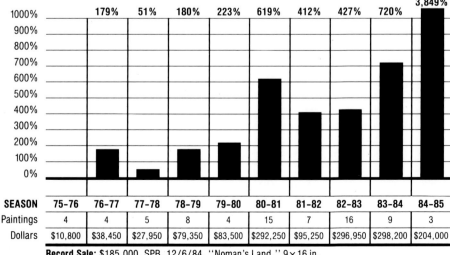

10-Year Average Change From Base Years '75-'76: 666%

SEASON	75-76	76-77	77-78	78-79	79-80	80-81	81-82	82-83	83-84	84-85
		179%	51%	180%	223%	619%	412%	427%	720%	3,849%
Paintings	4	4	5	8	4	15	7	16	9	3
Dollars	$10,800	$38,450	$27,950	$79,350	$83,500	$292,250	$95,250	$296,950	$298,200	$204,000

Record Sale: $185,000, SPB, 12/6/84, ''Noman's Land,'' 9 × 16 in.

198

The Coming Storm, 10 x 18 in., signed l.r. Courtesy of Henry B. Holt, Inc., Essex Fells, New Jersey.

Study on the Massachusetts Coast, 5 x 12 in. Courtesy of John H. Garzoli Gallery, San Francisco, California.

Berkshire Mountains, which yielded numerous studies from nature. Gifford wrote that these studies, " . . . together with the great admiration I felt for the works of Cole, developed a strong interest in Landscape art, and opened my eyes to a keener perception and more intelligent enjoyment of Nature. . . . Having once enjoyed the absolute freedom of the Landscape painter's life, I was unable to return to portrait painting."

The direction he took was decidedly out of step with the predominant tradition. Unlike Cole, Gifford intended to paint landscapes without the aid of heroic or religious subjects or of transplanted European affectations.

Gifford worked in the New York area until 1855, when he left for Europe to travel and study for three years. In England, Gifford met the dean of British art critics, John Ruskin; in Italy he traveled with American painter Albert Bierstadt.

The most important feature of the trip was his exposure to works of J.M.W. Turner and of the barbizon painters. Like the Hudson River School, Gifford could not accept Turner's propensity to permit light to dissolve matter. Gifford also disliked what he called the "slovenly" aspect of the barbizon landscapes.

Gifford returned in 1858, and soon exhibited a changed, matured style. Working slowly and on a small scale, he balanced minute detail with a graceful sense of overall atmosphere. The brush strokes are not evident, and his forms are clearly delineated, but the specifics of topography are sacrificed to the play of light.

Gifford and other mid-century painters who studied the effect of light on atmosphere, mountains, and bodies of water, are known as luminists. A feature of Gifford's mature work was his method of finishing canvases: using multiple layers of a translucent varnish, he would coat his paintings in an attempt to achieve verisimilitude through a "veiling" of tones.

Gifford continued to travel. From 1868 to 1879, he went abroad again—this time traveling not only in Europe but in parts of the Middle East. The following year, he journeyed with the painters Worthington Whittredge and John F. Kensett to the Colorado Rockies.

Gifford died in 1880, and was honored by a memorial exhibition at the Metropolitan Museum of Art.

MEMBERSHIPS
Century Club
National Academy of Design
Union League

PUBLIC COLLECTIONS
Adirondack Museum, Blue Mountain Lake,
  New York
Corcoran Gallery, Washington, D.C.
Metropolitan Museum of Art, New York City
National Gallery of Art, Washington, D.C.
New-York Historical Society, New York City
Newark Museum, New Jersey
Toledo Museum of Art, Ohio

THOMAS HICKS
(1823-1890)

Portraitist Thomas Hicks's talent was recognized early in his life. He was born in Newtown, Pennsylvania in 1823. By age 13, he was already painting and studying under his cousin, painter Edward Hicks. He went on to study at the Pennsylvania Academy of the Fine Arts and the National Academy of Design.

In 1845, Hicks traveled through Europe and eventually settled in Paris to study in the studio of Thomas Couture. Hicks may never have fully absorbed Couture's academic strength, but he did learn the use of symbolism in painting from Couture, and adopted his dark tonalism.

The landscapes and portraits Hicks produced before his training in Paris are praised for their simplicity. After his exposure to Couture, his paintings lost their sense of innocence.

Returning to New York City in 1849, Hicks established himself as a popular portrait artist. He painted the likenesses of such notables as *Hamilton Fish* (1852, City of New York); *Oliver Wendell Holmes* (1858, Boston Athenaeum); *Harriet Beecher Stowe, Henry Ward Beecher* and *Henry Wadsworth Longfellow* (dates unknown, United States Capitol, Washington, D.C.); and *Abraham Lincoln* (an engraving).

Although Hicks never gained extraordinary recognition as a fine artist, his talent for realistically stylized portraits brought him considerable success until his death in 1890.

MEMBERSHIPS
National Academy of Design

PUBLIC COLLECTIONS
Boston Athenaeum
Metropolitan Museum of Art, New York City
New-York Historical Society, New York City
United States Capitol, Washington, D.C.

The Musicale, Barber Shop, Trenton Falls, N.Y., 1866, 25 x 30⅛ in., signed l.r.
Courtesy of North Carolina Museum of Art, Raleigh.

Eliza Ann Coles Neilson, 1859, 33¼ x 26 in. Courtesy of Kennedy Galleries, New York, New York.

SEASON	75-76	76-77	77-78	78-79	79-80	80-81	81-82	82-83	83-84	84-85
Paintings				1		2	1			1
Dollars				$500		$4,000	$1,100			$2,808

Record Sale: $3,000, CH, 6/26/81, "Portrait of John C. Calhoun," 26 × 20 in.

WILLIAM M. HART

(1823-1894)

Hudson River School landscape artist William M. Hart was born in Paisley, Scotland. He emigrated to the United States with his family in 1831; they settled in Albany, New York. The artist was apprenticed to a carriage maker, but by the time he was 18 he began to paint portraits.

Soon after 1849, Hart left Albany and traveled widely throughout the United States, painting in New York, Virginia and Michigan, where he spent three years. After a brief visit to Scotland, he returned to Albany in 1847, and in 1854 opened a studio in New York City. Later he moved to Brooklyn, where he became the first president of the Brooklyn Academy of Design in 1854. His last years were spent in Mount Vernon, New York.

Both Hart and his brother, James McDougal Hart, who worked separately, were considered leading landscape painters of the second generation of the Hudson River School. William Hart painted in the style of Asher B. Durand, one of the leading landscape artists of the period, although his work lacked Durand's monumentality.

William Hart's earlier works were painted in a detailed and meticulous manner, while his later works were more broadly conceived. One of the founders (and later president) of the American Water Color Society, Hart also painted a number of small, dramatic seascapes of

Landscape, 1883, 16½ x 13½ in., signed l.r. Courtesy of M. Knoedler & Co., Inc., New York, New York.

Sunlight & Shadow, 8¾ x 14¼ in., signed l.l. Courtesy of M. Knoedler & Co., Inc., New York, New York.

the coast of Maine, suggesting the influence of popular German artist Andreas Achenbach of Dusseldorf.

But Hart's favorite subject matter was a herd of cattle drinking at a stream. According to the style of the day, Hart blended the real and the ideal to give an atmosphere of peace and serenity. Contemporary critics spoke of his ability to be "faithful to nature" and yet convey "a poetic sentiment." His paintings were engraved over and over again for the gift books and art journals of his time.

MEMBERSHIPS
American Water Color Society
Brooklyn Academy of Design
National Academy of Design

PUBLIC COLLECTIONS
Albany Institute of History and Art, New York
Metropolitan Museum of Art, New York City
National Academy of Design, New York City
New-York Historical Society, New York City
Vassar College

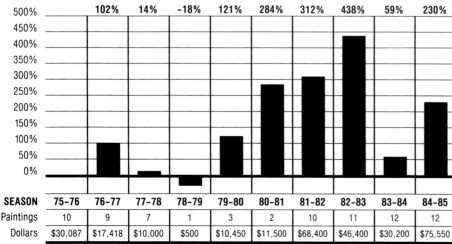

10-Year Average Change From Base Years '75-'76: 154%

	102%	14%	-18%	121%	284%	312%	438%	59%	230%
SEASON	75-76	76-77	77-78	78-79	79-80	80-81	81-82	82-83	83-84	84-85
Paintings	10	9	7	1	3	2	10	11	12	12
Dollars	$30,087	$17,418	$10,000	$500	$10,450	$11,500	$68,400	$46,400	$30,200	$75,550

Record Sale: $35,000, CH, 12/7/84, "The Months of the Year," 25 x 41 in.

JASPER CROPSEY
(1823-1900)

Jasper Cropsey was a mid-nineteenth-century painter and architect known for his detailed, romantic autumn landscapes. A member of the Hudson River School, he reached his artistic peak in 1860 with a nine-foot-long canvas of a New York autumn. Its brilliant colors stunned many of the English viewers to whom it was presented in London.

Cropsey was born on Staten Island, New York, in 1823. He was trained in mechanical drafting and apprenticed at age 15 to architect Joseph Trench. He developed a strong interest in painting and took lessons in painting watercolors.

In 1841, he began doing landscapes in oil, painting scenes of the White Mountains, the Catskill Mountains and areas around Greenwood Lake, New Jersey, as well as literary and thematic landscapes. In 1842 he left Trench's office to devote himself to painting, although he continued to work as an architect.

In *The Spirit of War* (1851, National Gallery of Art) Cropsey represents war as a mighty medieval fortress set among fantastic geological peaks against a phenomenal sunset. Allegorical paintings like this one, dark and turbulent, were remarkably similar to those of Thomas Cole.

Cropsey went to Europe in 1847 for two years; beginning in 1856, he lived in England for seven years. There, he painted one of his greatest works, *Autumn—On the Hudson River* (1860, National Gallery of Art), which received

Lake Scene, 16 x 30 in., signed l.r. Courtesy of Vose Galleries of Boston, Inc., Massachusetts.

The Hudson, 1877, 12 x 20 in., signed l.l. Courtesy of Vose Galleries of Boston, Inc., Massachusetts.

critical raves and rated Cropsey an audience with Queen Victoria.

From then on, Cropsey specialized in fall scenes, earning the nickname "America's painter of autumn." He was inclined toward precise detail and had a tendency to be repetitive. In the later years of his life, Cropsey settled on the Hudson River at Hastings, New York, painting oil and watercolor views of the river many times over.

He continued some architectural work throughout his life; among his designs was the Victorian-style Sixth Avenue elevated station in New York City.

Cropsey died in 1900.

PUBLIC COLLECTIONS
Harvard University
Metropolitan Museum of Art, New York City
National Gallery of Art, Washington, D.C.
New-York Historical Society, New York City

10-Year Average Change From Base Years '75-'76: 146%

	-9%	-18%	-36%	101%	451%	120%	291%	234%	327%

SEASON	75-76	76-77	77-78	78-79	79-80	80-81	81-82	82-83	83-84	84-85
Paintings	4	9	14	13	15	19	16	24	14	12
Dollars	$16,550	$37,028	$139,550	$56,550	$179,750	$863,900	$244,600	$552,570	$255,450	$388,850

Record Sale: $600,000, SPB, 4/23/81, "Backwoods of America," 42 x 70 in.

SUSAN C. WATERS
(1823-1900)

Susan C. Waters began her career in the mid-1840s as an itinerant portrait painter, but she is best known for her animal and still-life painting. A transition can be seen in her work between folk art and a higher degree of sophistication.

In her early portrait of *Francis and Sarah Johnson* (1844, Arnot Art Museum, Elmira, New York), a serious little boy and girl sit side by side in stiff poses, one holding a cat and the other a basket of fruit. By 1845 her portraits are much more professional—more loosely composed, their expressions softer. The artist was especially skilled at rendering lace, as in *Woman in Black* (ca. 1845, New York State Historical Association, Cooperstown).

Waters's portraits date from 1843 to 1845; none have been found after this, except for one painted in the late nineteenth century, *The Explorer* (ca. 1875-1900, private collection).

Waters was born in Binghamton, New York in 1823. The family moved to Friendsville, Pennsylvania when she was a child. There Susan and her sister attended a female seminary where Susan, at age 15, made drawings for her natural history class to help pay tuition.

In 1841, when she was 18, she married William C. Waters, a Quaker who encouraged her work and accompanied her as she painted portraits throughout Southern New York State and Pennsylvania.

Waters did no painting at all for a long period. When she settled in Bordentown, New Jersey in 1866, where she remained for 23 years, she concentrated on still lifes and animals. Sheep were kept in a pen in her backyard. *Sheep in a Landscape* (ca. 1875-1900) is typical of her work at this time.

By 1876, Waters was successful enough to exhibit two paintings in the Centennial Exposition in Philadelphia.

She died in Trenton, New Jersey in 1900.

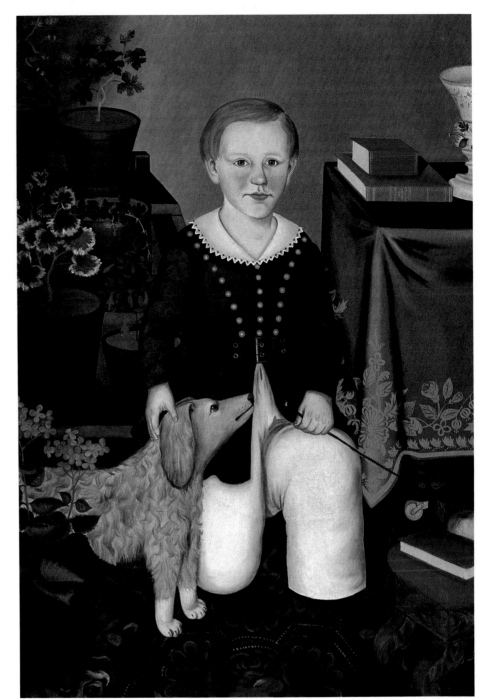

Portrait of a Boy with Dog, ca. 1845, 43½ x 29½ in. Courtesy of Wunderlich and Company, Inc., New York, New York.

SEASON	75-76	76-77	77-78	78-79	79-80	80-81	81-82	82-83	83-84	84-85
Paintings						4	1		3	
Dollars						$71,700	$650		$8,600	

Record Sale: $33,000, SPB, 4/30/81, ''The Downs Children,'' 42 × 50 in.

THOMAS WATERMAN WOOD

(1823-1903)

Thomas Waterman Wood, a genre painter and etcher, was born in Montpelier, Vermont in 1823. He is best known for his sentimental scenes of rural life, and for a series of paintings that depict the life of American blacks at the time of the Civil War.

Wood's formal training began when he traveled to Boston at age 23 to study with Chester Harding. He worked as a portraitist in New York City, Quebec, Washington, D.C. and Baltimore, where he settled briefly. In 1858, he departed on a two-year study tour of Europe that included visits to London, Paris and Dusseldorf.

On his return, he worked as a portrait painter in Nashville, Tennessee and Louisville, Kentucky. He settled permanently in New York City in 1867.

Wood was a sensitive portrait painter, though he achieved greater acclaim for his genre scenes. His tone, style and traditional subject matter in the latter were characteristic of an earlier period.

Wood's interest in themes of work, domestic life, American blacks and American Indians is characteristic of the approach used by the Dusseldorf school. He painted the genre scenes in his studio, after completing many preliminary studies for which he employed models. Over time, Wood's technique progressed from artisan-like craftsmanship to a dull style of near-photographic detail.

Portrait of a Young Boy, 1894, 9½ x 7½ in., signed l.r. Courtesy of Taggart, Jorgensen, & Putnam Gallery, Washington, D.C.

Among the most ambitious of his paintings is *The Village Post Office* (1873, New York State Historical Society). Here, Wood's rough technique is combined perfectly with a rural theme. His sentimentality is not forced, but rather shown through quiet observation of the scene.

A group of three paintings entitled *War Episodes* shows black participation in the Civil War, and the transformation from slavery to freedom: *The Contraband,* 1865; *The Volunteer,* 1866; and *The Veteran,* 1866 (all at the Metropolitan Museum of Art). After showing the group at the National Academy of Design in 1867, Wood received public and critical attention, and was elected to membership in the Academy.

In his later years, Wood lived year-round at his summer home in Montpelier. He established the Wood Art Gallery in his hometown to house a collection of his works, including a number of copies of old masters he painted.

Wood died in 1903.

MEMBERSHIPS
American Watercolor Society
National Academy of Design
New York Etching Club

PUBLIC COLLECTIONS
J.B. Speed Art Museum, Louisville
Metropolitan Museum of Art, New York City
New York State Historical Society,
   Cooperstown
Wood Art Gallery, Montpelier, Vermont

10-Year Average Change From Base Years '77-'78: 150%

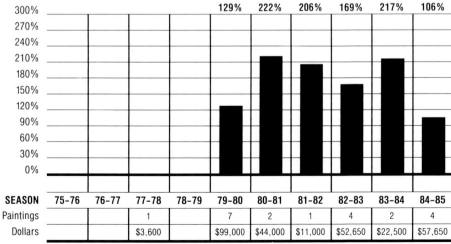

SEASON	75-76	76-77	77-78	78-79	79-80	80-81	81-82	82-83	83-84	84-85
					129%	222%	206%	169%	217%	106%
Paintings			1		7	2	1	4	2	4
Dollars			$3,600		$99,000	$44,000	$11,000	$52,650	$22,500	$57,650

Record Sale: $46,000, SPB, 12/6/84, ''Politics in the Workshops,'' 27 x 22 in.

204

WALTER M. BRACKETT

(1823-1919)

During the late nineteenth century, Walter M. Brackett achieved great notoriety as an accomplished still-life specialist. Although he painted a number of portraits during his career, Brackett is best known for his careful renderings of fish and game. During the 1860s, this highly specialized genre of still-life painting was popular with sportsmen who acquired these paintings as trophies.

Brackett was born in Unity, Maine in 1823, the younger brother of sculptor Edward A. Brackett. He settled in Boston, where he supported a family and began a career as a professional artist in 1843. Devoted to portraiture early in his career, Brackett specialized in depicting varieties of fish by the early 1860s.

In 1873, Brackett submitted a series of four works, illustrating a catch of fish, for exhibition in London's famous Crystal Palace. These paintings established Brackett as an artist of international reputation and brought favorable comparisons to Leonidas Rolfe, England's leading painter of fish subjects.

Brackett's still lifes of fish and game were greatly admired in his day because of their fidelity to nature and their picturesque, pleasant sensibility. The artist's careful renderings of such varieties as Lake Ontario whitefish and landlocked salmon were popular among the cultivated gentlemen of the era.

Before his death in Boston in 1919, Brackett exhibited in numerous galleries and cultural organizations, including: the Boston Atheneum, from 1846 to 1869; the Apollo Association, 1852; and the National Academy of Design, 1860 and 1865.

Captain Joseph Pitty Couthouy, ca. 1852, 190¼ x 157 in. Courtesy of The Boston Athenaeum, Massachusetts.

MEMBERSHIPS
National Academy of Design

SEASON	75-76	76-77	77-78	78-79	79-80	80-81	81-82	82-83	83-84	84-85
Paintings	1				1	1		1	1	1
Dollars	$500				$625	$1,800		$800	$15,000	$2,800

Record Sale: $15,000, D.NY, 9/29/83, "The Rise.The Leap.The Last Struggle.Land," 20 x 32 in.

WILLIAM MORRIS HUNT
(1824-1879)

William Morris Hunt was influential in introducing continental trends to the United States, particularly in Boston before the Civil War. Through his lectures, teaching and painting—and his unstinting admiration for such French masters as Thomas Couture and barbizon painter Jean-Francois Millet—Hunt shaped artistic tastes in Boston.

Vermont-born Hunt studied sculpture at Harvard University with Henry Kirke Brown before his European studies. He briefly attended the Dusseldorf Academy, but rebelled against the rigid training there, settling in Paris around 1847 to study with Couture.

It was with Couture that Hunt developed his preference for making quick sketches in a flash of inspiration, rather than using intermediate studies as the underdrawing for a painting. Hunt was more interested in conveying artistic insight than in drawing accurate details, a tendency that challenged the traditions of American realism.

Hunt was also profoundly influenced by Millet, and through him the softly-modeled French barbizon style was introduced into Boston after Hunt settled there in 1855.

Hunt painted a series of remarkable portraits in the 1860s, including a highly expressive self-portrait. He traveled in Europe again in 1866, and in the early 1870s, he opened an art school for women in Boston. In 1872, fire destroyed his studio, along with his French collection and many of his own paintings.

When Hunt started over, it was with a looser brush and brighter colors. His best known work from this era, *Gloucester Harbor* (1877, Museum of Fine Arts, Boston) captures the shimmering light of the bay. In 1878, Hunt did important murals for the state capitol in Albany, New York, but they were badly damaged by dampness soon after completion.

A year after he completed this exhausting undertaking, Hunt drowned in the Isles of Shoals in New Hampshire. It is thought that, melancholy from professional misfortunes, he may have killed himself.

MEMBERSHIPS
National Academy of Design

PUBLIC COLLECTIONS
Museum of Fine Arts, Boston
Philadelphia Museum of Art
Metropolitan Museum of Art, New York City
State Capitol, Albany, New York

Magnolia Mass, 1878, 36 x 29 in. Courtesy of Vose Galleries of Boston, Inc., Massachusetts.

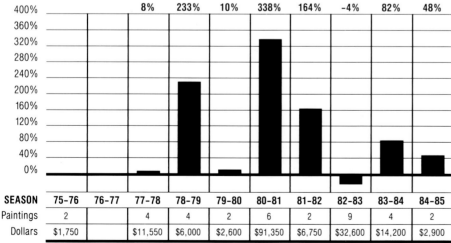

10-Year Average Change From Base Years '75-'76: 98%

| | 8% | 233% | 10% | 338% | 164% | -4% | 82% | 48% |

SEASON	75-76	76-77	77-78	78-79	79-80	80-81	81-82	82-83	83-84	84-85
Paintings	2		4	4	2	6	2	9	4	2
Dollars	$1,750		$11,550	$6,000	$2,600	$91,350	$6,750	$32,600	$14,200	$2,900

Record Sale: $53,000, S.BM, 11/20/80, "The Belated Kid," 54 x 38 in.

206

CHRISTIAN SCHUSSELE

(1824-1879)

Christian Schussele, genre, history and portrait painter, is noted for his role in establishing the Pennsylvania Academy of the Fine Arts in Philadelphia as a leading teaching institution.

Born in 1824 (some sources say 1826) in the Alsace, Schussele studied art in Strasbourg and Paris before coming to Philadelphia in 1848.

He was one of the earliest artists in America to work in the new medium of chromolithography. Schussele supported his family through lithography and wood engravings, but he preferred painting. In 1854, a John Sartain print after one of his paintings gained popular attention, and Schussele turned to painting full-time.

His work is academic, in the classic mode, with mannered composition and sound figure construction. It appealed to the popular taste of the time.

In 1868, Schussele became professor of drawing and painting at the Pennsylvania Academy. Despite failing health, he remained a highly respected teacher there until his death in 1879. He was president of the Artists' Fund Society for several years.

Schussele made portraits of many prominent Americans. His best-known history painting is *Benjamin Franklin before the Council, London, 1773* (date and location unknown). Also familiar is *Men of Progress* (1862, Pennsylvania Academy of the Fine Arts), an imaginary gathering of 18 great American inventors.

In 1876, Schussele named his former student, Thomas Eakins, as his assistant. After his death in 1879 at Merchantville, New Jersey, Schussele was succeeded at the Academy by Eakins, who continued Schussele's emphasis on figure painting.

Men of Progress, 1862, 51⅜ x 76¾ in., signed l.l. Courtesy of National Portrait Gallery, Washington, D.C.

MEMBERSHIPS
Pennsylvania Academy of the Fine Arts
Artists' Fund Society

PUBLIC COLLECTIONS
New-York Historical Society, New York City
Pennsylvania Academy of the Fine Arts,
 Philadelphia
Philadelphia Museum of Art

SEASON	75-76	76-77	77-78	78-79	79-80	80-81	81-82	82-83	83-84	84-85
Paintings				1	1	2			1	
Dollars				$700	$700	$19,200			$6,000	

Record Sale: $18,000, S.BM, 7/17/80, "Washington Irving & His Literary Friends," 52 × 78 in.

GEORGE LAFAYETTE CLOUGH
(1824-1901)

George Lafayette Clough was a notable New York landscape painter of the nineteenth century. His numerous naturalistic landscapes are of the Hudson River School.

Born in Auburn, New York in 1824, Clough was one of six children raised by a widowed mother. Although he was basically self-taught, Clough probably received some early training from local portrait painter Randall Palmer. Around 1844, Clough set up his own studio above a store in Auburn. Soon afterward painter Charles Loring Elliott came to Auburn to paint a commissioned portrait; he asked Clough to lend him the studio. Clough and Elliott became friends and Clough studied with Elliott in Auburn and New York City.

Clough went to Europe to study in the early 1850s. He copied paintings at the Louvre, and went to Holland, Germany and Italy. When Clough returned to America, he began to concentrate on landscapes.

Pastoral landscapes were his primary subject. While most of his paintings depicted the area around Auburn, Clough also painted throughout Pennsylvania, Eastern Ohio and New England.

Sawmill, Glen Cove, L.I., 23 x 40 in., signed l.l. Courtesy of Vose Galleries of Boston, Inc., Massachusetts.

Rounout Creek, 1871, 24 x 36 in., signed l.c. Courtesy of Henry B. Holt, Inc., Essex Fells, New Jersey.

During the 1860s and 1870s, Clough painted urban scenes, often using New York City as a subject. He also painted some genre scenes around 1870. Toward the end of the 1870s, Clough again concentrated on landscapes.

All Clough's paintings were rather academic. He painted sensitive, emotional scenes, with an emphasis on the natural lighting and atmosphere of each.

Clough died in Auburn in 1901.

MEMBERSHIPS
Art Club
Brooklyn Brush and Palette Club

PUBLIC COLLECTIONS
Carnegie Institute, Pittsburgh

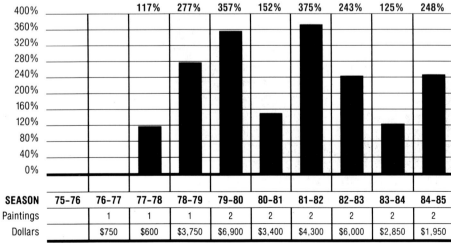

10-Year Average Change From Base Years '76-'77: 210%

	75-76	76-77	77-78	78-79	79-80	80-81	81-82	82-83	83-84	84-85
			117%	277%	357%	152%	375%	243%	125%	248%
SEASON	75-76	76-77	77-78	78-79	79-80	80-81	81-82	82-83	83-84	84-85
Paintings		1	1	1	2	2	2	2	2	2
Dollars		$750	$600	$3,750	$6,900	$3,400	$4,300	$6,000	$2,850	$1,950

Record Sale: $5,500, SPB, 3/17/80, "Two Children by a Pond," 25 x 37 in.

208

EASTMAN JOHNSON
(1824-1906)

Eastman Johnson, portrait and genre painter, was perhaps the most prominent and successful of the many American artists who came to the fore at the time of the Civil War.

The son of a successful politician, Johnson was born in Lovell, Maine in 1824. Johnson eschewed higher education, choosing instead to apprentice in John H. Bufford's Boston lithography studio. The apprenticeship was short-lived.

In his late teens and early twenties, Johnson established himself as a portraitist, limiting himself to black-and-white renderings. His popular success was furthered by the patronage of his family's friends in Boston and Washington, D.C.

In 1849, Johnson traveled to Dusseldorf, Germany, where he lived for two years, sharing a studio with Emanuel Leutze. Ultimately finding German painting too bland, Johnson studied for four years at the Hague. There, he became known as the "American Rembrandt"—an image he fostered by attending society balls dressed as a seventeenth-century Dutch burgher.

Turning down the post of court painter to the Hague, Johnson studied in Paris, where he was influenced by the then-popular French Victorian genre style. He returned to the United States in 1859 and ultimately settled in New York City.

Johnson used his genre skills to depict

The Lord is my Shepherd, 1863, 16⅝ x 13⅛ in., signed l.l. Courtesy of National Museum of American Art, Smithsonian Institution, Gift of Francis P. Garvan.

Southern slavery in a series of paintings. The most famous, *Old Kentucky Home* (1859, New-York Historical Society), shows poignantly the state of Southern social structure on the eve of the Civil War, juxtaposing the slave quarters with the owner's mansion. The painting brought Johnson acceptance from both pro and anti-abolitionists and won the

painter election to the National Academy of Design.

During the 1870s, Johnson painted a series of outdoor genre scenes, using maple-sugar camps and Nantucket cranberry harvests as his inspiration. In these paintings, Johnson retains his sharp attention to detail, though his brushstrokes are broader and shorter. His *In the Fields* (1870, location unknown) is almost impressionistic in tone.

As Johnson's popularity as a genre painter waned during the last 20 years of his life, the artist successfully returned to portrait painting. His favorite subjects were wealthy New York families and public figures, among them John Quincy Adams, Daniel Webster and Ralph Waldo Emerson.

Johnson continued painting until his death in New York City in 1906.

MEMBERSHIPS
National Academy of Design

PUBLIC COLLECTIONS
Metropolitan Museum of Art, New York City
New-York Historical Society, New York City

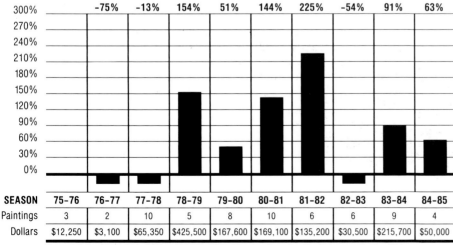

10-Year Average Change From Base Years '75-'76: 59%

	-75%	-13%	154%	51%	144%	225%	-54%	91%	63%

SEASON	75-76	76-77	77-78	78-79	79-80	80-81	81-82	82-83	83-84	84-85
Paintings	3	2	10	5	8	10	6	6	9	4
Dollars	$12,250	$3,100	$65,350	$425,500	$167,600	$169,100	$135,200	$30,500	$215,700	$50,000

Record Sale: $370,000, SPB, 4/20/79, "Washington Crossing the Delaware," 40 × 68 in.

209

RICHARD CATON WOODVILLE
(1825-1855)

Genre painter Richard Caton Woodville combined techniques perfected in Europe with subjects drawn from American life. The paintings he produced during his brief career were highly esteemed for their meticulous detail and fine finish.

Woodville was born in Baltimore in 1825 to a well-to-do family. He may have had some early training in art from Alfred Jacob Miller, later known for his Western paintings. Although Woodville's early sketches showed artistic promise, his family wanted him to become a doctor. He enrolled in medical school, but continued to draw and paint. He also studied the art collection of Baltimorean Robert Gilmore, which included representative works of the Dutch and Flemish schools, as well as the work of genre painter William Sidney Mount, which may have influenced Woodville's later direction.

Woodville's earliest known genre piece is *Soldier's Experience* (1844, Walters), in pencil and watercolor. He exhibited *Scene in a Bar-room* (1845, location unknown) at the National Academy of Design in 1845, and that same year left for Europe to study art. He settled in Dusseldorf, where he was the pupil of portraitist Karl Ferdinand Sohn. Some pencil-and-chalk studies on tinted paper from this period survive.

During the five years he studied with Sohn, Woodville acquired mastery of the techniques which distinguished his best work: precisely rendered still-life elements and skillful use of light and shadow. Among the best-known of the paintings he sent back to the United States are *War News from Mexico* (1848, National Academy of Design) and *Politics in an Oyster House* (1848, Walters). Both used settings and characters typical of Woodville's native Baltimore in small, tightly composed conversational groups.

The Artist's Gallery, 1853, 20 x 24 in., signed verso. Courtesy of Raydon Gallery, New York, New York.

The Sailor's Wedding (1852, Walters) represents the best of Woodville's mature style, with its dramatic posing of major and minor characters and its wealth of detail.

Woodville spent some time in Paris after 1850. He then settled in London, where he died of an overdose of morphine—a death officially listed as accidental—in 1855. His son of the same name became a successful illustrator.

PUBLIC COLLECTIONS
Corcoran Gallery of Art, Washington, D.C.
National Academy of Design, New York City
Walters Art Gallery, Baltimore

SEASON	75-76	76-77	77-78	78-79	79-80	80-81	81-82	82-83	83-84	84-85
Paintings										1
Dollars										$5,000

Record Sale: $5,000, SPB, 10/19/84, "Conquered but Not Subdued," 36 × 24 in.

GEORGE HENRY HALL

(1825-1913)

A largely self-taught artist, George Henry Hall was known for his detailed still lifes of fruit and flowers.

Hall was born in Manchester, New Hampshire in 1825, and grew up in Boston. In 1849, he made the first of many trips to Europe. He visited Paris, and studied with Eastman Johnson in Dusseldorf. In 1852, he returned to America and settled in New York City. Hall continued to travel frequently and often set his exotic genre paintings in Spain, Italy or Egypt.

In about 1857, he began painting fruit and flower still lifes. He was much admired and financially successful in his day, as mentioned in the famous *Book of the Artist* by Henry R. Tuckerman, published in 1867. (The author seems impressed that Hall received $12,000 for an auction of 75 small paintings in 1865.)

Hall's fruits and flowers emphasized the rich abundance of nature and demonstrated scientific knowledge of his subject matter. The exactitude of his paintings was much admired. A critic writing for *The Independent* said, "His still-life pictures are his best, and in the really picturesque delineation of fruit and flowers he has few superiors in the country. . . . ''

Hall was influenced by the writings of John Ruskin, who praised pre-raphaelite William Henry Hunt for his "simple love of our summer fruit and flower."

Still Life: Four Peaches, 1863, 8 x 10 in., signed l.r. Courtesy of Henry B. Holt, Inc., Essex Fells, New Jersey.

Although Hall often set his still lifes upon the conventional highly-polished tabletop, he preferred a natural setting—fruit or flowers against a natural background framed by the sky. Because of his penchant for placing small, tender fruit subjects in a casual outdoor setting, he became his generation's best-known advocate of the Ruskin approach.

One of Hall's favorite subjects was raspberries. *Raspberries in a Gauntlet* (date and location unknown) illustrates both his romanticism and his allegiance to the principles of Ruskin. Round, lush raspberries are pictured pouring out of a gauntlet (a medieval armored glove) against a natural background. The armor becomes a perfect foil for the succulent raspberries, perhaps exemplifying the contrast between man and nature.

MEMBERSHIPS
National Academy of Design

PUBLIC COLLECTIONS
Brooklyn Museum
Museum of Fine Arts, Boston

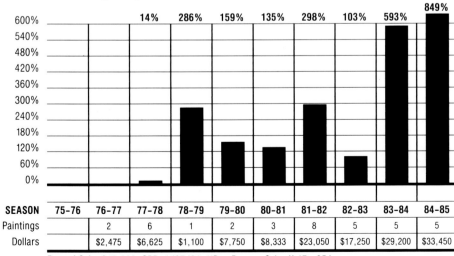

10-Year Average Change From Base Years '76–'77: 271%

SEASON	75-76	76-77	77-78	78-79	79-80	80-81	81-82	82-83	83-84	84-85
		14%	286%	159%	135%	298%	103%	593%	849%
Paintings		2	6	1	2	3	8	5	5	5
Dollars		$2,475	$6,625	$1,100	$7,750	$8,333	$23,050	$17,250	$29,200	$33,450

Record Sale: $18,000, SPB, 1/27/84, "Rug Bazaar, Cairo," 47 × 35 in.

GEORGE INNESS
(1825-1894)

A Thunderstorm, 1869, 30 x 45½ in., signed l.r. Courtesy of Vose Galleries of Boston, Inc., Massachusetts.

Many rank George Inness with Homer, Eakins and Ryder as a master of nineteenth-century American painting. Certainly he profoundly influenced the landscape painters who followed him.

Inness's early work was very much in the prevailing style of the Hudson River School. Several trips to Europe brought him into contact with the work of the barbizon painters and brought stronger color and a new looseness into his own compositions. In his late work, however, from 1880 on, he achieved the melding of the natural world with the spiritual that he sought, and created landscapes of extraordinary power.

Inness was born in Newburgh, New York, in 1825. He suffered from epilepsy, a condition that always affected his health. Because of it his formal education was sketchy. He was raised in Newark, New Jersey, had a brief stint running a grocery store for his father and was apprenticed for two years to an engraver in New York City.

His only training in the basics of painting came from an itinerant painter and from Regis Gignoux, an academic French painter who was working in Brooklyn at the time. Neither of them had a lasting effect on Inness, who always maintained that he was self-taught.

The work of Cole and Durand and prints of the old masters were his true models; he sought to surpass them. Prevented by his epilepsy from taking long hikes in the wild, he chose pastoral scenes close to home. Even in the 1840s, however, he did not portray what he saw literally. He tried to project his own vision into his paintings.

By 1850, his reputation was solid enough for a patron to send him to Italy to study. He returned to New York in 1852, but went back to Europe two years later, this time to France. It was then that he came under the barbizon influence. Rousseau, Daubigny and Corot became his new idols.

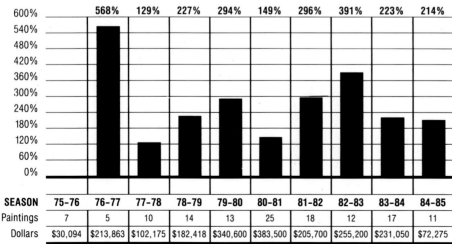

10-Year Average Change From Base Years '75-'76: 249%

SEASON	75-76	76-77	77-78	78-79	79-80	80-81	81-82	82-83	83-84	84-85
		568%	129%	227%	294%	149%	296%	391%	223%	214%
Paintings	7	5	10	14	13	25	18	12	17	11
Dollars	$30,094	$213,863	$102,175	$182,418	$340,600	$383,500	$205,700	$255,200	$231,050	$72,275

Record Sale: $200,000, PB, 10/28/76, "Path Through Florida Pines," 42 × 32 in.

212

Milking Time, ca. 1867, 29½ x 45 in., signed l.r. Courtesy of Henry B. Holt, Inc., Essex Fells, New Jersey.

New Yorkers were not impressed by the new direction of his work, however. Irritated, he moved to Medfield, near Boston, for five years. Later he returned to New Jersey and settled, surrounded by the countryside he had loved as a boy.

Through the 1860s Inness's most successful works were panoramas, full of light and almost lyrical color. To avoid foreground detail, he moved protruding objects, such as trees and animals, into the middle distance where they did not have to be sharply defined. Often mist obscured the distance.

In 1863, he was introduced to the writings of Emmanuel Swedenborg, the Scandanavian theologian. It was a landmark in his life. Here at last was a faith that reinforced his own notion that there was a direct correlation between the real world and the spiritual. He was striving to realize this connection in his work.

His interest in Swedenborg influenced his late work more and more. His forms became more and more indistinct, almost as if they were poised midway between the natural world and a heavenly world. In his best paintings an almost abstract quality appeared.

Inness was a frenzied painter, according to his son, who also became a painter. He would work and rework a canvas, sometimes painting an entirely different imaginary scene on top of an almost-finished work. After a night of frantic painting he sometimes would collapse, from either exhaustion or epilepsy. On a recuperative trip to Scotland, he died in 1894.

While the quality of Inness's output varied widely, his best paintings stand as some of the finest landscapes ever painted in America.

MEMBERSHIPS
National Academy of Design

PUBLIC COLLECTIONS
Art Institute of Chicago
Cincinnati Art Museum
Delaware Art Museum, Wilmington
Metropolitan Museum of Art, New York City
Montclair Art Museum, New Jersey
Museum of Fine Arts, Boston
National Gallery of Art, Washington, D.C.
Nelson Gallery, Atkins Museum of Fine Arts, Kansas City, Missouri
Phillips Collection, Washington, D.C.
Wadsworth Atheneum, Hartford, Connecticut

FREDERICK RONDEL
(1826-1892)

Narragansett Bay, Rhode Island, 1871, 22 x 36 in., signed l.l. Courtesy of Driscoll & Walsh, Fine Art, Boston, Massachusetts.

A highly respected academician and the only formal instructor of Winslow Homer, Frederick Rondel is noted for his landscape, marine and animal paintings in oil.

Born in Paris in 1826, Rondel studied there under Theodore Gudin and then under Gudin's pupil, Auguste Jugelet, both romantic marine and landscape painters. He came to the United States as a young man and was in Boston from 1855 to 1857 and in South Malden, Massachusetts in 1858, although he also maintained a studio in New York City.

In 1860, Rondel moved to New York City and became an associate member of the National Academy of Design. He left for an extensive stay in Europe in 1862, returning in 1868 to teach at the National Academy.

Rondel's most famous pupil was Winslow Homer. Rondel is credited with teaching him how to use brush and pigment when Homer began painting in oils.

Combining broad, deep perspective and clear, subtle light, Rondel's landscape and marine paintings reflect the romanticism of Gudin and Jugelet, his teachers. But the subjects of his paintings are American, scenes of New York City and the New England countryside where he lived and worked. They are exemplified by *Waiting for the Pilot* (location unknown), a large view of New York Harbor painted between 1872 and 1874.

Rondel's works have been exhibited at the National Academy of Design in New York City, at the Pennsylvania Academy of the Fine Arts in Philadelphia and at the Boston Athanaeum. He died in 1892.

MEMBERSHIPS
National Academy of Design

SEASON	75-76	76-77	77-78	78-79	79-80	80-81	81-82	82-83	83-84	84-85
Paintings	1		1		1	4	8	1	2	4
Dollars	$1,400		$6,000		$550	$7,200	$13,100	$2,300	$3,100	$6,100

Record Sale: $6,000, PB, 11/8/77, "On the Farm," 30 × 50 in.

GEORGE HETZEL
(1826-1906)

Landscape, portrait and still-life painter George Hetzel was one of Pennsylvania's most significant artists of the nineteenth century. From his base in Pittsburgh, he painted highly detailed, realistic views of nature, moving increasingly in the latter part of his career to impressionistic concerns with light. He was also very popular as a portraitist, noted for his sensitivity. All of his work possesses a quality of benevolent quiet and pensiveness.

Hetzel moved to Pittsburgh with his family when he was two. As a boy, he was apprenticed to a house and sign painter, later gaining experience as a muralist for river boats, cafes and a penitentiary. With the money he earned from interior decorating, Hetzel went to Germany in 1847 to study for two years at the Dusseldorf Academy. On his return in 1850, Hetzel painted very precise, representational portraits with smooth, even strokes, following the current Dusseldorf style.

In the late 1850s, Hetzel joined a group of Pittsburgh painters at the mountain retreat called Scalp Level and began to paint very precise landscapes—bucolic scenes of pleasant beauty. Throughout the 1850s and 1860s, he continued to rely on realistic detail to convey texture and reflected light. It wasn't until the next decade that Hetzel began to use his brush more freely.

Hetzel taught at the Pittsburgh School of Design for Women, and was the only

Landscape-River Ford in Woods, 1872, 9½ x 13 in., signed l.r. Courtesy of the Reading Public Museum, Pennsylvania.

Pittsburgh artist represented at the 1876 Centennial exposition held in Philadelphia. He died in 1906.

PUBLIC COLLECTIONS
Philadelphia Museum of Art

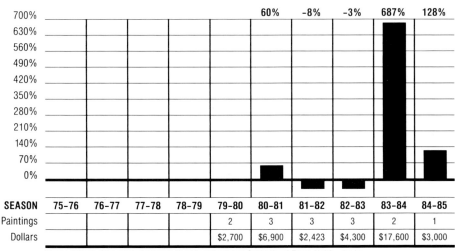

10-Year Average Change From Base Years '79-'80: 144%

	75–76	76–77	77–78	78–79	79–80	80–81	81–82	82–83	83–84	84–85
						60%	-8%	-3%	687%	128%
SEASON										
Paintings					2	3	3	3	2	1
Dollars					$2,700	$6,900	$2,423	$4,300	$17,600	$3,000

Record Sale: $11,000, SPB, 12/8/83, "Tabletop Still Life of Fruit," 22 × 34 in.

FREDERIC EDWIN CHURCH

(1826-1900)

Campfire in Maine Wilderness, 17¼ x 25¼ in., signed l.c. Photograph courtesy of The Gerald Peters Gallery, Santa Fe, New Mexico.

Frederic Edwin Church was one of the most famous landscapists of two continents in the 1850s and 1860s. His huge canvases are extravaganzas of nature in its extremes, painted with scientific exactitude. At their best, they are marvelous weddings of light, form and detail.

Church's career was meteoric, taking off when he was barely in his twenties, soaring in his thirties. Abruptly, in his late forties, Church's fame was eclipsed by a turnaround in public taste and by his own physical afflictions. It was never restored in his lifetime.

Born in 1826 in Hartford, Connecticut to a wealthy family, Church demonstrated early talent. In 1844, he became the pupil of the leading landscapist, Thomas Cole. A year later, at age 19, Church made his debut at the National Academy of Design and was named an associate member.

He established a studio in New York City in 1848 and took his first pupil, William Stillman.

Ebullient, physically energetic and brilliant, Church developed an approach to landscape painting significantly different from the accepted landscapists, Cole and Asher Durand, of the Hudson River School. Church shed much of Cole's romanticism and allegory. He adopted Durand's realism and took it to new heights. Church believed the artist could capture the essence of nature by studying the natural sciences and, by bridging the division between light and form, create what he called "organic unity."

In 1853, he made his first trip to South America. During his seven months' travel in Colombia and Ecuador, Church painted views of volcanoes, jungles and the snow-capped Andes Mountains, journeying 600 miles up the Magdalena River.

His South American paintings were acclaimed at the National Academy of Design in 1855. The artist's first major painting from this trip, *Andes of Ecuador* (1855, Reynolda House), was a sensation. Perhaps his best-known works are *Niagara Falls* (1857, Corcoran Gallery) and *Heart of the Andes* (1859, Metropolitan Museum of Art).

In 1861, Church traveled to the Arctic to paint massive canvases of glittering icebergs and seas. After a later trip to Jamaica and the tropics, he produced landscapes that some critics now fault as melodramatic.

In 1867, Church finally visited the Old World—Europe, the Mediterranean and North Africa. He began to work in spare, vigorous masses, with a new intensity of manner.

Some believe Church's new approach might eventually have created a second ascent to popularity, but in 1877 inflammatory rheumatism began to cripple the artist's right hand. Church attempted to educate his left.

For the remaining 23 years of his life, Church divided his time between his fabulous Moorish-inspired home, "Olana," on the Hudson River, his camp near Mt. Katahdin, Maine, and travel in Mexico. Though his work was depreciated and unsought, he continued to produce numerous good oil sketches.

After his death in 1900, virtually forgotten as an artist, Church was honored by an exhibition at the Metropolitan Museum of Art.

MEMBERSHIPS
National Academy of Design

PUBLIC COLLECTIONS
Cleveland Museum of Art
Cooper-Hewitt Museum, New York City
Corcoran Gallery, Washington, D.C.
Metropolitan Museum of Art, New York City
Museum of Fine Arts, Boston
Reading Public Museum and Gallery, Pennsylvania
Reynolda House, Winston-Salem, North Carolina

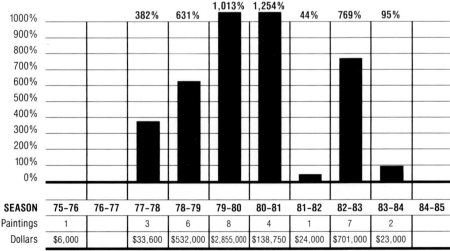

10-Year Average Change From Base Years '75-'76: 524%

SEASON	75-76	76-77	77-78	78-79	79-80	80-81	81-82	82-83	83-84	84-85
			382%	631%	1,013%	1,254%	44%	769%	95%	
Paintings	1		3	6	8	4	1	7	2	
Dollars	$6,000		$33,600	$532,000	$2,855,000	$138,750	$24,000	$701,000	$23,000	

Record Sale: $2,500,000, SPB, 10/25/79, "The Icebergs" 64 × 112 in.

LEMUEL MAYNARD WILES
(1826-1905)

Scene at Silver Lake, 11½ x 19½ in., signed l.l. Courtesy of Perry Public Library, New Jersey.

The many Western landscapes painted by Lemuel Maynard Wiles resulted from a large collection of color studies he accumulated during his 1873 and 1874 travels in California and Colorado, by way of Panama. His sketches of the old mission churches and cathedrals of the West are valuable records.

In addition to his successful work as a landscape painter in the tradition of the Hudson River School, Wiles enjoyed a long career as a respected teacher. No doubt his example motivated his only son, Irving, to become a renowned portrait painter. The rewarding relationship between father and son contributed greatly to their individual careers.

Lemuel Maynard Wiles was born in 1826 in Perry, New York, a town in the Mohawk Valley. After graduating from the New York State Normal School in 1847, he went on to study art for three years under William S. Hart in Albany, New York, where he also taught art at Albany Academy, and under Jasper F. Cropsey in New York City.

He concentrated mainly on painting from 1850 to 1857, then taught art in the Utica public schools. Irving was born seven years after his marriage to Rachel Ramsey in 1854.

The family moved to New York City in 1861, and by 1864 he had his own art studio on Washington Square, in the building occupied by painter-inventor Samuel F.B. Morse. Wiles later shared the studio with his son.

Wiles was director of the College of Fine Arts at Ingham University at LeRoy, New York from 1876 to 1888, and was responsible for organizing the art department at Peabody College in Nashville, Tennessee in 1893. He also founded the Silver Lake Art School in Ingham, near Perry, New York. He and his son conducted summer classes in the late 1890s and early 1900s at Peconic, Long Island.

Pikes Peak in Colorado and San Juan Capistrano and Yosemite in California were the subjects of some of Wiles's Western landscapes. He also traveled widely in Europe.

A double portrait of Lemuel and Rachel Wiles, painted by their son, won medals in 1893, 1900 and 1901. Lemuel Wiles died in New York City in 1905.

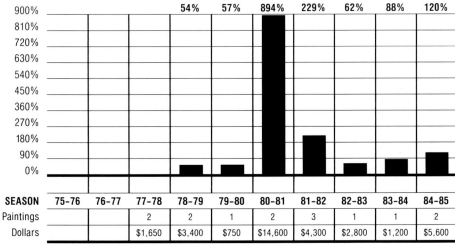

10-Year Average Change From Base Years '77-'78: 188%

	75-76	76-77	77-78	78-79	79-80	80-81	81-82	82-83	83-84	84-85
				54%	57%	894%	229%	62%	88%	120%
SEASON	75-76	76-77	77-78	78-79	79-80	80-81	81-82	82-83	83-84	84-85
Paintings			2	2	1	2	3	1	1	2
Dollars			$1,650	$3,400	$750	$14,600	$4,300	$2,800	$1,200	$5,600

Record Sale: $12,000, B.P, 11/22/80, "Hudson River, New York," 15 x 20 in.

217

JOHN BUNYAN BRISTOL

(1826-1909)

Long Island, 1868, signed l.r. Photograph courtesy of M. Knoedler & Co., Inc., New York, New York.

John Bunyan Bristol compares well with his contemporaries in refined, naturalistic landscape art. With little formal instruction, Bristol produced a consistently high quality of work, focusing on the mountains and lakes of New England and other Northern regions of the United States. He painted scenes in the Berkshire Mountains, along the New Jersey coast, around Lake George and Lake Champlain and in many other areas.

Bristol's compositions typically combine land and water views, displaying a luminous quality not unlike the earlier work of Kensett and Durand, with whom Bristol has been compared. Tuckerman's *Book of the Artist* describes Bristol as a "modest and assiduous" artist. He was, like other landscape artists of his era, highly accurate in detail.

Born in Hillsdale, New York, Bristol took a four-week course of instruction from portrait painter Henry Ary, but otherwise he taught himself from nature. He traveled widely along the Eastern seaboard gathering material, and in 1859 went to Florida, producing several semi-tropical paintings of the St. John's River and St. Augustine. In 1892, he married and settled in New York City, spending his summers in New England and other Northern states.

MEMBERSHIPS
National Academy of Design

PUBLIC COLLECTIONS
Peabody Institute, Baltimore

SEASON	75-76	76-77	77-78	78-79	79-80	80-81	81-82	82-83	83-84	84-85
Paintings					1	4	4	5	8	6
Dollars					$1,500	$7,350	$7,900	$7,990	$15,730	$7,350

Record Sale: $4,200, CH, 1/23/84, "Duck Hunting," 24 × 44 in.

JOHN W. EHNINGER
(1827-1889)

October, 1867, 43¼ x 54⅛ in., signed l.r. Courtesy of National Museum of American Art, Smithsonian Institution, Museum Purchase.

John Ehninger was a mid-nineteenth-century genre painter and illustrator best known for his paintings of familiar American folkloric themes, and for illustrations of literary works by Washington Irving and Henry Wadsworth Longfellow. In addition, he is known to have produced a number of landscapes, portraits and historical paintings.

John Ehninger was born in New York City, the only son of an old Dutch family. After graduating from Columbia College in 1847, he traveled to Europe, where he studied under Sohn and Lessing at the Dusseldorf Academy and with Couture in Paris. Although the exact chronology of Ehninger's studies is unclear, he seems to have studied in Europe until at least 1853, and is said to have returned there several times in his later career.

In the academies of Europe, Ehninger and other genre painters of his generation learned to paint scenes realistic in detail, but literary, historical or sentimental in conception. Ehninger's own paintings, though finely executed, were highly sentimental and embodied many popular subjects: examples are *Yankee Peddler* (1853, Newark Museum), *Old Kentucky Home* (1863, Shelburne Museum), and *The Turkey Shoot* (1879, Museum of Fine Arts, Boston).

Ehninger was elected an associate of the National Academy of Design in 1854, and a full academician in 1859. During the 1850s and 1860s, he exhibited regularly at many private Eastern galleries, as well as at the National Academy.

He published his first illustrations in the early 1850s, for an edition of the stories of Washington Irving. In 1859, Ehninger introduced a new method of photographic printmaking, the cliche verre, to the United States, in a published portfolio that included his own paintings, as well as the work of his contemporaries Durand, Kensett, Leutze and Eastman Johnson.

Ehninger spent his later career in Saratoga Springs, New York, where he and his wife were active in nonprofessional theater. The artist died in Saratoga Springs in 1889.

MEMBERSHIPS
National Academy of Design

PUBLIC COLLECTIONS
Museum of Fine Arts, Boston
Newark Museum, New Jersey
National Collection of Fine Art,
   Washington, D.C.
Shelburne Museum, Vermont

SEASON	75-76	76-77	77-78	78-79	79-80	80-81	81-82	82-83	83-84	84-85
Paintings								1		
Dollars								$13,000		

Record Sale: $13,000, SPB, 10/22/82, "Fife and Drum," 14 × 12 in.

JOSEPH RUSLING MEEKER
(1827-1889)

Joseph Rusling Meeker was a landscape painter and portraitist trained in the tradition of the Hudson River School. However, he chose to spend most of his life in the West and South, seeking out-of-the-way and unusual scenes to paint.

He is best known for his landscapes of the swamps and bayous of Louisiana. He was particularly interested in the visual effect of bright sunlight filtered through dense swamp foliage and reflected on dark, still water.

Meeker was born in Newark, New Jersey in 1827. While a student at the National Academy of Design, he was influenced by landscapist Asher Durand, one of his teachers. He also studied portrait painting under Charles Loring Elliott.

He painted for several years in Buffalo, New York and then worked in Louisville, Kentucky from 1852 to 1859. He was living and painting in St. Louis when the Civil War broke out in 1861. Soon after, he joined the Union Navy to serve as paymaster aboard a gunboat on the Mississippi. It was then that he came to know the entire length of the lower river, its tributaries and the swamps and bayous of Louisiana. He was fascinated by the dank, mysterious atmosphere of these wetlands and spent as much time as possible sketching them.

Meeker returned to St. Louis after the war and painted much of his best work at his studio there. He made periodic trips back to Louisiana, however, to refresh his memory of the pale light and eerie stillness of the bayous. Nearly all of his paintings of them were done between 1871 and 1879.

Meeker also traveled north along the Mississippi and Ohio Rivers and around the Great Lakes. He painted a number of portraits of Indian chiefs along the way. When not traveling, he continued to make his home in St. Louis until his death in 1889.

Near the Atchafalaya, 1878, 27 x 22 in., signed l.r. Courtesy of Vose Galleries of Boston, Inc., Massachusetts.

MEMBERSHIPS
St. Louis Art Society
St. Louis Sketch Club

PUBLIC COLLECTIONS
St. Louis Art Museum
Tulane University Library, New Orleans

SEASON	75-76	76-77	77-78	78-79	79-80	80-81	81-82	82-83	83-84	84-85
Paintings					3		3			3
Dollars					$8,400		$14,800			$9,900

Record Sale: $7,500, SPB, 1/31/85, "Swamp Landscape," 21 × 30 in.

FRANCIS BLACKWELL MAYER
(1827-1899)

During his life, Francis Blackwell Mayer established his reputation as a painter of colonial subjects. Today, however, the artist is better known for his renderings of the Plains Indians—watercolors and drawings valued more for their ethnological significance than for their artistic merit.

Mayer was born in 1827 in Baltimore, and studied there under Alfred Miller. In 1851, he traveled to the Minnesota Territory, observing and sketching the Sioux Indians. Artistically promising but technically uncertain, these sketches—along with Mayer's diary notes—were later reproduced in his book, *With Pen and Pencil on the Frontier in 1851,* published in 1932. One of the Minnesota paintings, *Treaty of Traverse des Sioux* (1851, Minnesota Historical Society) would later serve as valuable source material for artist Francis D. Millet.

Seemingly unaffected by the Civil War, Mayer spent the years from 1863 to 1870 abroad, studying with Charles Gleyre and Gustav Brion in Paris.

Returning to Annapolis, Maryland, where he lived until his death in 1899, Mayer painted landscapes and colonial genre scenes depicting daily activities.

Typical of much Civil War-period genre painting, many of Mayer's scenes are humorously anecdotal or vaguely moral. In his *Leisure and Labor* (1859, Corcoran Gallery of Art), Mayer juxtaposes the leisure and working classes in a setting which stresses their mutual dependence.

Independence (Squire Jack Porter), 1858, 12 x 15⅞ in., signed l.r. Courtesy of National Museum of American Art, Smithsonian Institution, Harriet Lane Johnston Collection.

PUBLIC COLLECTIONS
Cincinnati Art Museum
Corcoran Gallery of Art,
　Washington, D.C.
Metropolitan Museum of Art,
　New York City
Minnesota Historical Society, St. Paul
Peabody Institute, Baltimore

SEASON	75-76	76-77	77-78	78-79	79-80	80-81	81-82	82-83	83-84	84-85
Paintings							1		2	
Dollars							$1,500		$26,700	

Record Sale: $26,000, CH, 6/1/84, "The Invasion," 16 × 13 in.

MARY JANE PEALE
(1827-1902)

Mary Jane Peale, a painter of portraits and still lifes, spent her entire life as a professional artist. It was a remarkable feat, as women of her era were not expected to work outside their homes. However, Peale grew up in a liberated home in which female Peales were encouraged to achieve.

She was born in New York City in 1827 where her father, Rubens Peale, managed one of the three museums established on the East coast by his father, artist-naturalist Charles Willson Peale.

As a young lady, she studied portraiture with her uncle, Rembrandt, and the famed Thomas Sully. She also was exposed to natural history and science in the Peale museums.

In later years, her still-life compositions would reflect this background. Her style has been called "botanic-derivative," and was practiced mainly by members of the Peale family in a continuous still-life tradition.

Female artists were then limited to painting ornamental objects, but Peale built a career as a portrait painter in New York City and later produced misty flower studies. These were exhibited at the Pennsylvania Academy of the Fine Arts with paintings by other Peale women. She was in Paris in the late 1860s, and enrolled at the Academy a decade later.

Peale eventually returned to the family farm in Pottsville, Pennsylvania, where her father had retired when his museum failed. The loving daughter taught her father how to paint (his poor eyesight had prevented an artistic career), and together they executed numerous still lifes.

She remained single and died in Pottsville in 1902.

Portrait of a Woman with a Yellow Hat, 1859, 27⅛ x 22⅛ in. Courtesy of The Peale Museum, Baltimore, Maryland.

PUBLIC COLLECTIONS
University of Pennsylvania, Philadelphia

SEASON	75-76	76-77	77-78	78-79	79-80	80-81	81-82	82-83	83-84	84-85
Paintings	2				2		2	1	1	1
Dollars	$1,900				$4,500		$3,000	$3,000	$8,000	$5,250

Record Sale: $8,000, P.NY, 10/13/83, "George and Martha Washington," 30 × 25 in.

DAVID JOHNSON
(1827-1908)

David Johnson was a successful landscape painter of the Hudson River School. His fine draftsmanship and rich colors portrayed picturesque scenes of upper New York State and New England.

He was born in New York City in 1827. Although he spent most of his professional life there, his frequent journeys to the Hudson River Valley (particularly the Fort Putnam and West Point areas) and New England inspired some of his best landscapes.

Johnson studied the great European landscape artists and had a few lessons from American landscapist Jasper F. Cropsey. He said that his greatest teacher, however, was nature, and his intense realism and richly-painted rocks and trees attest to this.

He first exhibited at the National Academy of Design and the American Art Union in 1849, and was made a member of the National Academy in 1861.

At the Centennial Exhibition in Philadelphia in 1876, Johnson exhibited *Scenery on the Housatonic* and *A Brook Study, Orange County, New York* (dates and locations unknown) and received an award. His *View of the Adroscoggin River, Maine* (1869-1870, Museum of Fine Arts, Houston) demonstrates his exceptional ability with detail and color.

His best work can be compared with that of John F. Kensett, but in later years Johnson's skills declined. Influenced by the barbizon style, his work became monotonous and less articulate.

Under the Oak and Beside the Brook, New York Country Scene, 21 x 17 in., signed l.l. Courtesy of Kennedy Galleries, New York, New York.

Johnson died in 1908 at Walden, New York. His landscapes and several fine still lifes are not well known, but his work is beginning to find new attention and appreciation.

MEMBERSHIPS
Artists' Fund Society
National Academy of Design

PUBLIC COLLECTIONS
Museum of Fine Arts, Houston, Texas

10-Year Average Change From Base Years '75-'76: 67%

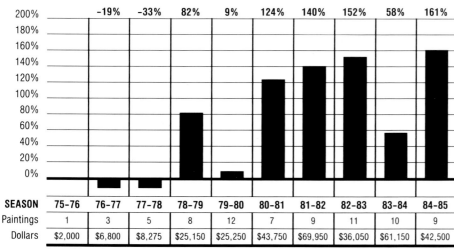

SEASON	75-76	76-77	77-78	78-79	79-80	80-81	81-82	82-83	83-84	84-85
		-19%	-33%	82%	9%	124%	140%	152%	58%	161%
Paintings	1	3	5	8	12	7	9	11	10	9
Dollars	$2,000	$6,800	$8,275	$25,150	$25,250	$43,750	$69,950	$36,050	$61,150	$42,500

Record Sale: $29,000, SPB, 5/30/84, "Eagle Cliff, Franconia Notch, New Hampshire," 27 x 46 in.

CHARLES WIMAR
(1828-1861)

German-born Charles Wimar, in his short career, was among the first group of artists to specialize in American Indian life.

Wimar died young, at 34. He left behind about 50 identified works (17 of them made abroad), including one watercolor and four sketchbooks.

His chief legacy was the Western Academy of Art, which he founded in 1860. It was St. Louis, Missouri's first art museum, and the first art institution west of the Mississippi.

Wimar had early difficulties with proportion and perspective. He worked in the tight linear style of his Dusseldorf training, using vivid color effects that verged on the lurid. His subjects often were manipulated into sentimental melodrama (perhaps in imitation of George Catlin). Improvements in some of his later works indicate these shortcomings might have been overcome had he lived longer.

Wimar's best work is *Indians Approaching Fort Union* (1859, Washington University). It is sure in execution, and impressive in its unified design, fine panoramic sense and luminosity of color.

Born in 1828 at Siegburg, Germany, the artist was christened Karl (or Carl) Ferdinand Wimar. In 1843, he came to St. Louis, then a frontier fur-trading town.

During his apprenticeship to Leon de Pomarede from 1846 to 1850, Wimar accompanied the artist up to the Mississippi to St. Anthony Falls, Minnesota, to prepare a proposed panoramic series that never materialized.

From 1852 to 1856, Wimar studied in Dusseldorf, Germany with Emmanuel Leutze and Josef Fay. Of the Western paintings Wimar sent back for American sales, only 12 have been located.

After his return to St. Louis, Wimar went on several rugged journeys—up the Missouri River several times and, in

Flatboatmen on the Mississippi, 1854, 19¼ x 23⅝ in., signed l.r. Courtesy of Amon Carter Museum, Fort Worth, Texas.

1858, 300 miles up the Yellowstone River. His sketchbooks from these trips have a documentary value which is lost in the dramatics of his finished paintings.

Wimar's work was popular, and he exhibited at the annual St. Louis exhibitions. In 1861, he married, and was commissioned to decorate the interior dome of the old St. Louis courthouse. He died of tuberculosis within a year. The courthouse paintings are largely gone, destroyed by deterioration, poor maintenance and inadequacies in the artist's technical skills.

MEMBERSHIPS
Western Academy of Art

PUBLIC COLLECTIONS
Missouri Historical Society, St. Louis
Peabody Museum, Harvard University, Boston
St. Louis County Courthouse, Missouri
University of Michigan Museum, Ann Arbor
Washington University, Gallery of Art, St. Louis

SEASON	75-76	76-77	77-78	78-79	79-80	80-81	81-82	82-83	83-84	84-85
Paintings	2					1			1	
Dollars	$16,100					$12,000			$1,700	

Record Sale: $14,000, SB, 5/11/76, "Funeral Raft of Dead Chieftain," 11 × 16 in.

JERVIS McENTEE
(1828-1891)

Roman Compagna. Courtesy of Henry B. Holt, Inc., Essex Fells, New Jersey.

Landscape painter Jervis McEntee was born in Rondout, New York in the Hudson Valley, in 1828; he died in 1891, in the same community. The nearby Catskill Mountains were reflected in his paintings of rural New York State.

His artistic career was influenced by a friend, Henry Pickering, and by artist Frederic E. Church. Pickering was a cultured man and a poet, who boarded with the McEntee family and spent considerable time with young Jervis. At age 22, McEntee went to New York City; he studied with Church during the winter of 1850.

McEntee married a minister's daughter in 1854 and tried his hand unsuccessfully at business in Rondout, before returning to art as a profession. In 1858, he opened a studio in New York City. Spending winters in the city, he returned in the summers to river-valley and mountain locations, his prime subjects.

At the beginning of the Civil War, McEntee enlisted in the Union Army. In 1868, he toured Europe with artist Sanford R. Gifford.

McEntee's landscapes are characterized by the colors of autumn and winter. He usually painted small views rather than wide panoramas. They are simple, naturalistic and detailed, and critics have noted the presence of a melancholy mood, perhaps even a feeling of desolation.

He added an unusual touch to his painting *The Melancholy Days Have Come* (1861, National Academy of Design), by attaching part of "The Death of the Flowers," a poem by William Cullen Bryant which complemented the painting. *Melancholy Days* enlarged McEntee's reputation. Another notable painting was *Eastern Sky at Sunset* (date unknown, Corcoran Art Gallery).

Elected an associate member of the National Academy in 1860, McEntee became a full member in 1861. He died in 1891.

MEMBERSHIPS
National Academy of Design

PUBLIC COLLECTIONS
Corcoran Art Gallery, Washington, D.C.
National Academy of Design, New York City
Peabody Institute, Baltimore

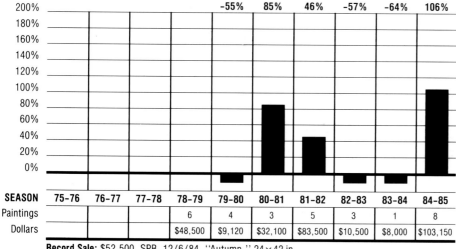

10-Year Average Change From Base Years '78-'79: 9%

				-55%	85%	46%	-57%	-64%	106%

SEASON	75-76	76-77	77-78	78-79	79-80	80-81	81-82	82-83	83-84	84-85
Paintings				6	4	3	5	3	1	8
Dollars				$48,500	$9,120	$32,100	$83,500	$10,500	$8,000	$103,150

Record Sale: $52,500, SPB, 12/6/84, "Autumn," 24 × 42 in.

JOHN RASMUSSEN

(1828-1895)

John Rasmussen was one of three American folk artists who, as a result of their association with the Berks County Almshouse in Shillington, Pennsylvania, have come to be known as the Pennsylvania Almshouse Painters. Although virtually unknown in their time, their work has been preserved in a small number of private and public collections.

Rasmussen was a German immigrant who came to the United States around 1865. He was listed in Reading, Pennsylvania directories as a painter by occupation, but his only known works were painted after his committal to the Berks County Almshouse in 1879. There, Rasmussen joined another German immigrant, Charles Hofmann, a drunkard and vagrant who painted large landscapes of the grounds of the Berks County, Montgomery County and Schuylkill County almshouses. Between 1865 and his death in 1882, Hofmann had gained a few local patrons for his accurate and sunny portrayals of the almshouses and their surroundings.

After his committal to the Berks County Almshouse, Rasmussen imitated Hofmann's example, and began painting views of the almshouse grounds. Although his works are distinct in execution from Hofmann's, Rasmussen adopted Hofmann's chosen media (oils on tin), painted some of the same views, and even obtained the support of some of Hofmann's patrons, before his death in 1895.

Hofmann and Rasmussen were followed in 1892 by another German pauper, Louis Mader, who painted a number of the almshouse views originated by Hofmann. The work of all three painters was the subject of a retrospective in 1968, sponsored by the Abby Aldrich Rockefeller Folk Art Collection of Williamsburg, Virginia.

Berks County Almshouse, ca. 1880-1881, 31 x 39 in. Courtesy of Abby Aldrich Rockefeller Folk Art Center, Williamsburg, Virginia.

PUBLIC COLLECTIONS
Abby Aldrich Rockefeller Folk Art Collection, Williamsburg, Virginia
Reading Public Museum and Art Gallery, Pennsylvania

SEASON	75-76	76-77	77-78	78-79	79-80	80-81	81-82	82-83	83-84	84-85
Paintings							1			
Dollars							$38,000			

Record Sale: $38,000, CH, 6/3/82, "Surroundings of Berks County Almshouse," 31 × 38 in.

226

JOHN O'BRIEN INMAN
(1828-1896)

Portraitist and genre painter John O'Brien Inman was the son of painter Henry Inman. Although his reputation has been overshadowed by that of his father, the younger Inman had a successful artistic career.

Born in 1828 in New York City, Inman studied under his father, who painted landscapes and miniatures, as well as portraits and genre scenes. By 1853, the younger Inman was exhibiting at the National Academy of Design. In his youth, he worked as a portrait painter in the South and West; later he moved his studio to New York City, where he specialized in small genre pieces and flower paintings.

Inman was elected an associate of the National Academy of Design in 1865. The following year, he moved to Europe and opened a studio in Rome. He remained abroad until 1878, when he returned for a while to New York. While in Europe, he executed a number of sentimental genre scenes with local settings. He died in Fordham, New York, in 1896.

Inman's work is admired for its technical skill and, in the case of his later works, for its reflection of European influences. One of his best-known works is *Moonlight Skating—Central Park, the Lake and Terrace* (ca. 1878, Museum of the City of New York). Discovered in the early 1940s, the painting was hailed for its treatment of the night scene and for the accomplished and lively figures, each

Basket of Flowers, 1865, 12¾ x 18 in., signed l.r. Photograph Courtesy of Kennedy Galleries, New York, New York.

A Glass of Port, 9¾ x 7½ in., signed l.l. Courtesy of Vose Galleries of Boston, Inc., Boston, Massachusetts.

executed with characteristic detail. Two small oils—*A Pet* (1862, location unknown) and *A Flower Necklace* (1869, location unknown) demonstrate Inman's skill in genre painting.

MEMBERSHIPS
National Academy of Design

PUBLIC COLLECTIONS
Museum of the City of New York
National Museum of American Art, Washington, D.C.
New-York Historical Society, New York City

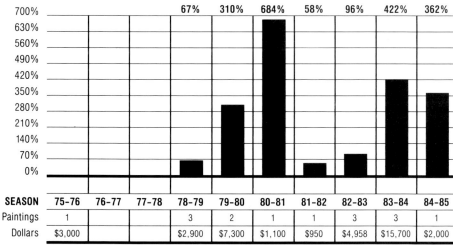

10-Year Average Change From Base Years '75-'76: 250%

| | | | 67% | 310% | 684% | 58% | 96% | 422% | 362% |

SEASON	75-76	76-77	77-78	78-79	79-80	80-81	81-82	82-83	83-84	84-85
Paintings	1			3	2	1	1	3	3	1
Dollars	$3,000			$2,900	$7,300	$1,100	$950	$4,958	$15,700	$2,000

Record Sale: $10,000, SPB, 12/8/83, "Fishermen Near Beached Boats," 9 × 12 in.

WILLIAM MASON BROWN

(1828-1898)

A landscape painter in his early career, William Mason Brown gained wide popularity for his later meticulously detailed still lifes.

Born in 1828 in Troy, New York, Brown studied with the leading portraitist there, Abel Buel Moore. In 1850, Brown moved to Newark, New Jersey, where he began to paint landscapes. In 1858, he moved to Brooklyn.

Brown's landscapes at that time were in the flowing style of romanticism, looking back to the work of Thomas Cole. His abrupt turn in the early 1860s to painting still lifes is attributed to his sale of *A Basket of Peaches Upset* for $2,000 to New York City dealer William Schaus.

The work reflects radical changes in the artist's approach and technique, substituting for the broad brushwork of the landscapes a meticulous, near-photographic effect.

The precision of this photographic style was exceptionally well suited to the new printing process of chromolithography, and it may be that the artist adapted his technique to fit the limitations of the process. His work was lithographed by Currier & Ives, and the widely distributed reproductions enhanced Brown's reputation as one of the leading mid-nineteenth-century painters in this exacting mode.

Brown's *Raspberries* (1873, location unknown) was chosen as representative of the best American still-life painting by Governor Horace Fairbanks of Vermont for the new St. Johnsbury Athenaeum and Art Gallery.

Still Life with Peaches, 20 x 15 in., signed l.l. Courtesy of Henry B. Holt, Inc., Essex Fells, New Jersey.

Brown, who followed the acute study of nature advised by English critic John Ruskin, often painted his still-life fruits and flowers in natural settings, placed in carefully "artless" arrangements. The artistic appeal of Brown's botanical still lifes is in the glowing textural clarity and compelling, almost surreal, opulence of the colors.

Brown's work continued in demand, and he exhibited at the National Academy of Design in New York City annually from 1859 to 1890. He died in 1898 in Brooklyn.

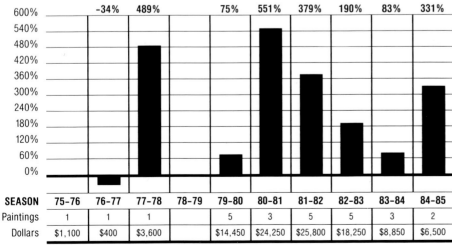

10-Year Average Change From Base Years '75-'76: 229%

		-34%	489%		75%	551%	379%	190%	83%	331%
SEASON	75-76	76-77	77-78	78-79	79-80	80-81	81-82	82-83	83-84	84-85
Paintings	1	1	1		5	3	5	5	3	2
Dollars	$1,100	$400	$3,600		$14,450	$24,250	$25,800	$18,250	$8,850	$6,500

Record Sale: $16,000, CH, 12/5/80, "Still Life," 22 × 18 in.

PUBLIC COLLECTIONS
Peabody Institute, Baltimore
Pennsylvania Academy of the Fine Arts, Philadelphia
J.B. Speed Art Museum, Louisville, Kentucky

EDWARD M. BANNISTER
(1828-1901)

Edward Bannister was a black artist who achieved a lofty standing in New England society. He was a deeply religious man with a strong sense of social purpose; he transferred his beliefs into his landscapes throughout a prolific, if somewhat sketchy, career.

Bannister was born in St. Andrews, New Brunswick, and lost both his parents by the time he was 16. He and his older brother were taken in by Harris Hutch, who introduced Bannister to the classics in literature, music and art. He drew often during these years, doodling with charcoal and crayon at every opportunity.

Bannister moved to Boston in 1848, probably after spending some time at sea, working his way along the Eastern seaboard. He eventually achieved skill as a barber, which enabled him to enjoy a higher status than many of Boston's blacks.

During the 1850s, he was a member of the Crispus Attucks Choir and the Histrionics Club, a black drama group. He met and married Christiana Carteaux, who operated several fashionable hair salons frequented by Boston's elite.

Although accounts are unclear, Bannister was able to establish his artistic credentials, thanks in large measure to the financial freedom offered by his wife's prosperous business. He attended the Lowell Institute evening division, one of the few blacks able to do so.

Seaweed Gatherers, ca. 1898, 24 x 19⅞ in., signed l.r. Courtesy of National Museum of American Art, Smithsonian Institution, Gift of H. Alan and Melvin Frank.

Little of his work during this period has survived. One painting, *Dorchester, Massachusetts* (1856, National Museum of American Art), however, shows his weakness in spatial relations at this stage. In spite of this flaw, he managed to capture much of the town's quaintness.

In 1870, the Bannisters moved to Providence, Rhode Island. The city was home to a growing number of pastoral-landscape artists influenced by the French barbizon style, and in this atmosphere Bannister matured and flourished. Like painters of the French school, he saw the rural landscape as an affirmation of harmony and spirituality. Unlike them, however, he did not react strongly to industrialized society.

Despite his failing health and the public's declining interest in his work, Bannister continued to be productive up to his death in 1901. The National Museum of American Art has uncovered 27 paintings dating from the 1890s.

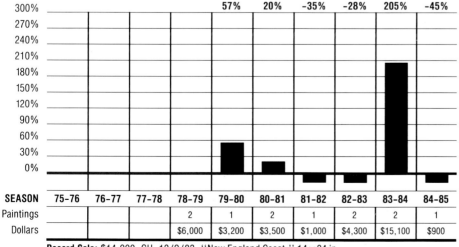

10-Year Average Change From Base Years '78-'79: 25%

			57%	20%	-35%	-28%	205%	-45%

SEASON	75-76	76-77	77-78	78-79	79-80	80-81	81-82	82-83	83-84	84-85
Paintings				2	1	2	1	2	2	1
Dollars				$6,000	$3,200	$3,500	$1,000	$4,300	$15,100	$900

Record Sale: $14,000, CH, 12/9/83, "New England Coast," 14 x 24 in.

MEMBERSHIPS
Providence Art Club

PUBLIC COLLECTIONS
Frederick Douglass Institute, Washington, D.C.
National Museum of American Art, Washington, D.C.
Rhode Island School of Design, Providence

JAMES McDOUGAL HART
(1828-1901)

A leading landscape painter of the second generation of the Hudson River School, James McDougal Hart was born in 1828 in Kilmarnock, Scotland. His family emigrated to Albany, New York in 1831. There, at age 15, he was apprenticed to a sign painter. Following the example of his older brother, William M. Hart, he decided to become an artist.

In 1851, Hart traveled to Dusseldorf, where he studied with Schirmer, a leading landscape painter. Schirmer's calmly ordered hills and valleys provided a life-long model for Hart's work.

Hart returned to the United States in 1852 and moved to New York City. In 1853, he went back to Albany. Finally, in 1857, he settled permanently in New York City. His work was frequently exhibited in the chief galleries of New York City, Philadelphia, Boston and Baltimore.

His gently colored compositions were praised for their accurate drawing and their emphasis on the "poetry of nature." As the artist commented, "I strive to reproduce the feeling produced by the original scenes themselves. . . . "

Hart often portrayed cattle standing in rivers, as did his brother, William. However, during the 1840s and 1850s, he painted a number of large panoramic landscapes, idyllic scenes peopled with schoolchildren and farmers depicted in

Summer, 36 x 70 in., signed l.r. Courtesy of Vose Galleries of Boston, Inc., Massachusetts.

Pastoral Landscape, 1884, 28 x 40 in., signed l.r. Courtesy of Henry B. Holt, Inc., Essex Fells, New Jersey.

meticulous detail. These luminous scenes glorified the conception of America as a rural Eden.

Later, during the 1860s, the artist painted several impressive landscapes depicting specific topography and capturing a quality of real light evocative of barbizon artist Constant Troyon. In the 1870s and later, the Adirondack Mountains were a favorite setting for his paintings.

In 1866, the artist married painter Marie Theresa Gorsuch. Their son, William Gorsuch Hart, also became a painter. In addition to William and James Hart, the Hart family produced another painter, the artists' sister, Julie Hart Beers Kempson, who was one of the few female professional landscape painters of her time.

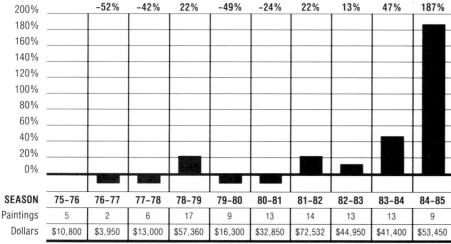

10-Year Average Change From Base Years '75-'76: 12%

	75-76	76-77	77-78	78-79	79-80	80-81	81-82	82-83	83-84	84-85
		-52%	-42%	22%	-49%	-24%	22%	13%	47%	187%
SEASON	75-76	76-77	77-78	78-79	79-80	80-81	81-82	82-83	83-84	84-85
Paintings	5	2	6	17	9	13	14	13	13	9
Dollars	$10,800	$3,950	$13,000	$57,360	$16,300	$32,850	$72,532	$44,950	$41,400	$53,450

Record Sale: $24,000, SPB, 4/20/79, "Winter on the Hudson," 34 × 71 in.

MEMBERSHIPS
National Academy of Design

PUBLIC COLLECTIONS
Brooklyn Museum
Corcoran Art Gallery, Washington, D.C.
Metropolitan Museum of Art, New York City
New York State Historical Association, Cooperstown
Vassar College

BENJAMIN FRANKLIN REINHART
(1829-1885)

Benjamin Franklin Reinhart was born near Waynesburg, Pennsylvania in 1829. He showed his artistic talent at an early age: by age 15 he was studying painting in Pittsburgh, and by age 18 he was in New York City at the National Academy of Design.

Between 1847 and 1848, Reinhart began to travel to find subject matter for his paintings. He visited parts of the Midwest, including Ohio, where he lived briefly.

By 1850, his growing interest in historical painting prompted Reinhart to study the fundamentals of that genre in Rome, Dusseldorf and Paris, before returning to New York City in 1853. Although he set up a permanent studio there, his frequent trips to the Midwest and South provided the scenery for some of his historical and landscape paintings. *The Emigrant Train Bedding Down for the Night* (1867, Corcoran Gallery), depicting a small wagon train settling into a prairie camp, could have been painted from studies made during these trips. In 1859, his travels South led him to establish a studio in New Orleans.

In 1861, Reinhart went to England, where he had success as a portrait artist. He stayed there for seven years, painting the likenesses of such people as Tennyson and Carlyle, as well as British nobility.

He returned to New York City in 1868, set up a studio, and spent most of the remainder of his life there. He died in Philadelphia in 1885.

MEMBERSHIPS
National Academy of Design

PUBLIC COLLECTIONS
Corcoran Gallery of Art, Washington, D.C.

Johnston, Joseph Eggleston, 11¾ x 9¾ in., signed l.l. Courtesy of National Portrait Gallery, Washington, D.C.

SEASON	75-76	76-77	77-78	78-79	79-80	80-81	81-82	82-83	83-84	84-85
Paintings								1	1	1
Dollars								$13,000	$6,500	$550

Record Sale: $13,000, SPB, 10/22/82, "The Chase," 16 × 20 in.

WILLIAM (KARL WILHELM) HAHN
(1829-1887)

William Hahn was an important California landscape and genre painter of the 1870s and 1880s. His work received new attention following its inclusion in the Metropolitan Museum of Art's 1939 "Life in America" exhibition.

Hahn was born in Ebersbach, Saxony, Germany in 1829. At 14, he was a pupil of Julius Huebner at the Royal Academy in Dresden. He also studied art in Dusseldorf, Paris and Naples. It is not known for certain when he emigrated to the United States, but by 1871 he was in New York City, exhibiting at the National Academy of Design.

For a short time in 1872, Hahn worked with William Keith in Boston. He then took a studio in San Francisco's Mercantile Library Building, where he was one of a group of painters that included Keith, Virgil Williams and Thomas Hill.

Hahn's paintings—which were well received by the public and by his fellow artists and sold well during his lifetime—were of two sorts: scenic landscapes and genre paintings.

Hahn made sketching trips to the Lake Tahoe area, Yosemite, the High Sierras, the Napa Valley, the redwood forests and the old Spanish settlements in California. His sketches led to paintings such as *Yosemite Valley from Gla-*

Game for Camp, 1882, 24 x 16¼ in., signed l.r. Courtesy of John H. Garzoli Gallery, San Francisco, California.

cier Point (1874, location unknown), which shows tourists admiring a spectacular view. He depicted the still-wild side of Western outdoor life, as in *Mexican Cattle Drivers* (1881, Kennedy Galleries) and *Return from the Bear Hunt* (1882, Oakland Museum).

Even better known than his landscapes, however, were Hahn's genre paintings, which portrayed detailed scenes of everyday California life. Typical are *Learning the Lesson (Children Playing School)* (1881, Oakland Museum) and *A Day at the Seashore* (date unknown, Kennedy Galleries). In 1873, Hahn's oil painting of the San Francisco market sold for $2,500.

Hahn exhibited at the San Francisco Art Association and the Graphics Sketching Club; he also gave art lessons. He worked in New York City in 1878, but returned to San Francisco. He died in 1887 in Dresden, where he had gone in the course of a long visit to Europe.

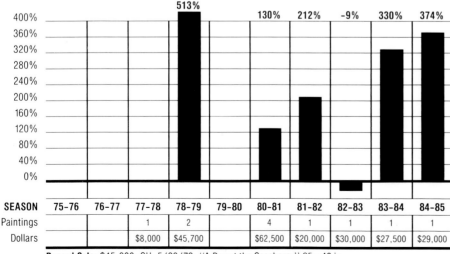

10-Year Average Change From Base Years '77-'78: 221%

				513%		130%	212%	-9%	330%	374%

SEASON	75-76	76-77	77-78	78-79	79-80	80-81	81-82	82-83	83-84	84-85
Paintings			1	2		4	1	1	1	1
Dollars			$8,000	$45,700		$62,500	$20,000	$30,000	$27,500	$29,000

Record Sale: $45,000, CH, 5/23/79, "A Day at the Seashore," 25 × 40 in.

PUBLIC COLLECTIONS
Dresden Museum
Hudson River Museum, Yonkers, New York
Oakland Museum
San Francisco Museum of Fine Art

WALTER GOULD
(1829-1893)

Although Walter Gould was born in Philadelphia in 1829, the artist's most notable portrait and genre paintings are oriental in character, reflecting the 44 years in which he lived abroad.

Gould studied drawing and painting in his native city under John Rubens Smith and Thomas Sully. When he was 14, his work was exhibited at Philadelphia's Artists' Fund Society, where he was later granted membership. Almost all of Gould's early portraits—painted in Pennsylvania and Virginia—were destroyed during the Civil War.

In 1849, Gould moved to Italy. With the exception of brief studies in Paris and travels in Asia, he lived there the remainder of his life.

Eastern travels inspired most of his work. While in Asia Minor in 1851, the artist painted portaits of Kossuth, the imprisoned governor of Hungary, and his friends and political followers. Later in Constantinople, his portrait subjects included the Grand Vizier, Richid Pasha and English ambassador Sir Strafford Canning.

In addition to his portraits, Gould also painted oriental-style genre scenes.

Gould died in Florence in 1893.

MEMBERSHIPS
Artists' Fund Society, Philadelphia

Louis Kossuth, 185í, 31 x 25¼ in., signed verso. Courtesy of The Historical Society of Pennsylvania, Philadelphia.

SEASON	75-76	76-77	77-78	78-79	79-80	80-81	81-82	82-83	83-84	84-85
Paintings						1				
Dollars						$15,000				

Record Sale: $15,000, SPB, 6/19/81, "Islamic Scene," 36 × 30 in.

EDWARD MORAN
(1829-1901)

Edward Moran was an English-born marine painter known for his Turneresque seascapes and paintings of American history.

Moran was born at Bolton-le Moor, Lancashire, one of four brothers who became artists. When he was 15, Moran emigrated to the United States with his family, to settle in Maryland. Originally trained as a weaver, Moran turned from that trade to study painting with Paul Weber and marine painter James Hamilton in Philadelphia. By 1857 he was an established artist, along with his younger brother, Thomas.

Moran was encouraged to paint marine subjects by Hamilton. These included fishermen at work, seascapes, vessels, and a series of scenes from American maritime history. The marine paintings are dramatically conceived, with brilliant sunsets and vibrant blue-green seas, recalling the glowing color of Joseph M.W. Turner. In one of his paintings, Moran placed the Statue of Liberty as a symbol on the horizon, silhouetted against a glowing sunset, with a wide expanse of New York Harbor spread out beneath the sky.

In 1861, Moran visited England for six months with his brother, Thomas. They came under the influence of Turner's work, which was on display in London. Moran moved to New York City in 1871 where he opened a studio and spent the rest of his life.

A visit to France in 1878 interested

Early Dawn, N.Y. Harbor, ca. 1860, 14 x 22 in., signed l.r. Courtesy of Wunderlich and Company, Inc., New York, New York.

Fishing Boats Beating Up to Windward, 1858, 29¾ x 45 in., signed l.l. Courtesy of National Museum of American Art, Smithsonian Institution, Bequest of Mabel Johnson Langhorne.

him in painting the figure, and after that date figures appear more prominently in his work than previously. The last 10 years of Moran's life were spent painting a series of 13 historical marine paintings.

MEMBERSHIPS
National Academy of Design
Pennsylvania American Federation of Arts

PUBLIC COLLECTIONS
Butler Institute of American Art,
  Youngstown, Ohio
Chrysler Museum, Norfolk, Virginia
Milwaukee Art Museum
Museum of the City of New York
National Museum of American Art, Washington, D.C.
United States Naval Academy Museum,
  Annapolis, Maryland

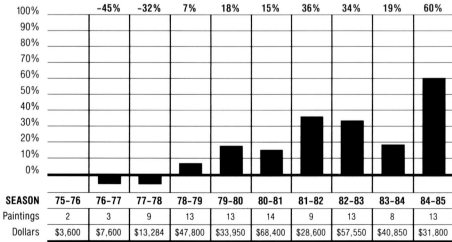

10-Year Average Change From Base Years '75–'76: 11%

	-45%	-32%	7%	18%	15%	36%	34%	19%	60%

SEASON	75-76	76-77	77-78	78-79	79-80	80-81	81-82	82-83	83-84	84-85
Paintings	2	3	9	13	13	14	9	13	8	13
Dollars	$3,600	$7,600	$13,284	$47,800	$33,950	$68,400	$28,600	$57,550	$40,850	$31,800

Record Sale: $26,000, CH, 5/23/79, "The Calm After the Storm," 40 x 63 in.

234

ROBERT SPEAR DUNNING
(1829-1905)

Robert Spear Dunning was a founder of the Fall River School, which emphasized still-life paintings. However, his influence reached well beyond the small industrial town of Fall River in Southeastern Massachusetts.

Born in 1829 in Brunswick, Maine, Dunning was brought to Fall River at age five and educated in the public schools. His first jobs were in the local cotton mills and, for three years, as a seaman on a ship that worked along the coast.

He became an art student of James Roberts in Maine, and then followed a well-trodden path to the National Academy of Design in New York City. At the Academy, he studied under Daniel Huntington, focusing on figure and portrait painting.

In 1852, he returned to Fall River, where he established a studio. He painted portraits and landscapes, but in 1865 his interest turned to still-life painting, which brought him notice and critical acclaim. Fruit was his best subject; local historians describe how he badgered the town's fruit-seller to save the most beautiful specimens for him.

Dunning's pictures were exhibited at the National Academy of Design from 1850 to 1880, and at the American Art Union in 1850, as well as the Boston Art Club and in local exhibitions.

Dunning searched for perfection in his paintings, which usually meant that he was slow to complete them. He once remarked that the first picture he finished on time was a commissioned copy of a Gilbert Stuart painting of George Washington. He was paid $1,000 for the copy, with money raised from the Washington Society of Fall River and by subscriptions. The painting is now in the Fall River library.

The Fall River Evening Drawing School, founded in 1870 by Dunning and his friend, John E. Grouard, was the predecessor of the now famous Fall River School. Students there included

Still Life, 1882, 29½ x 36 in., signed l.r. Courtesy of Vose Galleries of Boston, Inc., Massachusetts.

Bryant Chapin, Franklin H. Miller, Albert F. Monroe, Abbie Luella Zuill and Herbert Cash, all painters of still life. Dunning emphasized individuality in his teaching. He taught by example and insisted that students use the best materials available.

He died in 1905.

MEMBERSHIPS
National Academy of Design

PUBLIC COLLECTIONS
Public Library and Historical Society, Fall River, Massachusetts
Town Hall, Swansea, Massachusetts

SEASON	75-76	76-77	77-78	78-79	79-80	80-81	81-82	82-83	83-84	84-85
Paintings			1			2	1	2	3	2
Dollars			$750			$2,200	$7,000	$16,750	$65,900	$180,000

Record Sale: $170,000, D.NY, 10/24/84, "Cherries in Basket and Hat," 20 × 26 in.

THOMAS HILL
(1829-1908)

Thomas Hill specialized in paintings of spectacular Western mountain landscapes. Identified as a painter of the Rocky Mountains, he was often called "The Artist of Yosemite."

Though renowned for his huge paintings of the Yosemite Valley, Hill painted landscapes of all sizes, with Yellowstone National Park, Donner Lake, the Grand Canyon, and the Rocky and Sierra Mountains as other subjects. Hill was prolific: his speed and facility in turning out canvases astonished his colleagues.

Hill's famous heroic-sized landscapes, however mannered their magnificence, have stunning impact; reaction to them is seldom neutral. Critics have deplored what they see as formula studio-coloring, overbearing technique, and exaggerated artiness. Others commend the paintings for their grandeur, dignity and ability to inspire awe.

Hill was born in England in 1829. His family moved to Taunton, Massachusetts in 1841. He was apprenticed to a coach painter in Boston and later worked for decorators. During 1853, at the Philadelphia Academy of the Fine Arts, Hill studied portraiture and still-life painting and then successfully supported himself at both.

He moved to the West Coast in 1861, where he earned praise for his pictures, mostly portraits and figure-paintings. While he studied in Paris in 1866 and 1867, his teachers redirected him to landscape painting. However, his depic-

Half Dome and the Royal Arches, Yosemite, 30 x 46 in., signed l.r. Courtesy of John H. Garzoli Gallery, San Francisco, California.

Picnic, Mount Chocora, ca. 1872, 30 x 42½ in., signed l.r. Courtesy of John H. Garzoli Gallery, San Francisco, California.

tions of the White Mountains did not attract attention in Boston upon his return there. In 1870, Hill settled again in San Francisco, where success awaited.

He was active in the art community and helped set up the California School of Design, the first art school on the Coast. In later years, Hill moved to a studio in Yosemite, at Wawona. He was stricken by paralysis in 1898; his death by suicide occurred in 1908 at Raymond, near the Yosemite Valley.

Hill's most famous work is *The Driving of the Last Spike* (date unknown), a massive 8-by-11-foot painting depicting the completion of the Central-Pacific Railroad. It is owned by the State of California.

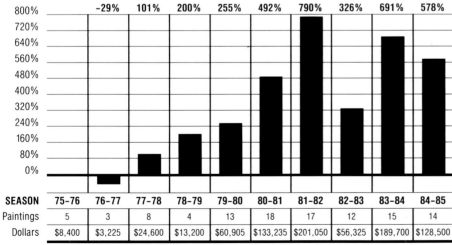

10-Year Average Change From Base Years '75-'76: 340%

	-29%	101%	200%	255%	492%	790%	326%	691%	578%
SEASON	75-76	76-77	77-78	78-79	79-80	80-81	81-82	82-83	83-84	84-85
Paintings	5	3	8	4	13	18	17	12	15	14
Dollars	$8,400	$3,225	$24,600	$13,200	$60,905	$133,235	$201,050	$56,325	$189,700	$128,500

Record Sale: $55,000, BB.SF, 10/3/81, "Summer Festivities by a Mountain Lake," 30 x 42 in.

MEMBERSHIPS
Boston Art Club
San Francisco Art Association

PUBLIC COLLECTIONS
Oakland Museum
University of Kansas Museum of Art

JOSEPH H. HIDLEY

(1830-1872)

Although virtually unrecognized during his lifetime, Joseph H. Hidley is now regarded as a sensitive painter of rural life in nineteenth-century America. A self-taught folk painter of townscapes, Hidley was born in 1830 in Greenbush, New York.

Hidley led a difficult and impoverished life. He was the only survivor of four children when his father died in 1834. He spent his childhood with various relatives in the small towns surrounding his birthplace, before settling in the town of Poestenkill, New York. He married in 1853 and had six children, but only three survived infancy.

Hidley made a meager income as a housepainter, carpenter, handyman, church sexton, taxidermist and artist. In addition to his townscapes and religious paintings, Hidley created wood carvings and decorative arrangements of dried flowers and stuffed birds.

Hidley's townscapes and rural landscapes reflect his intuitive understanding of paint, color and form. His work also reveals his desire to record changes in daily life over time.

His painting technique consisted of three stages. First, he applied a ground coat of light cream-colored paint to the panel, in order to unify and add brilliance to the overpainting. Secondly, he sketched the composition in pencil and painted over this with many layers of thin paint. Finally, he followed the natural contours of forms with short, controlled brushstrokes.

Hidley's most distinguished paintings are four views of Poestenkill on wood panels. The earliest of these is dated May 10, 1862, and is painted from a natural elevation. In the three later paintings, Hidley employed an imaginary aerial viewpoint in order to record as much as possible of the town.

After Hidley died of consumption in 1872, his paintings remained unknown outside the area of Poestenkill for

Poestenkill, NY: Winter, 1868, 18¾ x 25⅜ in. signed l.r. Courtesy of Abby Aldrich Rockefeller Folk Art Center, Williamsburg, Virginia.

almost 70 years. In 1941, they were introduced to the modern public at the Carnegie Institute in Pittsburgh. Since that time, they have gained wide recognition.

PUBLIC COLLECTIONS
Abby Aldrich Rockefeller Folk Art Center,
   Williamsburg, Virginia

SEASON	75-76	76-77	77-78	78-79	79-80	80-81	81-82	82-83	83-84	84-85
Paintings						1				
Dollars						$65,000				

Record Sale: $65,000, SPB, 11/21/80, ''Poestenkill, New York,'' 19 × 29 in.

WILLIAM JACOB HAYS
(1830-1875)

William Jacob Hays was born in New York City in 1830 and lived there most of his life. He studied with John Rubens Smith and exhibited at the American Art-Union in 1848. He began to exhibit at the National Academy of Design in 1850. His *Head of a Bull-Dog* (1852) established him as a noted painter of animals. Meticulous attention to the specifics of his subjects became one of his hallmarks. In 1852, he was elected an associate member of the Academy.

Hays was an accredited naturalist, with writings published in professional journals. He took pride in accurately depicting plant life.

Hays traveled in the Adirondacks, Nova Scotia and England. During a five-month trip up the Missouri River, through the Great Plains, the Dakotas and Montana to the Yellowstone River, he faithfully pictured on two small sketch pads Western animals, plants, landscapes and a few portraits. He communicated the dramatic immensity of the buffalo in *The Herd on the Move* (1862, Gilcrease Institute, Tulsa), and *The Stampede* (date and location unknown).

Returning to New York City, he transformed his sketches into an important body of dramatic, artistic and authentic documentation of the West before the white man's impact. New York collector Marshall O. Roberts owned several of his important works. Some of Hays's paintings were lithographically reproduced.

Race horses, game birds, fish, fruit and flowers, especially orchids, were among his subjects. He resigned from the National Academy of Design in 1857 and ceased exhibiting before his death at age 45.

Buffalo Hunt, 1872, 25½ x 47½ in., signed l.r. Courtesy of Wunderlich and Company, Inc., New York, New York.

Prairie Dog Village, 1860, 25½ x 47½ in., signed l.r. Photograph Courtesy of Kennedy Galleries, New York, New York.

MEMBERSHIPS
National Academy of Design

PUBLIC COLLECTIONS
City Art Museum, St. Louis
Corcoran Gallery of Art, Washington, D.C.
Gilcrease Institute, Tulsa
New York Public Library

SEASON	75-76	76-77	77-78	78-79	79-80	80-81	81-82	82-83	83-84	84-85
Paintings						2		1		
Dollars						$5,600		$29,000		

Record Sale: $29,000, S.W, 10/3/82, ''Flushing the Covey,'' 35 × 45 in.

GEORGE COCHRAN LAMBDIN
(1830-1896)

George Cochran Lambdin is remembered today primarily for his numerous and popular floral paintings, but in his own time he was also highly regarded as a painter of sentimental genre scenes.

Lambdin was born in Pittsburgh in 1830, the son of James Reid Lambdin, a successful portraitist from whom he received his early artistic training. He was taken to Philadelphia at age eight and lived there for the rest of his life, except for a brief residence in New York City and trips to Europe in 1855 and 1870.

Lambdin began exhibiting at the Pennsylvania Academy of the Fine Arts in 1848. His first successes were genre paintings, sentimental scenes of childhood, bereavement, or Civil War subjects. Typical is *The Dead Wife* (1860, location unknown), in which a young man kneels at the bedside of a young woman, clasping her hand. A number of these early paintings included flowers, usually roses, pointing toward the next stage of Lambdin's career.

Lambdin turned to still life in 1857 and began concentrating on floral themes during the 1860s. He settled in Germantown, near Philadelphia, and cultivated a garden famous for its roses. From 1870 on, his paintings of flowers, especially roses, were extremely popular and were widely reproduced as chromolithographs.

Still Life: White, Yellow and Pink Roses, 1877, 23½ x 11½ in., signed l.l. Courtesy of Kennedy Galleries, New York, New York.

Lambdin's floral paintings fall into two categories. One group consists of bouquet pictures, showing flowers painted with confidence and exuberance against rather simple backgrounds, as in *Still Life: Vase of Flowers* (1873, Museum of Fine Arts, Boston), or against black enamel. The other category is flowers—again, usually roses—growing in gardens. These "natural setting" paintings often show the rose's life cycle, from bud to aging bloom, an evolutionary theme popular at the time.

Lambdin was elected to the National Academy of Design in 1868. He died in 1896.

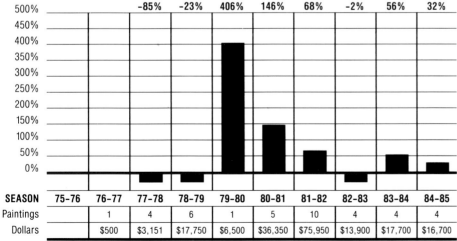

10-Year Average Change From Base Years '76-'77: 66%

		−85%	−23%	406%	146%	68%	−2%	56%	32%

SEASON	75-76	76-77	77-78	78-79	79-80	80-81	81-82	82-83	83-84	84-85
Paintings		1	4	6	1	5	10	4	4	4
Dollars		$500	$3,151	$17,750	$6,500	$36,350	$75,950	$13,900	$17,700	$16,700

Record Sale: $39,000, SPB, 4/23/82, "Wind on the Lily Pond," 16 × 20 in.

ALBERT BIERSTADT
(1830-1902)

The Sierra Nevada in California, 1868, 72 x 120 in., signed l.r. Courtesy of National Museum of American Art, Smithsonian Institution, Bequest of Helen Huntington Hull.

Like most painters of the Rocky Mountains in the nineteenth century, landscape painter Albert Bierstadt was foreign-born; he was born in 1830 in Solingen, near Dusseldorf, Germany. He and his family emigrated to the United States when he was two. He grew up in New Bedford, Massachusetts.

Without an audacity of spirit and a talent for taking infinite pains, Bierstadt might not have become such a phenomenal success. The young Bierstadt had neither the early brilliant talent nor the obsession with art that characterizes most great artists, though he always engaged in art as a pastime.

In 1853, however, despite the discouragement of family and friends, Bierstadt returned to Dusseldorf, to study under the landscape painters Andreas Aschenbach and Karl Friedman Lessing. Under the influence of the Dusseldorf school, and in the company of his fellow painters Emmanuel Gottlieb Leutze and T. Washington Whittredge, Bierstadt learned the attention to detail, the respect for drawing, and the numerous tricks and effects of technique which he utilized, essentially unchanged, for the rest of his life.

Bierstadt traveled through Germany, Switzerland and Italy during his four years of European study, and produced some competent and pleasing paintings of acceptably picturesque Old World scenes. After his return to the United States in 1857, he traveled and painted in

the White Mountains of New Hampshire. He also began to employ a camera, then not used much by artists. It was not until 1858 that he was to discover the subject matter which he would make his own.

In that year, Bierstadt joined a surveying expedition to the American West led by Colonel Frederick W. Lander. Bierstadt made numerous studies, working swiftly, of the spectacular Western scenery, Indians and wildlife. He endlessly compared the sights of the raw new country to things he had already seen in Europe, reducing the elements of each view to conventions he had already learned to employ. When he returned from his adventurous journey, he patiently set to work in his studio to pro-

duce grand paintings of the West which filled a seemingly insatiable hunger of the American and European public.

Much of the continent was unexplored and as foreign to these people as the moon; Bierstadt's stunning vistas of stately mountains and relentless waterfalls surpassed their romantic dreams. Bierstadt began to enjoy a financial success sufficient to enable him to build a 35-room "studio" on the banks of the Hudson River. He made another trip to the West in 1863, and the material he garnered brought him to the peak of his career.

Bierstadt is considered a member of the Hudson River School of artists because of the grand scale and attention to detail of his landscapes, but in both locale and technique he is actually very different. Before his death in New York City in 1902, radical changes in public taste made him an anachronism in his own time, but his work has retained an important place in the history of American art.

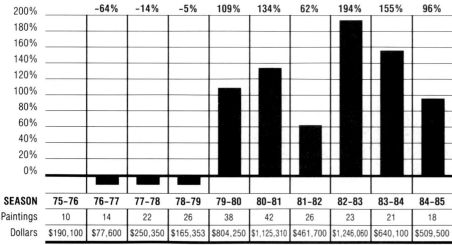

10-Year Average Change From Base Years '75–'76: 67%

SEASON	75–76	76–77	77–78	78–79	79–80	80–81	81–82	82–83	83–84	84–85
		−64%	−14%	−5%	109%	134%	62%	194%	155%	96%
Paintings	10	14	22	26	38	42	26	23	21	18
Dollars	$190,100	$77,600	$250,350	$165,353	$804,250	$1,125,310	$461,700	$1,246,060	$640,100	$509,500

Record Sale: $720,000, SPB, 6/2/83, "The Last of the Buffalo," 26 × 36 in.

CHARLES S. RALEIGH
(1830-1925)

Marine painter Charles S. Raleigh, active during the last quarter of the nineteenth century, executed a series of paintings of nautical subjects and ships. He is best known for his vivid, fanciful depictions of New Bedford whaling expeditions.

Charles Sidney Raleigh, born in Gloucester, England in 1830, ran away to sea at age 10. After serving aboard ship in various capacities, Raleigh landed in Bourne, Massachusetts. His transition to landsman was made during the early 1870s in New Bedford, Massachusetts, where he married and set up a studio; he returned to Bourne in 1881.

In 1879 Raleigh painted a panoramic series depicting the traditions of New Bedford whalemen (New Bedford Whaling Museum). One of the vignettes in this panorama shows a weary, lanced whale about to turn on his attackers, and another depicts the final peeling-off of the whale's blubber. The local New Bedford ship masters supplied Raleigh with all of the necessary details, as the artist himself, despite many years at sea, had no direct experience with whaling.

In addition to his action-filled narratives of various whaling expeditions, Raleigh executed a number of intricately detailed renderings of ships. An early example is *Western Star* (1878, Marine Arts, Salem, Massachusetts), a clear, concise depiction of a coastal ship. In a more mature work, entitled *Belle of the Sea* (1892, Mystic Seaport, Connecticut), Raleigh demonstrated his remarkable ability to record visual fact and create an atmospheric seascape. This painting demonstrates knowledge of rigging and shipboard protocol. The artist is known to have challenged sailors to find inaccuracies in paintings such as this.

Julia Frances, 1891, 22 x 30 in., signed l.l. Courtesy of Oliphant and Company, LTD., New York, New York.

By his own estimation, Raleigh created approximately 1,100 marine paintings, 400 of which were illustrations of whaling ships. His panoramic paintings provided an educational novelty during an age when the New England Atheneum lectures were waning in popularity. Raleigh died in 1925.

PUBLIC COLLECTIONS
Mystic Seaport Museum, Connecticut
New Bedford Whaling Museum,
    New Bedford, Massachusetts

SEASON	75-76	76-77	77-78	78-79	79-80	80-81	81-82	82-83	83-84	84-85
Paintings				1		1		2		
Dollars				$1,900		$1,300		$13,000		

Record Sale: $8,000, RB.HM, 11/27/82, "The Ship 'Celia'," 26 × 46 in.

LOUIS REMY MIGNOT
(1831-1870)

Louis Remy Mignot was an American Creole who enjoyed a brief but widely traveled artistic career, until his death at age 39. Best known for his tropical landscapes painted in Ecuador, Mignot is also remembered for his paintings of the Southern United States and of the upstate New York region.

Mignot was born the son of a confectioner in Charleston, South Carolina. It is believed that he had early instruction in Charleston, before traveling to the Netherlands in 1850 for three years of study at the Hague under Andreas Schelfhout.

Returning to the United States, Mignot established his studio in New York City, and began to make his reputation with landscapes of the upstate New York region, painted in the style of the Hudson River School.

In 1857, Mignot accompanied Frederick E. Church on his second trip to South America. Together, the artists traveled from Panama to Ecuador, where they spent 10 weeks painting village and mountain scenes.

Returning to New York in 1958, Mignot received critical praise for his South American landscapes. At the same time, he continued to paint landscapes of the Southeastern and Northeastern United States, and to execute the landscape backgrounds for prominent New York figurative artists such as John Ehninger and Eastman Johnson.

In 1862, with the outbreak of the Civil War, Mignot moved from New York to London, where he continued to lead a successful career, exhibiting at the Royal Academy and the 1867 Paris Exposition.

Mignot's career was unfortunately cut short in 1870 during a trip to France, when he became an accidental casualty of the Franco-Prussian War. Mistakenly imprisoned during the siege of Paris, he was eventually released, but died of smallpox shortly after his return to his home in Brighton, England. It is believed he contracted the disease while in confinement.

South American Scene, 15⅜ x 23⅛ in., signed l.l. The Art Museum, Princeton University, New Jersey, Gift of Mr. and Mrs. Stuart P. Feld.

10-Year Average Change From Base Years '75-'76: 1,090%

SEASON	75-76	76-77	77-78	78-79	79-80	80-81	81-82	82-83	83-84	84-85
			26%		215%	3,504%	492%	2,148%	1,970%	368%
Paintings	1		1		4	1	4	3	3	2
Dollars	$800		$900		$23,250	$4,800	$21,500	$30,940	$14,320	$9,500

Record Sale: $28,000, CH, 3/18/83, "On the Orinoco, Venezuela," 11 x 18 in.

242

JOHN GEORGE BROWN
(1831-1913)

John George Brown's sentimentalized portrayals of street urchins, reproduced by the thousands, made him the richest and most celebrated genre painter in turn-of-the-century America.

Born in Durham, England in 1831, Brown studied art in England and Scotland before coming to America in 1853. He was a glassblower in Brooklyn, and a student at the National Academy of Design in New York City. He opened a studio there in 1860, when his painting *His First Cigar* launched his national reputation.

Brown exploited his considerable talent to supply the Victorian taste for his specialty—adept (copyrighted) pictures of young white shoeshiners, vendors and servants.

From the 1860s on, his reputation as "the boot-black Raphael" never flagged. Toward the end of his life, his yearly income averaged $40,000. Originals sold for $500 to $700. Royalties from just one lithograph, distributed with packaged tea, totalled $25,000.

Though he claimed the successful formula of "contemporary truth" for his pictures, none gave doting collectors or wealthy patrons cause for social alarm. He falsified his subjects, who were in reality minority immigrants whose lives were often wretched struggles for survival.

Brown's street juveniles are invariably cheerful, spunky tykes—never sick, sad, emaciated, hungry or noticeably foreign.

Shoeshine Boy, 1880, 20 x 11 in., signed l.l. Courtesy of John H. Garzoli Gallery, San Francisco, California.

Their ragged clothing is picturesque, their grime cosmetic. They are undeniably appealing. Even the most uneven of Brown's popularized works show painterly skill and sound training.

Brown realized he was pressured by his buying public into subjects and techniques below his true ability; the pictures he painted for pleasure, using his full range of artistry, are straightforward and distinguished. Most are of country scenes and outdoor pastimes, with none of the contrived look of his commercialized "trademark" paintings.

Brown's *View of the Palisades* (1867, private collection) is a delightful and unaccustomed departure from his genre work. Showing boats on a calm, open bend of the Hudson, it is broadly painted, expansive in feeling, with crisp detail and care in every brushstroke.

Brown died in 1913 in New York City.

MEMBERSHIPS
National Academy of Design
American Water Color Society

PUBLIC COLLECTIONS
Corcoran Art Gallery, Washington, D.C.
Metropolitan Museum of Art, New York City
Museum of Fine Arts, Boston
Peabody Institute of the City of Baltimore
G.W.V. Smith Art Gallery, Springfield, Massachusetts

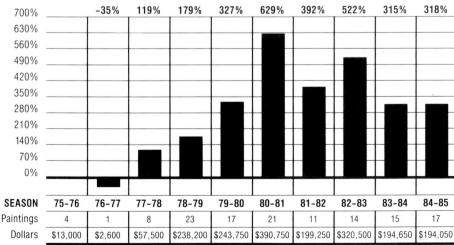

10-Year Average Change From Base Years '75-'76: 277%

	-35%	119%	179%	327%	629%	392%	522%	315%	318%

SEASON	75-76	76-77	77-78	78-79	79-80	80-81	81-82	82-83	83-84	84-85
Paintings	4	1	8	23	17	21	11	14	15	17
Dollars	$13,000	$2,600	$57,500	$238,200	$243,750	$390,750	$199,250	$320,500	$194,650	$194,050

Record Sale: $105,000, SPB, 4/25/80, "The Sidewalk Dance," 40 × 60 in.

HARRISON B. BROWN
(1831-1915)

Portland Lights, 1863, 28 x 40 in. Courtesy of Vose Galleries of Boston, Inc., Massachusetts.

Harrison Bird Brown turned a modest beginning as a sign painter into a successful career as one of the most celebrated landscape painters in Maine during the second half of the nineteenth century. Brown spent the greatest portion of his life in Maine, and his works often depicted the wholesome outdoor environment of his home state.

Brown was born in Portland, Maine in 1831, at a time when landscape painting enjoyed immense popularity, due mainly to the earlier influence of Charles Codman (1800-1842). Codman's paintings were widely collected for their keenly romantic sentiments. It is likely that Brown, as an apprentice sign and banner painter, saw examples of Codman's poetic landscape paintings.

By the time he was 21, Brown had completed an apprenticeship with Forbes and Wilson, a firm of house and ship painters located on Fore Street, near Portland's harbor. He immediately opened his own sign and banner establishment.

By 1858, having become a skilled commercial painter, Brown discarded his business to concentrate solely on fine art. His decision proved fruitful; between 1858 and 1860, the National Academy of Design in New York City exhibited six of his landscapes (five of which were borrowed from owners for the exhibition).

Oakland (1860, Portland Museum of Art) and *Autumn in the White Moun-* *tains* (1870, Portland Museum of Art) are two of Brown's popular works depicting the scenic beauty of Maine. His best-known paintings were of the Casco Bay, Maine area. Brown's sensitive handling of thin color produced effects of light and atmosphere reminiscent of John Frederick Kensett's technique.

Brown's election to the presidency of the Portland Society of Art in 1892 indicated his stature among his contemporaries in the New England art world.

He moved to London in 1892, where he continued to paint, living there until his death in 1915.

MEMBERSHIPS
Portland Society of Art

PUBLIC COLLECTIONS
Portland Museum of Art, Maine

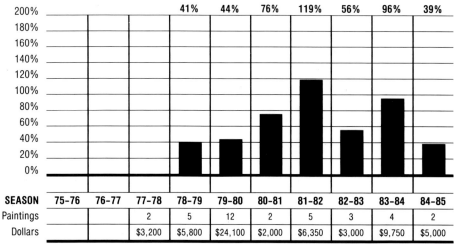

10-Year Average Change From Base Years '77-'78: 59%

SEASON	75-76	76-77	77-78	78-79	79-80	80-81	81-82	82-83	83-84	84-85
				41%	44%	76%	119%	56%	96%	39%
Paintings			2	5	12	2	5	3	4	2
Dollars			$3,200	$5,800	$24,100	$2,000	$6,350	$3,000	$9,750	$5,000

Record Sale: $7,500, CH, 5/22/80, "Valley Farm," 17 x 22 in.

ENOCH WOOD PERRY

(1831-1915)

Enoch Wood Perry, popular portraitist and landscapist, became best known for his genre paintings in the post-Civil War period. Genre painters, whose subject is everyday life, enjoyed an American heyday during the late nineteenth century, and Perry was one of the most skilled and successful.

His work reflects sound academic virtues—strongly drawn contrasts of light, solid modeling and exactitude in form. His middle-career genre paintings are especially extravagant in detail, forming valuable, authentic records of American interiors of Perry's period.

Born in Boston in 1831, Perry went to New Orleans in his youth. From 1848 to 1852, Perry clerked in a grocery and saved $1,100 for art study in Europe.

From 1852 to 1854, he studied with Emanuel Leutze in Dusseldorf, concentrating on anatomy and proportion. Two further years of study with Thomas Couture in Paris greatly influenced the young artist.

At 24, Perry was named United States consul in Venice. On his return to America, his Venetian scenes in the 1858 National Academy of Design exhibition earned his associate membership and launched his lucrative career.

After a year in Philadelphia, Perry opened a New Orleans studio in 1860. His growing list of illustrious portraits included *Senator John Slidell* (1860, Louisiana State Museum) and *Jefferson Davis* (1861, Louisiana State Museum).

Oriental Interior (San Francisco), 1863, 16 x 12¾ in., signed l.r. Collection of William Hurlbut, Photograph courtesy of Kennedy Galleries, New York, New York.

The Civil War over, Perry traveled to Hawaii, where he painted landscapes and portraits of native royalty. Later in Utah, he sold portraits (one of Brigham Young) and landscapes for more than $11,000 in a four-month period.

About 1868, he settled in New York City. Many of his paintings were reproduced in magazines, such as *Harper's Weekly* and Sheldon's *American Painting.* Ulysses S. Grant was among his portrait subjects. Perry's best genre work is typified by the tremendously popular *The True American* (1875, Metropolitan Museum of Art).

Perry's late-career work shows less anecdotal, more painterly elements, reflecting the impressionist influence. He died in 1915 in New York City.

MEMBERSHIPS
American Water Color Society
National Academy of Design

PUBLIC COLLECTIONS
Bishop Museum, Honolulu, Hawaii
Buffalo Fine Arts Academy
The Cabildo, New Orleans
Louisiana State Museum
Metropolitan Museum of Art, New York City

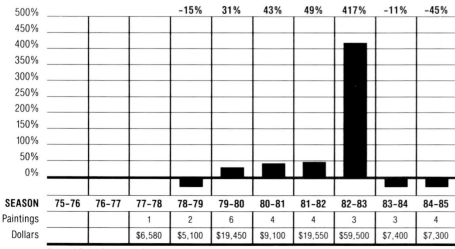

10-Year Average Change From Base Years '77-'78: 59%

			-15%	31%	43%	49%	417%	-11%	-45%
SEASON	75-76	76-77	77-78	78-79	79-80	80-81	81-82	82-83	83-84	84-85
Paintings			1	2	6	4	4	3	3	4
Dollars			$6,580	$5,100	$19,450	$9,100	$19,550	$59,500	$7,400	$7,300

Record Sale: $42,000, CH, 3/18/83, "Mother and Child," 29 x 37 in.

JOHN BRADLEY

(Active 1832-1847)

John Bradley, an English-born portrait painter, was active in and around New York City from 1832 to 1847. Approximately 30 works have been attributed to Bradley. They bear the signatures "I. Bradley," "John Bradley," or "Drawn by I. Bradley from Great Britton." Other paintings traditionally considered to be Bradley's work have not been authoritatively attributed to the artist.

Immigration records suggest that Bradley entered the country in 1826 from Ireland. An 1831 portrait of an unidentified woman and *The Cellist* (1832, Phillips Collection) are Bradley's earliest identified works. They represent his only known full-length portraits of adults, and are of a somewhat smaller size than the remainder of his known paintings.

Yet Bradley's style is firmly established in these early portraits. He depicts the sitter with objects significant to his or her interests and pursuits. His paintings are similar to the conversation pieces that were popular in Britain but rare in the United States.

Bradley's portraits have a sharp, hard, defined quality. He relies on silhouette to present detail of facial features, particularly of the nose. Bradley's self-taught style is evident in the way he contours figures with lighter tones or white outlines, making them appear to jump away from his dark backgrounds. His style is in direct contrast to the conventional procedure of darkly outlining or shadowing figures to give the impression of depth.

Bradley chose clear, bright colors. His reds, greens, blues and golds have a jewel-like clarity. Toward the end of his career, as photography became popular, Bradley toned down his colors to more somber shades. Despite the change, his paintings remain vibrant.

Little Girl in Lavender, ca. 1840, 33⅞ x 27⅜ in., signed l.r. Courtesy of National Gallery of Art, Washington, D.C. Gift of Edgar William and Bernice Chrysler Garbisch.

Bradley chose to paint children full-figure, to better capture the spirit of the subjects by including their dress and playthings in elaborate detail. This attention to detail is evident in all of the artist's work. In *Margaretta Bowne Crawford* (date unknown, Monmouth County Historical Society), sheet music is so clearly painted that it could be played.

Bradley apparently did not travel far from New York City, where he had several addresses until 1847. Most of his subjects were from New York City, Staten Island or New Jersey.

PUBLIC COLLECTIONS
Abby Aldrich Rockefeller Folk Art Collection,
   Williamsburg, Virginia
Allen Memorial Art Museum,
   Oberlin College, Ohio
Monmouth County Historical Society,
   Freehold, New Jersey
National Gallery of Art, Washington, D.C.
National Gallery of Canada, Ottawa, Ontario
Staten Island Historical Society, New York

SEASON	75-76	76-77	77-78	78-79	79-80	80-81	81-82	82-83	83-84	84-85
Paintings				1		1				
Dollars				$43,000		$21,000				

Record Sale: $43,000, SPB, 1/27/79, "Child in a Green Dress," 33 × 26 in.

WILLIAM BRADFORD
(1823-1892)

William Bradford, a marine painter of the nineteenth century, was celebrated on both sides of the Atlantic for his arctic scenes. In several trips to Labrador, including exploratory polar expeditions, Bradford photographed and made original studies of this frozen world.

He saw remarkable colors in icebergs—blue, green, purple and gray, shot through with saffron. He painted sailing vessels fishing in the icy waters. He is also known for his remarkably accurate representations of coastal scenes in New England, Nova Scotia and Labrador.

On at least one occasion, Bradford was stranded for two weeks on an ice-locked ship, surrounded by a field of frozen water for 500 miles in all directions. Wearing a sealskin coat, he spent the time drawing and photographing icebergs.

Born a Quaker in Fairhaven, Massachusetts in 1823, Bradford liked art from an early age, but was educated more practically in business. Eight years after his start in commerce, he was bankrupt—a fortunate circumstance for the young artist-to-be, because he permanently turned his back on business and took up painting as a career. Since he lived in a seaport town, ships were available subjects. Bradford painted many of them, selling the portraits for a good income.

Bradford was primarily self-taught, but he also trained with Albert Van Beest; they shared a studio and collabo-

Whaler off the Vineyard—Outward Bound, 1859, 16 x 24 in., signed l.r. Courtesy of National Museum of American Art, Smithsonian Institution, Museum Purchase.

The Wreck of an Emigrant Ship on the Coast of New England, 51 x 77 in., signed l.r. Photograph courtesy of Hirschl & Adler Galleries, Inc., New York, New York.

rated on some paintings. Van Beest, however, had a more passionate style than Bradford, who could spend days painting a single group of rocks, making sure that they were faithfully drawn and colored. After two years, the duo separated.

Bradford extended his studies of ships to views of shore and sea, visiting picturesque regions along the North Atlantic coastline. So accurate are his representations that anyone familiar with it can immediately identify the scene of a Bradford painting.

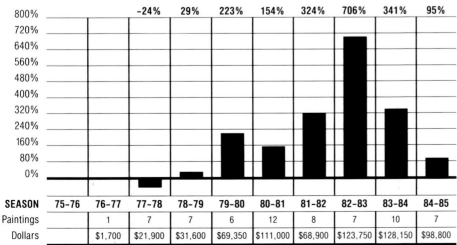

10-Year Average Change From Base Years '76-'77: 205%

		−24%	29%	223%	154%	324%	706%	341%	95%
800%									
720%									
640%									
560%									
480%									
400%									
320%									
240%									
160%									
80%									
0%									
SEASON	75-76	76-77	77-78	78-79	79-80	80-81	81-82	82-83	83-84	84-85
Paintings		1	7	7	6	12	8	7	10	7
Dollars		$1,700	$21,900	$31,600	$69,350	$111,000	$68,900	$123,750	$128,150	$98,800

Record Sale: $70,000, CH, 12/3/82, "Stowing Sails," 14 x 20 in.

PUBLIC COLLECTIONS
Art Institute of Chicago
Metropolitan Museum of Art, New York City

247

ROBERT HOPKIN
(1832-1909)

Robert Hopkin, a prominent figure in the Detroit art community during the late nineteenth century, was a landscape and scene painter whose best work reflects his lifelong interest in the sea.

Hopkin was born in Glasgow, Scotland. As a child, he was encouraged by his father, an amateur artist, to copy prints and illustrations. He also sketched local seascapes.

When he was 11, Hopkin's family moved to Detroit, where he was soon apprenticed to a carriage painter who directed him toward an artistic career. He received commissions for decorative art—murals, panels in trains, and theater scenery. Without formal training, Hopkin learned from other artists, such as Frederick E. Cohen, who taught him color mixing.

In 1870, Hopkin moved to Chicago. He returned to Detroit the following year, after many of his paintings were destroyed in the great Chicago fire. He was eventually able to make a living with easel painting, which he preferred to decorative work.

Hopkin painted many views of the Great Lakes, the Detroit River and the sea, although he also painted landscapes and animals. He worked in both watercolor and oil. His work was widely exhibited and an art club was founded in his honor. He died in 1909 in Detroit.

On Lake St. Clair, 1875, 14 x 24½ in. Collection of The Montgomery Museum of Fine Arts, Alabama.

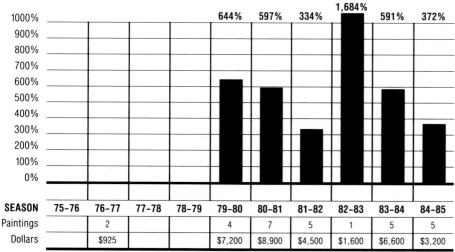

10-Year Average Change From Base Years '76-'77: 603%

SEASON	75-76	76-77	77-78	78-79	79-80	80-81	81-82	82-83	83-84	84-85
					644%	597%	334%	1,684%	591%	372%
Paintings		2			4	7	5	1	5	5
Dollars		$925			$7,200	$8,900	$4,500	$1,600	$6,600	$3,200

Record Sale: $2,500, DM.D, 5/17/81, "Seashore Scene with Clan," 38 × 48 in.

248

GEORGE WASHINGTON NICHOLSON
(1832-1912)

Landscape artist George Washington Nicholson spent much of his life without recognition. Recently, there has been new interest in his work. Many of his paintings, fine examples of turn-of-the-century American art, are unlocated; the artist had a penchant for giving them away. Others on loan were never returned to his estate. Fortunately, however, he signed and dated his paintings.

Born in Salem County, New Jersey in 1832, he lived and painted in Philadelphia, except for his last few years. He spent these in Hammonton, New Jersey, where he died in 1912.

A young man from a rural background, Nicholson wanted to travel. His wanderlust took him to England, France and Egypt. He recorded his impressions in sketches. One of these, *Windsor Castle,* was exhibited in 1867 at the Pennsylvania Academy of the Fine Arts.

Returning home, he painted landscapes, historical scenes and an occasional still life. In France, he had studied with Isabey, who may have influenced his landscape technique, and his landscapes were regularly exhibited at the Haseltine Art Galleries. A fine oil, *Winter Morning* (date and location unknown), displays his talent as a master winter-scene painter. Another striking painting, *Washington Crossing the Delaware* (date unknown), hangs in the Pennsylvania Statehouse in Harrisburg.

Coastal Scene, 20 x 36 in., signed l.l. Courtesy of Henry B. Holt, Inc., Essex Fells, New Jersey.

Marine Scene, 10½ x 15 in., signed l.l. Courtesy of Newman Galleries, Philadelphia, Pennsylvania.

Although he lived and worked quietly, Nicholson had admirers. When he moved to the pine air of Hammonton for his son's health, an art dealer named Deschonde visited him regularly to buy paintings for his museum in Chester, Pennsylvania.

Nicholson is known to have been an artist of enormous output; there are still hundreds of paintings for collectors to locate. Recent finds have been acquired by the Newman Galleries in Philadelphia, and in 1972 a painting surfaced in London where it sold at Christie's.

Nicholson died in 1912.

MEMBERSHIPS
Pennsylvania Academy of the Fine Arts

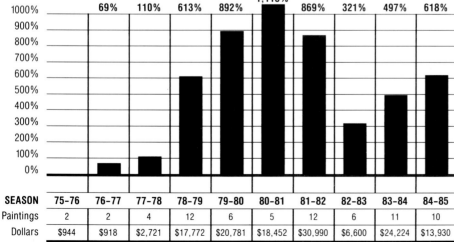

10-Year Average Change From Base Years '75-'76: 510%

SEASON	75-76	76-77	77-78	78-79	79-80	80-81	81-82	82-83	83-84	84-85
		69%	110%	613%	892%	1,113%	869%	321%	497%	618%
Paintings	2	2	4	12	6	5	12	6	11	10
Dollars	$944	$918	$2,721	$17,772	$20,781	$18,452	$30,990	$6,600	$24,224	$13,930

Record Sale: $11,300, S, 2/6/80, "After Day's Toil," 34 x 56 in.

249

JAMES RENWICK BREVOORT
(1832-1918)

Half Moon Cove, Gloucester Bay, 1871, 8¾ x 14½ in., signed l.r. Private Collection, Courtesy of Adams Davidson Galleries Inc., Washington, D.C.

Even as a child, James Renwick Brevoort was sketching scenes in the rural Yonkers, New York countryside, foretelling a time when he would use numerous drawings in correlation with his works in oil and watercolor.

Born in 1832, he began at age 18 to study architecture under the aegis of his cousin, James Renwick, a prominent architect. In 1854, Brevoort was awarded a certificate in architecture from New York University.

He remained in New York City, and his interests returned to painting. Before long, Brevoort was exhibiting at the National Academy of Design, and studying there with Thomas S. Cummings. Brevoort's subject matter was often the traditional landscape view typical of the later years of the Hudson River School. Like other artists of the period, he left the city during the summers to find appropriate subject matter in rural Connecticut and upper New York State.

By the late 1850s, the titles of his paintings reflected his absorption in seasons, weather and the time of day; these continued to be variants in his landscapes. In the 1860s, he was influenced by Samuel Colman's work in watercolor, an appropriate medium for the shimmering quality of "native impressionism," which developed during the 1870s in works created by the Hudson River School.

Harvest Scene with Storm Coming Up (ca. 1862, Hudson River Museum) is perhaps his best-known work, and is certainly among the largest at 32 by 48 inches. It shows distant hills and clouds, with a creek and trees in the foreground; in the middle distance are farm workers and a wagon. The vista dwarfs the human figures.

In 1861, Brevoort was named an associate member of the National Academy of Design; two years later he was made a full member. In 1872, he was named professor of perspective at the National Academy.

Brevoort lost his first wife, and in 1873 married Marie Louise Bascom, an artist and first medalist of the National Academy School. In February of that year, he auctioned off the contents of his studio, including works by other artists, selling more than 150 landscapes. By the end of the year, he and his second wife were in Europe. Until 1880, he lived in Florence, where there was a colony of American artists. English moors and European scenes were among his subjects. After his return to the United States, he continued to make visits abroad.

From 1856 to 1890, Brevoort's works were exhibited at the National Academy. He also exhibited at the Boston Athenaeum, the Brooklyn Art Association, and the Pennsylvania Academy of the Fine Arts. For three years, from 1916 to 1918, his work was displayed at the Yonkers Art Association, which he helped establish.

Brevoort died in Yonkers in 1918.

PUBLIC COLLECTIONS
Corcoran Gallery of Art, Washington, D.C.
Hudson River Museum, Yonkers, New York
National Academy of Design, New York City
George Walter Vincent Smith Art Museum,
   Springfield, Massachusetts

SEASON	75-76	76-77	77-78	78-79	79-80	80-81	81-82	82-83	83-84	84-85
Paintings				5		1	1	1		2
Dollars				$7,500		$700	$700	$800		$2,250

Record Sale: $3,100, S.BM, 5/22/79, "Haying," 19 × 36 in.

SAMUEL COLMAN
(1832-1920)

Samuel Colman was a second-generation painter of the Hudson River School and a recorder of the American West. His landscapes, often large in size, portray mountains, rivers, lakes and wagon-train life. He also painted European scenes.

Colman was a many-faceted man: etcher, collector and authority on oriental art and porcelains. He did some interior design and worked with Louis Comfort Tiffany and John LaFarge in the 1880s. He wrote two books on art, *Nature's Harmonic Unity* and *Proportional Form.*

Colman was born in Portland, Maine in 1832. His father was a fine-arts bookseller and publisher who moved to New York City while Samuel, Jr. was still a boy. His store on Broadway became a center for artists and literary types.

In New York, Colman studied painting under Hudson River School painter Asher B. Durand. At age 18 he showed his first painting, *Morning,* at the National Academy of Design; in 1860 he was already an associate, and by 1862 he had become a full academician. He exhibited at the Boston Athenaeum, the Maryland Historical Society, and the Pennsylvania Academy of the Fine Arts.

From 1860 to 1862 and from 1871 to 1875, Colman traveled in France, Italy, Spain and Morocco, studying and painting. His oils before 1870 are characterized by a lucid style indicative of an affinity for watercolor, which he also

Morning Glories, ca. 1890, 16¾ x 12¼ in., signed l.c. Courtesy of Fogg Art Museum, Harvard University, Cambridge, Massachusetts, Bequest-Mrs. William Hayes Fogg.

used. His later work shows the influence of the barbizon painters in bucolic, unpopulated scenes, broadly executed.

In *View of the Catskills, New York State* (ca. 1864, location unknown), Colman's colors are exceedingly delicate; the mountains are rendered in smoky lavenders and pinks, while the trees, rocks and grasses are counterpointed in russets and greens. His paintings often feature one major natural or man-made form, as in *Storm King on the Hudson*

(1866, National Museum of American Art, Washington, D.C.).

Beginning in about 1870, Colman started traveling to the West to paint. Typical of his work at this time is *Ships of the Plains* (1872, Union League Club, New York City). The dramatic *Green River, Wyoming* (1871, Museum of Fine Arts, Boston), showing a turn in the river bounded on one side by huge bluffs, illustrates the suitability of watercolor for vast subjects. *The Emigrant Train, Colorado* (1872, St. Johnsbury Athenaeum, Vermont) depicts a quiet moment in the lives of travelers moving West—animals being watered by a stream and people walking about and stretching their legs.

Colman died in New York City in 1920.

MEMBERSHIPS
American Water Color Society
National Academy of Design

PUBLIC COLLECTIONS
Chicago Art Institute
Hudson River Museum, Yonkers, New York
Metropolitan Museum of Art, New York City
Museum of Fine Arts, Boston
National Academy of Design, New York City
National Museum of American Art, Washington, D.C.
St. Johnsbury Athenaeum, Vermont
Union League Club, New York City

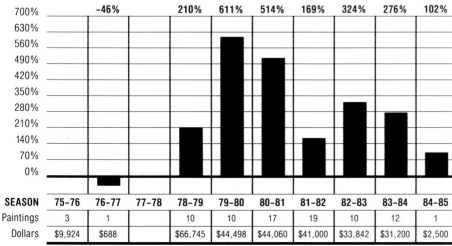

10-Year Average Change From Base Years '75-'76: 240%

	-46%		210%	611%	514%	169%	324%	276%	102%
SEASON	75-76	76-77	77-78	78-79	79-80	80-81	81-82	82-83	83-84	84-85
Paintings	3	1		10	10	17	19	10	12	1
Dollars	$9,924	$688		$66,745	$44,498	$44,060	$41,000	$33,842	$31,200	$2,500

Record Sale: $28,000, SPB, 4/20/79, "Solomon's Temple, Colorado," 20 x 26 in.

251

JOHN ROSS KEY

(1832-1920)

John Ross Key was a landscape painter and illustrator. He was the grandson of Francis Scott Key, the author of "The Star Spangled Banner." Most sources agree that he was born in 1832 in Hagerstown, Maryland:

After studying in Munich and Paris, Key spent his life working in various American cities: Baltimore, Boston, Charleston, Chicago, New York City and San Francisco.

In 1854, Key was a draftsman for the United States Coast and Geodetic Survey. In 1863, he served with the federal corps of engineers in Charleston, South Carolina. There he recorded the siege of the Confederate city with his illustrations.

After the war, Key worked in New York City, Boston and San Francisco. From 1870 to 1873, he lived in San Francisco and painted many landscapes of Northern California. These paintings were reproduced as chromolithographs by Louis Prang during the 1870s. The subjects included Lake Tahoe, Mariposa Big Trees, Point Lobos, the Yosemite Half Dome and the Golden Gate Bridge.

Key exhibited at the National Academy of Design, the Pennsylvania Academy of the Fine Arts, and the Boston Athenaeum. In 1877 he exhibited at least 100 works in Boston. The critics praised the show, saying that Key's "charcoal drawings are among the best ever shown in Boston, firm and masterly, strong and graceful."

Key died in Baltimore in 1920.

Courtesy of Vose Galleries of Boston, Inc., Massachusetts.

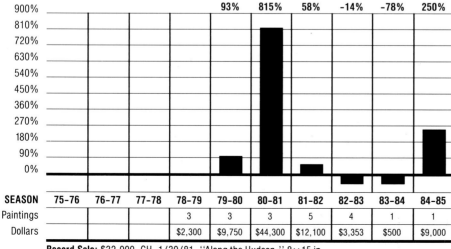

10-Year Average Change From Base Years '78-'79: 161%

SEASON	75-76	76-77	77-78	78-79	79-80	80-81	81-82	82-83	83-84	84-85
					93%	815%	58%	-14%	-78%	250%
Paintings				3	3	3	5	4	1	1
Dollars				$2,300	$9,750	$44,300	$12,100	$3,353	$500	$9,000

Record Sale: $32,000, CH, 1/30/81, "Along the Hudson," 8 × 15 in.

MEMBERSHIPS
Boston Art Club
Society of Washington Artists

PUBLIC COLLECTIONS
Amon Carter Museum of Western Art, Fort Worth
Corcoran Gallery of Art, Washington, D.C.

THOMAS HOPE
(1832-1926)

A musician as well as a painter, Thomas Hope seems to have turned to full-time serious painting relatively late in life. Although he first studied at the Pennsylvania Academy of the Fine Arts in Philadelphia shortly after the Civil War, a card preserved in a family scrap book indicates that he did not actually graduate from the Academy until 1881, when he was nearly 50.

As well as being a portrait painter, Hope did landscapes, genre paintings and many extremely realistic small still lifes. An old newspaper clipping mentions that in eight small works exhibited by Hope, "we see on canvas papes of tobacco, newspapers, coins and bank notes so real in treatment that we feel like grasping."

Hope was born in Sussex, England in 1832. As a young man he studied both music and art, and showed an early interest in painting still lifes. In 1864, he and his young family and Thomas Campbell, a boyhood friend and fellow art student, embarked for America.

The Civil War had already been raging for three years and Hope must have enlisted in the 17th Connecticut Volunteers almost immediately after his arrival in this country. He served as a musician until the end of the war.

After demobilization he settled in Philadelphia, and began studying art at the Pennsylvania Academy under popular artist George F. Bensell. Just why 15 years passed before he graduated is unknown, but it seems likely that he may have been working as a bandmaster to support his family in the interim.

One of his first works was exhibited at the National Academy of Design in 1882 and was well received. Around this time he moved to South Norwalk, Connecticut. Along with painting, he also taught cornet to musicians in the Philharmonic Society of South Norwalk.

Washington the Boy Hero, ca. 1850, 27 x 34 in. Courtesy of Independence National Historical Park Service, Philadelphia, Pennsylvania.

Hope exhibited regularly in Philadelphia, Boston and New York City. In 1916, he moved to Devon, Connecticut. Although illness reduced his activity after 1919, he continued to paint for several years. He completed a landscape of a favorite mill near Wilton, Connecticut in 1923, just three years before he died at age 94.

SEASON	75-76	76-77	77-78	78-79	79-80	80-81	81-82	82-83	83-84	84-85
Paintings						3			5	1
Dollars						$7,200			$10,850	$1,500

Record Sale: $4,250, SPB, 1/27/84, "Still Life of Apple and Wine," 19 × 27 in.

AARON DRAPER SHATTUCK
(1832-1928)

Aaron Draper Shattuck, a landscape, portrait and animal painter, was closely associated with the White Mountain School. Though he was quite popular with his contemporary public, today his works are relatively unknown; they remain privately held in collections of his descendants. Shattuck also was a successful inventor.

Born in Francestown, New Hampshire in 1832, Shattuck first studied portrait and landscape painting with Alexander Ransome in Boston. By 1852, Shattuck had moved to New York City with his teacher. There he enrolled in classes at the National Academy of Design, financing his studies with portrait commissions.

Beginning in 1854, Shattuck, like other second-generation members of the Hudson River School, made summer sketching trips in New York State and New England. He then painted romantic mountain scenes of trees, rocks and water during the winter in his New York City studio.

He was popular with fellow artists John F. Kensett, James D. Smillie, Samuel Coleman, Asher B. Durand and William Sidney Mount. He collaborated with Durand and Mount on several paintings. Shattuck spent a summer at Coleman's New Hampshire camp in 1956, and later married Coleman's sister.

Shattuck's work is not flashy, but quietly romantic. He preferred to paint on small canvases, giving a feel of intimacy to the work. His paintings have a photographic quality, in part because of the scientific precision with which he rendered foreground detail. Shattuck was equally adept at suggestion in his treatment of backgrounds.

By 1861, Shattuck was a member of the National Academy of Design. He moved from New York City to Ganby, Connecticut in 1870. During this period, he achieved recognition as a cattle and sheep painter.

Shattuck was stricken with a serious illness in 1888, after which he painted virtually nothing. At the time of his death in 1928, he was the oldest living member of the National Academy of Design. At that time, more than 600 of his paintings remained in his studio, representing 37 years of painting.

Deer Going to Water, 1860, 17½ x 29 in., signed l.l. Photograph courtesy of M. Knoedler & Co., Inc., New York, New York.

MEMBERSHIPS
National Academy of Design

PUBLIC COLLECTIONS
Vassar College Art Gallery, Poughkeepsie, New York

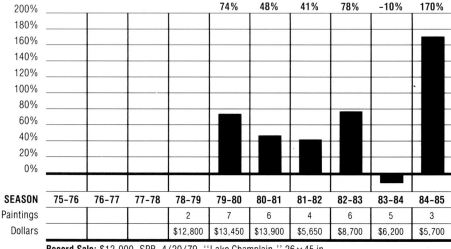

10-Year Average Change From Base Years '78-'79: 57%

SEASON	75-76	76-77	77-78	78-79	79-80	80-81	81-82	82-83	83-84	84-85
					74%	48%	41%	78%	-10%	170%
Paintings				2	7	6	4	6	5	3
Dollars				$12,800	$13,450	$13,900	$5,650	$8,700	$6,200	$5,700

Record Sale: $12,000, SPB, 4/20/79, "Lake Champlain," 26 x 45 in.

254

Connecticut Landscape, 14 x 22 in., signed l.l. Courtesy of Driscoll & Walsh, Fine Art, Boston, Massachusetts.

New Hampshire Farm, 1855, signed l.r. Courtesy of Vose Galleries of Boston, Inc., Massachusetts.

255

HERMANN HERZOG
(1832-1932)

Hermann Herzog was born in Bremen, Germany in 1832. His artistic production commenced early and continued throughout his 100-year life span.

Possessing recognizable talent in childhood, Herzog received guidance and acclaim early in life; his career developed rapidly. Modest and happy with his artistic gifts, Herzog rarely entered competitions. Herzog studied in Dusseldorf with Johann Wilhem Schirmer and then with renowned Norwegian landscape painter Hans Gude. Herzog traveled and painted with Gude in Norway and later captured many of Western Europe's beauty spots on his canvases.

His ability soon attracted European royalty; Queen Victoria and Czar Alexander II were among his clients. Early earnings and wise investments relieved him of the financial and psychological sufferings endured by many artists.

In the 1860's, Herzog emigrated to America, choosing Philadelphia for his home. His interest and energy soon led him to paint many landscapes throughout the United States and Mexico. Contemporaries observed that Herzog could sense the best time of the day and season to catch a scene at the peak of its beauty. His style was realistic and included an aesthetic tempering of mood, with soft and pleasing effects. He numbered and catalogued a thousand paintings.

Following Herzog's death in 1932, his family retained a large group of his paintings. Release of this group to the

Falls-Yosemite Valley, 25 x 20 in., signed l.r. Courtesy of John H. Garzoli Gallery, San Francisco, California.

art market in the 1970s spurred interest and demand for Herzog's work in the United States and Europe.

PUBLIC COLLECTIONS
Metropolitan Museum of Art, New York City
Reading Public Museum and Art Gallery, Pennsylvania

10-Year Average Change From Base Years '80–'81: 18%

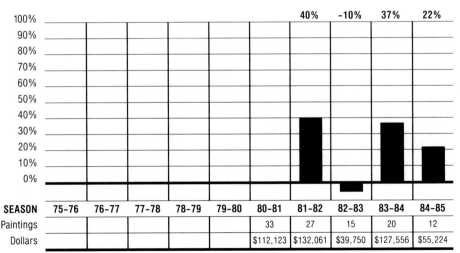

SEASON	75-76	76-77	77-78	78-79	79-80	80-81	81-82	82-83	83-84	84-85
							40%	-10%	37%	22%
Paintings						33	27	15	20	12
Dollars						$112,123	$132,061	$39,750	$127,556	$55,224

Record Sale: $45,000, CH, 6/3/82, "Niagara from the Museum," 32×46 in.

LOUIS MAURER

(1832-1932)

Trotting Cracks on the Snow, 1858, signed l.r. Courtesy of The Harry T. Peters Collection, Museum of the City of New York.

Louis Maurer, one of a group of European-trained artists who worked for Currier and Ives during the mid-nineteenth century, was a lithographer and painter whose long career spanned several phases. An accomplished artist in his own right, he was also the father of painter Alfred H. Maurer.

Louis Maurer was born in Biebrich-on-the-Rhine, Germany in 1832. He studied drafting and animal anatomy in Mainz, where he also learned lithography, cabinet-making and ivory carving.

In 1851, he emigrated to New York City.

Soon Maurer went to work as a staff artist for Currier and Ives at $5 a week. He designed, drew and lithographed sporting and outdoor prints, alone or together with fellow artists such as Fanny Palmer, John Cameron and Arthur Fitzwilliam Tait. Maurer's best-known work of this period is his series "The Life of a Fireman"; he also frequently used the American trotting horse as a subject. With Tait, he worked on a series of American Indian subjects.

In 1860 or 1861, Maurer went to work for Major and Knapp, and from 1872 until 1884 he headed his own successful lithography firm, Maurer and Heppenheimer. He studied at the Gotham Art School and the National Academy of Design, beginning at age 50, and after his retirement in 1884 he devoted himself to painting. He toured the West as Buffalo Bill Cody's guest in 1885; a second trip West inspired Rocky Mountain landscapes and animal paintings.

At age 99, Maurer had his first one-man exhibition, in New York City. He died a year later.

SEASON	75-76	76-77	77-78	78-79	79-80	80-81	81-82	82-83	83-84	84-85
Paintings					1	1	1		2	
Dollars					$21,000	$4,250	$44,000		$105,000	

Record Sale: $60,000, CH, 6/8/84, "Trotting Contest," 57 × 96 in.

PUBLIC COLLECTIONS
Amon Carter Museum of Western Art, Fort Worth, Texas

GEORGE HENRY BOUGHTON
(1833-1905)

Recognized as a leading landscape and genre painter in the United States and abroad, George Henry Boughton had the ability to express sentiment and pathos on canvas. He illustrated editions of Washington Irving's *Rip Van Winkle* and *History of New York* and Nathaniel Hawthorne's *Scarlet Letter*. In his landscapes, he painted scenes of England, Brittany and The Netherlands.

Though he was born near Norwich, England in 1833 and lived in London for the second half of his life, Boughton's formative years as a self-taught artist began in Albany, New York, where his family settled in 1839.

At age 19 he was a landscape painter, whose paintings were being praised. The American Art-Union purchased his third or fourth picture. Through the encouragement of that institution, where he exhibited in 1852, he was able to study in England for six months.

If ever there were a painter who could tell a story with genuine sentiment, using soft tones and colors, it was Boughton. A London critic once declared that he "has learnt the secret of putting natural feeling into rustic figures, which has been almost entirely wanting to English painters."

Many of his works were of small size; notable among them is one entitled *Passing into the Shade* (date and location unknown), a woodland scene with two aged peasant women. Other paintings such as *Hop-Pickers Returning* (date

Alone, 30 x 20 in., signed l.r. Courtesy of Grand Central Art Galleries, Inc., New York, New York.

and location unknown), *Through the Fields* (date and location unknown), and *Coming through the Rye* (date and

location unknown), reflect his narrative approach. *Pilgrims Going to Church* (1867, New-York Historical Society) recalls a past era with historical accuracy.

In 1857, Boughton exhibited at the Washington Art Association, and from 1859 to 1860 he worked in New York City. In 1861, he went to Paris to study on his own; the French influence was subsequently reflected in his style.

Boughton established a studio in London in 1861, and continued his career in England until his death in 1905.

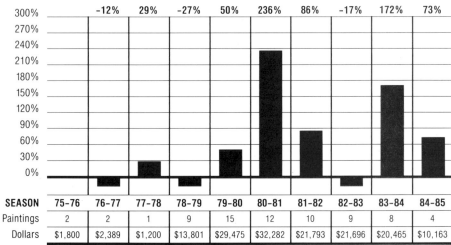

10-Year Average Change From Base Years '75-'76: 59%

	-12%	29%	-27%	50%	236%	86%	-17%	172%	73%

SEASON	75-76	76-77	77-78	78-79	79-80	80-81	81-82	82-83	83-84	84-85
Paintings	2	2	1	9	15	12	10	9	8	4
Dollars	$1,800	$2,389	$1,200	$13,801	$29,475	$32,282	$21,793	$21,696	$20,465	$10,163

Record Sale: $5,500, CH, 4/24/81, "By the Sea," 18 x 11 in.

WILLIAM TROST RICHARDS
(1833-1905)

William Trost Richards combined in his works the grandeur, atmosphere and light of the American painter, the interest in the minutiae of nature of the pre-raphaelites, and the precision and technique of the Dusseldorf School. He was a landscape artist for much of his life and is most remembered for his coastal seascapes.

Born in Philadelphia in 1833, Richards began to draw when very young. Despite circumstances that forced him at age 13 to drop out of school and support his family by designing chandeliers and gas fixtures, he studied privately, along with William Stanley Haseltine, under German artist Paul Weber. He may also have attended classes at the Pennsylvania Academy of the Fine Arts.

By 1853, Richards felt ready to devote all his time to art. He set out for Europe, probably in the company of his studio-mate, painter Alexander Lawrie, and Haseltine. Traveling through Florence, Rome and Paris, he encountered American artists Hiram Powers, Emanuel Gottlieb Leutze and Albert Bierstadt. He returned from Europe in 1856 with high regard for the uplifting works of native American landscape artists, such as John F. Kensett and Frederic Edwin Church.

In 1856, he married Anna Matlack and honeymooned and sketched at Niagara Falls. They later settled in German-

Approaching Storm, 1891, 41¼ x 32½ in., signed l.l. Courtesy of Taggart, Jorgensen, & Putman Gallery, Washington, D.C.

town, Pennsylvania, on the outskirts of Philadelphia. Richards devoted his attention from then through the Civil War to meticulous, naturalistic landscapes, many with literary themes. He was particularly influenced by an exhibition of the works of pre-raphaelite painters in Philadelphia in 1858.

His paintings of this period are charming; they combine, oddly, an obsessive camera-like precision with grand atmospheric effects. He worked out-of-doors as much as possible, in Pennsylvania, the Adirondacks and the Catskills.

At the end of the Civil War, from 1866 to 1867, Richards traveled with his family in Europe. After that, he began to paint his masterful coastal seascapes, which ideally reconcile his love of sharp detail with the larger scale.

He began in the 1870s to spend the summers and paint in Newport, Rhode Island. He also traveled frequently to England for further subjects and markets. In 1890, he moved permanently to Newport, where he died in 1905.

MEMBERSHIPS
Forensic and Literary Circle of Philadelphia
National Academy of Design

PUBLIC COLLECTIONS
Bowdoin College, Brunswick, Maine
Brooklyn Museum
Cooper-Hewitt Museum of Decorative Arts and Design, New York City
Corcoran Gallery, Washington, D.C.
Metropolitan Museum of Art, New York City
Newark Museum, New Jersey
University of Washington, Seattle

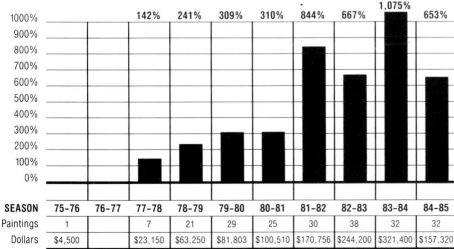

10-Year Average Change From Base Years '75-'76: 471%

| | 142% | 241% | 309% | 310% | 844% | 667% | 1,075% | 653% |

SEASON	75-76	76-77	77-78	78-79	79-80	80-81	81-82	82-83	83-84	84-85
Paintings	1		7	21	29	25	30	38	32	32
Dollars	$4,500		$23,150	$63,250	$81,803	$100,510	$170,756	$244,200	$321,400	$157,320

Record Sale: $170,000, SPB, 5/30/84, "Mackerel Cove, Jamestown, Rhode Island," 26 x 47 in.

JAMES DAVID SMILLIE
(1833-1909)

On the Boquet, Elizabethtown, 1868, 18 x 24 in., signed l.r. Courtesy of Henry B. Holt, Inc., Essex Fells, New Jersey.

James David Smillie was the eldest son in a family of engravers and painters. His etchings, dry points, aquatints and lithographs were probably his most significant contributions to the art of his period, but in his later years he also achieved some status as a landscape painter. Like that of his younger brother, George, also a landscapist, his work was influenced by the earlier Hudson River School of painters. His landscapes, however, had a certain dryness, probably a carry-over from his years as an engraver.

Smillie was born in New York City in 1833. His father was a well-known engraver and, working with him, James made his first engraving plate when he was eight. He collaborated with his father until he was 31, working largely on bank-note vignettes. In 1857, the pair also made the engravings for Emory's *Mexican Boundary Survey.*

Even after taking up painting, Smillie continued his interest in engraving. For Volume 1 of *Picturesque America,* published in 1872, he wrote the section on the Yosemite Valley and illustrated it with some 20 engravings. He also wrote various articles on engraving.

After a trip to Europe in 1864, he turned to landscape painting. His favorite scenes were mountains, and he painted many of the noted American ranges in the East and West. On a second trip to France in 1884, he painted the cliffs and shores around Entretat, already made familiar by such artists as Courbet and Monet. In color and composition these are reminiscent of the Western landscapes of Thomas Moran, who had accompanied Smillie on at least one of his trips to the American West.

Aside from his occasional travels, Smillie spent his entire life in New York City and died there in 1909.

10-Year Average Change From Base Years '77-'78: 363%

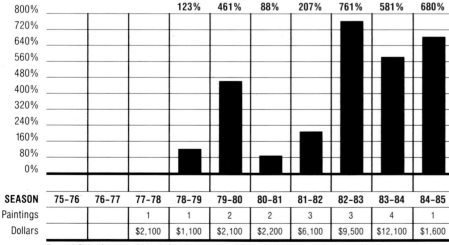

SEASON	75-76	76-77	77-78	78-79	79-80	80-81	81-82	82-83	83-84	84-85
			123%	461%	88%	207%	761%	581%	680%	
Paintings			1	1	2	2	3	3	4	1
Dollars			$2,100	$1,100	$2,100	$2,200	$6,100	$9,500	$12,100	$1,600

Record Sale: $7,500, SPB, 6/22/84, "Home of G.H. Van Valkenburgh," 15 x 22 in.

MEMBERSHIPS
American Watercolor Society
National Academy of Design
New York Etching Club

PUBLIC COLLECTIONS
Amon Carter Museum, Fort Worth
Corcoran Gallery of Art, Washington, D.C.
Museum of Fine Arts, Boston
New York Public Library, New York City
Oakland Museum, California

NORTON BUSH
(1834-1894)

Tropical River, 1892, 22 x 36 in., signed l.l. Courtesy of John H. Garzoli Gallery, San Francisco, California.

Norton Bush was first noted for his portraits, marine views and landscapes of the East Coast and California. Later in his career, after visiting Central and South America, Bush devoted himself to his favorite topic—painting tropical scenery.

Born in Rochester, New York, Bush first studied art in his native city under James Harris. He studied with Jasper F. Cropsey after moving to New York City. At age 19, Bush moved to California, making San Francisco his permanent home. In 1868, he opened a studio in that city.

During a visit to Panama in 1868, Bush obtained material for a series of landscapes he painted for the late William C. Ralston. These paintings were hung on the walls of the Sharon residence in Belmont, California.

On a trip to Peru, where he made sketches of Mount Chimborazo, Bush also crossed the Andes, drawing the famous volcano El Miste, Mount Meiggs, and other exotic scenes.

Bush was a frequent contributor to exhibitions held in San Francisco and at the state fairs in Sacramento. He also exhibited at the National Academy of Design in 1852 and 1871.

Elected a member of the San Francisco Art Association in 1874 and a director in 1878, Bush died in San Francisco in 1894.

SEASON	75-76	76-77	77-78	78-79	79-80	80-81	81-82	82-83	83-84	84-85
Paintings	2			4	2	2	4	4	8	
Dollars	$1,750			$3,800	$2,000	$12,100	$9,500	$5,300	$30,400	

Record Sale: $10,000, CH, 4/24/81, "On the San Juan," 20 x 36 in.

MEMBERSHIPS
San Francisco Art Association

JAMES ABBOTT
McNEILL
WHISTLER
(1834-1903)

Lady of the Lang Lijsen. Courtesy of Philadelphia Museum of Art, Pennsylvania,
The John G. Johnson Collection.

One of his era's most outspoken proponents of art for art's sake, James A.M. Whistler thumbed his nose at conventional Victorian notions of storytelling in painting. The subtle harmonies of his misty, impressionist landscapes—and of his portraits, which were more compositions of muted colors than actual representations of the sitters—baffled the public and outraged critics at first. In the end, however, he was recognized as one of the most original and influential painters of the nineteenth century.

In many ways his later work paved the way for the abstract art that emerged some 50 years later. Moreover, his representational etchings now are considered by some the finest since Rembrandt.

Whistler was born in 1834 in Lowell, Massachusetts. His father, a civil engineer, took the family to Russia in 1843, while he supervised construction of the first railroad between St. Petersburg and Moscow. Following the aristocratic Russian custom, the young Whistler grew up speaking French. He also had his first art training at the Imperial Academy of the Fine Arts.

When his father died, the family returned to the United States and, in 1851, Whistler entered the military academy at West Point. He excelled in drawing, but failed chemistry and was expelled in 1853.

He worked for a time for the United States Geodetic Survey and, while there, learned the fundamentals of map etching with astonishing speed. In 1855, he went to Paris, intent on becoming a painter, and never returned to his homeland. He soon met and fell under the influence of Courbet. Much of his early work was realistic, like Courbet's, but by the late 1860s he had rejected realism and developed his own poetic style.

Whistler loved the bohemian life of Paris. He loved playing the part of the artist and attracting attention with his outrageous remarks. Even so, in 1859 he moved to London permanently, although he went back to Paris frequently.

A set of etchings executed before he left France, and another set of the Thames River executed several years after Whistler came to London, clearly established his supremacy in that field. He was captivated by Japanese art, and its economy of means was reflected in his masterful ability to suggest a whole scene by using only the merest indications of its elements.

The first of his great paintings to reflect this Japanese influence through flattened planes and monochromatic colors was *The White Girl* (1862, National Gallery of Art), a full-length portrait of his mistress, Joanna Heffernan.

Believing that color, like music, could suggest moods, Whistler began in 1866 to use musical nomenclature for his work, both new and old. *The White Girl,* for example, was renamed *Symphony in White, No. 1.* His most famous portrait, that of his mother, was titled simply *An Arrangement in Black and Grey, No. 1* (1871, Louvre).

As Whistler's work became more abstract, critical reaction became harsher. In 1877, when John Ruskin, England's leading critic, accused him of "flinging a pot of paint in the public's face," Whistler sued him for libel. He won the case, but was awarded only a farthing. The court costs bankrupted him and many of his paintings were sold at ridiculously low prices.

A commission to do two series of etchings of Venice in 1880 saved him financially. The etchings themselves, which eloquently capture the magic of that city, are considered the finest he ever did.

In the two decades before his death in London in 1903, Whistler finally received serious recognition from critics, art patrons and the public.

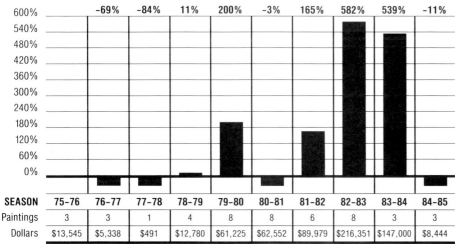

10-Year Average Change From Base Years '75-'76: 133%

	-69%	-84%	11%	200%	-3%	165%	582%	539%	-11%
SEASON	75-76	76-77	77-78	78-79	79-80	80-81	81-82	82-83	83-84	84-85
Paintings	3	3	1	4	8	8	6	8	3	3
Dollars	$13,545	$5,338	$491	$12,780	$61,225	$62,552	$89,979	$216,351	$147,000	$8,444

Record Sale: $75,000, CH, 12/9/83, "The Sea, Pourville," 6 × 9 in.

MARCUS WATERMAN
(1834-1914)

Solitary, independent and imaginative, landscape and figure artist Marcus Waterman chose his own path and followed his own muse, while other artists pursued the various movements and trends that came and went during his lifetime. His subjects encompassed the New England forest, the Cape Cod shore, Europe, North Africa and fantastic lands seen only by his mind's eye. His paintings are distinguished by an exquisite harmony of color and light, and by a sense of isolation and remoteness.

Born in Providence, Rhode Island in 1834, Waterman received little formal art education. He graduated from Brown University in 1857, and moved to New York City, painting there until 1874. In that year, he moved to Boston. While living in Boston, he traveled widely, finding his subjects in some of the most desolate areas of the world, including the wild forests of Vermont and the exotic landscape of Algeria. The more alien and picturesque the locale, the more he felt at home. In 1900, he moved to Italy, and died in Moderno in 1914.

Waterman apparently received some instruction from California's Yosemite Valley painter Thomas Hill, and from influential teacher and landscape artist William Morris Hunt, but they had little influence on his style. He pursued his own agenda, making innumerable color studies, examining the effects of light in all circumstances. Apparently blessed with an eidetic or photographic memory, he never forgot the details of any scene he had studied, and could examine a forest scene in his mind as if he were in front of it.

His landscapes are richly atmospheric, dramatic and moody. The series of scenes from the *Arabian Nights* he produced while he was in Algeria epitomize his originality; though they are romantic, storytelling pictures, they are untarnished by self-conscious cuteness, being instead distinguished by their perspective and detachment.

Dutch Country Scene, 17 x 23½ in., signed l.l. Courtesy of Raydon Gallery, New York, New York.

MEMBERSHIPS
American Watercolor Society
Artists Fund Society
National Academy of Design

SEASON	75-76	76-77	77-78	78-79	79-80	80-81	81-82	82-83	83-84	84-85
Paintings			2				3	1	3	1
Dollars			$1,350				$3,450	$600	$3,850	$2,400

Record Sale: $2,500, S.BM, 2/29/84, "Banana Seller," 18 × 14 in.

FRANCIS A. SILVA
(1835-1886)

Born in 1835, Francis Silva was a marine painter known for exaggerating and intensifying natural effects of light and air for poetic purposes. For Silva, the subtle manipulation of light and atmosphere was an aesthetic device that transcended naturalism and became an almost abstract means of expressing sentiment. The style that Silva worked in was known as luminism, a poetry of nature that approached Emersonian transcendentalism.

As a schoolboy, Silva exhibited pen drawings at the American Institute, but he did not begin his art career until after service in the Seventh Regiment of the New York State Militia during the Civil War. Advancing from lieutenant to captain, Silva was soon stricken with "miasmatic disease." He was dishonorably discharged for desertion when he left his regiment, but was soon reinstated.

When he finally received an honorable discharge a year later, Silva married Margaret A. Watts in Keyport, New Jersey in 1868. His debut as a painter was at the National Academy of Design's annual exhibition of 1868-1869. Silva's earliest known painting, however, is *Cape Ann* (1870, Coe Kerr Gallery).

By 1870, Silva had evolved, for a self-taught artist, a remarkably skillful technique and a repertoire of marine subjects and atmospheric effects that varied little for the rest of his life. He evolved from the somewhat tentative

Kingston Point, Hudson River, 20 x 36 in., signed l.r. Courtesy of Vose Galleries of Boston, Inc., Massachusetts.

Dawn on the Coast, 11¾ x 24 in., signed l.l. Courtesy of Newman Galleries, Philadelphia, Pennsylvania.

handling of such early canvases as *Sunrise: Marine View* (1870, Hirschl and Adler Galleries) to the crisper forms of such later works as *View Near New London, Connecticut* (1877, Brooklyn Museum).

"We have few artists who are so accurate in drawing or so conscientious in the rendering of detail," an *Art Journal* critic wrote in 1880, "but it is to be regretted that he does not modify the occasional crudeness of the coloring of compositions which have so many excellent qualities."

Although his luminous technique led to his election to the American Water Color Society in 1872, he was primarily known for his late paintings, which were nearly impressionist in feeling. Just before he died in 1886, Silva painted *A Summer Afternoon at Long Branch* (1885, National Gallery of Art), considered his masterpiece.

MEMBERSHIPS
American Water Color Society

PUBLIC COLLECTIONS
Broad Street Trust, Boston
Brooklyn Museum
National Gallery of Art, Washington, D.C.
Peabody Museum of Salem, Massachusetts

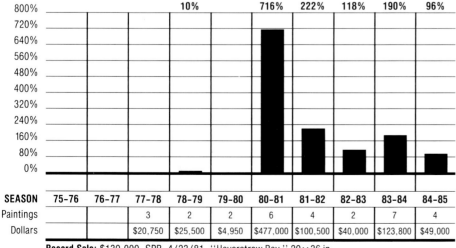

10-Year Average Change From Base Years '77-'78: 169%

		10%			716%	222%	118%	190%	96%
SEASON	75-76	76-77	77-78	78-79	79-80	80-81	81-82	82-83	83-84	84-85
Paintings			3	2	2	6	4	2	7	4
Dollars			$20,750	$25,500	$4,950	$477,000	$100,500	$40,000	$123,800	$49,000

Record Sale: $130,000, SPB, 4/23/81, "Haverstraw Bay," 20 x 36 in.

265

JAMES CRAWFORD THOM
(1835-1898)

The Acorn, 6 x 11½ in., signed l.r. Courtesy of National Museum of American Art, Smithsonian Institution, Gift of John Gellatly.

James Crawford Thom was a talented genre and landscape painter of the second half of the nineteenth century.

The son of a noted Scottish sculptor who was active in the United States, he was born in 1835 in New York City, but with a brother spent his youth on a farm near Ramapo, New York.

At age 18, Thom was admitted to the National Academy of Design in New York City. In 1859, James McCormack sponsored his trip to France, where he studied with Thomas Couture, Pierre Edouard Frere, Corot and Henri Picou. He moved to Ecouen, near Paris, to study with Frere, whose typical subjects were the peasants and their children at work and play in the picturesque French countryside.

In early 1866, Thom moved with his wife and son to London. He began to exhibit regularly at a number of galleries; between 1866 and 1873, his fame gradually increased.

In 1873, his paintings were being exhibited in major cities in the United States, and Thom and his wife and five children returned to New York City to live.

His best work was of children, whom he portrayed lovingly in natural settings. His landscapes were generally of the Hudson River School.

Thom won no major honors or awards in the United States. Although he had been a student and an exhibitor at the National Academy of Design, he was never elected to membership.

Thom moved his family to Atlantic Highlands, New Jersey, where he painted children boating and having snowball fights in that rural town.

During the last decade of his life, Thom remained as productive as ever, with his usual skill and precision. He died in 1898 in Atlantic Highlands after a bout with pneumonia.

Though his paintings did not bring him lasting fame, a retrospective of Thom's work in East Brunswick, New Jersey in October of 1983 was favorably received.

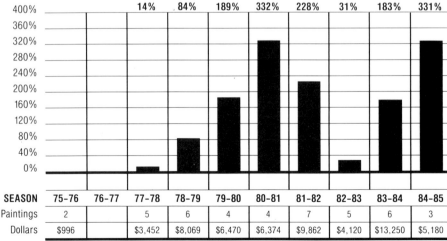

10-Year Average Change From Base Years '75–'76: 155%

SEASON	75-76	76-77	77-78	78-79	79-80	80-81	81-82	82-83	83-84	84-85
			14%	84%	189%	332%	228%	31%	183%	331%
Paintings	2		5	6	4	4	7	5	6	3
Dollars	$996		$3,452	$8,069	$6,470	$6,374	$9,862	$4,120	$13,250	$5,180

Record Sale: $4,200, P.NY, 10/13/83, ''Feeding the Ducks,'' 30×41 in.

266

WILLIAM STANLEY HASELTINE
(1835-1900)

Indian Rock, Narragansett, Rhode Island, 1863, 22 x 38¼ in., signed l.r. Photograph courtesy of Hirschl & Adler Galleries, Inc., New York, New York.

Expatriate painter William Stanley Haseltine was an important landscapist whose precise attention to geological formations adds a strong sense of reality to his coastal scenes of New England and Italy.

Born into an artistic Philadelphia family in 1835, Haseltine studied there under German artist Paul Weber. After graduating from Harvard in 1854, he followed Weber to Germany, where he studied in Dusseldorf. Haseltine became an important member of the American group in that city; in 1857, he and his fellow American students made a sketching trip down the Rhine and into Italy.

Upon his return to the United States in 1858, he was elected to the National Academy of Design. In the following years, he painted his finest pictures, coastal views of New England.

Haseltine's German training endowed him with a precise sense of line. But it is his extraordinary attention to the detail of coastal rocks and his sense of light that bring his paintings to life, as in *Indian Rock* (date and location unknown). His inland landscapes also rely upon conscientious observations of nature to produce a crisp, true rendering of a scene, as in *Near Hyde Park—Hudson River / July 30, 1860* (Museum of Fine Arts, Boston).

In 1866, he returned to Europe, studying for a time with barbizon land-scape painters in Paris before settling in Rome. Haseltine remained in Rome until his death in 1900, making occasional trips to the United States.

Like other expatriates, Haseltine produced Italian landscapes for the American market. In these late paintings, he replaced the cool palette of his New England landscapes with the warmer hues of Italy.

MEMBERSHIPS
National Academy of Design

PUBLIC COLLECTIONS
Museum of Fine Arts, Boston

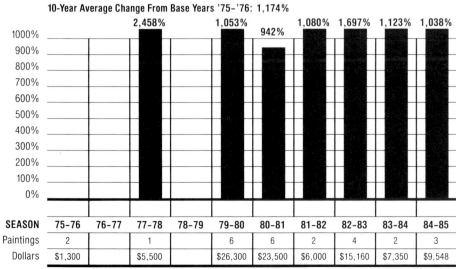

10-Year Average Change From Base Years '75-'76: 1,174%

SEASON	75-76	76-77	77-78	78-79	79-80	80-81	81-82	82-83	83-84	84-85
			2,458%		1,053%	942%	1,080%	1,697%	1,123%	1,038%
Paintings	2		1		6	6	2	4	2	3
Dollars	$1,300		$5,500		$26,300	$23,500	$6,000	$15,160	$7,350	$9,548

Record Sale: $14,000, SPB, 4/23/81, "Mediterranean Coastal Town," 32 x 56 in.

267

JOHN HENRY DOLPH
(1835-1903)

Gray Day at the Coast, 1875, 32 x 48 in., signed l.l. Courtesy of Raydon Gallery, New York, New York.

Sometimes called "the Landseer of America," John Henry Dolph earned a considerable reputation producing masterful, and sometimes humorous, paintings of dogs and cats.

Dolph was born in Fort Ann, New York in 1835. He began his career as a portrait painter in Detroit during the late 1850s. By 1865, he had moved to New York City, and had begun to attract attention with his scenes of American rural life.

Dolph spent approximately five years studying in Antwerp and Paris. In Antwerp, he was tutored by Von Kuyck in animal painting.

Dolph returned to New York City in the early 1870s. In 1875, he produced a rendering of a Persian cat, and decided he would specialize in paintings of cats and dogs from that point on. He was known to weave subtle humor into these paintings, as in his interpretation of La Fontaine's fable, "The Rat Retired from the World." Another painting, *High Life* (date and location unknown), which depicted the comfortable existence of a wealthy family's pets, was whimsically enhanced by *Low Life* (date and location unknown), showing a litter of barnyard kittens.

Dolph was made an associate of the National Academy of Design in 1877, and a full member in 1898. In 1901, he was awarded a bronze medal at the Pan-American Exposition in Buffalo, New York.

Dolph's singularity of subject matter was apparently inspired by his great fondness for animals. When he was felled by the heart disease that had troubled him for years, Dolph spent his last days regretting that he would be unable to complete a painting of a favorite dog.

Dolph died at the home of a friend in New York in 1903. His work is held at the Pennsylvania Academy of the Fine Arts.

MEMBERSHIPS
Kit-Kat Club
Lotus Club
National Academy of Design
Salmagundi Club

PUBLIC COLLECTIONS
Pennsylvania Academy of the Fine Arts, Philadelphia

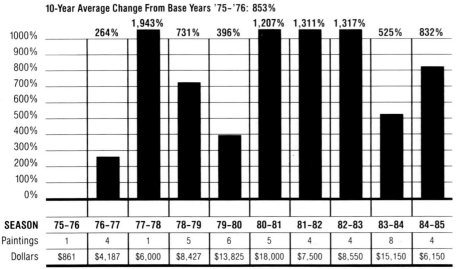

10-Year Average Change From Base Years '75–'76: 853%

SEASON	75–76	76–77	77–78	78–79	79–80	80–81	81–82	82–83	83–84	84–85
		264%	1,943%	731%	396%	1,207%	1,311%	1,317%	525%	832%
Paintings	1	4	1	5	6	5	4	4	8	4
Dollars	$861	$4,187	$6,000	$8,427	$13,825	$18,000	$7,500	$8,550	$15,150	$6,150

Record Sale: $11,500, SPB, 6/19/81, "Kitten Watching Goldfish," 28 × 21 in.

268

EDMUND DARCH LEWIS
(1835-1910)

Edmund Darch Lewis enjoyed a career as one of the nineteenth century's most financially successful landscape painters.

Born in Philadelphia in 1835, Lewis studied painting for five years under Paul Weber. He first exhibited at the Pennsylvania Academy of the Fine Arts in 1854. Later his paintings were exhibited at the National Academy of Design and the Boston Athenaeum.

Lewis, who lived in Philadelphia until his death in 1910, chose scenes from Philadelphia, New York and New England as his chief subjects.

His early picturesque Pennsylvania and Delaware Water Gap pictures were fresh in color and became immensely popular.

Their mass appeal caused Lewis to increase production to the point of painting two or three pictures a day. His quickly painted works were considered potboilers; reportedly, the trained eye could detect the hurriedness of their execution, but it was less apparent to the layman.

Lewis sold his work as rapidly as it was painted. His paintings were sought out and accepted at every major exhibition in the country. For a while, his oil and watercolor sales exceeded every other painter's in the country.

Lewis built a tapestry gallery filled with antique collections. The success he enjoyed as a painter followed him as a collector. After he had long established himself as an artist, Lewis had equal acclaim as a noted connoisseur of furniture and china.

He died in 1910.

Lake in the Afternoon, 24 x 42 in., signed l.l. Courtesy of Henry B. Holt, Inc., Essex Fells, New Jersey.

10-Year Average Change From Base Years '75–'76: 158%

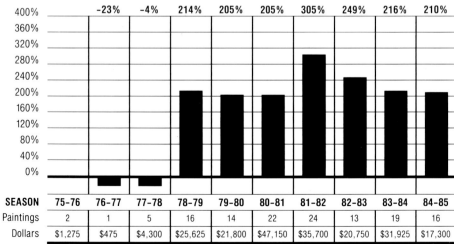

	-23%	-4%	214%	205%	205%	305%	249%	216%	210%

SEASON	75–76	76–77	77–78	78–79	79–80	80–81	81–82	82–83	83–84	84–85
Paintings	2	1	5	16	14	22	24	13	19	16
Dollars	$1,275	$475	$4,300	$25,625	$21,800	$47,150	$35,700	$20,750	$31,925	$17,300

Record Sale: $7,250, SPB, 10/21/83, "Lake Willoughby," 44 × 74 in.

JOHN
LA FARGE
(1835-1910)

Visit of Nicodemus to Christ, 1880, 42¾ x 35½ in., signed l.r. Courtesy of National Museum of American Art, Smithsonian Institution, Washington, D.C. Gift of William T. Evans.

Upper-class, well-educated and cosmopolitan, John La Farge was regarded as one of the most cultured and sophisticated artists of his time. Today he is known not only for still-life and landscape paintings, but for his murals, stained-glass design and writings. Stylistically, La Farge is considered somewhere between the romanticism of his mentor, William Morris Hunt, and the American impressionists.

La Farge was born in New York City. After graduating from Mount St. Mary's College in Maryland, he studied law. In 1856 he made a visit to Paris and for a very brief time took some lessons in painting with prominent French artist Thomas Couture. Before returning home, La Farge visited England; there, he was impressed by the pre-raphaelites' efforts to express romantic ideas in naturalistic terms.

In 1859, La Farge returned to the United States and spent the year with artist William Morris Hunt in Newport. Throughout the next decade, he became interested in the study of optics and, like the French impressionists, explored the properties of light and color. In addition, La Farge was interested in Japanese art and was one of the first American artists to write about its aesthetic significance.

During the 1860s, La Farge executed several important landscapes, although he was primarily interested in still lifes and floral studies. Characteristic of his floral still lifes is the masterwork *Flowers on a Window Ledge* (1862, Corcoran Gallery of Art). It demonstrates his concern with light, as the flowers are suffused with the light from the outdoors beyond the window. The water lily, in particular, featured prominently in many of La Farge's finest works.

Short of cash, La Farge agreed in 1865 to accept a commission from prosperous Bostonian Charles Freeland. Before falling gravely ill, La Farge completed three of six panels in Freeland's dining room.

Although incapacitated for nearly two years, he undertook several major, if disparate, projects during the 1870s, including watercolors, book illustrations, mural paintings and stained-glass designs.

In 1876, La Farge was invited by architect Henry Hobson Richardson to design the interior of Trinity Church in Boston. In his design, he revived the neglected principles of Venetian mural painting and the workshop tradition of the old masters. Within the next decade, he completed murals for St. Thomas's Church (1877 to 1878), the Church of the Incarnation (1885) and the Church of the Ascension (1886 to 1888), all in New York City.

La Farge's predilection for mystical, spiritual ideals led him to undertake extended voyages in the Orient and South Seas. He accompanied writer Henry Adams to Japan in 1886 and Tahiti in 1890. La Farge, like French artist Paul Gauguin, drew inspiration from the exotic, tropical landscape. Works such as *Maua, Our Boatman* (1891, Addison Gallery of Art) demonstrate his skill in rendering an evocative, atmospheric landscape, and his ability to combine still life and portraiture.

During his prolific career, La Farge published several books, including *Considerations on Painting* (1895) and *An Artist's Letters from Japan* (1877).

He died in Providence, Rhode Island in 1910.

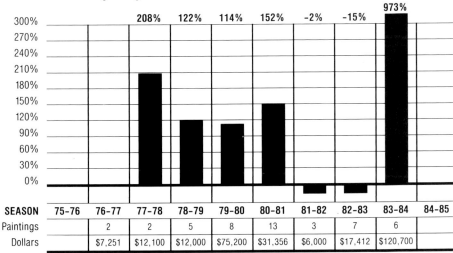

10-Year Average Change From Base Years '76-'77: 194%

SEASON	75-76	76-77	77-78	78-79	79-80	80-81	81-82	82-83	83-84	84-85
		208%	122%	114%	152%	-2%	-15%	973%	
Paintings		2	2	5	8	13	3	7	6	
Dollars		$7,251	$12,100	$12,000	$75,200	$31,356	$6,000	$17,412	$120,700	

Record Sale: $67,500, SPB, 12/8/83, "Hollyhocks," 34 × 16 in.

GEORGE HENRY STORY
(1835-1922)

George Henry Story was a painter equally adept at landscapes, portraits and genre scenes. He also served for many years as curator of paintings at both the Metropolitan Museum of Art in New York City and the Wadsworth Atheneum in Hartford, Connecticut. He painted portraits of many prominent New Yorkers, but perhaps his best-known were several of Abraham Lincoln as president.

Born in New Haven, Connecticut in 1835, Story apprenticed himself at age 15 for three years to a local wood-carver. After that he studied for three more years under portrait painters Charles Hines and Louis Bail. He finished off his art training with a year in Europe.

On his return, he worked successively in Portland, Maine, Washington, D.C. and Cuba before settling in New York City.

In Washington he came to know Lincoln. It was Story, in fact, who posed Lincoln for the first official photograph taken after he became president. Story made pencil sketches of Lincoln at that time and later, when he was commissioned to paint a portrait of the president, he arranged with Lincoln's secretary to be admitted to the Oval Office to make further sketches of him at work. He did this for three days.

"After each sitting I returned to my room," Story wrote later, "and worked upon my picture with my sitter as vividly in mind almost as though he were in my actual presence."

The Scissors Grinder, signed l.l. Courtesy of Thomas Gilcrease Institute of American History and Art, Tulsa, Oklahoma.

He held his curatorial post at the Metropolitan from 1889 to 1906, when he became curator emeritus. In 1904 and 1905, he was also acting director of the museum. He was appointed curator of painting at the Wadsworth Atheneum in 1899, and held that position until his death in New York in 1922.

MEMBERSHIPS
Artists' Fund Society
National Academy of Design

PUBLIC COLLECTIONS
National Gallery of Art, Washington, D.C.
Metropolitan Museum of Art, New York City
Wadsworth Atheneum, Hartford, Connecticut

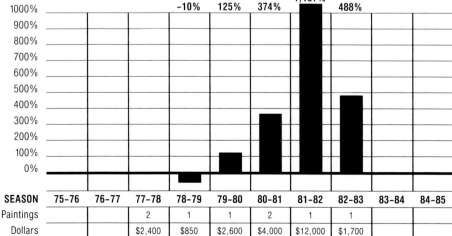

· 10-Year Average Change From Base Years '77-'78: 362%

SEASON	75-76	76-77	77-78	78-79	79-80	80-81	81-82	82-83	83-84	84-85
				-10%	125%	374%	1,197%	488%		
Paintings			2	1	1	2	1	1		
Dollars			$2,400	$850	$2,600	$4,000	$12,000	$1,700		

Record Sale: $12,000, CH, 12/11/81, "Playing Soldiers," 24 × 16 in.

FIDELIA BRIDGES
(1835-1923)

Fidelia Bridges was a painter of nature, working first in oils and later in watercolor. Instead of capturing the broad vista, however, she preferred the close-up examination of small segments of the natural world. Birds and·flowers were her favorites, and she recorded them with botanical and scientific accuracy.

She was born in Salem, Massachusetts in 1835, the daughter of a sea captain in the China trade who died in Canton when she was 14. When her mother died soon after, Bridges became a mother's helper for a kindly Quaker family in Brooklyn, a relationship that grew into lifelong friendship.

Later she met Anne Whitney, a budding sculptor, who encouraged her to take up painting. Moving to Philadelphia, Bridges studied under William Trost Richards, who painted in the style of the English pre-raphaelites. He helped her develop her exquisite sense of detail.

In 1867, Bridges went to Rome for a year to study, sharing quarters for a time with Anne Whitney and another painter, later traveling on her own. On her return, she concentrated more and more on painting in watercolor. She also did illustrations for magazines.

In time she adopted an almost oriental simplification of her backgrounds, often leaving the paper white where before it might have been busy with plants or leaves.

In 1892, Bridges moved to Canaan, Connecticut to be near friends. After 1900 she continued to sketch, but retired from the art world. She lived a quiet, pleasant life in Canaan until her death in 1923.

MEMBERSHIPS
American Watercolor Society
National Academy of Design

(Birds), 1874, 13 x 9½ in., signed l.r. Courtesy of Henry B. Holt, Inc., Essex Fells, New Jersey.

SEASON	75-76	76-77	77-78	78-79	79-80	80-81	81-82	82-83	83-84	84-85
Paintings							1	1		2
Dollars							$1,300	$1,000		$2,068

Record Sale: $1,600, YG.P, 11/24/84, "Birds in Snow," 8 × 6 in.

ALEXANDER H. WYANT
(1836-1892)

Housatonic Valley, 1880-1890, 24⅛ x 36⅛ in. Courtesy of National Museum of American Art, Smithsonian Institution, Gift of William T. Evans.

Alexander H. Wyant was a landscape painter whose work was in vogue throughout his long career. His grand portrayals of American Eastern mountains and woodlands earned for him a reputation as a significant artist of the late Hudson River School. Moreover, he was among the handful of landscape artists—the boldest being his mentor and contemporary, George Inness—who pushed beyond the strictures of the school's meticulous realism, experimenting with approaches and techniques that led to impressionism.

Wyant's characteristic departures from the formulas of the Hudson River School were in his use of a more subtle palette in depicting light and shadow, tonal delicacy and freer brushwork. The effect is softer, luminous, more personal, almost always subdued in mood, compared to the hard, literal, typically grandiose brilliance associated with the school.

Born to an itinerant farmer in Ohio, Wyant was apprenticed to a sign painter and harness maker, but wanted to be an artist. In Cincinnati, in 1857, he saw landscapes by George Inness that so fired his ambition that he went to New York City to meet Inness. With his help and that of Cincinnati art patron Nicholas Longworth, Wyant enrolled for a year of study at the National Academy of Design in 1860.

In 1865, Wyant studied in Karlesruhe, under Norwegian artist Hans Fredrik Gude, who had trained at the Dusseldorf School. After visiting England, where he was greatly influenced by the work of J.M.W. Turner, Wyant returned to open a New York City studio in 1867.

During an expedition to Arizona and New Mexico in 1873, Wyant experienced a stroke which paralyzed his right hand, forcing him to paint with his left for the remaining two decades of his career. The enforced left-handedness apparently hastened Wyant's progression toward a looser technique, freer brushwork, greater use of implied forms, further retreat from detail and the somber tonalities and impressionism that characterize his mature work.

These developments were in fortunate alignment with changing public taste; Wyant's popular recognition and stream of commissions continued unabated. He divided his time between his New York City studio and the Adirondack and Catskill Mountains he knew so well. In 1889, he moved to Arkville, New York, in the Catskills. He died in 1892.

Wyant's work is sometimes faulted by modern critics for repetitiveness in composition and mood and for a lack of vigor. Most concede his importance in the movement from the impersonal objectivism of the Hudson River School toward the subjective freedoms of American impressionism.

MEMBERSHIPS
American Water Color Society
National Academy of Design

PUBLIC COLLECTIONS
Brooklyn Museum
Metropolitan Museum of Art, New York City
Montclair Art Museum, New Jersey
National Gallery of Art, Washington, D.C.
St. Louis Art Museum
Toledo Museum of Art, Ohio
Worcester Art Museum, Massachusetts

SEASON	75-76	76-77	77-78	78-79	79-80	80-81	81-82	82-83	83-84	84-85
Paintings	6	4	9	27	18	12	18	11	1	15
Dollars	$22,675	$9,700	$18,950	$49,916	$53,906	$23,550	$48,250	$84,902	$900	$38,700

Record Sale: $52,000, SPB, 6/23/83, "Riverscape," 33 × 60 in.

HOMER DODGE MARTIN
(1836-1897)

Homer Martin was a landscape painter whose style evolved over the years from an early Hudson River School realism to the near-impressionism of his final paintings. He is remembered today as a painter who struggled all his life to overcome a variety of handicaps, producing his finest work at the very end of his life.

Born in Albany, New York, Homer Martin was largely self-taught. Around 1852 he studied briefly with landscapist James Hart. In the early 1860s, Martin moved to New York City, where he began painting cool and somber studies of the upstate New York region. Melancholy in mood, his paintings of this period reflect the cold and unforgiving side of nature, as in *Lake Sanford* (1870, Century Association, New York).

Martin struggled for many years to overcome his lack of early training, as well as a variety of ailments ranging from melancholy to chronic eczema to the deteriorating vision that left him almost blind at the end of his life. Nonetheless, his stoic nature and dedication to art led him through a variety of influences to the discovery of his personal vision.

Martin's later influences included landscapes of the barbizon painters and plein-air studies of the early impressionists. He made two trips to Europe, traveling to England in 1876, and living in Normandy from 1881 to 1886. Although he painted little in Europe, each time he returned to the United States with renewed creativity.

Martin painted his finest works at the end of his life, apparently reconciled to his steadily declining health. His late masterpiece, *The Harp of the Winds* (1895, Metropolitan Museum of Art), a remembered view of the Seine River, is notable for its peaceful composition and plein-air clarity.

Homer Martin died in 1897 in St. Paul, Minnesota.

The Giant, Dead River Pond, 1886 (Adirondacks), 18 x 30 in., signed l.l. Collection of Robert H. Solem, Photograph courtesy of Kennedy Galleries, New York, New York.

MEMBERSHIPS
National Academy of Design
Society of American Artists

PUBLIC COLLECTIONS
Metropolitan Museum of Art,
New York City

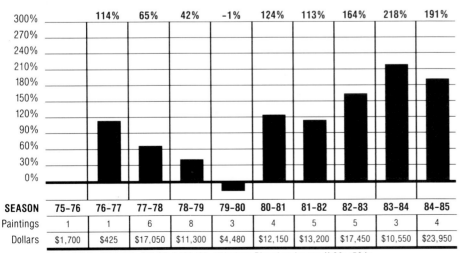

10-Year Average Change From Base Years '75-'76: 103%

	114%	65%	42%	-1%	124%	113%	164%	218%	191%

SEASON	75-76	76-77	77-78	78-79	79-80	80-81	81-82	82-83	83-84	84-85
Paintings	1	1	6	8	3	4	5	5	3	4
Dollars	$1,700	$425	$17,050	$11,300	$4,480	$12,150	$13,200	$17,450	$10,550	$23,950

Record Sale: $18,000, BB.SF, 2/28/85, "Hudson River Landscape," 38 × 50 in.

RANSOM HOLDREDGE
(1836-1899)

Russian River Valley, 30 x 49¾ in., signed l.l. Courtesy of Vose Galleries of Boston, Inc., Massachusetts.

A painter of Western mountain landscapes, Indians and seascapes, Ransom Holdredge was hailed by the San Francisco press as one of the ranking artists of his day. Some critics put his work above that of his contemporary William Keith. His early paintings were bright, very much in the style of the Hudson River School.

He was born in 1836 in New York City and went to San Francisco as a young man. He worked there for many years as a draftsman at the Mare Island Navy Yard. Without formal art training, he began sketching and painting around the bay and in the Sierra Nevada Mountains.

Later Holdredge studied with area artists and exhibited locally, always signing his name "Holdridge." On vacations he went to the Southwest, the Rockies and Canada to paint, frequently including Indians in his landscapes.

In 1874, Holdredge and a friend sold enough paintings to finance a trip to France to study. On his return to the United States two years later, he worked for a time as a staff artist for *Scribner's Magazine.* It is said that he was with United States troops when General Custer was massacred at Little Big Horn.

After his trip to France, Holdredge's paintings moved more toward the barbizon style. His work became darker. He used a palette knife to get a thick impasto.

Although his landscapes sold well, at heart Holdredge wanted to be a portrait painter. Disappointed and frustrated at not achieving this goal, he began to drink heavily. When he died, in 1899, he was penniless.

MEMBERSHIPS
Bohemian Club
San Francisco Art Association

PUBLIC COLLECTIONS
Oakland Art Museum, California

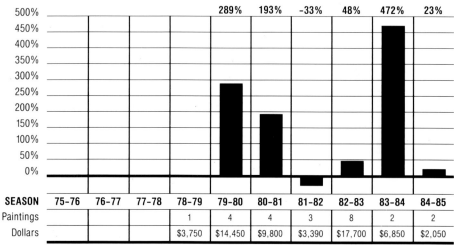

10-Year Average Change From Base Years '78-'79: 142%

				289%	193%	-33%	48%	472%	23%
SEASON	75-76	76-77	77-78	78-79	79-80	80-81	81-82	82-83	83-84	84-85
Paintings				1	4	4	3	8	2	2
Dollars				$3,750	$14,450	$9,800	$3,390	$17,700	$6,850	$2,050

Record Sale: $7,000, SPB, 6/24/80, "Flathead Squaws in Camp, Montana," 23 x 40 in.

ANDREW MELROSE
(1836-1901)

New Jersey artist Andrew Melrose painted traditional, atmospheric landscapes inspired by travels in Europe, South America and various regions of the United States. Many of his best paintings are views of New York State and New Jersey, especially regions of the Hudson River Valley and New York Harbor. Melrose typically painted in an indigenous American style of landscape painting which may be characterized as romantic realism.

A self-taught artist, Andrew Melrose was born in Selkirk, Scotland in 1836. Although few records exist of his activity prior to the Civil War, it is thought that Melrose emigrated to the United States about 1856.

In the two decades after 1865, he worked out of New Jersey, where he maintained studios in Hoboken and Guttenberg. Searching for inspiring subject matter, Melrose traveled to various Southern and Western areas of the United States, the British Isles and Austria.

In 1880 or 1881, Melrose visited the mountain regions of North Carolina. In addition to being impressed with the natural grandeur of that region, he was interested by certain aspects of rural life. In his painting *The Whiskey Still by Moonlight* (1880, Robert P. Coggins Collection of American Art, Marietta, Georgia), the artist depicts men producing corn whiskey against a backdrop of dark, forested hills and somber moon-

The Ox Bow, 24 x 42 in., signed l.l. Courtesy of Wunderlich and Company, Inc., New York, New York.

light. Melrose rendered many of his Southern landscapes, which typically included views of the mountains of North Carolina or the Shenandoah Valley, in soft, atmospheric terms.

In about 1887, Melrose executed an oil painting entitled *New York Harbor and the Battery* (location unknown), from which he later produced a series of chromolithographs. This bright and airy view of the harbor recalls a long tradition of scenic landscape painting that goes back to the early nineteenth century. Melrose's concern for rendering the effects of light and atmosphere signals a trend toward a lighter palette and looser brushstroke. These stylistic developments suggest the influence of the French impressionists in his mature work.

Melrose was a frequent exhibitor at the National Academy of Design between 1868 and 1883. He died in West New York, New Jersey in 1901.

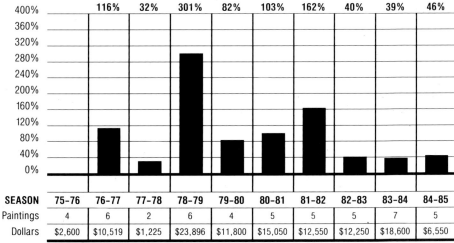

10-Year Average Change From Base Years '75-'76: 92%

SEASON	75-76	76-77	77-78	78-79	79-80	80-81	81-82	82-83	83-84	84-85
		116%	32%	301%	82%	103%	162%	40%	39%	46%
Paintings	4	6	2	6	4	5	5	5	7	5
Dollars	$2,600	$10,519	$1,225	$23,896	$11,800	$15,050	$12,550	$12,250	$18,600	$6,550

Record Sale: $10,000, SPB, 10/27/78, "Sunset on the Valley of the Shenandoah," 22 x 36 in.

PUBLIC COLLECTIONS
Allen Memorial Art Museum,
  Oberlin College, Ohio
New-York Historical Society, New York City
Robert P. Coggins Collection of American
  Art, Marietta, Georgia
White House, Washington, D.C.

277

GILBERT D. MUNGER
(1836?-1903)

Niagara Falls, 1903. Courtesy of Private Collection.

The career of Gilbert D. Munger exemplifies an art-historical rarity. He was a major painter of the American West, and later an expatriate whose work was collected by European patrons and praised by art critics, yet he died virtually unknown in his own country. Until recently, he remained unnoticed and unpublished.

Gilbert Munger was born in the village of North Madison, Connecticut in 1836 or 1837. His family included several artists.

His formal education ended about 1850 when he began work as an engraver for the Smithsonian Institution. During this early period, he taught himself the rudiments of art, and after the Civil War he began to exhibit at the National Academy of Design. One of his early patrons was noted Western explorer Clarence King. In 1869, he won high praise from one New York City critic for his painting of Niagara Falls.

That year Munger left New York for the West, with his close friend, artist John Ross Key. Munger remained in California until 1871. He painted Yosemite and Mt. Shasta. His work in California was highly praised by art critics, and he was patronized by wealthy Californians such as William C. Ralston, who bought his *Minnehaha Falls* (date and location unknown), reputedly for $5,000. Munger revisited California and the West in 1872.

During the mid-1870s, Munger was presumably back in New York, and it is believed he left for Europe about 1877. He did not return until 1893. He lived first in England, where he exhibited at the Royal Academy, among other places.

Around 1885 or 1886, he moved to France, where he remained until 1893. His whereabouts and work in France remain even more mysterious than his English period. From what is known, it appears that Munger shifted his style away from the tight naturalism of the Hudson River School toward the barbizon style—quiet domestic landscapes that are glowing and mysterious. He also visited Venice and painted a number of scenes there.

In 1893, Munger returned to New York City, and he exhibited a work at the Columbian Exhibition in Chicago. During his last decade, he produced some of his finest works, many of which are at the Tweed Museum of Art in Duluth, Minnesota, the largest repository of his work in the United States. He painted in upstate New York, along the old Erie Canal near Cazanovia.

His last work was a major six-by-10-foot painting of *Niagara Falls,* showing both the American and Canadian views. It was praised as his masterpiece. Munger died in Washington, D.C., where he had begun his career half a century earlier, just as he put the finishing strokes on his large painting of the falls.

Today, with the reassessment of American painting of the nineteenth century, Gilbert Munger emerges as an artist whose career offers interesting parallels to those of Albert Bierstadt and Thomas Moran. His paintings, which once languished in obscurity, are increasingly sought by collectors, and it is now recognized that Munger is one of the few artists of the second half of the nineteenth century who successfully made the transition from the style of the Hudson River School to the barbizon mode, and later to impressionism.

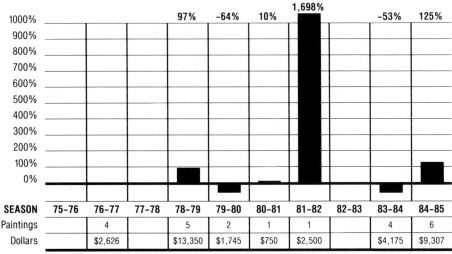

10-Year Average Change From Base Years '76-'77: 259%

				97%	−64%	10%	1,698%		−53%	125%

SEASON	75-76	76-77	77-78	78-79	79-80	80-81	81-82	82-83	83-84	84-85
Paintings		4		5	2	1	1		4	6
Dollars		$2,626		$13,350	$1,745	$750	$2,500		$4,175	$9,307

Record Sale: $3,600, SPB, 3/12/79, "Venice at Sunrise," 22 × 32 in.

PUBLIC COLLECTIONS
Heckscher Museum, Huntington, New York
Oakland Museum of Art
Tweed Museum of Art,
　University of Minnesota, Duluth
William Benton Museum of Art,
　University of Connecticut
Yale University Art Gallery

ARCHIBALD WILLARD

(1836-1918)

Archibald Willard created a picture that rose to far greater prominence than himself. His *Spirit of '76* is instantly recognizable, but few people know who painted it.

Originally conceived as a humorous sketch of three musicians prancing around during a Fourth of July parade, *Yankee Doodle,* as it was known, struck a patriotic chord during and after the Centennial Exposition in Philadelphia. Willard was catapulted to fame and fortune.

Archibald Willard was born in 1836 in Bedford, Ohio. He possessed a gift for humor that appeared in his art, as evidenced by the conception of *Yankee Doodle.*

After the Civil War, Willard met photographer J.F. Ryder, who would prove instrumental in his success. Willard eventually sent Ryder two caricatures, *Pluck 1* and *Pluck 2,* showing a dog chasing a rabbit while pulling a wagonload of children. When Ryder placed them in the window of his studio, they attracted such attention that he had them copyrighted and photographed.

Ryder now suggested that Willard create something for the Centennial. Willard came up with the three musicians, using his father and two acquaintances as models. After his father's death in 1874, he adopted a more serious approach to the work; its final tone was reverent.

Ryder made chromolithographs of the finished painting. Through good business acumen, he created a market for *Yankee Doodle,* and made a tidy profit, despite the picture's lack of attention and poor visibility in the Centennial's gallery.

After the Centennial, Willard exhibited *Yankee Doodle* around the country. In Boston, it acquired a new name, *The Spirit of '76.*

Willard remained prolific for the rest of the century, working as an illustrator

Spirit of '76, 1876, signed l.l. The original painting hangs in the Selectmen's Room, Abbot Hall, Marblehead, Massachusetts.

and muralist and producing additional patriotic paintings. *The Spirit of '76,* however, always seemed to be in the forefront of his career, overshadowing everything else. And he was able to enjoy, however dubious, the benefits and adulation it produced until his death in 1918.

PUBLIC COLLECTIONS
Abbott Hall, Marblehead, Massachusetts
Fayette County Historical Society, Ohio
Washington Court House, Washington, Ohio

SEASON	75-76	76-77	77-78	78-79	79-80	80-81	81-82	82-83	83-84	84-85
Paintings			1			1				
Dollars			$1,900			$150,000				

Record Sale: $150,000, B.P., 11/22/80, "The Spirit of '76," 24 × 18 in.

WINSLOW HOMER
(1836-1910)

One of the towering figures of American art, Winslow Homer was a supreme exponent of nature painting—he painted what he saw exactly as he saw it. He began as an illustrator and produced wood-block illustrations that were perhaps the best ever done in this country. In middle age he took up watercolor painting and raised that medium to a level of excellence never seen before. And the marine paintings in both oil and watercolor of his solitary mature years rank with the finest anywhere.

Born in Boston in 1836, he spent most of his boyhood across the Charles River in Cambridge. His mother, an amateur watercolorist, encouraged his early interest is sketching. At age 19 he was apprenticed to a Boston lithographer for two years, but loathed it.

He became a free-lance illustrator, first for *Ballou's Pictorial* in Boston and then for *Harper's Weekly* in New York City, where he moved in 1859. Aside from some night courses in drawing at the National Academy of Design and a few brief lessons in landscape painting, he was self-taught.

When the Civil War started, *Harper's Weekly* sent him on assignments to the front. Not interested in the romance or drama of war, he depicted it dispassionately, often showing soldiers in mundane activities. Many historians consider Homer's war reportage equal to the photographs of Mathew Brady.

It was not until after the war that he

Beach Scene, 11½ x 9½ in., signed l.r. Courtesy of Vose Galleries of Boston, Inc., Massachusetts.

began painting seriously. One of his first major works, *Prisoners from the Front* (1866, Metropolitan Museum of Art), showing three dejected Confederate soldiers being interrogated by a dapper Union officer, immediately attracted attention.

In 1866 and 1867, Homer spent 10 months in Paris, but French painting had little influence on him. Many of his oils after his return, however, were plein-air scenes of girls playing croquet and boys rollicking in the fields, such as *Snap the Whip* (1872, Butler Institute of American Art), as full of light and air as the work of any of the French impressionists. Along with these he did many

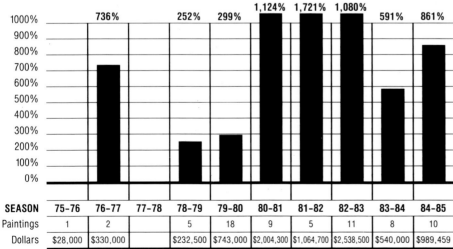

10-Year Average Change From Base Years '75-'76: 740%

SEASON	75-76	76-77	77-78	78-79	79-80	80-81	81-82	82-83	83-84	84-85
		736%		252%	299%	1,124%	1,721%	1,080%	591%	861%
Paintings	1	2		5	18	9	5	11	8	10
Dollars	$28,000	$330,000		$232,500	$743,000	$2,004,300	$1,064,700	$2,538,500	$540,000	$989,459

Record Sale: $1,700,000, SPB, 10/17/80, "The Signal of Distress," 24 × 38 in.

Entering the First Rapids, 1897, 13½ x 20½ in., signed l.l. Photograph courtesy of The Gerald Peters Gallery, Santa Fe, New Mexico.

The Dinner Horn, 1888, 19¼ x 13¼ in., signed l.l. Courtesy of Vose Galleries of Boston, Inc., Massachusetts.

paintings of hunting and fishing, sports that he loved. In 1873, he began painting in watercolor. From then on, he used it as often as he did oils.

A stay on the North Sea coast of England in 1881 and 1882 marked a major turning point in Homer's career. He began to paint the sea and the men and women who struggled against it, themes that preoccupied him for the balance of his life. His work took on a new emotional dimension, depth of color and atmosphere.

Returning to the United States, Homer built a studio on the rock coast at Prout's Neck, Maine. Although he still took hunting and fishing trips, and continued to paint in the Adirondack Mountains, Canada, Bermuda, the Bahamas and Cuba, his attention was focused on the sea. His work now was filled with the majestic power of the waves.

In Homer's mature watercolors of the West Indies, such as *The Gulf Stream* (1899, Metropolitan Museum of Art), perhaps the best-known of all his work, he attained the pinnacle of his creative genius. Full of vitality, light, space and magnificent color, brilliant in design, these were the work of a true master.

Homer was showered with honors in his final years, but, by now almost a recluse, he ignored them and continued to work. He died in Prout's Neck in 1910.

MEMBERSHIPS
American Watercolor Society
National Academy of Design
National Institute of Arts and Letters

PUBLIC COLLECTIONS
Butler Institute of American Art, Youngstown, Ohio
Delaware Art Museum, Wilmington
Denver Art Museum, Colorado
Metropolitan Museum of Art, New York City
Museum of Fine Arts, Boston
National Gallery of Art, Washington, D.C.
Pennsylvania Academy of the Fine Arts, Philadelphia
Philadelphia Museum of Art
St. Louis Art Museum
Sterling and Francine Clark Art Institute, Williamstown, Massachusetts
Whitney Museum of American Art, New York City

ELIHU VEDDER
(1836-1923)

Although he made his home in Rome for most of his adult life, Elihu Vedder always considered himself an American artist. He had a long career as a symbolist painter, muralist and illustrator, but it was a group of visionary paintings done before he was 30 that gained him lasting attention. In startling contrast to the prevailing Victorian academic art of the day, these highly original evocations of almost mystically lonely landscapes foreshadowed the work of the surrealists who were to come several generations later.

Vedder was born in New York City in 1836, but spent his childhood in Schenectady, New York, and in Cuba and Jamaica, where his father worked as a dentist. He showed an early interest in art and began to study it at age 12. After a brief stint of working for an architect, he studied with genre painter Tomkins H. Matteson. When he was 20 he went to Europe for five years, studying in Paris, Florence and Dusseldorf.

He returned to America in 1861 and settled into the bohemian life of artists and writers in Greenwich Village, making a living as best he could by designing greeting cards and comic valentines, and by illustrating books and magazines. It was during this period, when the United States was torn by the Civil War, that he conceived his most haunting and imaginative fantasies.

Some now speculate that the sense of isolation and melancholy in these works

A Music Party, Venetian Figures on the Terrace, 1868, 12¾ x 21 in., signed l.r.
Courtesy of Vose Galleries of Boston, Inc., Massachusetts.

reflected the trauma the nation was suffering because of the war. Scholars who have studied Vedder's life, however, tend to think of them more as manifestations of a "cultivated weirdness" pose that Vedder and some of his drinking friends struck, despite the horrors of the war.

Whatever the cause, four or five paintings of the early 1860s, executed with precise, almost surreal naturalism, convey an eerie sense of loneliness and despair which puzzled viewers of the day. In *The Lair of the Sea Serpent* (1864, Museum of Fine Arts, Boston), an otherwise placid seascape is defiled by a huge, slithery monster sprawled

across the top of the dunes, one eye staring fixedly at the viewer.

In 1866, Vedder returned to Rome and resided there until his death in 1923. He painted some lovely, free landscapes of the Italian countryside, but for the most part concentrated on allegorical and symbolist scenes reminiscent of some of the old masters.

Many think that the finest work of Vedder's mature years is his beautifully imaginative illustrations for the *Rubaiyat of Omar Khayyam,* done in 1884. In the 1890s he painted important, but mannered, murals for the art gallery at Bowdoin College in Maine (1894) and in the Library of Congress in Washington, D.C. (1896-1877). Most critics agree, however, that these are bleak and contrived when compared to the eccentric fantasies of his youth.

MEMBERSHIPS
American Academy of Arts and Letters
American Society of Mural Painters
Century Association
National Academy of Design

PUBLIC COLLECTIONS
Art Institute of Chicago
Brooklyn Museum
Corcoran Gallery of Art, Washington, D.C.
Fine Arts Museums of San Francisco
Hudson River Museum, New York
Library of Congress, Washington, D.C.
Los Angeles County Museum
Metropolitan Museum of Art, New York City
Museum of Fine Arts, Boston
Worcester Museum of Art, Massachusetts

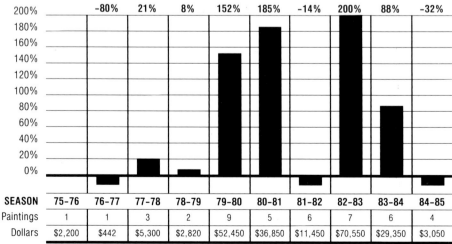

10-Year Average Change From Base Years '75-'76: 53%

	-80%	21%	8%	152%	185%	-14%	200%	88%	-32%
SEASON	75-76	76-77	77-78	78-79	79-80	80-81	81-82	82-83	83-84	84-85
Paintings	1	1	3	2	9	5	6	7	6	4
Dollars	$2,200	$442	$5,300	$2,820	$52,450	$36,850	$11,450	$70,550	$29,350	$3,050

Record Sale: $32,200, CH, 9/30/82, "For the Lost Pliades," 18 × 10 in.

GEORGE FREDERICK BENSELL
(1837-1879)

Philadelphia painter and poet George Frederick Bensell is recognized for his skillful renderings of historical subjects, genre scenes and portraits.

Bensell was born in Philadelphia in 1837, and seems to have spent his life there. Artist Edmund Birckhead Bensell was his brother. A student of John Lambdin, George Bensell developed considerable skill in using crayon and oil. By mid-century, the artist's career was flourishing, and he exhibited annually at the Pennsylvania Academy of the Fine Arts from 1856 to 1868. He was a founder and active member of the Philadelphia Sketch Club.

One of Bensell's earliest known works, executed when he was 19 years of age, is a drawing of *Ann Newbury Diggs* (ca. 1856, Historical Society of Pennsylvania). Other portraits include *Thomas Livezey* and *Mrs. Thomas Livezey* (1860-1875, Germantown Historical Society) and *Frederick Smith* (1877, Pennsylvania Academy of the Fine Arts).

Bensell combined genre and landscape in a work entitled *Indians Camping at Riverside* (1867, location unknown). Bensell's Indians are of the Eastern frontier, and were probably a product of his imagination. *Autumn Landscape* (date unknown, Pennsylvania Academy of the Fine Arts) is representative of his landscapes.

St. Genevieve of Brabant in the Forest, 1860-1870, 50½ x 40⅛ in., signed l.l. Courtesy of National Museum of American Art, Smithsonian Institution, Museum Purchase.

Also in 1867, Bensell collaborated with fellow Philadelphian Samuel Diffield in writing a 22-page poem called "The Artist's Dream" (1867, Historical Society of Pennsylvania).

Bensell's talent never reached full maturation; he died in mid-career at age 42.

PUBLIC COLLECTIONS
Germantown Historical Society, Pennsylvania
Historical Society of Pennsylvania, Philadelphia
Pennsylvania Academy of the Fine Arts,
 Philadelphia

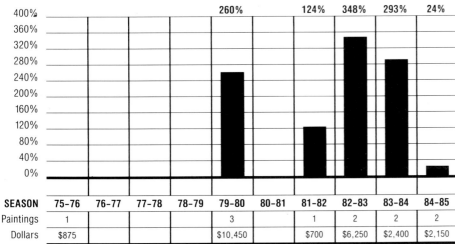

10-Year Average Change From Base Years '75-'76: 175%

	260%		124%	348%	293%	24%

SEASON	75-76	76-77	77-78	78-79	79-80	80-81	81-82	82-83	83-84	84-85
Paintings	1				3		1	2	2	2
Dollars	$875				$10,450		$700	$6,250	$2,400	$2,150

Record Sale: $7,250, SPB, 4/25/80, "Mountain Stream," 50 × 40 in.

283

JOSEPH FOXCROFT COLE
(1837-1892)

Born in Jay, Maine in 1837, landscape painter Joseph Foxcroft Cole moved to Boston with his family while he was still a boy. After leaving school, he was apprenticed for a time, along with his contemporary, Winslow Homer, at J.G. Bufford's lithography shop.

In 1860 he went to France for the first time and studied for several summers with Emile Lambinet, whose landscapes of Normandy were popular at the time. In winter he studied drawing at the Ecole des Beaux Arts.

On his return to Boston, Cole met William Morris Hunt, perhaps the strongest advocate of the barbizon style of landscape painting in Boston. Hunt urged Cole to go back to France for even more training in that style. Hunt himself bought several of Cole's paintings and urged others to buy them so that, by 1865, Cole was able to return to Paris. He became a pupil of Charles Jacque, and through him met such barbizon stalwarts as Troyon, Daubigny, Corot and Diaz.

Cole exhibited regularly at the Paris Salon and at the Royal Academy in London, as well as in shows in the United States. Many of the paintings of his middle years were of grazing cows and sheep, done, as one critic wrote, "in delicate gradations of color, with quiet, slumberous distances. . . ."

In 1877 Cole built a house in Winchester, Massachusetts; except for brief visits to Europe and California (the latter for

Later Afternoon Near Providence, 1879, 18 x 26⅛ in., signed l.r. Courtesy of National Museum of American Art, Smithsonian Institution, Gift of William T. Evans.

his wife's health) he spent most of his time there until his death in 1892. Many of his later paintings were of rugged New England hillsides. Others were of the misty marshes and pastures near his home on Mystic Lake and around Providence, Rhode Island.

In his final years, Cole's work became lighter in tone and began to show influences of Monet and the impressionists.

PUBLIC COLLECTIONS
Museum of Fine Arts, Boston
Walker Art Museum, Bowdoin, Maine

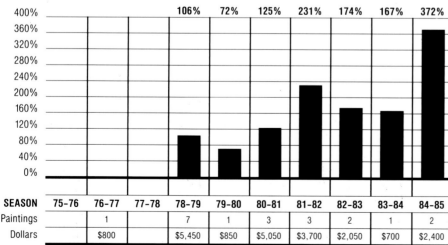

10-Year Average Change From Base Years '76-'77: 156%

	75-76	76-77	77-78	78-79	79-80	80-81	81-82	82-83	83-84	84-85
				106%	72%	125%	231%	174%	167%	372%
SEASON	75-76	76-77	77-78	78-79	79-80	80-81	81-82	82-83	83-84	84-85
Paintings		1		7	1	3	3	2	1	2
Dollars		$800		$5,450	$850	$5,050	$3,700	$2,050	$700	$2,400

Record Sale: $2,600, CH, 12/5/80, "California Landscape," 18 × 26 in.

CLEVELAND ROCKWELL
(1837-1907)

As a surveyor and mapmaker for the United States Coast Geodetic Survey, Cleveland Rockwell sketched and painted. Late in life, he turned to painting fulltime. The result was a matchless pictorial record of the Northern California and Oregon coastlines and estuaries as they looked in the late nineteenth century, and of the early ocean- and river-fishing operations that flourished in and around the mouths of the Columbia and Willamette Rivers.

Rockwell was born in Youngstown, Ohio in 1837. He was educated at the Polytechnic School in Troy, New York, where he received his first art training. Later he took courses in drawing and design while studying for a degree in mechanical engineering at the University of the City of New York.

As a student in New York (and later, when he had time off from geodetic surveys) Rockwell had ample opportunity to visit exhibitions and study the work of contemporary marine and landscape painters. Perhaps the greatest influence on him, however, was Baron Friedrich von Humboldt, the great German naturalist, statesman and explorer. In von Humboldt's view, landscape painting should be a melding of science and a painter's creative power.

Rockwell joined the Coast Geodetic Survey in 1857, and was assigned first to chart parts of New York harbor. In 1861, when the Civil War started, he was working along the coasts of South Caro-

Straits of the Farallones, 1868, 12 x 18 in., signed l.r. Collection of Mrs. Margaret Bewley. Photograph courtesy of Nan & Roy Farrington Jones, Ross, CA.

lina and Georgia. During the war, he spent most of his time on projects for the Union Army. On Sherman's march through Georgia, he was attached to the general's staff to survey Confederate installations and their approaches.

After a tour in Colombia, South America, surveying the Magdalena River, Rockwell was transferred to California in 1868. For the next 24 years, until his retirement in 1892, his work took him up and down the coasts of Northern California and Oregon.

Rockwell painted scenes that he knew intimately in every sort of light and weather. His early work, both in watercolor and oils, tended to be somber in tone. His later work was considerably brighter, although he never gave himself free rein in use of color. In some of his oils he laid down the pigment as a thin wash, almost like watercolor. There were no clashes of color in his work. Everything was controlled.

After his retirement from government service, Rockwell made his home in Portland, Oregon, and continued to paint until his death in 1907.

10-Year Average Change From Base Years '79-'80: 86%

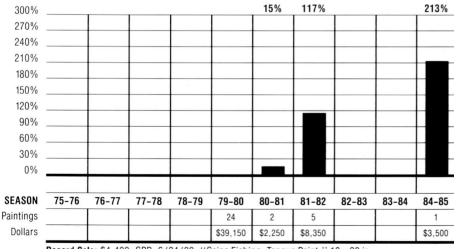

SEASON	75-76	76-77	77-78	78-79	79-80	80-81	81-82	82-83	83-84	84-85
						15%	117%			213%
Paintings					24	2	5			1
Dollars					$39,150	$2,250	$8,350			$3,500

Record Sale: $4,400, SPB, 6/24/80, "Seine Fishing, Tongue Point," 10 x 20 in.

MEMBERSHIPS
Oregon Art Association
Sketch Club of Portland

PUBLIC COLLECTIONS
Flavel Museum, Astoria, Oregon

ALFRED THOMSON BRICHER
(1837-1908)

Narragansett Beach The Turn of the Tide, 1870, 20 x 40 in., signed l.l. Private Collection, Photograph courtesy of Vose Galleries of Boston, Inc., Massachusetts.

Untitled. Courtesy of Henry B. Holt, Inc., Essex Fells, New Jersey.

One of the last of the luminist painters, Alfred Thomson Bricher was known principally for oil and watercolor paintings of the coast of New England. He brought to a close the cult of nature painting that was started by Thomas Cole and was carried on by such men as Martin Johnson Heade, Frederic Edwin Church and William Haseltine. Many of his sweeping panoramas of the coastline, although well done, suffered from a sameness of format in the opinion of some critics.

Bricher was born in Portsmouth, New Hampshire in 1837. As a teenager he went to Boston to find a job in business and spent his spare time painting at the Lowell Institute. In 1858, he began painting full-time. For the next 10 years, he worked in Boston and Newburyport, north of Boston.

In 1871, he moved to New York and settled on Staten Island. Every summer, however, he went North to sketch and paint on Grand Manan Island and on the shores of Massachusetts and Rhode Island. His particular strength was his ability to capture the translucent appearance of the sea and the crispness of the horizon under a luminous sky.

While Bricher displayed a sure linear touch in his oil paintings, there was a greater freedom in his watercolors. His subject matter in the watercolor was more varied, too. Some of his female figures in the medium bear comparison to those that Winslow Homer was painting in the 1870s.

Bricher died in New Dorp on Staten Island in 1908. In the years that followed, his work was largely forgotten. By the 1980s he had been rediscovered, and now he is looked upon as one of the better marine painters of his time.

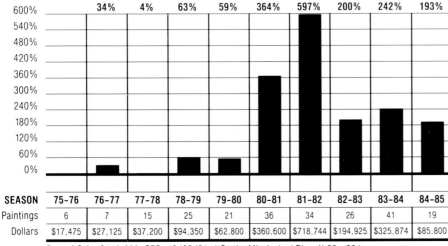

10-Year Average Change From Base Years '75-'76: 176%

	75-76	76-77	77-78	78-79	79-80	80-81	81-82	82-83	83-84	84-85
		34%	4%	63%	59%	364%	597%	200%	242%	193%
SEASON	75-76	76-77	77-78	78-79	79-80	80-81	81-82	82-83	83-84	84-85
Paintings	6	7	15	25	21	36	34	26	41	19
Dollars	$17,475	$27,125	$37,200	$94,350	$62,800	$360,600	$718,744	$194,925	$325,874	$85,800

Record Sale: $110,000, SPB, 10/22/81, "On the Mississippi River," 20 x 38 in.

PUBLIC COLLECTIONS
Indianapolis Museum of Art
Metropolitan Museum of Art, New York City

286

SAMUEL S. CARR
(1837-1908)

Samuel Carr was a skillful painter of children, seashore life and pastoral subjects. In his beach scenes, largely painted between 1879 and 1881, he used certain figure shapes repeatedly, reversing them, turning them this way and that. Often the figures would not even be looking at each other. He created an odd effect by doing this, which gave the paintings an eerie stillness.

Most of Carr's pastoral scenes date from the 1890s. Carr and Clinton Loveridge, with whom he shared a studio, made their living from these very competent and peaceful landscapes filled with cattle, sheep or goats, depicting different times of day or different seasons. They were typical of the popular taste of the second half of the nineteenth century.

What Carr painted most frequently were children and their various pastimes. The paintings were charming and warm, and the activities depicted were always happy ones. A typical title is *Children's Parade* (date unknown, Paterson Free Public Library).

Little is known of Carr's life. He was born in England in 1837, and came to this country at approximately age 28. At the Cooper Union in New York City, a record shows his attendance in a class of mechanical drawing in 1865.

He lived in Brooklyn from 1870 to 1907 with Annie and John Bond, his sister and brother-in-law. He remained a bachelor all his life. At one time he was

Her Pets, 14 x 20 in., signed l.l. Courtesy of Vose Galleries of Boston, Inc., Massachusetts.

president of the Brooklyn Art Club, and he was a member of a Masonic Lodge. Carr died in 1908.

MEMBERSHIPS
Brooklyn Art Club

PUBLIC COLLECTIONS
New Britain Museum of American Art,
  Connecticut
Paterson Free Public Library, New Jersey
Smith College, Northampton, Massachusetts
Clark Art Institute, Williamstown, Massachusetts

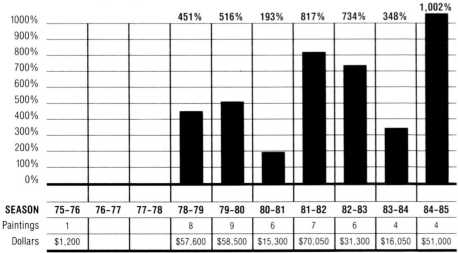

10-Year Average Change From Base Years '75-'76: 508%

SEASON	75-76	76-77	77-78	78-79	79-80	80-81	81-82	82-83	83-84	84-85
				451%	516%	193%	817%	734%	348%	1,002%
Paintings	1			8	9	6	7	6	4	4
Dollars	$1,200			$57,600	$58,500	$15,300	$70,050	$31,300	$16,050	$51,000

Record Sale: $31,000, SPB, 12/6/84, "Little Drummer Boy," 20 x 16 in.

287

MAX WEYL
(1837-1914)

A founder and leader of the Washington School of landscape painting, Max Weyl was one of the most popular and best-known artists of his day in the capital.

Largely self-taught, Weyl painted much in the manner of the Hudson River School in his early years. After a trip to Europe in middle age, his work turned toward the direction of the barbizon mode; for years, in fact, his admirers called him the "American Daubigny." From the 1890s on, however, it was George Inness, the master landscapist, who had the most profound influence on Weyl's work.

Weyl was born in Muhlen-am-Neckar, near Wurttemberg, Germany in 1837. As a boy, he was apprenticed to a watchmaker and, after emigrating to America, he made his living as an itinerant watch repairman. In 1861, however, he settled permanently in Washington, D.C. and opened a small jewelry store.

Through the 1860s, he experimented with painting as a hobby, trying still lifes of fruit and flowers at first. In 1870, he finally worked up enough courage to hang several of his small paintings in the window of his shop.

A great boost to his career came when Samuel Kauffmann, publisher of the Washington *Evening Star* and president of the board of trustees of the Corcoran Gallery of Art, stopped in to have his watch repaired, admired a small landscape and bought it. Over the years, Kauffmann became a regular patron.

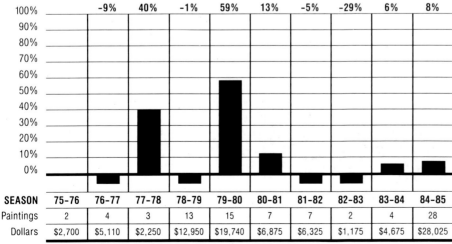

Hollyhocks, 1881, 25½ x 16½ in., signed l.r. Courtesy of National Museum of American Art, Smithsonian Institution, Gift of St. Yves, Amelia and Rene.

It was not until 1878, however, that Weyl listed himself in the city directory simply as an artist. His first exhibition of landscapes in 1879 sold well enough to pay for a trip to Europe to visit museums and studios. It was after this trip that the barbizon influence became so apparent in his work.

Weyl's star was in the ascendancy through the 1880s and 1890s. The Brazilian ambassador, a noted collector, bought 14 of his paintings. So did other wealthy collectors. Later, both Mrs. Grover Cleveland and the first Mrs. Woodrow Wilson bought his landscapes for the White House.

In the 20 years before his death in 1914, Weyl was known particularly for his poetic paintings of the scenic Rock Creek valley at the edge of Washington, and of the wide tidal marshes of the Potomac River. In these paintings, his handling of light was most like that of Inness. His Rock Creek landscapes became so popular, however, that he repeated many to a formula.

10-Year Average Change From Base Years '75-'76: 8%

	75-76	76-77	77-78	78-79	79-80	80-81	81-82	82-83	83-84	84-85
		-9%	40%	-1%	59%	13%	-5%	-29%	6%	8%
SEASON	75-76	76-77	77-78	78-79	79-80	80-81	81-82	82-83	83-84	84-85
Paintings	2	4	3	13	15	7	7	2	4	28
Dollars	$2,700	$5,110	$2,250	$12,950	$19,740	$6,875	$6,325	$1,175	$4,675	$28,025

Record Sale: $3,600, W.W, 3/2/85, "Turkey Farm," 24 × 36 in.

MEMBERSHIPS
Washington Art Club

PUBLIC COLLECTIONS
Corcoran Gallery of Art, Washington, D.C.
National Gallery of Art, Washington, D.C.

EDWARD GAY
(1837-1928)

Edward Gay was a productive landscape painter who does not fit into any particular category or school. He learned technique from several artists with whom he studied, but was not markedly influenced by them. His paintings depicted what he saw—no more, no less. He did not romanticize or idealize.

Born in Ireland in 1837, Gay came to America with his parents in 1848 in the wake of the Potato Famine. They settled in Albany, New York. He had to go to work as a boy, but showed a talent for drawing. Encouraged by the Hart brothers and George Boughton, all successful local painters, he began to study with them.

In 1862, at the urging of the Harts, he went to Karlsruhe, Germany to continue his studies under Johann Schirmer and Karl Friedrich Lessing, both conventional historical painters. Although he learned much, Gay felt that he was wasting his time.

When he returned to the United States in 1864, he began painting the large landscapes which were then in vogue. Three years later, with his wife and growing family, he moved to Mount Vernon, just north of New York City. The area was open farmland, with sunny meadows and orchards stretching along Long Island Sound. These were the scenes that Gay painted for much of his life.

In 1905, he built a summer home at Cragsmoor in upstate New York and painted there, as well as on frequent

Summer at Sound Beach, 1906, 33 x 43½ in., signed l.l. Courtesy of Montclair Art Museum, New Jersey.

trips to Europe. It was for his paintings of the rivers, fields and shores near Mount Vernon, where he died in 1928, however, that he was best known.

MEMBERSHIPS
Lotos Club
National Academy of Design
New York Water Color Club

PUBLIC COLLECTIONS
Layton School of Art, Milwaukee
Metropolitan Museum of Art, New York City
Minnesota Museum of Art, St. Paul
Mt. Vernon Public Library, New York

10-Year Average Change From Base Years '75–'76: 62%

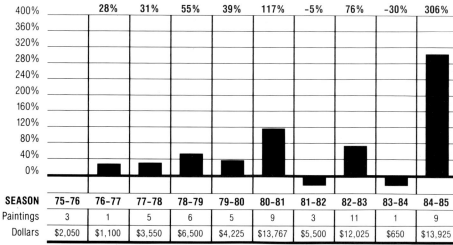

SEASON	75-76	76-77	77-78	78-79	79-80	80-81	81-82	82-83	83-84	84-85
		28%	31%	55%	39%	117%	–5%	76%	–30%	306%
Paintings	3	1	5	6	5	9	3	11	1	9
Dollars	$2,050	$1,100	$3,550	$6,500	$4,225	$13,767	$5,500	$12,025	$650	$13,925

Record Sale: $4,000, CH, 12/7/84, "Poughkeepsie, Sunday Morning," 16 × 14 in.

THOMAS MORAN
(1837-1926)

Thomas Moran's panoramic landscape paintings of the West, which captured the spirit and magnitude of that little-known wilderness, influenced the United States Congress to establish Yellowstone National Park and the national park system. Congress bought his *The Grand Canyon of the Yellowstone* (1872) and *Chasm of the Colorado* (1873) for $10,000 apiece. Mount Moran, in the Grand Teton Mountains, was named for him by appreciative officials. He also worked as an etcher, engraver and lithographer.

Moran was born in Bolton, Lancashire, England in 1837. His talented family came to the United States when Thomas was seven; of the seven children, three of his brothers—Edward, John and Peter—became artists of renown.

In Philadelphia, young Moran worked for a wood engraver, sketching designs on wood blocks for printing and experimenting in various media in his spare time. Edward, his older brother, shared a studio with him and served as his teacher. By age 21, Thomas Moran's determination to become an artist was rewarded by his exhibition of an oil painting at the Pennsylvania Academy of the Fine Arts.

In the 1850s, Moran was introduced to the work of J.M.W. Turner, the noted English landscape artist, by James Hamilton (known as "the American Turner"). But Turner's full influence on Moran's work came after a European study trip taken with his new wife, Mary Nimmo (who later became an etcher of note), and his brother Edward in 1862. Moran was greatly impressed by Turner and French landscape painter Claude Lorrain.

Inspired by Turner, Moran returned to the United States to " . . . paint as an American on an American basis." And this he did, for throughout his long life the great American West compelled him to return many times; in 1923, at age 86, he made his last Western trip. Moran's Western scenes, at which he was prolific until his very last years, were often reproduced on calendars.

Scribner's Monthly commissioned Moran to illustrate the first scientific expedition to the Yellowstone Valley in 1870. This work was completed on a small scale in his Eastern studio.

In 1871, Moran joined the Ferdinand V. Hayden Geological Survey Expedition to the Yellowstone Territory, and on seeing the magnificent grandeur of the area his inspiration soared. In 1876, Louis Prang of Boston issued a portfolio of 15 large chromolithograph illustrations by Moran from a report of the Hayden expedition.

Pioneer photographer William Henry Jackson also joined the expedition, and his photographs supported Moran's "Turneresque" watercolors when Congress decided to declare Yellowstone a national park, saving the territory from exploitation.

Another important expedition took place in 1873, for which Moran was the official artist. It was led by Major John Wesley Powell through the Grand Canyon region.

Perhaps *The Grand Canyon* (1915) best exemplifies the many years of Moran's intimate association with beautiful natural phenomena. It reflects his ability to idealize the reality of space and the subtle changes of light and air; the panoramic spread captures rock formations, plateaus, and degrees of moisture.

Moran lived in Newark, New Jersey in 1872, but New York City eventually became his permanent base until later years. Well established by 1884, he was one of the first artists to build a summer home in East Hampton, a Long Island resort. *Windy Hilltop—Amagansett, Long Island* (1901) is typical of his work in that area, where he also painted *The Much Resounding Sea* (1884), part of a series on breakers. Figures were rarely included in his work; however, on a visit to New Mexico he did paint Indians in their surroundings.

Moran lived in Santa Barbara, California from 1916 until his death in 1926.

MEMBERSHIPS
American Water Color Society
Artists' Fund Society
National Academy of Design
New York Etching Club
Pennsylvania Academy of the Fine Arts
Society of Etchers

PUBLIC COLLECTIONS
Cooper-Hewitt Museum of Decorative Arts and Design, New York City
Thomas Gilcrease Institute of American History and Art, Tulsa
Los Angeles County Museum of Art
Metropolitan Museum of Art, New York City
Milwaukee Art Center, Wisconsin
Museum of Fine Arts, Boston
National Museum of American Art, Washington, D.C.
Newark Museum, New Jersey
Philadelphia Museum of Art
Rockwell Gallery, Corning, New York
Smithsonian Institution, Washington, D.C.

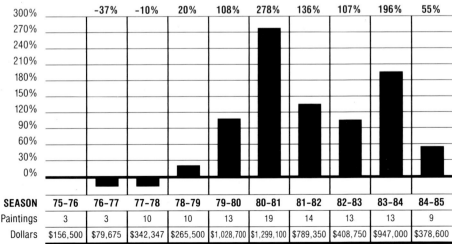

10-Year Average Change From Base Years '75-'76: 85%

	-37%	-10%	20%	108%	278%	136%	107%	196%	55%
SEASON	75-76	76-77	77-78	78-79	79-80	80-81	81-82	82-83	83-84	84-85
Paintings	3	3	10	10	13	19	14	13	13	9
Dollars	$156,500	$79,675	$342,347	$265,500	$1,028,700	$1,299,100	$789,350	$408,750	$947,000	$378,600

Record Sale: $650,000, CH, 5/22/80, "Children of the Mountain," 62 × 52 in.

Green River Wyoming, 1907, 20 x 28½ in., signed l.l. Photograph courtesy of The Gerald Peters Gallery, Santa Fe, New Mexico.

CARL C. BRENNER
(1838-1888)

Carl Christian Brenner did not list his profession as landscape painter until age 40. Yet at his death just before his fiftieth birthday, the local press called him Kentucky's greatest artist, and the *London Magazine of Art* ran an obituary on him.

He was born in Lauterecken, Bavaria in 1838. His art teacher, Philipp Frohlich, managed to have him accepted at the Munich Art Academy before he was 14, so he must have displayed considerable talent at that point. However, his father, a glazier, was determined that he follow that profession. Indeed, following his emigration to the United States at age 15, Brenner made his living as a glazier, sign painter and ornamental painter.

Brenner settled permanently in Louisville, Kentucky. In 1878, this cautious family man finally changed his professional designation to landscape painter (and his name from Charles to Carl), and made the commitment to art. He had already been working as an artist for some time.

In 1863, he had produced a panorama of Civil War scenes for the Masonic Hall in Louisville. He had also exhibited at the Louisville Exposition of 1873, the Centennial Exposition of 1876 in Philadelphia, and the Pennsylvania Academy of the Fine Arts in Philadelphia in 1876.

Beginning in 1878, Brenner began to show his work widely, including regular exhibitions at the National Academy of Design in New York City. He also held annual auctions at his own studio.

Brenner's work was probably most influenced by Asher Durand; his stately landscapes followed the Hudson River School's depiction of the American countryside as immense and grand, dwarfing the spectator. What distinguished him from many others of that school was his extreme passion for working directly from nature. In the coldest weather he often painted deep in the

Beechwoods, 1878, 19 x 15 in., signed l.l. Courtesy of Raydon Gallery, New York, New York.

woods, even going so far as to use a portable hut with glass windows when the temperature was fiercest.

When he died in Louisville in 1888, he was beginning to receive substantial recognition; yet his reputation languished after his death until the J.B. Speed Art Museum held an exhibition of his work in 1947.

PUBLIC COLLECTIONS
Addison Gallery, Andover, Massachusetts
Corcoran Gallery of Art, Washington, D.C.
J.B. Speed Art Museum, Louisville, Kentucky

SEASON	75-76	76-77	77-78	78-79	79-80	80-81	81-82	82-83	83-84	84-85
Paintings					1	5	5	1		
Dollars					$2,750	$7,402	$8,200	$1,500		

Record Sale: $2,750, SPB, 6/24/80, "View of Budd's Inlet, Olympia, Washington," 16 × 30 in.

ALFRED CORNELIUS HOWLAND

(1838-1909)

Friendly Neighbors, ca. 1909, 16½ x 22⅝ in., signed l.l. Courtesy of National Museum of American Art, Smithsonian Institution, Gift of William T. Evans.

Landscape and genre painter Alfred Cornelius Howland was a gregarious man whose many friendships included some of the more important figures of the nineteenth-century art.

Howland was born in Walpole, New Hampshire in 1838, to parents who were solid members of the community and descendants of early American settlers. In 1855, he went to Boston to study art and work as an engraver. Two years later, he went to New York City and worked as a lithographic artist for a printing firm.

In 1860, Howland embarked on the serious study of art by enrolling in the renowned Academy in Dusseldorf, Germany. He stayed in Dusseldorf three years; during the latter two he studied under Albert Flamm. He then traveled to Paris, where he was introduced by the artist Corot to two of the greatest artists in Paris, both of whom became his friends: Theodore Rousseau and Jean Francois Millet. It is clear from Howland's work that he preferred the rustic mood, light and landscape of these barbizon painters to the tight, realistic style of the Dusseldorf School.

Howland returned to the United States permanently in 1865, wintering for the rest of his life in New York City and summering in Williamstown, Massachusetts. He was much admired for his sun-dappled, anecdotal landscapes and genre scenes, and became friendly with interpretive landscapist Homer D. Martin and the reclusive Winslow Homer. He died in Pasadena, California in 1909.

MEMBERSHIPS
Artists Fund Society of New York
Century Association
National Academy of Design

PUBLIC COLLECTIONS
Layton Art Gallery, Milwaukee, Wisconsin
Naval Academy, Annapolis, Maryland
Yale University, New Haven, Connecticut

10-Year Average Change From Base Years '75-'76: 92%

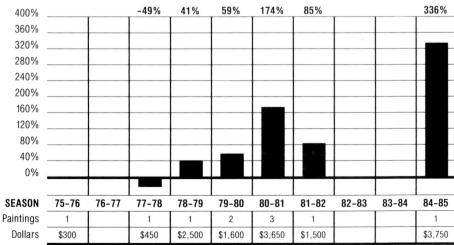

SEASON	75-76	76-77	77-78	78-79	79-80	80-81	81-82	82-83	83-84	84-85
			-49%	41%	59%	174%	85%			336%
Paintings	1		1	1	2	3	1			1
Dollars	$300		$450	$2,500	$1,600	$3,650	$1,500			$3,750

Record Sale: $3,750, D.NY, 4/24/85, "Farmyard Scene," 14 x 18 in.

WALTER SHIRLAW
(1838-1909)

Walter Shirlaw was a prominent painter, engraver, teacher and illustrator of the late nineteenth century. Although best known for his paintings and illustrations of the American West, Shirlaw was also noted as a painter of portraits, genre paintings, nudes and murals and as a designer of stained-glass windows.

Shirlaw was born in Scotland and raised in New York City. He worked for several years as an apprentice mapmaker and banknote engraver, before entering the National Academy of Design in the late 1850s. He exhibited at both the National and Pennsylvania Academies in 1861, and was active in New York and Philadelphia until around 1865, when he accepted a job with the Western Engraving and Banknote Company in Chicago.

From 1865 to 1870, Shirlaw continued to paint while supporting himself as a banknote engraver. He was active in the founding of the Art Institute of Chicago, and in 1869 he spent six months sketching in the Rocky Mountains.

In 1870, Shirlaw traveled to Munich, where he studied for the next seven years under Lindenschmidt, Raab, Wagner and von Ramberg. In 1876, his painting *Toning the Bell* (date and location unknown), was exhibited at the Philadelphia Centennial Exhibition. In 1878, *Sheep Shearing in the Bavarian Highland* (date and location unknown) received an honorable mention at the Paris Exhibition.

Diana, 10 x 16 in., signed l.l. Courtesy of Frederic I. Thaler Gallery, Cornwall Bridge, Connecticut.

In 1877, Shirlaw returned to the United States, settling in New York City. He exhibited there regularly and was elected a member of the National Academy of Design in 1888. He traveled widely, and was instrumental in the founding of the Society of American Artists (of which he was the first president) and the Art Students League, where he was an influential teacher.

In 1890, Shirlaw made his second trip West, as a participant in census survey of the Indian tribes. The influence of his Munich training is evident in the broad, expressionistic brushstrokes of the resulting paintings. Returning to New York, he maintained an active career until his death in 1909.

MEMBERSHIPS
National Academy of Design
Society of American Artists

PUBLIC COLLECTIONS
Art Institute of Chicago
Indianapolis Museum of Art
Library of Congress, Washington, D.C.
Museum of Fine Arts, Boston
National Museum of American Art,
  Washington, D.C.
St. Louis Art Museum

10-Year Average Change From Base Years '77-'78: 344%

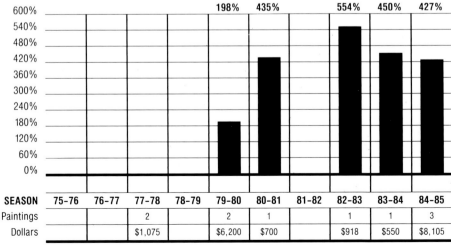

SEASON	75-76	76-77	77-78	78-79	79-80	80-81	81-82	82-83	83-84	84-85
					198%	435%		554%	450%	427%
Paintings			2		2	1		1	1	3
Dollars			$1,075		$6,200	$700		$918	$550	$8,105

Record Sale: $5,000, S.W, 9/23/79, "Eager for the Fray," 66 × 32 in.

294

WILLIAM KEITH
(1838-1911)

William Keith, an important member of the Rocky Mountain School, was known for his dramatic landscapes of the American Northwest, and for his more intimate pastoral studies of meadows and groves in the barbizon style.

Born in Aberdeenshire, Scotland, William Keith emigrated to the United States in 1850. At age 18, he was apprenticed as an engraver to Harper and Brothers, making his first trip to California two years later as a Harper's engraver.

After a visit to Scotland, Keith returned to San Francisco, where he opened his own engraving shop and began painting under the tutelage of his wife. He first exhibited his paintings in 1864 in San Francisco.

In 1868, he received the first in a series of major commissions when the Northern Pacific Railroad commissioned him to paint landscapes along its route. Around the same time, he was commissioned by the Oregon Navigation and Railroad Company to paint a series of landscapes, including Mt. Ranier, Mt. Hood and various scenes along the Columbia River.

Like other members of the Rocky Mountain School, Keith painted landscapes which tended to emphasize the dramatic and monumental aspects of the American Northwest. While his earlier works were painted in a light and buoyant manner, his work grew darker and more solemn over the years.

Mt. Ranier, 1878, 30¼ x 25¼ in., signed l.r. Courtesy of Vose Galleries of Boston, Inc., Massachusetts.

Among the major influences on Keith's later work were his admiration for the old masters and his friendship with painter George Inness (a follower of Emanuel Swedenborg), who encouraged Keith to explore the subjective and mystical aspects of nature.

Keith traveled regularly to Europe throughout his career, to study painting in Dusseldorf, Munich, London and Amsterdam. From 1883 to 1885, he maintained a studio in Munich, where he began to study portraiture. Returning to the United States, he spent several years in New Orleans before moving back to San Francisco. He was also a close friend of the noted naturalist and environmentalist John Muir.

Keith lost nearly 2,000 of his paintings and drawings in the San Francisco earthquake and fire of 1906. Because of this, examples of his earlier work are somewhat rare. He continued painting until his death in Berkeley, in 1911.

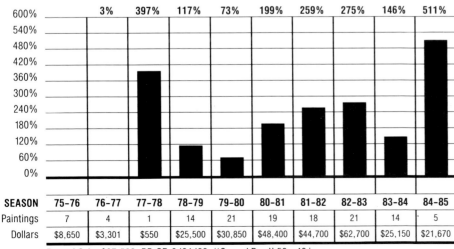

10-Year Average Change From Base Years '75-'76: 198%

		3%	397%	117%	73%	199%	259%	275%	146%	511%
SEASON	75-76	76-77	77-78	78-79	79-80	80-81	81-82	82-83	83-84	84-85
Paintings	7	4	1	14	21	19	18	21	14	5
Dollars	$8,650	$3,301	$550	$25,500	$30,850	$48,400	$44,700	$62,700	$25,150	$21,670

Record Sale: $27,500, BB.SF, 3/24/83, ''Carmel Bay,'' 50 × 40 in.

PUBLIC COLLECTIONS
Art Institute of Chicago
Brooklyn Museum
National Gallery of Art, Washington, D.C.

CARDUCIUS PLANTAGENET REAM
(1838-1917)

Carducius Plantagenet Ream was a highly successful still-life painter. Specializing in exquisitely executed pictures of fruit, Ream achieved international recognition during his lifetime.

Born in 1838 near Lancaster, Ohio, Ream was primarily self-taught as an artist. After attending public schools, Ream studied in Paris, London, Munich and New York City.

Ream's subjects included sensuously painted plums, apples, grapes, peaches and raspberries, among other fruits. The fruit was often displayed in glass or china dishes, and seen with serving utensils. Louis Prang and Company reproduced some of these dessert paintings as chromolithographs. They were highlighted in Prang's catalogue, and advertised as perfect pieces for the dining room.

In addition to his numerous still lifes, Ream painted some landscapes, marine paintings, figure studies and portraits. He always painted in oils, and was adept at capturing the colors and textures of his subjects. The lighting in his paintings caressed the edges of objects. Ream's work, harmonious and beautiful, reflected his deep love for nature.

After working in New York City during the mid-1870s, Ream settled in Chicago in 1878. He was a member of the Academy of Design and the Art Institute in Chicago.

Peaches, 1880, 12¼ x 24⅛ in., signed l.r. Photograph courtesy of the Brandywine River Museum, Chadds Ford, Pennsylvania, Anonymous Collection.

Still Life, signed l.r. Courtesy of Henry B. Holt, Inc., Essex Fells, New Jersey.

Ream repeatedly exhibited at the Royal Academy in London and in various American exhibitions. He was the first Chicago painter to have one of his works included in the permanent collection of the Art Institute of Chicago.

Ream died in 1917 in Chicago.

MEMBERSHIPS
Academy of Design
Art Institute of Chicago

PUBLIC COLLECTIONS
Art Institute of Chicago

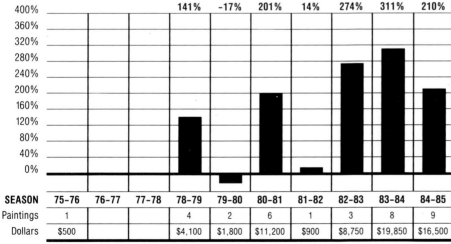

10-Year Average Change From Base Years '75-'76: 142%

				141%	–17%	201%	14%	274%	311%	210%
SEASON	75–76	76–77	77–78	78–79	79–80	80–81	81–82	82–83	83–84	84–85
Paintings	1			4	2	6	1	3	8	9
Dollars	$500			$4,100	$1,800	$11,200	$900	$8,750	$19,850	$16,500

Record Sale: $4,800, CH, 12/9/83, "Still Life with Fruit and Pitcher," 13 × 11 in.

WILLIAM AIKEN WALKER
(1838-1921)

William Aiken Walker was a Southern painter who specialized in genre scenes of black field hands, although he also painted some portraits, still lifes and landscapes. Although lacking in insight or emotional depth, his paintings are accurate in detail—perhaps because he often used a camera to capture scenes—and competently executed.

Walker was born in Charleston, South Carolina in 1838. He enlisted in the Confederate Army during the Civil War; his duties included map-making and sketching the defenses of Charleston. He was largely self-taught, although he studied in Dusseldorf sometime during the 1860s.

After the war, Walker lived at various times in Charleston, Baltimore and New Orleans. He led a wandering life, spending part of each year in the new resort communities of the South, at Arden, North Carolina, or Ponce Park, Florida. He painted many small studies of black laborers, such as *Cabin Scene with Cotton Picker* (date and location unknown) and *Man, Two Boys and Dog in Cotton Field* (date and location unknown). Some of his larger canvases approach the folk art style.

During a stay in Galveston, Texas, Walker painted *View of Galveston Harbor* (1874, Rosenberg Library, Galveston). Larger in scale than most of Walker's work, this painting patriotically emphasizes the prosperity of the American port. Walker painted an increasing number of landscapes after 1890. He also executed many examples of the then-popular fish and game study, particularly during the 1860s and after 1900. Currier & Ives made lithographs of several of his paintings during the 1880s.

Walker died in Charleston in 1921.

Plantation Economy in the Old South, 22 x 42 in., signed l.l. Courtesy of Robert M. Hicklin Jr., Inc., Spartansburg, South Carolina.

PUBLIC COLLECTIONS
Museum of Fine Arts, Boston
Rosenberg Library, Galveston

10-Year Average Change From Base Years '75-'76: 99%

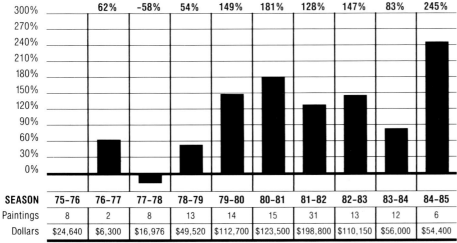

	62%	-58%	54%	149%	181%	128%	147%	83%	245%
SEASON	75-76	76-77	77-78	78-79	79-80	80-81	81-82	82-83	83-84	84-85
Paintings	8	2	8	13	14	15	31	13	12	6
Dollars	$24,640	$6,300	$16,976	$49,520	$112,700	$123,500	$198,800	$110,150	$56,000	$54,400

Record Sale: $58,000, P.NY, 10/11/79, "The Bombardment of Fort Sumter," 20 × 36 in.

EDWIN DEAKIN
(1838?-1923?)

Edwin Deakin was an English-born landscape and architectural painter who specialized in detailed and accomplished paintings of the old Spanish missions of California, but also executed still lifes.

As far as is known, Deakin was born in 1838 or 1840 in Sheffield, England. Established in England and France as an architectural painter, he emigrated to the United States in 1869. He found work in Chicago as a painter of memorial portraits of Civil War heroes, and in 1870 he opened a landscape and portrait studio in San Francisco.

Deakin became involved in the lively San Francisco art community. He joined the Bohemian Club; one of his closest friends was well-known still-life painter Samuel Marsden Brookes. In 1874, Deakin painted a portrait of Brookes at work in his studio (Fine Arts Museum of San Francisco).

Between 1870 and 1899, Deakin painted at least 21 scenes of the Spanish missions of California; they are prized for their historical as well as aesthetic values. A good example is *Mission Dolores* (ca. 1880, California Historical Society). He also painted rural landscapes in California and Idaho, such as *Farming in the Livermore Valley* (date and location unknown).

Deakin produced a number of still lifes. *Still-Life Kitchen Corner* (date and location unknown) emphasizes a meal in preparation, rather than a static collection of objects. *Homage to Flora* (1903, location unknown) was inspired by the artist's own garden.

Deakin may have been active as late as 1920. He probably died in 1923.

Grapes, 1896, 24 x 16 in., signed l.l. Courtesy of Maxwell Galleries, LTD., San Francisco, California.

MEMBERSHIPS
Bohemian Club

PUBLIC COLLECTIONS
California Historical Society, Sacramento
Fine Arts Museum of San Francisco
M.H. de Young Memorial Museum, San Francisco

SEASON	75-76	76-77	77-78	78-79	79-80	80-81	81-82	82-83	83-84	84-85
Paintings								5	4	4
Dollars								$7,350	$13,000	$8,750

Record Sale: $3,500, B, 5/24/84, "Rue des Chartres, Old Paris," 24 × 16 in.

ROBERT C. MINOR
(1839-1904)

Robert Minor was a late-nineteenth-century landscape artist, and one of the chief American exponents of the French barbizon style of landscape painting. He is remembered as a painter of poetic landscapes in France, Belgium, England and the Adirondack region of upper New York State.

Minor was born in New York City. He resisted his father's wishes that he become a businessman; instead, Minor chose to pursue the study of painting, first under Alfred C. Howland in New York, and then, in the mid-1860s, at the artists' colony at Barbizon, where he came under the influence of Narcisse Diaz and Camille Corot.

Following his stay at Barbizon, Minor went on to the Antwerp Academy in Belgium, where he studied with von Luppen, Boulanger and others. During this time, he traveled widely in Germany and Italy. He exhibited paintings at the Paris Salon of 1872, and at the Royal Academy and the Grosvenor Gallery while painting landscapes in England during 1873 and 1874.

Returning to New York City in 1874, Minor opened a studio on Washington Square, and began to establish his reputation in the United States as a sympathetic interpreter of nature in the barbizon mode. He exhibited regularly at the National Academy of Design, and received praise for both European and American landscapes.

River Landscape, ca. 1903, 22 x 30½ in., signed l.r. Courtesy of Florence Griswold Museum, Lyme Historical Society, Old Lyme, Connecticut. Donated in memory of Charles Davis White.

Minor remained active in Europe and America until shortly before his death. He was elected an associate of the National Academy of Design in 1888, and a full academician in 1897. His final years were spent in failing health at his home in Waterford, Connecticut, where he died in 1904.

MEMBERSHIPS
National Academy of Design
Salmagundi Club
Societe Artistique et Litteraire
  of Antwerp
Society of American Artists
Society of Landscape Painters

PUBLIC COLLECTIONS
National Museum of American Art, Washington, D.C.

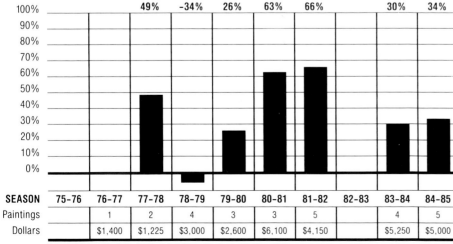

10-Year Average Change From Base Years '76-'77: 29%

SEASON	75-76	76-77	77-78	78-79	79-80	80-81	81-82	82-83	83-84	84-85
			49%	-34%	26%	63%	66%		30%	34%
Paintings		1	2	4	3	3	5		4	5
Dollars		$1,400	$1,225	$3,000	$2,600	$6,100	$4,150		$5,250	$5,000

Record Sale: $3,250, SPB, 1/29/81, ''Autumn,'' 55 × 19 in.

JOHN LINTON CHAPMAN
(1839-1905)

Judging by his work, J. Linton Chapman was a talented painter and illustrator, but he seems to have had little or no ambition. He was content to drift through much of his life. He lived abroad with his family as a boy and young man, and many of his paintings were of the Italian countryside and of crumbling Roman ruins.

He was born in 1839 in Washington, D.C., the son of John Gadsby Chapman, a popular painter of landscapes and portraits whose best-known work today is his *The Baptism of Pocahontas* in the United States Capitol. The elder Chapman also was known for *The American Drawing Book,* which became a classic instruction book for generations of would-be artists.

In 1848, the Chapman family moved to Europe and lived there for many years. It was only natural that J. Linton and his brother, Conrad Wise Chapman, should study under their father and follow him as painters. Conrad, however, had the motivation to make a name for himself. When the Civil War broke out in the United States, Conrad returned to fight for the Confederacy; he went to Mexico after the war and fell in love with the lush beauty of that country.

In 1866, Conrad made plans with Linton to open a large photographic establishment in Mexico, but nothing materialized. Instead, Conrad went to Paris to study under Gerome, whom he admired. Linton remained in Italy, painting meticulously detailed landscapes of ruined aqueducts and other vestiges of imperial Rome.

Linton returned to New York in 1878 and worked in and around the city for the rest of his life. He married, but the marriage failed. He seems to have been known principally for a tendency to live beyond his means. One friend commented that he seemed not to have the

Roman Coliseum, 30 x 40 in., signed l.l. Courtesy of Raydon Gallery, New York, New York.

slightest idea of how to take care of himself. He continued to paint Italian landscapes, but interspersed them with scenes of such American landmarks as the Erie Canal.

In 1897, Linton did the illustrations for *Diomed; the Life, Travels and Observations of a Dog,* written by John Wise, a relative of an old friend of his father. Linton Chapman died destitute in Westchester, New York in 1905. It was not until the following year that funds were raised for his burial.

PUBLIC COLLECTIONS
Butler Institute of American Art,
 Youngstown, Ohio
Charleston Art Gallery, West Virginia
Heckscher Museum, Huntington, New York

SEASON	75-76	76-77	77-78	78-79	79-80	80-81	81-82	82-83	83-84	84-85
Paintings	1	1		2	1	2	1		1	
Dollars	$2,600	$600		$3,746	$3,000	$21,000	$1,600		$9,000	

Record Sale: $13,000, CH, 6/26/81, "Via Appia," 28 x 72 in.

HENRY BACON
(1839-1912)

Henry Bacon, schooled as a figure painter in the conservative French tradition of the latter part of the nineteenth century, is noted principally for his watercolor paintings of Normandy and Egypt.

Little is known of his early life and education. He was born in 1839 in Haverhill, Massachusetts. At age 18, he enlisted in the U.S. Army during the Civil War, serving as both a soldier and a field artist for *Leslie's Weekly*.

Badly wounded, Bacon left the Army and went with his young wife, Lizzie, to Paris in 1864. He was one of the first Americans to be admitted to the reformed Ecole des Beaux-Arts, where he studied under Alexandre Cabanel and, later, Edouard Frere, both representatives of conservative academic painting in France.

From these masters, Bacon learned to paint in oils in a highly finished manner; his smooth brushstrokes, softly outlined figures and rich colors derived from the French academic tradition.

The unusual composition of *On Shipboard* (1877, location unknown) reflects the structural experiments of these artists in the 1860s and 1870s. Bacon helped popularize the shipboard theme by exhibiting many such subjects for some 20 years at the salons of Paris and at the National Academy of Design in New York City. He used the oblique angles and cropping effects developed in French painting at the time.

Lady with Violin (Sleeping), 1897, 36 x 26 in., signed l.l. Courtesy of Vose Galleries of Boston, Inc., Massachusetts.

As a figure painter, Bacon was noted for good drawing, interest and a variety of subjects. He painted shore scenes, as well as peasant subjects in Normandy and Italy.

The well-traveled painter turned exclusively to watercolors in 1895, spending much of his time working in London, Italy, Ceylon, Greece and Egypt, where he spent the last 15 years of his life before dying in Cairo in 1912 at age 73.

After 1895, Bacon emerged as an exponent of the use of watercolor in pure washes, without opaque body color. He continued to paint watercolors the rest of his life, winning high acclaim in that medium. His work has some of the qualities of La Farge and Fortuny, but it possesses an artistic distinction of its own.

10-Year Average Change From Base Years '75-'76: 83%

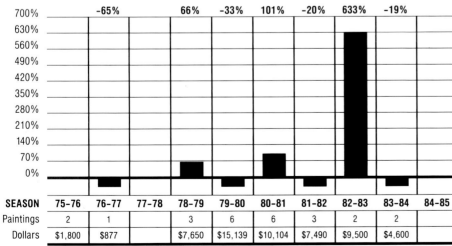

	-65%		66%	-33%	101%	-20%	633%	-19%	
SEASON	75-76	76-77	77-78	78-79	79-80	80-81	81-82	82-83	83-84	84-85
Paintings	2	1		3	6	6	3	2	2	
Dollars	$1,800	$877		$7,650	$15,139	$10,104	$7,490	$9,500	$4,600	

Record Sale: $9,000, CH, 12/3/82, "Bedtime," 14 x 10 in.

MEMBERSHIPS
National Academy of Design

PUBLIC COLLECTIONS
Corcoran Gallery of Art, Washington, D.C.
Museum of Fine Arts, Boston

JAMES BRADE SWORD

(1839-1915)

James Brade Sword was a landscape, portrait and genre painter who traveled widely in the United States, but lived and worked in Philadelphia once he became a painter. His paintings were well composed and often had touches of quiet sentiment. Many of his genre canvases involved children and sportsmen in the field. Views of the shore and of the sea were also recurring themes in his work.

Sword was born in Philadelphia in 1839, but spent his boyhood with his family in Macao, China. He was back in Philadelphia for high school, however, and immediately afterward went to work for a civil engineer.

He was involved with the enlargement of the Union Canal from Lebanon to Reading, Pennsylvania; the federal government's survey of Atchafalaya Bay in Louisiana; and the construction of a railroad tunnel through Broad Mountain in Mahoney Valley in upstate Pennsylvania.

While working on these projects, Sword tried his hand at sketching the surroundings. He enjoyed it, and in 1861 he began studying at the Pennsylvania Academy of the Fine Arts. In 1863, he turned to painting seriously, and studied for a time with landscape painter George W. Nicholson.

He painted in the Adirondacks; around Newport, Rhode Island; along the New Jersey shore; and in many parts of Eastern Pennsylvania. His paintings reflected popular tastes and were fre-

Cranberry Picking at Cape Cod, 25 x 35 in., signed l.r. Courtesy of Arvest Galleries, Inc., Boston, Massachusetts.

quently exhibited in Philadelphia and New York City. In 1911, he was commissioned by Congress to paint a portrait of former Speaker of the House J. W. Jones, which hangs in the Capitol in Washington.

Sword was one of the founders of the Art Club of Philadelphia, and was active in art circles in the city until his death in 1915.

MEMBERSHIPS
Art Club of Philadelphia
Artists' Fund Society
Philadelphia Society of Artists

PUBLIC COLLECTIONS
United States Capitol, Washington, D.C.
University of Pennsylvania, Philadelphia

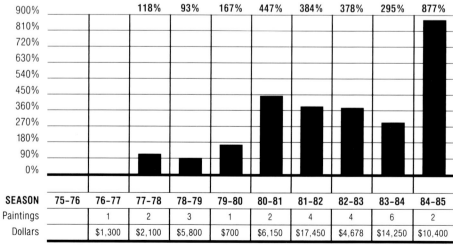

10-Year Average Change From Base Years '76-'77: 307%

		118%	93%	167%	447%	384%	378%	295%	877%
SEASON	75-76	76-77	77-78	78-79	79-80	80-81	81-82	82-83	83-84	84-85
Paintings		1	2	3	1	2	4	4	6	2
Dollars		$1,300	$2,100	$5,800	$700	$6,150	$17,450	$4,678	$14,250	$10,400

Record Sale: $9,800, CH, 1/23/85, "Sleighing on Frozen Lake," 20 x 36 in.

XANTHUS RUSSELL SMITH

(1839-1929)

The son of painters Russell and Mary Wilson Smith, Xanthus Smith came by his artistic ability quite naturally. Art was encouraged in the Smith family, and Xanthus became his father's equal in skill.

Xanthus Russell Smith was born in Philadelphia in 1839. In 1848, he and his father went on a sketching trip to New Hampshire's White Mountains. The entire Smith family traveled in Europe in 1851 and 1852, painting and sketching.

Smith studied painting at the Pennsylvania Academy of the Fine Arts in Philadelphia, and at the Royal Academy in London. His first commission, in 1854, was a painting of a neighbor's house outside Philadelphia. He also studied medicine at the University of Pennsylvania from 1856 to 1858. During the same period, he exhibited landscapes at the Academy.

While Smith served in the navy during the Civil War, he made several official and unofficial sketches. Following his discharge in 1865, he took a sketching trip to Gettysburg, which laid the foundation for his later paintings of battle scenes.

Between 1869 and 1876, Smith was commissioned to do paintings of marine subjects and Civil War battle scenes. He painted *The Battle of the "Monitor" and the "Merrimac"* (date unknown) for the Union Club in Philadelphia, and produced a 30-foot-long canvas of a beach scene of Cape May, New Jersey for the Pennsylvania Railroad Company.

Later in his career, Smith favored portrait painting, then became interested in photography. During the 1880s and 1890s, he wrote several articles on photography and its relation to art; his writing schedule eventually eclipsed his work in painting. Smith died near Philadelphia in 1929.

Battle of the Monitor and Merrimac, 7 x 12 in., signed l.l. Courtesy of Vose Galleries of Boston, Inc., Massachusetts.

Rebel Rain "Tennessee" attacking the U.S. ships "Richmond" and "Lackawanna", 7 x 12 in. Courtesy of Vose Galleries of Boston, Inc., Massachusetts.

SEASON	75-76	76-77	77-78	78-79	79-80	80-81	81-82	82-83	83-84	84-85
Paintings		1	2		2			1		3
Dollars		$4,250	$2,400		$27,000			$3,500		$45,000

Record Sale: $26,000, SPB, 12/6/84, "Blockade Runner Beached," 12 × 18 in.

WORDSWORTH THOMPSON
(1840-1896)

Historical painter Wordsworth Thompson is known for his colonial scenes and sketches. He also depicted the early days of the Civil War.

Born in Baltimore in 1840, he was educated at Maryland's Newton University. He studied law with his father, but gave it up to pursue a career in art.

At the beginning of the Civil War, Thompson became interested in the drama of military life in Virginia and became a sketch artist for *Harper's Weekly* and the *Illustrated London News*.

He left for Paris in 1861 and studied with several teachers before enrolling at the Ecole des Beaux Arts in 1864. He exhibited at the Paris Salon in 1865. While in Europe, he traveled on foot through Italy and Germany before returning in 1868 to New York City, where he set up a studio.

Thompson exhibited at the National Academy of Design in 1868. He became an associate of the Academy in 1875 with his painting *The Ruins of the Palace of St. Cloud in the Winter of 1871* (date and location unknown), his first picture to attract wide attention in America. His brilliant color, careful draftsmanship, and attention to historical fact show the influences of his European training.

In 1876, Thompson sent paintings to the Philadelphia Centennial. He also participated in the Paris Exposition of

North African Desert Outpost, 1893, 18 x 28 in., signed l.l. Courtesy of Raydon Gallery, New York, New York.

1878 and became a member of the newly organized Society of American Artists.

Of the 125 paintings sold in the National Academy by Thompson, more than 40 were of colonial revolutionary subjects. He also spent 18 years making trips to Spain, Morocco and Asia Minor, where he constantly sketched out-of-doors.

He died in 1896 in Summit, New Jersey, where he and his wife had lived for the last 12 years of his life.

MEMBERSHIPS
National Academy of Design
Society of American Artists

PUBLIC COLLECTIONS
Albright-Knox Art Gallery, Buffalo, New York
New-York Historical Society, New York City
Union League Club of New York

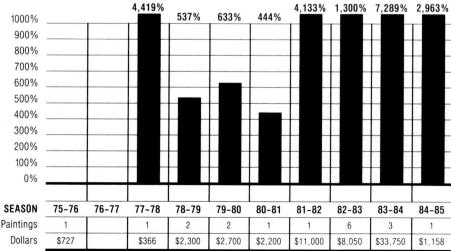

10-Year Average Change From Base Years '75-'76: 2,413%

SEASON	75-76	76-77	77-78	78-79	79-80	80-81	81-82	82-83	83-84	84-85
			4,419%	537%	633%	444%	4,133%	1,300%	7,289%	2,963%
Paintings	1		1	2	2	1	1	6	3	1
Dollars	$727		$366	$2,300	$2,700	$2,200	$11,000	$8,050	$33,750	$1,158

Record Sale: $23,000, SPB, 1/27/84, "The Port of Algeria," 22 × 36 in.

304

HARVEY YOUNG
(1840-1901)

Known primarily as a painter of the Rocky Mountains, Harvey Young developed a distinctive painting technique in his later years. He used opaque watercolor to capture the evanescent quality of sky, clouds and shadow.

Young was self-taught at first, and his early paintings seem almost formulaic. Later, however, after he had studied in Europe, his work assumed a rather Germanic romanticism. Eventually it took on many of the characteristics of the barbizon painters, with more intimate pastoral scenes taking precedence over the earlier landscapes of majestic mountains.

Young was born in 1840 in Post Mills, Vermont. Recent research has established that his full name was Harvey Otis Young, not Harvey B. Young, as many records show. At age 19, he went to California to prospect for gold. Six years later, when surface mining proved impractical, he went to San Francisco and found a job decorating carriages. After only six months, he opened his own studio, billing himself as a fine-arts painter.

By the mid-1900s, San Francisco was becoming a city of considerable wealth and culture, and good paintings were being exhibited with some frequency; presumably, Young studied these as guidelines for his own work. His early landscapes of the California mountains show traces of the Hudson River School style.

In 1869, he returned to the East coast, and the following year he made the first of six trips to study in Europe. Between stays in Europe he also went back to California, Nevada and Utah several times on sketching trips. He then painted mountain landscapes in his New York studio.

On a visit to Paris in 1876, he enrolled for a time at the Academie Julien, and also studied under Carolus-Duran. Like

Western, 20 x 30 in., signed l.r. Photograph courtesy of M. Knoedler & Co., Inc., New York, New York.

other Americans who now were flocking to Paris (rather than Munich) to study, he sketched conventional barbizon scenes at Fountainebleau. Two years later, he exhibited two paintings in the Paris Salon.

Young virtually abandoned painting for much of the 1880s, when he moved his family to Denver and went into silver mining. He prospered at first, but even-

tually lost most of a fortune and returned to painting. It was then that he adopted the wash and opaque watercolor technique he had been developing to catch the misty beauty of the Rockies.

In 1889, after a financial crisis, he moved to Colorado Springs and painted there until his death in 1901. His finest work was done in the final years of his life.

SEASON	75-76	76-77	77-78	78-79	79-80	80-81	81-82	82-83	83-84	84-85
Paintings			1	1	3	4	5	2	2	5
Dollars			$1,900	$3,000	$3,700	$5,800	$5,050	$4,650	$2,350	$6,100

Record Sale: $4,000, S.W, 2/27/83, "Platte River Valley," 19 × 29 in.

MEMBERSHIPS
Artists Club of Denver

PUBLIC COLLECTIONS
Copley Library, La Jolla, California
Denver Art Museum, Colorado
Oakland Art Museum, California
Penrose Public Library, Colorado Springs

THOMAS NAST
(1840-1902)

Thomas Nast, who created the elephant and donkey political emblems and the popular image of Santa Claus, is known as "the father of American political cartooning." He drew several thousand cartoons in his 25 years with *Harper's Weekly.* He is famous for his series attacking New York City's corrupt Tammany Hall politicians. The cartoons, and a *New York Times* crusade, destroyed Tammany in 1871.

Short, rotund and spirited, Nast in his political work was a fierce partisan or an unmerciful enemy. He is credited with helping to win a war and elect three presidents. Ulysses Grant said he was elected by "the sword of Sheridan and the pencil of Nast."

Nast was born in 1840, in Landau, Bavaria. His mother brought the family to New York City in 1846; his musician father arrived in 1850.

Nast studied briefly at the National Academy of Design, and in 1855, at age 15, he became a news illustrator for *Leslie's Illustrated Magazine.* By 1859, he was a contributor to *Harper's Weekly* and a member of the *New York Illustrated News* staff.

In 1860, the *News* sent him to England for the Heenan-Ayers fight. Borrowing money from Heenan, Nast went on to Italy and Garibaldi's revolution, sending back illustrated reports.

On his 1862 return, *Harper's* hired Nast full-time as a pictorial reporter. He became a major Civil War artist-correspondent. Lincoln called Nast "the Union's best 'recruiting sergeant.'"

Nast's cartooning increased with his attention to corruption and reform, though he continued to paint and draw. Many of his genre, literary and military works were exhibited from 1859 to 1870 at the National Academy of Design. He illustrated many books, including C. C. Moore's *A Visit from St. Nicholas.*

In 1888, Nast and *Harper's Weekly* parted, to the detriment of both. Nast

A Jolly Good Fellow, 1874, 62 x 42 in., signed l.l. Strong Museum, Rochester, New York.

took a fling at publishing (*Nast's Weekly,* 1892 to 1893), but the 1890s were not prosperous for him. In 1902, he accepted Theodore Roosevelt's appointment as consul in Guayaquil, Ecuador. He died of malaria five months later.

PUBLIC COLLECTIONS
Colorado Springs Courthouse, Colorado
Metropolitan Museum of Art, New York City
Museum of Fine Arts, Boston

SEASON	75-76	76-77	77-78	78-79	79-80	80-81	81-82	82-83	83-84	84-85
Paintings			1	1		2			1	
Dollars			$1,400	$60,000		$6,500			$800	

Record Sale: $60,000, SPB, 6/21/79, "Marching Through Georgia," 41 × 79 in.

306

R. SWAIN GIFFORD
(1840-1905)

Most remembered for his scenes of oriental life and landscape, Robert Swain Gifford was born in Massachusetts in 1840, on the island of Naushon near Martha's Vineyard. In his late teens he studied art in New Bedford, Massachusetts under Benjamin Russell and Dutch marine painter Albert Van Beest. He moved to Boston to begin his career in 1864, and established a studio there.

Gifford exhibited at the National Academy of Design for the first time in 1864; within two years, emboldened by his success, he packed up and moved to New York City. He became an associate member of the National Academy and began a series of far-ranging travels.

He painted in the Western United States in 1869, traveling through Oregon and California. He also voyaged to Europe, Egypt and the port of Algiers. One has only to scan a list of some of his titles to see his penchant for the most austere and mysterious aspects of nature: *The Griffin* (date and location unknown); *Edge of Field in Early Autumn* (1880, location unknown); *Lone Trees by the Water* (date and location unknown); *Quissett Moors* (1889, location unknown); *Sand Dunes, Naushon* (1881, location unknown).

Gifford belonged to many of the more important artists' associations of the United States and England. He died in New York City in 1905.

Nonquitt Cliff, 1882, 22 x 40 in., signed l.l. Courtesy of Raydon Gallery, New York, New York.

MEMBERSHIPS
American Water Color Society
National Academy of Design
National Arts Club
Royal Society of Painters and Etchers
Society of American Artists
Society of London Painters
Tile Club

PUBLIC COLLECTIONS
Corcoran Gallery of Art, Washington, D.C.

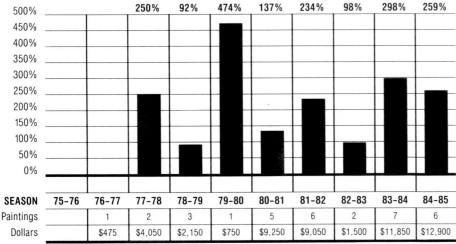

10-Year Average Change From Base Years '76-'77: 205%

	250%	92%	474%	137%	234%	98%	298%	259%

SEASON	75-76	76-77	77-78	78-79	79-80	80-81	81-82	82-83	83-84	84-85
Paintings		1	2	3	1	5	6	2	7	6
Dollars		$475	$4,050	$2,150	$750	$9,250	$9,050	$1,500	$11,850	$12,900

Record Sale: $7,000, SPB, 10/26/84, "Passing Shower, Newport," 30 x 50 in.

LABARRE GOODWIN
(1840-1910)

LaBarre Goodwin was one of nineteenth-century America's practitioners in the trompe l'oeil style.

Most scholars place him as a follower of William Michael Harnett, whose meticulously painted *After the Hunt* won plaudits and started a vogue when it was hung in a New York saloon in 1886. Others, however, maintain that Harnett was working in Munich when Goodwin was developing his own technique and that the two probably arrived at much the same style independently. Unquestionably, however, some hallmarks of Harnett's work, such as the floating feather and the trompe l'oeil signature carved into the wood, appear in Goodwin's work.

Richard Labarre Goodwin (who never used his first name) was born in Albany, New York in 1840, the son of a successful miniature and portrait painter. He began his career as an itinerant portrait painter in New York State, and began doing trompe l'oeil still lifes around 1881.

Goodwin was an habitual wanderer, traveling along the East Coast and through much of the frontier country of the West, painting wherever he happened to be. He loved to hunt, and braces of wildfowl and other game, along with a gun and perhaps a powder horn or some other accessory, became his standard subject matter.

Cabin Door Still Life, ca. 1886, 56¼ x 34⅛ in., signed l.l.
Courtesy of National Museum of American Art,
Smithsonian Institution, Museum Purchase in memory
of the Reverend F. Ward Denys.

Goodwin used a rustic door as a background for his compositions so often that his work was sometimes referred to as "cabin door" or "barn door" art. Occasionally he painted kitchen still lifes, but always with game as the feature of his composition.

Perhaps the painting for which Goodwin is best known is his *Theodore Roosevelt's Cabin Door* (1905, Museum of Fine Arts, Springfield). He made three versions; the whereabouts of the first is unknown. The door was exhibited at the Lewis and Clark Centennial in Oregon in 1905 and Goodwin borrowed it for his painting.

Goodwin gave up traveling and settled in Orange, New Jersey shortly before his death in 1910.

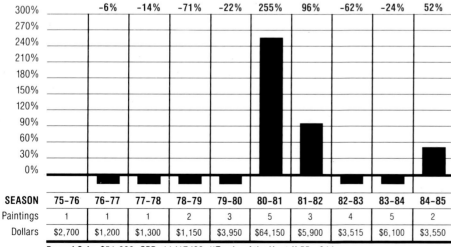

10-Year Average Change From Base Years '75–'76: 20%

	-6%	-14%	-71%	-22%	255%	96%	-62%	-24%	52%

SEASON	75–76	76–77	77–78	78–79	79–80	80–81	81–82	82–83	83–84	84–85
Paintings	1	1	1	2	3	5	3	4	5	2
Dollars	$2,700	$1,200	$1,300	$1,150	$3,950	$64,150	$5,900	$3,515	$6,100	$3,550

Record Sale: $51,000, SPB, 11/17/80, "Trophy of the Hunt," 55 × 34 in.

PUBLIC COLLECTIONS
Museum of Fine Arts, Springfield, Massachusetts
Stanford University, California
Vassar College, New York

GEORGE HENRY SMILLIE
(1840-1921)

A member of a respected family of engravers and painters, George Henry Smillie was a landscape painter whose work displayed many of the hallmarks of the Hudson River School, which by then had passed its prime. His paintings were marked by a brightness of color and poetic sentiment that were popular in his day, but which now cause critics to relegate him to a secondary rank in American landscape painting.

He made trips to many parts of the country, including one to the Rocky Mountains which provided him with material for many paintings. It is for his scenes of the farms and shoreline of Long Island and New England, however, that he is best known.

Smillie was born in New York City in 1840. His father, James Smillie, was a well-known line engraver, and as a boy George studied under him. He also studied painting with James McDougal Hart, an important landscape painter of the period. Two older brothers, James, Jr. and William, also became artists and engravers.

In 1871, Smillie made a trip to the Rocky Mountains and the Yosemite Valley of California, to sketch and paint. He used the material he gathered for years afterward for oils and watercolors. Most of his paintings were mountain landscapes, but some also included the Indians then native to the two regions.

Smillie also traveled to Florida to paint, but for most of his life he lived and worked in the New York City area. In 1881, he married Nellie Jacobs, a genre painter who had been a student of his brother James, and for many years the three shared a studio in suburban Bronxville. He died in Bronxville in 1921.

Florida Landscape, 1875, 18 x 32 in., signed l.l. Courtesy of Vose Galleries of Boston, Inc., Massachusetts.

MEMBERSHIPS
American Watercolor Society
National Academy of Design

PUBLIC COLLECTIONS
Corcoran Gallery of Art, Washington, D.C.
Metropolitan Museum of Art, New York City
Oakland Museum, California
Rhode Island School of Design, Providence

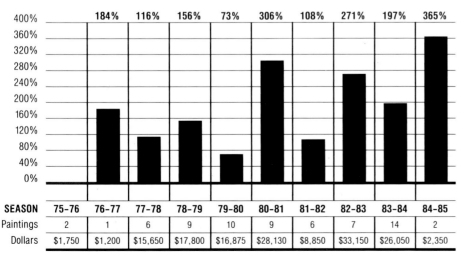

10-Year Average Change From Base Years '75-'76: 178%

	184%	116%	156%	73%	306%	108%	271%	197%	365%
SEASON	75-76	76-77	77-78	78-79	79-80	80-81	81-82	82-83	83-84	84-85
Paintings	2	1	6	9	10	9	6	7	14	2
Dollars	$1,750	$1,200	$15,650	$17,800	$16,875	$28,130	$8,850	$33,150	$26,050	$2,350

Record Sale: $11,000, CH, 12/3/82, "Near Elizabethtown," 28 x 52 in.

309

WILLIAM DE LA MONTAGNE CARY
(1840-1922)

The Trading Post, 12 x 25 in. Courtesy of Thomas Gilcrease Institute of American History and Art, Tulsa, Oklahoma.

William de la Montagne Cary was an important illustrator and genre painter. Although he began drawing at an early age, Cary's artistic future was sealed by an extraordinary cross-country odyssey.

Cary was born in 1840 in Tappan, New York, but spent most of his early life in New York City's Greenwich Village. While he was still a teenager, he contributed illustrations to major magazines, including *Harper's Weekly, Appleton's* and *Leslie's Weekly,* working at the time in pen-and-ink, oil and watercolor.

Although he would resume it later in his life, Cary's work as an illustrator ended when, at age 20, the artist and two New York friends decided to travel West.

Without jobs and with no particular destination in mind, the young New Yorkers followed the route of traders and trappers along the Missouri River, traveling by riverboat, flat-boat and wagon train. They eventually wound up in Oregon, journeyed South to San Francisco, and then returned to New York City via Panama at the outbreak of the Civil War.

For years, Cary maintained a studio in New York City and earned his living as a magazine and newspaper illustrator.

But the trip West never waned in significance. As exemplified by his *Trading on the Upper Missouri* (Thomas Gilcrease Institute of American History and Art), his travels enabled Cary to witness firsthand the river-based trading culture before the outbreak of the war. The adventure also inspired him to spend the next 50 years painting genre scenes of frontier and Indian life.

Cary made a second trip West in 1874, and it, too, resulted in innumerable paintings and sketches. In addition to drawing famous personages—Buffalo Bill, Sitting Bull and General Custer—Cary also painted canvases depicting the customs of ceremonies of the Plains Indians. These works, many of which were subsequently reproduced as magazine illustrations, are notable for their detailed verisimilitude.

An account of Cary's first trip West was preserved in a four-part 1895 serial in *Recreation* magazine, written by one of Cary's fellow-travelers and illustrated with Cary's drawings.

Cary died in Brookline, Massachusetts in 1922. A major collection of his paintings is housed in the Gilcrease Foundation in Tulsa, Oklahoma.

PUBLIC COLLECTIONS
Amon Carter Museum of Western Art,
  Fort Worth, Texas
Gilcrease Foundation, Tulsa, Oklahoma

SEASON	75-76	76-77	77-78	78-79	79-80	80-81	81-82	82-83	83-84	84-85
Paintings			1	2		1		1	2	
Dollars			$6,500	$2,700		$2,800		$18,000	$59,750	

Record Sale: $56,000, SPB, 5/31/84, ''Rounding Up Horses,'' 30 × 60 in.

DANIEL RIDGWAY KNIGHT
(1840-1924)

Hailing the Ferry, 1888, 64½ x 83 in., signed l.r. Courtesy of The Pennsylvania Academy of the Fine Arts, Philadelphia.

Daniel Ridgway Knight, a genre and figure painter, was born in Philadelphia. He studied at the Pennsylvania Academy of the Fine Arts, exhibiting there for the first time in 1858. In 1861, he founded the Philadelphia Sketch Club.

After saving his money for eight years, he went to Europe in 1872. He studied at the Ecole des Beaux Arts in Paris under Charles Gleyre, among whose other pupils were Joseph Woodwell, Pierce Francis Connelly, Renoir and Sisley. In 1876, he moved to Poissy to work under Jean Louis Meissonier, whose work idealized the French peasantry. Although Meissonier did not formally accept students, he allowed Knight to use his name when submitting his work to the Paris Salon, in order to facilitate acceptance of his paintings.

Knight's first peasant subject was shown at the Salon in 1875. *Market Day in Poissy* (1876, location unknown) shows how well the artist emulated Meissonier's crisp drawing and mastery of detail.

Although Knight's paintings were frequently exhibited in the United States, he remained in France for the rest of his life. During World War I, he served the French war effort as a pictorial propagandist. In 1924, he died in his home at Rolleboise-par-Bonniers in Seine-et-Oise.

At his best, Knight was in the first rank of plein-air painters of his time, following the example of Jules Breton and Bastien-Lepage. He traveled extensively in Normandy, where he completed many delightful studies and small works out of doors. One of his paintings, *Hailing the Ferry* (date and location unknown), has been called one of the most-copied paintings in America.

PUBLIC COLLECTIONS
Brooklyn Museum
Pennsylvania Academy of the Fine Arts,
  Philadelphia

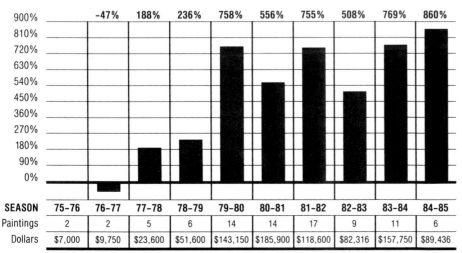

10-Year Average Change From Base Years '75-'76: 458%

	-47%	188%	236%	758%	556%	755%	508%	769%	860%
SEASON	75-76	76-77	77-78	78-79	79-80	80-81	81-82	82-83	83-84	84-85
Paintings	2	2	5	6	14	14	17	9	11	6
Dollars	$7,000	$9,750	$23,600	$51,600	$143,150	$185,900	$118,600	$82,316	$157,750	$89,436

Record Sale: $32,000, SPB, 1/25/80, "Garden Above the Seine," 32 × 26 in.

CHARLES CARYL COLEMAN
(1840-1928)

Although he spent most of his life in Italy, Charles Caryl Coleman exhibited in the United States and England. Early in his career he executed a number of portraits and figure paintings; later he specialized in landscape and architectural subjects.

Coleman was born in 1840 in Buffalo, New York. He studied art there under William H. Beard, then spent the years 1859 to 1862 in Paris. He returned to the United States to serve in the Union force during the Civil War, in which he was seriously wounded.

In 1866, Coleman returned to Europe with fellow painters William Morris Hunt and Elihu Vedder. He spent time in Paris and Brittany before moving to Rome, where he lived in the apartment that had been occupied by poet John Keats. Eventually Coleman settled in Capri, near Naples. He remained there for the rest of his life.

Among his early work is a study of his friend Vedder in Coleman's studio. Coleman was also commissioned to do a portrait of poet and essayist Walter Savage Landor. He is perhaps better known, however, for his architectural paintings, such as *The Bronze Horses of San Marco, Venice* (1876, Whitney Museum of American Art).

One of Coleman's favorite subjects was Mt. Vesuvius, which was visible from his villa on the island of Capri; Coleman portrayed the volcano's distur-

Studio Window, Island of Capri, 1897, 21 x 31½ in., signed l.r. Courtesy of John H. Garzoli Gallery, San Francisco, California.

bances and their effect on the landscape and the Bay of Naples with great fidelity. His treatments of this view include *Vesuvius from Pompeii* (date unknown, Detroit Institute of Arts) and *The Vesuvius Eruption of 1906* (date unknown, Brooklyn Museum).

Coleman worked not only in oils but also in watercolor and pastels. While he did not execute many still lifes, his floral paintings were recognized for their skillful composition and use of color.

He died in 1928 in Capri.

MEMBERSHIPS
National Academy of Design
National Arts Club
Newspaper Artists Association

PUBLIC COLLECTIONS
Albright-Knox Art Gallery, Buffalo, New York
Brooklyn Museum
Detroit Institute of the Arts
Museum of Fine Arts, Boston
Whitney Museum of American Art,
New York City

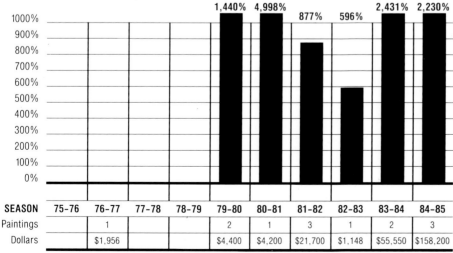

10-Year Average Change From Base Years '76-'77: 1,796%

SEASON	75-76	76-77	77-78	78-79	79-80	80-81	81-82	82-83	83-84	84-85
					1,440%	4,998%	877%	596%	2,431%	2,230%
Paintings		1			2	1	3	1	2	3
Dollars		$1,956			$4,400	$4,200	$21,700	$1,148	$55,550	$158,200

Record Sale: $155,000, D.NY, 10/24/84, "Quince Blossoms," 31 × 43 in.

ANDREW FISHER BUNNER
(1841-1897)

Andrew Fisher Bunner was a competent, but not particularly outstanding, landscape and marine painter. Many of the scenes he depicted were European. He was an excellent draftsman, however; perhaps his finest achievements were two groups of drawings of European scenes which his widow presented to the Metropolitan Museum of Art and the Corcoran Gallery of Art after his death.

Bunner was born in New York City in 1841. Little is known of his early life, or of any art training that he may have received in the United States before he went to Europe in 1871 to spend five years studying in Germany, France and Italy. His travels can be traced principally through the dates on his drawings of those countries.

Records of the National Academy of Design, of which he was an associate member, indicate that Bunner was active as a painter during the late 1860s, even before going to Europe. In 1866 and 1867, he painted landscapes of the Catskill Mountains, and in 1868 and 1870 he was painting scenes of Harper's Ferry and the countryside of West Virginia.

From 1879 until 1882, he lived in New York City and summered in the Hamptons in Eastern Long Island. A considerable number of his Long Island landscapes survive, as do seascapes of scenes along the shore of Great South Bay.

Bunner's spiritual home, however, seems to have been Venice. He lived there from 1883 until 1886 and painted more scenes there than in any of the other cities where he lived or visited. The morning light, the sunsets, everything about Venice attracted him and some of his best drawings were done there.

After his return to New York City, and until his death there in 1897, he continued to paint scenes of his favorite city.

Picnic Party at Lake George, 1874, 30½ x 24½ in. In the collection of The Corcoran Gallery of Art, Washington, D.C. Museum Purchase through a gift of the Honorable David Jayne Hill.

MEMBERSHIPS
American Watercolor Society
National Academy of Design
Salmagundi Club

PUBLIC COLLECTIONS
Corcoran Gallery of Art, Washington, D.C.
George Walter Vincent Smith Art Museum,
    Springfield, Massachusetts
Metropolitan Museum of Art, New York City
National Museum of American Art,
    Washington, D.C.
Parrish Art Museum,
    Southhampton, Long Island
Pennsylvania Academy of the Fine Arts,
    Philadelphia
William Penn Memorial Museum,
    Harrisburg, Pennsylvania

SEASON	75-76	76-77	77-78	78-79	79-80	80-81	81-82	82-83	83-84	84-85
Paintings						2	6	3	2	3
Dollars						$7,700	$9,800	$3,277	$3,558	$5,720

Record Sale: $6,000, SPB, 6/19/81, "Picnic by the Lake," 30 × 24 in.

PETER MORAN
(1841-1914)

Peter Moran was noted principally for his paintings and etchings of animals, although he occasionally did landscapes.

He was born in Bolton, Lancashire, England in 1841, the youngest of four brothers, and brought to the United States at age three.

When he graduated from grammar school, he was apprenticed to Herline and Hersel, lithographic printers in Philadelphia. His two older brothers, Edward and Thomas, were artists and maintained a studio there. Moran studied under them, but was also influenced by Rosa Bonheur and Constant Troyon. Except for a brief trip to England in 1863 to study the work of Landseer and other English animal painters, Peter Moran spent most of his professional life in his Philadelphia studio, where he worked with his wife, the former Emily Kelley, a painter and etcher.

In addition to his etchings and paintings of animals, Moran was interested in the theater. He painted scenery and acted bit parts.

Moran often traveled through the Western United States. These trips provided the subject matter for some of his works, including three illustrations for a report on the taxation of American Indians. He accompanied his brother Thomas on a trip to the Grand Teton Mountains in 1879. In 1881, he traveled with Captain Bourke on a trip to Indian pueblos in New Mexico and Arizona.

Santa Fe Traders, New Mexico, 1883, 7 x 11½ in., signed l.l. Courtesy of The Peters Corporation, Santa Fe, New Mexico.

His two brothers were more famous, but by the time of his death in 1914, Peter Moran had made his own significant and productive career as an artist.

MEMBERSHIPS
New York Society of Etchers
Philadelphia Arts and Crafts Guild
Philadelphia Society of Etchers

PUBLIC COLLECTIONS
Amon Carter Museum of Western Art,
  Fort Worth
Parrish Art Museum,
  Southampton, New York
Peabody Institute, Baltimore

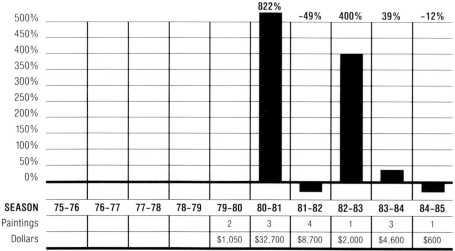

10-Year Average Change From Base Years '79-'80: 200%

SEASON	75-76	76-77	77-78	78-79	79-80	80-81	81-82	82-83	83-84	84-85
						822%	-49%	400%	39%	-12%
Paintings					2	3	4	1	3	1
Dollars					$1,050	$32,700	$8,700	$2,000	$4,600	$600

Record Sale: $28,000, CH, 4/24/81, "Stampede Pueblo of Jemez" 19 × 30 in.

314

ELBRIDGE WESLEY WEBBER
(1841-1914)

Little-known today, Elbridge Wesley Webber attained considerable success in the late 1870s for his seascapes, landscapes, animal pictures, still lifes and genre and Civil War scenes.

Self-taught, Webber developed a competent, realistic style. His oil paintings were popular and were reproduced often, but were uneven in quality. He was prolific; although he was capable of fine work, much of his output was conventional and undistinguished. His best work is unified and effectively subtle in color, as in *Kennebec River, Maine, Boat Shop* (date unknown, Peabody Museum).

Webber (who did not use his first name) was born in Gardiner, Maine in 1841. He was apprenticed in 1858 to sign and carriage painter J.C. Roberts of Boston. Wed in 1861, Webber returned to Gardiner in 1862 to enlist in Company B, of the Sixteenth Maine Volunteer Infantry Regiment.

He contracted a chronic intestinal disorder and saw little Civil War battle action. An amateur musician-composer, he played in the band and sketched until he was mustered out in 1865.

Apparently Webber was the only artist-soldier present at Lee's surrender at Appomattox, where he made first-hand sketches of historical value. Civil War scenes were a continuing staple of his career. Many were reproduced in leading magazines.

Webber's earliest known oil is *The Brook* (1866, location unknown). In 1870, he opened a Boston studio. By the mid-1870s, he had an established reputation, primarily for his New England landscapes and marine subjects.

Webber's palette was somber, and he pictured his subjects often at twilight or under overcast skies. A favorite theme was a coasting ship in half-light. A relative described his disposition as melancholy.

Hauling the Logs, 22 x 30⅛ in., signed l.r. Courtesy of Marbella Galleries, Inc., New York, New York.

Webber opened a studio in New York City in 1892, working hard to support his drinking habit. Divorced in 1896, he remarried in 1897. He maintained the two studios until his death in 1914 at his sister's Wollaston, Massachusetts home. He was buried in Gardiner.

MEMBERSHIPS
Boston Art Club

PUBLIC COLLECTIONS
Boston Athenaeum
Brooklyn Museum
New York Public Library, New York City
Peabody Museum of Salem, Massachusetts
Portland Museum of Art, Maine

SEASON	75-76	76-77	77-78	78-79	79-80	80-81	81-82	82-83	83-84	84-85
Paintings			3	12	7	8	5	5	10	6
Dollars			$2,075	$13,475	$9,025	$9,000	$7,350	$6,430	$15,350	$7,750

Record Sale: $3,500, CH, 1/29/82, "Shipping in a Harbour," 30 × 50 in.

JOHN JOSEPH ENNEKING
(1841-1916)

Not long after John J. Enneking died in 1916, he had been largely forgotten except by a few collectors, but at the height of his career he was one of the most popular landscape painters in New England. There has been a recent·resurgence of interest in Enneking's work, possibly because of his revival of interest in American impressionism. Having studied with Leon Bonnat and Charles-Francois Daubigny in France, Enneking was a bridge between the French and American schools of painting.

Enneking was born in 1841 in Minster, Ohio. He was the only child of Joseph and Margaretha Enneking, who owned a large farm about 40 miles north of Cincinnati. When both of his parents died in 1856 he went to live with an aunt and uncle in Cincinnati, where he attended Mount St. Mary's College in 1858 and studied drawing. In 1861 he joined the Union Army, but when he was injured he returned to Cincinnati to continue with his art career. He then went first to New York City and then to Boston, where he studied with Samuel Gerry.

In 1864, Enneking married Mary Eliot and built a house in Hyde Park, Massachusetts. In the late 1860s and early 1870s, he went on with his studies and began to earn money as an artist.

From 1872 to 1876, Enneking went to Europe with his family to study and paint. Enneking is said to have painted with Monet himself.

Landscape with Sheep, 1891, signed l.r. Courtesy of Vose Galleries of Boston, Inc., Massachusetts.

The Village, 1894, 18 x 24 in., signed l.r. Courtesy of Vose Galleries of Boston, Inc., Massachusetts.

Enneking's earliest work—from 1873 to 1876—is a vivid and exact representation of nature. His later paintings vary widely in style. There are many flowering orchard scenes which show a definite impressionist influence; they are lighter in tone and employ a looser brushwork, as in *Hillside Spring* (date unknown, Museum of Fine Arts, Boston).

His New England landscapes fall into several categories: November twilights, as in *Evening Gold* (date and location unknown); trout brooks, as in *Wight's Brook* (date and location unknown); and woodland and mountain scenes, as in *Saddle Back Mountain* (date and location unknown). Sometimes he painted interiors, but for these he used a darker palette and a more traditional style. *John G. Whittier's Ancestor's Home-*

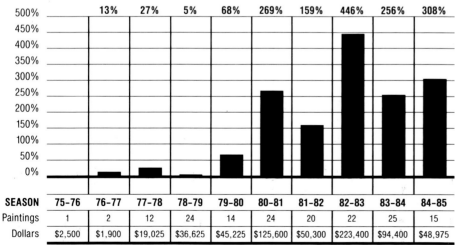

10-Year Average Change From Base Years '75-'76: 155%

	13%	27%	5%	68%	269%	159%	446%	256%	308%
SEASON	75-76	76-77	77-78	78-79	79-80	80-81	81-82	82-83	83-84	84-85
Paintings	1	2	12	24	14	24	20	22	25	15
Dollars	$2,500	$1,900	$19,025	$36,625	$45,225	$125,600	$50,300	$223,400	$94,400	$48,975

Record Sale: $110,000, SPB, 6/2/83, "Summer on the Lake," 18 × 24 in.

Landscape, signed l.r. Courtesy of Vose Galleries of Boston, Inc., Massachusetts.

stead (date and location unknown) is an example of his work in this mode.

Enneking's best pictures were the subdued autumnal scenes of dusk and twilight. Time of day is more important than location—this could be an influence of the barbizon painters. In addition to his studies with Daubigny, Enneking was acquainted with Camille Carot and Jean-Francois Millet.

Enneking's real forte was atmospheric painting: he captured humidity, mists, hazes, the wetness of winter. Like George Inness and George Fuller, he was interested in subordinating the forms of nature to light, color and feeling. In these mood paintings, the unity of effect is all-important.

He returned to Boston in 1876. In 1878, his first one-man show, at Wil-liams and Everett's Gallery, made his reputation there.

His most famous painting was an atypical work, a view of the first Church of Christ Scientist, commissioned for $10,000 as a gift for the founder of the Christian Science religion. The church is symbolically surrounded by sunset glow and clouds.

Enneking died in 1916.

MEMBERSHIPS
Boston Art Club
Connecticut Academy of Fine Arts
Copley Society
Salmagundi Club

PUBLIC COLLECTIONS
Museum of Fine Arts, Boston
Worcester Art Museum, Massachusetts

EDWARD LAMSON HENRY
(1841-1919)

A spiritually innocent artist in a time of intellectual and stylistic complexity, Edward Lamson Henry is best described as a visual historian who preserved the lifestyles of rural America in his genre and landscape paintings. He also painted portraits.

Born in South Carolina in 1841, Henry came to New York City as a child. He studied there with Walter M. Oddie; later, he attended the Pennsylvania Academy of the Fine Arts. He then went to Paris, where he worked under Charles Gleyre and Gustave Courbet.

Gleyre's influence led Henry to historical and genre painting, while Courbet's led him to observe and romanticize nature.

During the Civil War, Henry sketched with the Union army in Virginia. In 1871, he returned to Europe.

After his marriage in 1875, Henry made another trip to Europe. In the 1880s he built a summer home at Cragsmoor, near Ellenville, New York. Cragsmoor soon became an artists' colony, attracting George Inness, Jr., Arthur Keller, and many others. This group founded the Cragsmoor Free Library.

Although Henry tended to gloss over the rugged countryside of Cragsmoor and the harsh lives of its people, they inspired his finest work. His paintings were old-fashioned, anecdotal, authentic and brilliantly colored.

Henry's railroad scenes combined minute detail with a sense of open space.

Portrait of Mrs. Lydig and her Daughter, 1891, 19⅜ x 15¼ in., signed l.l. Photograph courtesy of Hirschl & Adler, Inc., New York, New York.

His collection of antique carriages and costumes, which served as models, was renowned; details were also documented through books, prints and photographs, and he worked directly from nature when possible. His portraits, especially those of black children, show a keen eye for character and a sensitivity to poverty and innocence.

While Henry's painting style remained consistent through his lifetime, his later work is less sharply defined and his palette is lighter, almost pastel.

Henry died at Cragsmoor in 1919.

PUBLIC COLLECTIONS
Corcoran Art Gallery, Washington, D.C.
Metropolitan Museum of Art, New York City
New York State Museum, Albany
Shelburne Museum Inc., Shelburne, Vermont

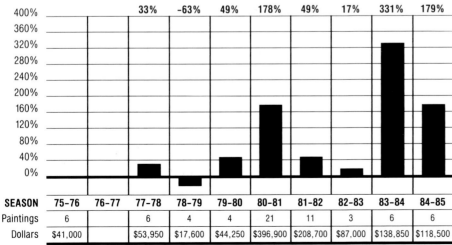

10-Year Average Change From Base Years '75-'76: 86%

		33%	-63%	49%	178%	49%	17%	331%	179%

SEASON	75-76	76-77	77-78	78-79	79-80	80-81	81-82	82-83	83-84	84-85
Paintings	6		6	4	4	21	11	3	6	6
Dollars	$41,000		$53,950	$17,600	$44,250	$396,900	$208,700	$87,000	$138,850	$118,500

Record Sale: $250,000, S.BM, 7/17/80, "Election Day 1844," 27 x 51 in.

HENRY MOSLER
(1841-1920)

Henry Mosler, a genre and figure painter, designer and engraver, was born in New York City in 1841.

His family moved to Cincinnati in 1851, where his father opened a lithography business. Mosler was apprenticed as a wood engraver, and began painting about 1858. He studied with James H. Beard from 1859 to 1861. Beginning in 1862, he followed the Union Army as an illustrator for *Harper's Weekly.*

Mosler went to Dusseldorf in 1863 to continue his artistic training. He came back to Cincinnati in 1866 after studying with Hebert in Paris. Returning to Europe in 1870, he lived at first in Munich, then in Paris.

Much of the artist's international reputation is based on his genre scenes of peasant life. He painted a series of Breton marriage scenes, which includes *Courtship* (date unknown, William R. Nelson Gallery of Art, Kansas City).

Mosler painted in Paris, using sketches and accessories collected on-site to produce Breton interiors and Normandy coastal scenes, as well as paintings of American Indians. Throughout his career, Mosler was an active teacher, one of the first to open his atelier to both sexes.

In 1879, his *Le Retour* (date unknown, Musee d'Orsay) received an honorable mention at the Paris Salon. Two weeks later, it was purchased for the Luxembourg Museum in Paris, making Mosler the first American to be so honored.

Children Rowing, 1866, 48 x 66 in., signed l.r. Collection of Procter and Gamble.

Mosler received other honors in Europe, including election to the French Academy and the Legion of Honor. He received a gold medal at the Salon and a silver medal at the Paris Exhibition in 1889.

Mosler returned to the United States in 1894, settling in New York City, where he remained until his death in 1920. However, he was not acclaimed in his native land. Though he became an associate member of the National Academy of Design in 1895, he was repeatedly passed over for full membership.

MEMBERSHIPS
French Academy
Legion of Honor
National Academy of Design

PUBLIC COLLECTIONS
Art Gallery of New South Wales,
  Sydney, Australia
Cincinnati Art Museum
Corcoran Gallery of Art,
  Washington, D.C.
Musee des Beaux-Arts de Grenoble,
  France
Musee d'Orsay, Paris
Metropolitan Museum of Art,
  New York City
Pennsylvania Academy of the Fine Arts,
  Philadelphia

10-Year Average Change From Base Years '78-'79: 255%

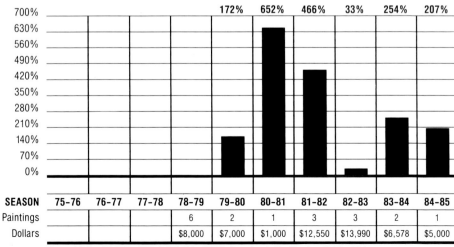

	172%	652%	466%	33%	254%	207%

SEASON	75-76	76-77	77-78	78-79	79-80	80-81	81-82	82-83	83-84	84-85
Paintings				6	2	1	3	3	2	1
Dollars				$8,000	$7,000	$1,000	$12,550	$13,990	$6,578	$5,000

Record Sale: $7,000, SPB, 9/23/81, "With Grandpa in the Garden," 22 x 25 in.

WILLIAM MARK FISHER

(1841-1923)

Although William Mark Fisher was born and raised in the United States, he failed to achieve fame as a landscape painter until he moved to England.

Born in 1841 in Boston, Fisher received instruction at an early age at the Lowell Institute in Massachusetts. He also studied under George Inness, who steered him from portraiture to landscape artistry.

At 20, Fisher went to Paris, studying at Gleyre's atelier. While working in France, he was influenced by the ideas of Monet and the younger school of French painters.

After a few years in France, Fisher returned to Boston, but found only slight success in the United States. Still looking to prove himself, he settled in England in 1877, and quickly established himself as one of the foremost landscape artists and animal painters.

The totality of Fisher's landscapes constituted the strength of his works. Figures were subordinated to landscape. Intent on producing realistic paintings, he was driven by a dogged desire to paint only what he saw. The picturesque was disregarded if it undermined reality.

Fisher's landscape preference came from his studies in France, where he traveled to various villages. His many paintings of the English countryside were distinguished by fine drawing and a sense of color. He also painted genre and cattle pieces.

Before his death in 1923, Fisher

The Hunt, 16 x 20 in. Courtesy of Vose Galleries of Boston, Inc., Massachusetts.

received medals' for work exhibited in Paris, Chicago and St. Louis expositions. In England, his peers bestowed on him three of the highest honors an artist can receive in that country: membership to the New English Art Club; election as president of the Essex Club; and full member status in the Royal Academy.

Fisher's best paintings included *Noon* (1872, Museum of Fine Arts, Boston), *On the Cam* (1876, Museum of Fine Arts, Boston), *The Meadows* (1877, Museum of Fine Arts, Boston) and *Feeding the Fowls* (date unknown, Tate Gallery).

MEMBERSHIPS
Essex Art Club
New English Art Club
Royal Academy

PUBLIC COLLECTIONS
Museum of Fine Arts, Boston
Tate Gallery, London

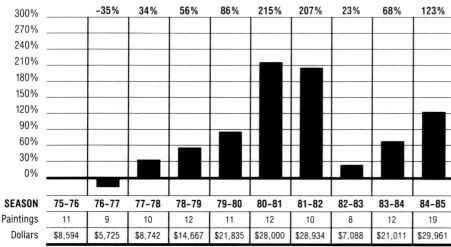

10-Year Average Change From Base Years '75-'76: 78%

SEASON	75-76	76-77	77-78	78-79	79-80	80-81	81-82	82-83	83-84	84-85
		-35%	34%	56%	86%	215%	207%	23%	68%	123%
Paintings	11	9	10	12	11	12	10	8	12	19
Dollars	$8,594	$5,725	$8,742	$14,667	$21,835	$28,000	$28,934	$7,088	$21,011	$29,961

Record Sale: $8,750, S, 5/15/85, "Pasturage," 30 × 50 in.

320

JOHN FERGUSON WEIR
(1841-1926)

Painter, sculptor, writer and teacher, John Ferguson Weir was born in West Point, New York in 1841. He painted American industrial pictures, impressionist scenes, academic portraits and landscapes reminiscent of the Hudson River School.

Although he was a prolific painter, Weir's reputation as an administrator exceeded his artistic endeavors. He was the first director of Yale University's School of Fine Arts, a position he held for more than 40 years from 1869 to 1913.

Son of Robert W. Weir, professor of drawing at West Point, and brother of impressionist painter Julian Alden Weir, he completed his education at West Point and studied painting in his father's studio.

At age 20, John F. Weir moved to New York's Tenth Street Studio Building where he became familiar with many of America's leading painters. *The Gun Foundry* of 1866 (Putnam County Historical Society) was one of America's first industrial pictures and won him election to the National Academy of Design. That painting and its companion, *Forging the Shaft* (1867, destroyed; replica of 1877 at Metropolitan Museum of Art), helped Weir achieve early fame.

These large paintings dramatically depict workmen against the fiery glow of the furnaces. Figures were modeled from local athletes and details of industrial interiors are exact.

After a year spent in Europe, where he painted panoramic landscapes, Weir returned to New Haven, Connecticut and assumed the post at Yale. There, Weir was lauded for his administrative efforts, for the acquisition in 1871 of the James Jarves collection of early Italian paintings, and for his sculptured portraits of Yale president Theodore Dwight Woolsey and Professor Benjamin Silliman the elder.

East Rock, New Haven, Connecticut, 25 x 30 in., signed l.r. Courtesy of Vose Galleries of Boston, Inc., Massachusetts.

In 1882, Weir published an article titled "American Arts: Its Progress and Prospects." His book *Human Destiny in the Light of Revelation* (1903) reveals his interest in religion.

Weir died in Providence, Rhode Island in 1926.

MEMBERSHIPS
National Academy of Design

PUBLIC COLLECTIONS
Corcoran Gallery, Washington, D.C.
Metropolitan Museum of Art, New York City
Museum of Fine Arts, Boston
Putnam County Historical Society,
 Cold Spring, New York

SEASON	75-76	76-77	77-78	78-79	79-80	80-81	81-82	82-83	83-84	84-85
Paintings			1		3	1	2	1	2	4
Dollars			$21,000		$15,000	$1,400	$5,300	$4,750	$2,800	$14,700

Record Sale: $21,000, PB, 10/27/77, "Artist's Studio," 25 × 30 in.

MARY SMITH
(1842-1878)

Mary Smith, daughter of noted land-scapist Russell Smith, was a painter of considerable skill who died at age 36. A true naturalist, she painted such denizens of the woods as opposum, birds, squirrels and rabbits. Her subtly textured paintings are characterized by brilliant color and a warm, earthy glow.

Born in 1842, Smith grew up at Edgehill, near Jenkintown, Pennsylvania. Together with her well-known father, Smith's mother was an accomplished artist who specialized in painting flowers, and her brother, Xanthus, was a prominent marine painter.

Smith began painting at age 14. Although she had no professional training, she benefited from the instruction of her mother and from the natural surroundings that formed so much of her imagery. Her early years were spent roaming the woods near her house, collecting natural objects and tending her flock of poultry (chickens figured prominently in many of her paintings). In describing his daughter's pursuits, Russell Smith wrote: "Such habits early in life no doubt laid the foundation of that strong love of nature that was more a passion that a predilection, and remained the ruling principle of her life and art" (*A Brief Sketch of the Life of Mary Smith, The Painter,* 1878).

From 1859 to 1869, Smith was a frequent exhibitor at the Pennsylvania Academy of the Fine Arts. In 1868, two of her paintings were shown at the National Academy of Design in New York City. She also exhibited at the Centennial International Exhibition in Philadelphia in 1876.

An oil painting entitled *Picking Cherries* (1872, Pennsylvania Academy of the Fine Arts) is a characteristic example of her finest work. It features an intimate grouping of her favorite subjects, chickens and baby chicks, softly rendered in brown and gold. This work demon-

Three Rabbits, 13⅝ x 20¼ in., signed l.l. Courtesy of Reading Public Museum, Pennsylvania.

strates her typical palette, composed of red, brown and yellow, with smaller amounts of contrasting black, white and blue.

After her mother's death in 1874, Smith continued to paint while managing her father's household. Her death in 1878 ended a promising career in the fine arts. Concerned about promoting the careers of women artists in the Philadelphia area, she designated a portion of her income from the sale of her paintings to finance an annual award. The Mary Smith prize was established in her memory and awarded each year until 1969 to the best work by a woman in the annual student exhibition of the Pennsylvania Academy of the Fine Arts.

PUBLIC COLLECTIONS
Pennsylvania Academy of the Fine Arts,
    Philadelphia

SEASON	75-76	76-77	77-78	78-79	79-80	80-81	81-82	82-83	83-84	84-85
Paintings			1		1		2	2		
Dollars			$1,600		$800		$5,700	$5,500		

Record Sale: $4,000, SPB, 7/1/82, "Springtime Feast," 22 × 26 in.

322

LOUIS MADER
(1842-1892?)

Louis Mader was the third of Pennsylvania's "Almshouse Painters" of the late nineteenth century (Charles Hofmann and John Rasmussen preceded him). He is also known for a set of murals painted in a house in Parkesburg, Pennsylvania.

Almost nothing is known of Mader's life, and little is known about his work. The legend in Parkesburg is that Mader, an itinerant, appeared one autumn day during the mid-nineteenth century and offered to paint several rooms in a house on Main Street in exchange for lodging. The house may have been a rectory. At any rate, Mader covered the walls of two rooms with 29 signed murals of geographic and historical scenes, ranging from Constantinople to Trenton, New Jersey. He also painted a trompe l'oeil ceiling, including polychrome fruit.

The murals, remarkably well preserved, were discovered by art historians in the 1960s, and installed in the Pennsylvania State Museum in Harrisburg. They suggest either that Mader had traveled in Europe, or perhaps that he had merely copied fashionable wallpapers and travel books.

In 1892, Mader was committed to the Berks County Almshouse for intemperance. Like Hofmann and Rasmussen, he painted a number of views portraying the almshouse as orderly and serene. His known paintings, all of which are on tin, appear to have been modeled on Hofmann's treatment of the institution.

PUBLIC COLLECTIONS
Pennsylvania State Museum, Harrisburg

Berks County Almshouse, 1895, 32⅝ x 39⅝ in., signed l.r. Courtesy of the National Gallery of Art, Washington, D.C. Gift of Edgar William and Bernice Chrysler Garbisch.

SEASON	75-76	76-77	77-78	78-79	79-80	80-81	81-82	82-83	83-84	84-85
Paintings						1		1		
Dollars						$10,000		$24,000		

Record Sale: $24,000, SPB, 1/27/83, "View of the Berks County Almshouse," 33 x 40 in.

EDWARD C. LEAVITT
(1842-1904)

Courtesy of Vose Galleries of Boston, Massachusetts.

Although Edward C. Leavitt's name is not included in most dictionaries of American art, he stands out in the late nineteenth century as Providence, Rhode Island's leading still-life painter. His work, emphasizing fruits, flowers, antiques and Victorian bric-a-brac resting on highly polished, carved tabletops, is known for its realistic, tangible quality. Leavitt paid great attention to texture and illuminated surfaces. His objects are sharply focused.

Taught by James Morgan Lewin, who dominated the school of still-life painting in nearby Fall River, Massachusetts, Leavitt seems to have spent most of his life in Providence. He was a prolific painter, a successful fruit and flower specialist who also did many other still lifes, including dead game and fish.

Unlike the poetic style of his teacher, Leavitt's objects are precisely drawn, realistic in detail and very carefully finished. He had a penchant for antiques, which seem to be included for their purely opulent effect, and his decorative compositions are marked by a multitude of diverse objects, often in costly bronze and silver.

Leavitt exhibited frequently at the National Academy of Design in the 1870s and 1890s. Thereafter, his quality declined, and the work of this productive and popular painter went into eclipse until the publication in 1971 of William H. Gerdt and Russell Burke's standard work in the field, *American Still-Life Painting*.

Leavitt died in 1904.

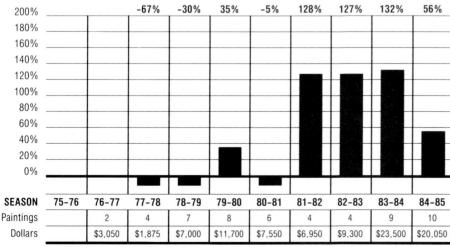

10-Year Average Change From Base Years '76-'77: 42%

SEASON	75-76	76-77	77-78	78-79	79-80	80-81	81-82	82-83	83-84	84-85
			-67%	-30%	35%	-5%	128%	127%	132%	56%
Paintings		2	4	7	8	6	4	4	9	10
Dollars		$3,050	$1,875	$7,000	$11,700	$7,550	$6,950	$9,300	$23,500	$20,050

Record Sale: $10,000, CH, 6/1/84, "Chinese Plums," 35 × 12 in.

FRANK HENRY SHAPLEIGH
(1842-1906)

Known as the "White Mountain artist," Frank Henry Shapleigh earned a handsome living and popular recognition for his landscapes.

The best-known are of familiar landmarks in New Hampshire's White Mountains. Shapleigh also produced paintings of St. Augustine, Florida scenes.

Besides landscapes in oil, Shapleigh did some portraiture and some late-career watercolors. His interest in antiques resulted in a late series of rustic interiors. A major part of Shapleigh's professional life was as a resort artist-in-residence, an occupation peculiar to the Victorian age in America. The affable resident-artists gave weekly studio receptions for their prospective clients, the wealthy patrons of the fashionable resorts.

The artist's summer studio, established in the early 1870s in the White Mountains, was moved into Crawford House, a hotel in Mount Washington Valley. There he held forth seasonally from 1877 to 1892. His studio in the spring and fall from 1886 on was in St. Augustine's Ponce de Leon, a luxurious hotel. He wintered in Boston.

Born in Boston in 1842, Shapleigh studied art at the old Lowell Institute of Design. He saw nine months' Civil War service with the 45th Massachusetts Regiment in 1863.

Shapleigh's first exhibited landscape was *A Quiet Lane* (date and location

The Presidential Range & Ammonoosuc River, 1885, 22 x 36 in., signed l.l. Courtesy of Vose Galleries of Boston, Inc., Massachusetts.

unknown) at the Boston Athenaeum in 1864.

He studied in Paris from 1867 to 1869 with Emile Lambinet, a pastoral landscapist who advocated painting directly from nature. On his return, Shapleigh shared a Boston studio with John Appleton Brown. He produced some large paintings of the Yosemite Valley and other scenes on a Western trip in 1870.

Shapleigh's career was well-established by the mid-1870s. In 1880, he did illustrations for W.W. Longfellow's works, as well as other books and magazines.

After a two-year European trip, the artist built a permanent home, "Maple Knoll," in Jackson, New Hampshire in 1896. He died there in 1906, having painted very little after 1897.

PUBLIC COLLECTIONS
Farnsworth Library and Art Museum, Rockland, Maine
Hood Museum of Art, Dartmouth College, Hanover, New Hampshire
New Britain Museum of American Art, Connecticut
Portland Museum of Art, Maine
University of New Hampshire, Durham

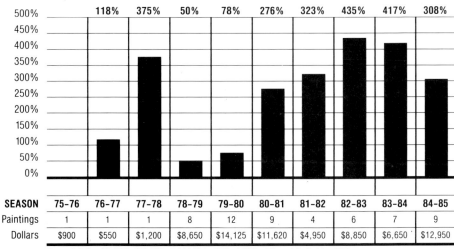

10-Year Average Change From Base Years '75-'76: 238%

	75-76	76-77	77-78	78-79	79-80	80-81	81-82	82-83	83-84	84-85
		118%	375%	50%	78%	276%	323%	435%	417%	308%
SEASON	75-76	76-77	77-78	78-79	79-80	80-81	81-82	82-83	83-84	84-85
Paintings	1	1	1	8	12	9	4	6	7	9
Dollars	$900	$550	$1,200	$8,650	$14,125	$11,620	$4,950	$8,850	$6,650	$12,950

Record Sale: $2,900, RB.HM, 8/14/84, "Wind Mill at Harwich," 14 x 24 in.

CARING FOR YOUR PAINTING COLLECTION

THOMAS BOWER

Everything deteriorates. Some objects by their nature or status are more long-lasting than others, but everything eventually suffers the ravages of time. Paintings are not exempt from this rule. Wood splits, pigments fade, canvas rots, oils dry and become brittle. Insects infest paintings, water stains them, mold and mildew discolor them and their surfaces deteriorate. These problems exclude man's myriad threats to the survival of works of art, from willful vandalism to the accidental broom-handle or foot through the canvas.

The loss of treasured works of art, although inevitable, can be postponed. By thinking before we act and considering the effects of what we are doing to a painting, we can add many years to its life. Taking it as a given that a painting will be looked at in a peopled environment and will be moved about, we must strike a balance between using it now and protecting it for future enjoyment.

This article discusses the maintenance of paintings created before the twentieth century and kept in private homes (museums have similar, but more exacting, standards to uphold). Hanging a painting in a sunny, humid room or other threatening situation is a prerogative of the private owner, but he or she should know what will happen to the painting as a result.

What follows are some suggestions about using and caring for paintings. A brief review of the various techniques used to create paintings will explain the logic behind the actions which will extend their useful life.

Canvas has probably been the most common surface on which artists have painted. It is usually made of cotton or linen, natural fibers which react to changes in their environment, such as variations in its temperature and humidity. The surface is usually sized and primed, processes which change a cloth surface that tends to sag into one that is hard, smooth and flat. The canvas has initially been pulled over a stretcher—an inner frame of wooden bars—to make it taut. Paint is applied to this prepared surface and allowed to dry and harden. (A note on stretchers: the wooden triangles in their corners are called keys. They may be pushed further into the corners to increase the tension on the canvas and keep its surface flat, but this must be done with care as too much tension can cause damage.)

Problems develop when, over time, the canvas and paint expand and contract at different rates in reaction to temperature and humidity. The canvas gradually becomes a less firm support, and the paint cannot maintain its brittle surface, cracking wherever the canvas has shifted under it. Paint can become so loose, in fact, that it will fall off. If the canvas is greatly weakened, it may be necessary to mount it on a new canvas or other stronger support by a process called relining.

Painting on rigid panels removes the problem of insufficient support. Panels made of wood and certain metals are hard and flat and do not deteriorate as rapidly as canvas. These surfaces present their own problems, however.

Wood panels do expand and contract with humidity, but much less than canvas, reducing the possibility of cracks in the paint surface. However, the wood itself may crack. Wood warps and splits because it grows in circles and we paint on flat surfaces. As it moves in response to variations in heat and humidity, its fibers start to pull in different directions at different rates; the whole surface may eventually warp, or even split. This process may occur gradually over a period of time, or tension can build up and cause the panel to split at a simple shock. To prevent this, wood-panel paintings have frequently been mounted on a grid of wooden bars called a cradle. The cradle provides strength in the way plywood does, by allowing expansions and contractions in different directions to counteract each other.

Metal panels, usually of copper, are among the oldest solid surfaces upon which people have painted in oil. They are hard, smooth and not chemically reactive when sealed with paint, but metal panels of any size are heavy. In addition, while paint can get into the pores of prepared canvases, it really only rests on the surface of metal panels. As the paint dries, adhesion decreases. If the panel is bent or poked or receives a hard shock, paint can easily flake.

What are the general characteristics of the paints that go onto these surfaces? Paints are pigments, usually finely ground minerals suspended in oil (or, for tempera, egg or egg yolk and water). These paints are viscous and adhesive when they are applied but harden and become brittle when they dry. If its surface support remains flat, however, paint is relatively stable and solid. After the artist has finished a painting, it can take months or years for oil paints to dry completely, depending on the thickness of the paint, although tempera dries almost immediately. Brightly colored pigments tend to be more fugitive in reaction to light than darker ones, but all will fade in varying degrees over time.

To protect and enhance their surfaces, paintings are frequently covered with various varnishes. Varnish holds much less dirt and dust than paint does; it also provides a surface which keeps oxygen and its darkening effects from oil paint. Varnishing doesn't eliminate ultraviolet rays and their effects, but without it their damage would be greater. Unfortunately, all varnishes yellow and darken as the years pass. They can, however, be removed periodically to clean and refresh a painting without affecting the paint surface. But because many solvents used to remove varnish will also dissolve paint surfaces, this cleaning should only be done by a trained professional conservator.

Presented with a properly varnished painting, how can you tell if it is properly framed? A frame is, first of all, a protective device to guard the edges of a painting. It should be broad and strong to enable the painting to be carried by its side or top, as this often happens—although the safest way to carry a painting is with a hand on each side. The painting should fit snugly in a frame, neither so tightly as to have to be forced in nor so loosely as to slip from side to side when handled. The frame's inner edge, against which the surface of the painting rests, is called the rabbit. It should be covered with a soft, non-reactive fabric, such as linen or felt. Metal straps (usually brass because it won't rust) are screwed into the frame and over a few inches of the back of the painting to hold it in. The number of these straps will vary with the size of the painting, but enough should be used that the painting feels secure. Paintings should never be nailed into frames. The vibration from nailing is damaging to the surface, and the rubbing against the inside of the frame which takes place during nailing is frequently damaging to the edges of the painting.

All paintings on canvas should have solid backings of cardboard or some similar material to protect them from possible damage or puncture from behind. Such backings also slow the reaction of the otherwise exposed canvas of the back of the painting to any temperature or humidity changes.

No painting should be illuminated with a picture light attached to the frame unless the arm of the light is sufficiently long that no warmth is felt on the surface of the painting no matter how long the light is on. Heat and light close to the surface of a painting, as with most picture lights, are major aging factors, frequently causing paint to fade and varnish to yellow or even to bubble.

For hanging a painting, its frame should be equipped with hinge-type hanging devices screwed into the back of the frame with wire drawn between the hangers. Hinges are preferred to screw eyes, which have a tendency to develop metal fatigue if they are re-used; in addition, when a painting is hung with screw eyes, all the weight of the frame and painting is put on one point, rather than being spread out as it is with the hinges. The painting should be hung on the wall from bent metal picture hangers, not from nails. A nail directs the weight of the picture toward pulling the nail down, but a picture hanger pushes the weight against the wall at a solid spot, not where it has been cracked by the entry of the nail.

Now that we know how to hang our paintings, we should consider where to hang them. Paintings should be hung in a space away from direct sunlight where the temperature range is between 68 and 72 degrees Fahrenheit, the relative humidity is 50 percent, plus or minus 5 percent, and any environmental change will occur very gradually. Interior walls away from windows are probably the best sites. Both sunlight and fluorescent lights possess damaging ultraviolet rays that cause varnish to yellow, paint pigment to fade and canvas to deteriorate. Protective sleeves and self-protecting tubes are available to eliminate ultraviolet rays from fluorescent lights, but their effectiveness diminishes over time, so it is wise to check the manufacturers' warranties if you use this form of lighting.

Exterior walls that are not well insulated can be dangerous to paintings, because the dampness of the wall can be transferred to the frame and the painting, resulting in mildew and the warping of wooden parts of the frame and stretcher. This can be somewhat reduced by placing spacers (such as pieces of cork) between the wall and the painting to increase the air circulation in that space. Equally dangerous, but for different reasons, are walls above radiators and fireplaces. The flow of hot, dry, dirty air up such a wall and over the face of a painting can age varnish, make paint more brittle, cover the painting's surface with the grime of smoke and dust, and seriously dry out the stretcher, making it loose. Other obvious areas to avoid are kitchens, because of the heat, humidity and grease that can hold dust on a painting's surface, and bathrooms, where humidity can lead to mold and mildew, which in turn deteriorate canvas and can cause some varnishes to become cloudy.

If your paintings are not going to be on view, how are they best housed? The same conditions needed to exhibit them safely are required for safe storage—with the addition of darkness. Individual bins lined with a continuous-filament carpet are a good alternative to a professional museum-type storage area. They provide a place that is dark and dry, where temperature changes are slow and the paintings are safe from moving objects and people. Paintings should be stored in a cool, dry area of your house or apartment, where there is good air circulation. Other possibilities are the interiors of closets away from heat and water pipes and from uninsulated exterior walls (such walls are too humid and possibly have insect pests). If they are stacked one against the other, paintings should be placed face to face and back to back, with the stretchers crossing. Put cardboard between them, being careful to avoid any pressure on the front or back of a painted surface.

Once they are properly stored, do not forget about your paintings. Pull them out and check for changes at least every few months. Photographs of the paintings, even simple snapshots, are a big help; what you are looking for is any change in the painting's appearance. Cleavage, which is paint lifting up from the surface of a painting, indicates a major problem. The painting should be placed flat with the face up until it can be treated. Save all paint chips that fall off the surface so your conservator can re-adhere them rather than having to inpaint them. Yellowish discoloration, pale clouding or crackling varnish are all signs of damage from light, heat or moisture. Dents or sags in the canvas may indicate that the painting is pulling away from the stretcher or that the keys in the back of the frame need to be tightened.

If your painting has suffered damage, do not attempt home remedies, such as cleaning the surface of a painting with potatoes, onions or bread. These substances may lighten a surface temporarily, but they leave a residue which ultimately stains and darkens.

As well as the preventive measures described here, there are a few actions you can take to prolong the life of your paintings. A periodic dusting of the surface with a clean, soft, long-bristled brush—stroking downward and back and forth from the top to the bottom—is useful. If some material has been freshly splattered onto the surface of a varnished painting, you might try removing it by blotting with an absorbent fabric, but don't rub. Usually, the smallest efforts are best.

The surface of a painting is very delicate; only a trained conservator should be allowed to make any change or correction in it. Your local museum will give you the names of conscientious conservators in your area. Ask to see examples of their work before allowing them to handle your art objects.

As it is related to the care of paintings, one aspect of security should not be overlooked. Always identify the objects you own with your name or with some particular marking; this will make it easier to claim or identify them if they should be stolen. Museums, conservators or police will be happy to advise you on this.

Owning a painting is both a long-term pleasure and a potential good investment. As with anything we treasure, paintings deserve proper care and forethought in their handling if they are to continue to satisfy us with their beauty and value. Here is a brief summary of these suggestions to help you preserve them:

Don't expose paintings to sunlight or unfiltered fluorescent light.
Don't use picture lights that attach to frames.
Don't hang paintings from nails.
Don't use home remedies to clean paintings.
Don't use one hand to carry a painting.
Don't place paintings above radiators or functioning fireplaces.
Don't touch a paint surface with bare hands.

Do maintain a temperature of 68 to 72 degrees Fahrenheit and a relative humidity of close to 50 percent where paintings are viewed or stored.
Do protect paintings from rapid changes in their environment.
Do examine paintings periodically for any surface changes.
Do use proper hanging devices.
Do use backing to protect the back of a painting.
Do gently dust paintings with a soft brush if they appear to need it and are in good condition.
Do seek the advice and services of a professional conservator when you have a question about the condition of a painting.

Thomas Bower has a degree in studio art from the University of Notre Dame and studied art history at Oberlin College. He has taught a course for the Smithsonian Institution resident associates entitled "Caring for the Private Art Collection."

GLOSSARY

A

Abstraction. Art which makes no direct, immediately discernible reference to recognizable objects. In abstract art, the formal arrangement of colors and forms is independent of, and more important than, the subject matter.

Academic. Pertaining to the arts as taught in academies and schools of art according to established rules. Since the high tide of conservatism in the late nineteenth century, the term has become synonymous with traditional thinking and opposition to fresh and innovative ideas in art.

Acrylic. A widely used water-based polymer paint. Because of its chemical composition, it combines the characteristics of traditional oil and watercolor paints and can be used for washes and for heavy impasto. It is relatively odorless, quick-drying and extremely resistant to deterioration.

Action painting. The vigorous, often improvisatory, gestural slash and drip paintings made most notably by Jackson Pollock, Willem de Kooning and Hans Hofmann. The term is often used to describe the entire abstract expressionist movement, including the more consciously planned canvases of Mark Rothko, Barnett Newman and others.

Aquatint. Like etching, a method of engraving which uses acid to eat into a metal plate. Unlike etching, however, it is a tone, rather than a line, process. The porous ground of the plate allows the acid to form a network of extremely fine lines, creating transparent effects comparable to those of watercolor painting.

Armory Show. The International Exhibition of Modern Art held in 1913 at the 69th Regiment Armory in New York City and later in Boston and Chicago. It introduced avant-garde European and contemporary American painting to the American public and critics. Enormous in scope (approximately 1,600 paintings) and highly controversial, it proved to be the turning point in the development and appreciation of modern art in the United States.

Art Institute of Chicago. Established in 1879 as an art school, it has grown into one of the major art institutions of the United States. Approximately 4,000 students attend its classes annually. Its collections—particularly of Spanish, Flemish, Dutch, French and American paintings and of Near Eastern and oriental decorative arts—place it among the outstanding museums of the world.

Art nouveau. A decorative linear style which appeared in all media throughout Europe and in the United States at the end of the nineteenth century. Characterized by sinuously curving organic forms, it was often used to depict mysterious landscapes, women and symbolist subjects.

Ashcan School. The work of a group of late-nineteenth- and early-twentieth-century realist American painters who, disdaining the prevailing aestheticism of the academics, determined to bring painting back into touch with the life of the common man. Often collectively called The Eight, they depicted the seamy life of the streets, taverns and prize-fight rings, thus gaining the distinctly derogatory designation of their school.

Assemblage. Mixed-media combinations of found objects (rather than traditional art objects of paint, canvas, carved stone and cast bronze). Primarily assembled, rather than painted, modeled or carved, these works question the nature of art and often break down the traditional distinctions between painting and sculpture.

B

Barbizon. The style developed by a group of landscape painters in mid-nineteenth-century France who lived and worked in Barbizon, a village on the edge of the forest of Fountainebleau. Opposed to the prevailing classical conventions of landscape painting, they strove to depict peasant life and the surrounding country-side exactly as it was, without prettification. The best-known of the group were Millet and Rousseau.

Baroque. An opulent style, religious in origin, that prevailed in the Roman Catholic countries of Europe, particularly in France and Italy, from the end of the sixteenth century until the early eighteenth century. In its truest form it was a union of architecture, painting and sculpture, all designed to evoke a strong emotional response. Through skillful use of substance, light, color and texture, baroque artists sought to create an illusion of the actuality and truth of a subject.

Bauhaus. A utopian school founded in 1919 in Weimar, Germany to promote the unity of the arts and harmony between craftsmanship and artistry in a modern technological society. The school moved to Dessau in 1925, was closed by Hitler in 1933, and has been continued in the United States at Harvard University and the Illinois Institute of Technology. The teachings of Josef Albers, first at the Black Mountain School and later at Yale University, promoted the Bauhaus ideal.

Blaue Reiter (Blue Rider). A pre-World War I artistic alliance established in Munich in 1911, it was founded by Vasily Kandinsky and Franz Marc, who also published the *Blaue Reiter Almanac*. The style of the group, which turned toward the symbolic semi-abstraction of bold and strident color, was used by American painter Marsden Hartley for his "German Officer" series. Together with Die Bruecke (the Bridge), established in Dresden in 1905, the Blaue Reiter composed the foundations of German expressionism.

Boston School. A group of American impressionist painters who studied or worked in Boston around 1900, several of whom were also members of The Ten. The dominant figures were Edmund C. Tarbell and Frank W. Benson. Although impressionist landscape paintings were popular in Boston as early as the late 1880s, the impressionist figure paintings of the Boston School were not well received there until after 1900.

Brandywine School. Initially a term used to denote the work of Howard Pyle and the many illustrators he taught and influenced through his hand-picked classes in Wilmington, Delaware and Chadds Ford, Pennsylvania, both located on the Brandywine River. Because several of the progeny of N.C. Wyeth, perhaps Pyle's best-known student, have continued to live in the area and paint in a distinctive representational manner, the term now has come also to include succeeding generations of the Wyeth family, most notably Andrew Wyeth, and similarly influenced local painters as well.

C

Ca. Abbreviation for circa, meaning "about" or "approximately."

Century Association. An organization founded in New York City in 1847 when members of the Sketch Club asked 100 men (hence the name) to form a new club oriented toward the arts. Its membership now includes educators and other professionals in addition to practicing artists. Its clubhouse, which includes galleries for frequent exhibitions, is at 7 West 43rd Street in Manhattan.

Chromolithography. A method of surface-printing lithographs in many colors which involves no engraving. A different stone or plate is used for each color and each is printed in exact register with the others. It is widely used, particularly for posters and other forms of commercial art.

Classical. A term used to describe art which conforms to the standards and principles established in ancient Greece and Rome. Generally speaking, such work is characterized by its simplicity, symmetry and dignity.

Color field. Organic, sensuous and joyous abstract painting developed in the United States during the 1960s in which color is both the form and the subject (also identified with post-painterly abstraction). The very large, fluid, stained or sprayed areas of color often allude to landscapes; some of them seem devoid of passion or emotional expression.

Constructivism. A radical movement begun in Russia by 1917 by the brothers Naum Gabo and Antoine Pevsner, who used industrial materials in three-dimensional sculpture. Transplanted to Paris and Germany, it was picked up by American artists; its formal anti-expressionism dominated American abstract art of the early 1930s.

Conte crayon. A proprietary name for a man-made chalk which is widely used in sketching. It is available in black, brown and red and was named for Nicholas Conte, who developed the first lead pencil in 1790.

Cos Cob, Connecticut. One of several communal art colonies which were developed by plein-air American impressionists in picturesque locales accessible by railroad (and later by automobile) from New York City. Other such colonies included Old Lyme, Connecticut, Appledore, Isle of Shoals, New Hampshire, and the Shinnecock Hills of Long Island, New York.

Cubism. A style which originated in the search by Picasso and Braque for methods of representation to replace the sensuous pictorial realism of the impressionists. Derived from the perceptual realism of Cezanne, cubism developed into an austere, very logical technique by which the permanent structure of an object was analyzed and then fragmented into planes to reveal its whole structure. Rather than depicting objects as they appear, the cubists superimposed several different views of the same object to express the idea of the object instead.

D

Dada, New York. A 1915 forerunner of the irreverent international avant-garde dada movement, led by French-born Marcel Duchamp, Cuban-born Francis Picabia and American-born Man Ray. The concepts underlying their activities, publications, paintings and readymades (nihilistic or ironic sculptures based on manufactured objects) became the basis for later pop and conceptual art.

Daguerrotype. The earliest successful photographic process. Developed in France by Louis Daguerre in the mid-nineteenth century, it made use of a silver or silver-covered copper plate which was made sensitive to light through the use of chemicals.

Decorative. A general term for all arts in which decoration is added to a functional object. In the context of painting, it frequently is applied to work that is intended to embellish or ornament a given space. Purists traditionally disdain decorative work as not a part of the fine arts of painting and sculpture.

Dusseldorf. Between 1840 and 1860 many prominent American artists—including Albert Bierstadt, George Caleb Bingham, Eastman Johnson, Emmanuel Leutze and Richard Caton Woodville—were attracted to the study of sentimental genre painting at the Dusseldorf Academy. The Dusseldorf style is typically hard and dry. After the Civil War, a shift toward realism led younger students to Munich and Paris instead.

E

The Eight. A group of eight relatively dissimilar realist painters, led by Robert Henri, who banded together in 1908 to exhibit their work independently after the work of three of them had been rejected for exhibition at the National Academy of Design. They exhibited together only once, but the name remained with them; they were also known as members of the Ashcan School. The Eight were Henri, William Glackens, George Luks, Everett Shinn, John Sloan, Arthur Davies, Ernest Lawson and Maurice Prendergast.

Encaustic. An ancient painting technique, mentioned by Pliny, in which colors were mixed with wax which in turn was heated so that the colors were absorbed into the wall. The same technique was used for a time in Egypt in the first century A.D. for small portraits on mummy cases. Leonardo da Vinci attempted without success to revive the process in the early sixteenth century, and several artists also attempted to use the method in the late nineteenth century.

Engraving. A term which has come to refer to all the processes for multiplying prints. While there are distinct differences between individual methods of engraving, the chief difference is between reproductive and original engravings. The former reproduce an idea or work of an artist other than the engraver, while original engravings are unique works of art created by engraver himself.

Etching. A widely used form of engraving in which the etcher draws on a copper plate which has been covered with an acid-impervious resinous ground, exposing the copper wherever he wants a line. When the plate is placed in an acid bath, the exposed parts are eaten away. By controlling the depth of the acid "bite," subtle variations in the strength of lines may be achieved. Prints are then made by inking the plate, removing the ink from its surface, and pressing paper onto the plate; the picture is made by the ink in the etched-away lines.

Expressionism. A late-nineteenth- and early-twentieth-century northern European movement away from the representation of the observed world to the expression of personal emotional intensity. Its subjective, exaggerated and distorted colors and forms were further developed in the abstract expressionism of Willem de Kooning and others and, in the 1980s, in the work of the neo-realists.

F

Fauvism. The spontaneous use of pure bright color (rather than tone), expressively applied with distortions in flat patterns. Work in this style by Henri Matisse and others was first exhibited in the Paris Salon d'Automne of 1905; the furor it aroused caused a critic to label these artists the "fauves" (wild beasts). Max Weber helped Matisse organize a short lived school in 1907, which was attended by Patrick Henry Bruce and other Americans.

Federal period. A phase of neo-classicism in design and architecture in the United States which lasted from approximately 1780 until approximately 1820. It was based primarily on the work of Robert and James Adam in England. Its most distinguishing features were: graceful, slender proportions; small but delicate ornaments; and curvilinear elements, such as eliptical rooms and sweeping circular staircases.

Folk art. Paintings, objects and decorations made in a distinctive or traditional manner by artists or craftsmen who have had no formal training. In general, it is looked upon as an autonomous tradition which is seldom affected by changes in fashion or trends in professional art.

Fourteenth Street School. A relatively small group of realist painters who, in the late 1920s and 1930s, had studios in the vicinity of Union Square and 14th Street in New York City. In sharply different styles they continued in the tradition of the Ashcan School and portrayed boisterous, vulgar crowds, lonely individuals and the hopelessness of people in breadlines. The group was founded by Kenneth Hayes Miller, but its most substantive work was done by Reginald Marsh, Raphael and Moses Soyer and Morris Kantor.

Futurism. An artistic program which arose in Italy shortly before the outbreak of World War I and sought to simulate the dynamism of the modern urban technological world through exploding faceted cubist form. Joseph Stella used the style for his monumental depictions of the Brooklyn Bridge.

G

Gouache. An opaque watercolor paint. The effects achieved with it are closer to those of oil paint than of watercolor. A disadvantage of gouache is the fact that it lightens as it dries.

H

Hudson River School. A succession of American painters who, between 1840 and the late nineteenth century, established for the first time a true tradition of landscape painting in the United States. Many of the scenes they painted were in the Hudson River Valley and the adjoining mountains of New York State and Vermont. Their work, derived from European romantic landscape painting, was marked by a meticulous rendering of detail and by an almost religious reverence for the magnificence of the American wilderness.

I

Impasto. A thick application of oil paint on canvas or a panel. The heaviness of the paint, often clearly showing the marks of individual brushstrokes, is thought to add character and vigor to the painting.

Impressionism. One of the most important artistic movements of the nineteenth century in France and in many ways the precursor of much of modern art. It began as a loose association of brilliantly innovative painters, such as Monet, Renoir and Sisley, whose primary purpose was to record their immediate emotional responses to a scene, rather than to create a conventional record of nature. The styles of impressionist painters varied widely, but they were united by their desire to capture the spontaneity of the moment and to avoid the constrictions of formal compositions.

L

Limner. A designation used originally in the Middle Ages for an illuminator of manuscripts. Beginning in the sixteenth century it took on new meaning to include painters of miniature portraits and sometimes painters in general. In this last context the term has been obsolete since the nineteenth century. Early American folk artists were sometimes called limners.

Lithography. The only major process of surface printing in which no engraving or cutting-out of the surface of the plate is involved. The design is put on the surface of a stone with a greasy chalk; the stone is wetted and then covered with a greasy ink, which is rejected by the wet surface and clings only to those areas which already are greasy.

Lotos Club (also Lotus Club). A New York City club dedicated to the cultivation of the arts. Since its founding in 1870 it has honored many distinguished writers, musicians, actors and others in the arts with testimonial dinners. Its quarters are at 5 East 66th Street.

Luminism. An effect that is obtained in painting when a light or reflective undercoat of paint is visible through a thin or transparent outer layer. The technique was developed in the mid-nineteenth century in America by painters, such as George Caleb Bingham, who had a particular interest in the character of light as an element in painting.

M

Macchiaioli. An important school of Italian painters who worked in Florence between 1850 and approximately 1865. In revolt against academic painting and influenced by the realism of Corot and Courbet, they employed individual touches or daubs of color to achieve their desired effect. Some of the group were landscape and genre painters, while others did costumed history scenes.

Magic realism. An American variant of surrealism which uses sharp focus and precise representation to portray imaginary subjects.

Mannerism. A sophisticated, sixteenth-century, elongated style used most elegantly in Italy and elsewhere for international court portraits. Seventeenth-century colonial portraits were often based on English prints of mannerist portraits and on Italian mannerist treatises filtered through England.

Minimal art. Reductive movements of the 1960s, including color-field painting, op art, hard-edge painting and serial imagery. They arose as a further development of the cool, formal, abstract expressionist art of Mark Rothko, Barnett Newman and others, and as a reaction against autobiographical gestural action painting.

Modernism. A term used to describe innovations in art brought about by two factors: a strong sense of detachment from the past and a deliberate desire to replace past aesthetic concepts with an artistic expression more in accord with the contemporary ideas and beliefs. Sometimes reaction to prevailing aesthetic concepts can take the form of a return to those of an earlier period. Although the requisite sense of detachment from the past has been especially strong through much of the twentieth century, the term "modernism" can be applied to innovations in any art period.

Munich School. A group of radical young German painters under the leadership of Wilhelm Liebl in Munich in the latter half of the nineteenth century. Their work was characterized by a choice of commonplace subject matter, loose and vigorous brushwork and a relatively dark and restricted palette. This style had a strong influence on many young Americans who came to Munich to study in the 1870s, notably Frank Duveneck and William Merritt Chase.

N

Nabis. Young French painters between 1889 and 1899 who were influenced by Eastern motifs, esoteric ideas and the art of Paul Gauguin. Their goal was to devise decorative techniques to adorn "a plane surface covered with colors brought together in a certain order." Their name comes from the Hebrew word for "prophet."

National Academy of Design. Founded in New York City in 1826 by Samuel F.B. Morse and others as a rebellion against the dictatorial administration of an earlier American Academy of Fine Arts. Over the years the National

Academy became a bastion of conservatism and the works of innovative young artists were frequently excluded from its exhibitions. Most trends in twentieth-century American art have developed independently of the Academy.

Neoclassicism. An eighteenth-century attempt to revive the classical art—and thereby the glory—of ancient Greece and Rome. In the United States it was consciously adopted for the art (especially the architecture) of the early republic.

New Deal Art. Art produced between 1933 and 1943 under the auspices of various government programs, including the Works Progress Administration's Federal Art Project (WPA/FAP) and the Treasury Relief Administration Project (TRAP), which employed more than 5,000 artists. The subject matter of most of the thousands of murals and easel paintings these programs generated was interpretations of the prescribed American scene.

New Hope School (Pennsylvania impressionists). A group of American landscape painters with strong inclinations toward impressionism who settled and painted in the region around New Hope, a small town on the Delaware River in rural Bucks County, Pennsylvania, for several generations beginning in 1898. Although he did not live in New Hope, Edward Redfield is considered the leader of the group. Because of their focus on scenes of the countryside and country life, the group now is looked upon as a rural counterpart to the urban Ashcan School of painters, with whom they were contemporaries.

New York School. The name given to the group of bold, highly innovative painters who lived and worked in New York City during the 1940s and 1950s and who collectively developed abstract expressionism. Also known as action painting, the work of this school had as far-reaching an effect on artists as cubism had had on earlier generations of painters.

O

Old Lyme impressionists. A loosely defined group of early-twentieth-century American impressionist landscape painters who worked in the area of Old Lyme, Connecticut, a picturesque old town at the mouth of the Connecticut River. Childe Hassam was one of the early members and the catalyst around whom the group coalesced. Several other members of The Ten, among them J. Alden Weir and John H. Twachtman, were also considered Old Lyme impressionists.

Op art. An abbreviation for optical art, a term first used to define work in "The Responsive Eye" exhibition at the Museum of Modern Art in 1965. It covers a broad range of sophisticated, geometric, abstract painting styles which exploit perceptual ambiguities and shock or distort what is perceived by the viewer.

Orientalism. In its earliest connotation, the interest in the exotic colors and savage passions of the Middle East and North Africa that first appeared in the work of Delacroix in the 1820s and later became an important element in romantic painting. In a later context, it refers to the influence of oriental art and design, particularly of Japanese prints, on the work of such painters as Whistler, Van Gogh and Gauguin after the United States gained access to Japanese ports in 1854. The universal values embodied in oriental art, calligraphy and philosophy have been adapted or reflected in American painting most recently in action painting and the work of some painters of the Northwest.

Orphism. A completely abstract type of color painting created by French artist Robert Delaunay in 1912-1913. His work contained no reference to the visual world; he believed that "color alone is form and subject."

P

Painterly. The tendency to depict form as patches of colored light and shade, in which edges merge into the background or into one another, best exemplified by the work of Rembrandt. Its opposite, linear, which denotes an emphasis on outline and drawing, is considered characteristically American.

Panorama. A complete depiction of a landscape or historical scene, often mounted on the inside of a large cylindrical surface, such as a curved wall or round room. It may also be a scene that is passed before a spectator in such a way as to show the various parts of the whole in continuous succession.

Pennsylvania Academy of the Fine Arts. The oldest continuously operative art institution in the United States. Modeled after the Royal Academy in London, it was founded in Philadelphia in 1805 by Charles Willson Peale, sculptor William Rush and a group of prominent local business and professional men. In addition to the Academy's continuing teaching functions, its museum is recognized for its comprehensive collection of American painting.

Photo-realism. Also known as superrealism, a style of figurative painting and sculpture of photographic exactitude that gained prominence in the United States and England during the 1960s and 1970s. It was usually characterized by banal contemporary subject matter and a glossy finish. Unlike naturalism, however, its aim was to create a sense of unreality through an almost hallucinatory wealth of detail and sometimes through altered scale.

Plein-air. The French phrase for "open air." The term refers to painting which is done outdoors, directly from nature. It is also used sometimes to describe a style of painting which conveys a feeling of openness and spontaneity.

Pop art. Art which uses symbols, images and objects of mass production and contemporary popular culture—normally seen on supermarket shelves, in mass-media advertising and in comic strips—in the context of the fine arts. It appeared in England in the mid-1950s, but reached its apex in the United States during the 1960s in the work of painters like Andy Warhol, Jasper Johns and Robert Rauschenberg and sculptors like Claes Oldenburg. Much of its effect on the viewer is based on the shock value of seeing the commonplace displayed as serious art.

Post-impressionism. A term invented by English art critic Roger Fry when he organized an exhibition in London of such modern French masters as Cezanne, Manet and Matisse in 1910. The term underscored the fact that these painters had rejected the principles of impressionism and had instead focused their attention on creating form rather than imitating natural form.

Post-modernism. A general term used to cover such contemporary phenomena as pop art and pop design, which appeared in the 1960s as a reaction against the values established by the acknowledged masters of modern art. The initiators of post-modernism felt that modern art and the functionalism of modern design did not fulfill the psychological and emotional needs of ordinary people as they were reflected in the popularity and near-universal acceptance of mass-produced consumer goods.

Pre-raphaelitism, American. An association, organized in 1863 in emulation of John Ruskin's British Pre-Raphaelite Brotherhood in order to promote landscape, still-life and nature painting with the photograph as a standard of accuracy. John William Hill and William Trost Richards were two of the members of the Association for the Advancement of Truth in Art who published the American pre-raphaelite manifesto in *The New Path*.

Precisionism. Known in the 1920s and the 1930s as cubist realism, the work of Charles Sheeler and other "immaculate" painters featured indigenous American subject matter executed in a sharp, precise linear manner, without figures or anecdotal elements.

Primitive art. A term which often is applied to paintings and other art in three distinctly different categories: 1) Dutch and Italian painters working before the Renaissance, or before about 1500 A.D. 2) The work of peoples, such as African blacks, Eskimos and Pacific islanders, whose art matured unaffected by any influence from the traditional great centers of culture. 3) The work of artists, primarily European and American, who have received little or no formal training, yet have developed their own unsophisticated, nontraditional style.

R

Realism. In one context, this term refers to the depiction of life as it is—even the squalid and ugly—instead of conventionally beautiful or idealized subjects. In another context, it means representational painting, as against that painting which is deliberately abstract or distorted. In the late nineteenth and early twentieth centuries, the term "social realism" was coined to apply to representational painting which contained a specific political or social message.

Regionalism. Associated with the patriotic efforts of Thomas Hart Benton and others, especially in the 1930s, to communicate something significant about America by making the legends of a region's shared past the subject matter of their art. Various areas of the country, including the Midwest, the Pacific Northwest and New York City, had their own brands of regionalism.

Rococo. A graceful, yet florid, style of interior decoration and ornamentation that replaced the excessive ostentation associated with Louis XIV and the Palace of Versailles after his death in 1715. It was characterized by curves and counter-curves, prettiness and gaiety. The style lasted in France only until the mid-eighteenth century, but flourished longer in Germany and Austria.

Romanticism. A cult of feeling and individual imagination which originated in mid-eighteenth-century English philosophy and spread throughout the arts in Europe. America's first romantic, Washington Allston, brought to the United States the inspiration to paint seascapes and landscapes imbued with the sublime power of nature, as well as moralistic history paintings.

S

Salon. For many years the only officially recognized exhibition of paintings in Paris. It derived its name from the fact that it was originally held in the Salon d'Apollon in the Louvre. It has undergone many transformations over the years, but for the most part its organizers have been traditionalists who have been hostile to and have excluded new and innovative paintings. In 1863, the outcry from those whose work had not been accepted was so vehement that Napoleon III ordered a special Salon des Refuses which was equally controversial and was held only once.

Scumbling. A technique in painting of softening or modifying the color of a surface by applying an upper layer of opaque color. The upper layer is thin or irregular enough to allow some of the color beneath to show through.

Serigraphy. A stenciling process more commonly known as silk-screen printing. Paint or ink is brushed over unmasked areas of stretched silk on which the design has been fixed. By using successive masks on the same screen, multi-colored prints can be achieved. The process is widely used in commercial art and in the textile industry.

Social realism. Direct and critical portrayals of social, political and economic issues in art works, particularly during the 1930s.

Surrealism. Based on the depiction of dreams and the subconscious, and founded by Frenchman Andre Breton in 1924, surrealistic art aims for "the systematic dismantling of establishment values." Its principle of automatism (the depiction of pure thought) helped pave the way for the improvisatory character of American action painting.

Synchromism. The sole modern movement founded by American artists before World War I. Synchromism means "with color," and Morgan Russell and Stanton MacDonald-Wright used color alone to generate form, meaning and composition. Their work was based in part on the color theory of French painter Robert Delaunay.

T

Tachism. A term coined in 1952 by French art critic Michel Tapie to describe paintings in which dabs and splotches of color appear to have been applied at random, with no regard for form or construction. It is now frequently applied to action painting and to any painting technique that strives to be completely spontaneous and instinctive.

Taos Colony. An art colony in Taos, New Mexico, which began in 1912 when a small group of painters, led by Henry Sharp, formed the Art Society of Taos. Tired of European traditions, these artists sought intrinsically American subjects to paint and found them in the local Spanish and Pueblo Indian cultures and in the spectacular scenery of the Southwest. Members of the original group continued to work until 1927, and Taos continues today as a popular center for artists.

Tempera. A method of painting on surfaces prepared with gesso in which dry pigments are mixed with egg yolks, whites or sometimes whole eggs to form a water-soluble yet binding medium. It was the commonest painting technique until the late fifteenth century. The medium dries almost immediately and is permanent.

The Ten. A group of 10 late-nineteenth-century Boston painters who exhibited together from 1898 until 1918. Initially they banded together to protest what they considered to be the too-strict academic tastes of the city. While the styles of these painters varied widely (some were not American impressionist painters at all), as a group they are now thought of generally as the Boston School of American impressionists.

Tonalism. A poetic, meditative style developed primarily between 1880 and 1910. Tonalist paintings often used intimate interiors or sylvan settings, depicted as if photographed behind a veil or shrouded in mist.

Trompe l'oeil. French for "deceive the eye." The term is applied to easel or decorative painting whose purpose is to fool the eye as to the composition or the reality of the objects represented—as with painted money that appears to be real, and the like. In easel painting the technique is normally restricted to surfaces in or near the plane of the picture.

SELECTED BIBLIOGRAPHY

AUCTION RECORDS

Hislop, Richard, ed. *Annual Art Sales Index*. Weybridge, Surrey, England: Art Sales Index Ltd. (Published annually.)

Leonard's Annual Index of Art Auctions. Newton, Massachusetts: Leonard's Index of Art Auctions. (Published annually.)

Mayer, E. *International Auction Records*. New York: Editions Publisol. (Published annually.)

DICTIONARIES

Baigell, Matthew. *Dictionary of American Art*. Reprint with corrections. New York: Harper and Row, 1982.

Brewington, Dorothy E.R. *Dictionary of Marine Artists*. Peabody Museum of Salem, Massachusetts and Mystic Seaport Museum, Connecticut, 1982.

Cummings, Paul. *Dictionary of Contemporary American Artists*. New York and London: St. Martin's and St. James, 1977.

Groce, George C., and David H. Wallace. *The New York Historical Society's Dictionary of Artists in America*. New Haven: Yale University Press, 1957.

Mantle Fielding's Dictionary of American Painters, Sculptors and Engravers. Revised by Glenn B. Opitz. Poughkeepsie, N.Y.: Apollo Book, 1983.

Murray, Peter and Linda. *Penguin Dictionary of Art & Artists*. Penguin Books, 1959.

Samuels, Peggy and Harold. *Illustrated Biographical Encyclopedia of Artists of the American West*. New York: Doubleday, 1976.

HISTORIES AND GENERAL REFERENCES

Ashton, Dore. *The New York School: A Cultural Reckoning*. New York: Viking Press, 1972.

Baigell, Matthew. *The American Scene: American Painting of the 1930s*. New York: Praeger, 1979.

_____. *A Concise History of American Painting and Sculpture*. New York: Harper and Row, 1984.

Barker, Virgil. *American Painting: History and Interpretation*. New York: Macmillan, 1951.

Berman, Greta, and Jeffrey Wechsler. *Realism and Realities: The Other Side of American Painting, 1940-1960*. New Brunswick: Rutgers University Art Gallery, 1981.

Bermingham, P. *American Art in the Barbizon Mood*. Washington, D.C., 1975.

Bizardel, Y. *American Painters in Paris*. New York, 1960.

Boyle, Richard. *American Impressionism*. Boston: New York Graphic Society, 1974.

Broder, Patricia Janis. *The American West: The Modern Vision*. Boston: New York Graphic Society/Little, Brown and Co., 1984.

_____. *Great Paintings of the Old American West*. New York: Abbeville Press, 1981.

Brown, Milton H. *American Art to 1900*. New York: Harry N. Abrams, 1978.

_____. *American Painting from the Armory Show to the Depression*. Princeton, N.J.: Princeton University Press, 1955.

Campbell, Mary Schmidt. *Tradition and Conflict: Images of a Turbulent Decade, 1963-1973*. New York: Studio Museum in Harlem, 1985.

Cohen, George M. *A History of American Art*. New York: Dell, 1971.

Corn, Wanda M. *Grant Wood: The Regionalist Vision*. New Haven: Yale University Press for the Minneapolis Institute of the Arts, 1983.

Czestochowski, John S. *The American Landscape Tradition: A Study and Gallery of Paintings*. New York: E.P. Dutton, 1982.

Davidson, Abraham A. *Early American Modernist Painting 1910-1935*. New York: Harper and Row, 1981.

Dunlap, William. *A History of the Rise and Progress of the Arts and Design in the United States*. New York, 1934. 2 Vols. Edited by Rita Weiss. Introduction by James T. Flexner. 3 Vols. New York: Dover Publications, 1969.

Fine, Elsa Honig. *The Afro-American Artists: A Search For Identity*. New York: Holt, Rinehart and Winston, 1973.

Flexner, James T. *American Painting: First Flowers of Our Wilderness*. Boston: Houghton and Mifflin, 1947.

_____. *American Painting: The Light of Distant Skies, 1760-1835*. New York: Harcourt Brace, 1954.

_____. *America's Old Masters: First Artists of the New World*. New York: Viking Press, 1939.

_____. *Nineteenth-Century American Painting*. New York: Putnam's, 1970.

_____. *That Wilder Image: The Painting of America's Native School from Thomas Cole to Winslow Homer*. Boston: Little, Brown, 1962.

Frankenstein, Alfred V. *After the Hunt: William Michael Harnett and Other American Still Life Painters, 1870-1900*. 2nd Edition. Berkeley and Los Angeles: University of California Press, 1969.

Hassrick, Peter. *Treasures of the Old West*. New York: Harry N. Abrams, Inc., 1984.

_____. *The Way West: The Art of Frontier America*. New York: Harry N. Abrams, Inc., 1977.

Hills, Patricia. *Social Concern and Urban Realism: American Painting of the 1930s*. Boston: Boston University Art Gallery, 1983.

Hoopes, Donelson. *The American Impressionists*. New York: Watson-Guptill, 1973.

Geldzahler, Henry. *American Painting of the Twentieth Century*. New York: The Metropolitan Museum of Art, distributed by the New York Graphic Society, 1965.

Gerdts, William. *American Impressionism*. New York: Abbeville Press, 1984.

Gerdts, William H., and Russell Burke. *American Still Life Painting*. New York: Praeger, 1971.

Gerdts, William H. *Down Garden Paths: The Floral Environment in American Art*. London and Toronto: Associated University Presses, 1983.

_____. *Painters of the Humble Truth: Masterpieces of American Still Life 1801-1939*. Columbia, Missouri: University of Missouri Press, 1981.

Goodrich, Lloyd, and John I. H. Baur. *American Art of Our Century*. New York: Praeger, 1961.

Greenberg, Clement. *Art and Culture: Critical Essays*. Boston: Beacon Press, 1961.

Harmsen, Dorothy. *American Western Art*. Harmsen Publishing Co., 1977.

Homer, William I. *Alfred Stieglitz and the American Avant-Garde*. Boston: New York Graphic Society, 1977.

Howat, John K. *The Hudson River and Its Painters*. New York: Viking Press, 1972.

Kenin, Richard. *Return to Albion: Americans In England, 1760-1940*. New York: Holt, Rinehart and Winston; Washington, D.C.: The National Portrait Gallery, Smithsonian Institution, 1979.

Larkin, Oliver W. *Art and Life in America*. New York: Holt, Rinehart and Winston, 1966.

Levin, Gail. *Synchromism and American Color Abstraction*. New York: Braziller, 1978.

Lewis, Samella. *Art: African American*. New York: Harcourt, Brace, Jovanovich, 1978.

Lipman, Jean, and Tom Armstrong, eds. *American Folk Painters of Three Centuries*. New York: Hudson Hills Press/Whitney Museum of American Art, 1980.

Marling, Karal Ann. *Wall-to-Wall America: A Cultural History of Post Office Murals in the Great Depression*. Minneapolis: University of Minnesota Press, 1983.

Meixner, Laura. *An International Episode: Millet, Monet and Their North American Counterparts*. Exhibition catalog. Memphis, Tennessee: Dixon Gallery and Gardens, 1982.

Miles, Ellen, ed. *Portrait Painting in America: The Nineteenth Century*. New York: Main Street/Universe Books, 1977.

Novak, Barbara. *American Painting of the 19th Century*. 2nd Edition. New York: Harper and Row, 1979.

_____. *Nature and Culture: American Landscape and Painting, 1825-1875*. New York: Oxford University Press, 1980.

Park, Marlene, and Gerald E. Markowitz. *New Deal for Art: The Government Art Projects of the 1930s With Examples from New York City and State*. Hamilton, New York: The Gallery Association of New York State, Inc., 1977.

Porter, James A. *Modern Negro Art*. New York: Dryden Press, 1943.

Portraits from "The Americans": The Democratic Experience—An Exhibit at the National Portrait Gallery Based on Daniel J. Boorstin's "The Americans". New York: Random House, 1975.

Portraits USA 1776-1976: An Exhibition Celebrating the Nation's Bicentennial. University Park, Pennsylvania: Museum of Art, Pennsylvania State University, 1976.

Prown, Jules D. *American Painting: From Its Beginnings to the Armory Show*. Cleveland, Ohio: World Publishing, 1969.

Quick, M. *American Expatriate Painters of the Late Nineteenth Century*. Dayton, Ohio, 1978.

Richardson, Edgar P. *American Romantic Painting*. Edited by Robert Freund. New York: E. Weyhe, 1944.

_____. *Painting In America, From 1502 to the Present*. New York: Thomas Crowell, 1965.

Ritchie, Andrew C. *Abstract Painting and Sculpture in America*. New York: Museum of Modern Art, 1969.

Rose, Barbara. *American Painting: The Twentieth Century*. Cleveland, Ohio: World Publishing, 1969.

Rossi, Paul, and David Hunt. *The Art of the Old West*. New York: Alfred A. Knopf, 1971.

Sandler, Irving. *The Triumph of American Painting: A History of Abstract Expressionism*. New York: Harper and Row, 1970.

Seitz, William C. *Abstract Expressionist Painting in America*. Cambridge, Massachusetts: Harvard University Press, 1983.

Sellin, David. *Americans in Brittany and Normandy, 1860-1910*. Phoenix Art Museum, 1982.

Shapiro, David. *Social Realism: Art as a Weapon*. Critical Studies in American Art. New York: Frederick Unger, 1973.

Sheldon, George W. *American Painters*. New York, 1879.

Soria, Regina. *Dictionary of Nineteenth Century American Painters in Italy: 1760-1914*. East Brunswick, New Jersey: Fairleigh University Press, 1982.

Stein, Roger B. *Seascape and the American Imagination*. New York: The Whitney Museum of American Art, 1975.

Sweeney, J. Gray. *Great Lakes Marine Painting of the Nineteenth Century*. Washington, D.C.: National Gallery of Art, 1980.

Tuckerman, Henry T. *The Book of the Artists: American Artist Life*. New York: Putnam's, 1867. Reprint. New York: James F. Carr, 1966.

Wein, Frances Stevenson, ed. *National Portrait Gallery Permanent Collection Illustrated Checklist.* Washington, D.C.: Smithsonian Institution Press, 1980.

Wilmerding, John. *American Art.* London and New York: Penguin Books, 1976.

_____, et al. *American Light: The Luminist Movement, 1850-1875.* Washington, D.C.: The National Gallery of Art, 1980.

_____. *A History of American Marine Painting.* Salem, Massachusetts: Little, Brown for the Peabody Museum of Salem, 1968.

Wynne, G. *Early Americans in Rome.* Rome, 1966.

PERIODICALS

American Art Journal, New York, New York.

Antiques, New York, New York.

Art & Antiques, New York, New York.

Art & Auction, New York, New York.

Art in America, New York, New York.

Art Journal, New York, New York.

ARTnews, New York, New York.

Art Students League News, New York, New York.

Maine Antique Digest, Waldoboro, Maine.

Winterthur Portfolio, Chicago, Illinois.

AUCTION HOUSES

CODE	AUCTION HOUSE
A	Aldridges—Bath
A.D	Adams—Dublin
A.R	D'Anjou—Rouen
A.T	Arnaune—Toulouse
AAA.S	Australian Art Auctions—Sydney
AG	Anderson & Garland—Newcastle
AMG.C	Appay, Mainon-Gairoared et G.—Cannes
AN.Z	Auktionshaus Am Neumarkt—Zurich
AW.H	Arno Winterberg—Heidelberg
B	Bonham—London
B.A	Paul Brandt—Amsterdam
B.G	Blache—Grenoble
B.M	Boscher—Morlaix
B.P	Barridoff Galleries—Portland
B.S	Bukowski—Stockholm
B.T	Beaumont—Tours
B.V	Blache—Versailles
BB	Richard Baker & Baker—Birkenhead
BB.SF	Butterfield & Butterfield—San Francisco
BC	Bannister & Co.—Haywards Heath
BFA	Barber's Fine Art—Woking
BL.N	Bailly, Loevenbruck—Nancy
BMM	Button, Menheinett & Mutton—Wadebridge
BR	Bracketts—Tunbridge Wells
BR.CS	Bretaudiere et Raynaud—Chalon-sur-Saone
BV	Bradley & Vaughan—Haywards Heath
BW	Biddle & Webb—Birmingham
C	Christie, Manson Woods—London
C.A	Campo—Antwerp
C.LIA	Calvet—L'Isle Adam
C.V	Chapelle—Versailles
CB	Charles Boardman & Son—Haverhill
CBS	Chrystal Brothers—Isle of Man
CE	Christie Edmiston—Glasgow
CG.P	Charles Galleries—Pontiac

CODE	AUCTION HOUSE
CG.V	Champion-Gondran—Vienna
CH	Christie—New York
CJ.N	Courchet, Palloc & Japhet—Nice
CL.E	Champin & Lombrail—Enghien
CR.T	Chassaing, Rivet—Toulouse
CS.L	Chenu & Scrive—Lyon
CSK	Christie's, South Kensington—London
D.B	Commissaires-Priseurs—Bordeaux
D.H	Dupuy—Honfleur
D.NY	William Doyle—New York
D.R	Denesle—Rouen
D.V	Dorotheum—Vienna
DA.B	Darmancier—Bourges
DA.R	Dapsens—Reims
DH	Dacre, Son & Hartley—Ilkley
DL.Se	Delpeint & Lemaitre—Saint Etienne
DM.D	Du Mouchelle—Detroit
DO.H	Dorling—Hamburg
DV.G	De Vos—Ghent
DWB	Dreweatt, Watson & Barton—Newbury
E	Edmiston—Glasgow
E.EDM	Eldred—East Dennis, Mass.
EC	Entwistle—Southport
EG	Elliott Green—Lymington
F.M	Finarte—Milan
F.P	Freemans—Philadelphia
F.R	Finarte—Rome
FB.M	Fraser Bros.—Montreal
FO.R	Fournier—Rouen
G	Grant—Stourport
G.G	Gaucher—Grenoble
G.L	Galateau—Limoges
G.S	Goodman—Sydney
G.SB	Guichard—Saint Brieuc
G.Z	Germann—Zurich
GA.L	Guillaumot & Albrand—Lyon
GC	Geering & Colyer—Hawkhurst
GD.B	Galerie Dobiaschofsky—Bern
GDA.G	Galerie D'Horlogerie Ancienne—Geneva

CODE	AUCTION HOUSE
GF.L	Galerie Fischer—Lucerne
GG.S	Geoff. Gray—Sydney
GG.TA	Gordon Galleries—Tel Aviv
GGL.L	Genin, Griffe, Leseuil—Lyon
GK.B	Galerie Kornfeld—Bern
GK.Z	Galerie Koller—Zurich
GM.B	Galerie Moderne—Bruxelles
GS.B	Galerie Stuker—Bern
GSP	Graves, Son & Pilcher—Hove
GT	Garrod Turner—Ipswich
GT.A	Gerrard-Tasset—Angouleme
GV.G	Goteborgs Auktionsverk—Goteborg
GV.P	Gilles Vergnault—Parthenay
H.AP	Hours—Aix-en-Provence
HB	Heathcote Ball—Leicester
HG.C	Hanzell Galleries—Chicago
HMA.L	Herment-Mochon & Anaf—Lyon
HN.H	Hauswedel & Nolte—Hamburg
HS	Henry Spencer—Retford
J	Jollys—Bath
J.M	Joel—Melbourne
JSS	Jackson, Stopps and Staff—London
JT	James Thompson—Kirkby
K.B	Kaczorowski—Brive-La Gaillarde
K.BB	Kohn—Bourg-en-Bresse
K.N	Klinger—Nurnberger
K.S	Kvalitetsauktion—Stockholm
KC	King & Chasemore—Pulborough
KC.R	King & Chasemore—Roermond
KF.M	Karl & Faber—Munich
KH.K	Kunsthallens Kunstauktioner—Copenhagen
KK.B	Kornfeld & Klipstein—Bern
KM.K	Kunsthaus Am Museum—Cologne

CODE	AUCTION HOUSE	CODE	AUCTION HOUSE	CODE	AUCTION HOUSE
KV.L	Kunstgalerij De Vuyst—Lokeren	PC	Phillips—Chester	VT.M	Villebrun & Tournel—Marseilles
KV.S	Kvalitetsauktion—Stockholm	PE	Phillips—Edinburgh	W.M	Weinmuller—Munich
L	Lane & Sons—Penzance	PG	Phillips—Glasgow	W.T	Waddington—Toronto
L.C	Lelieve—Chartres	PJ.M	Phillips-Jacoby—Montreal	W.W	Weschler—Washington
L.K	Lempertz—Cologne	PK	Phillips—Knowle	WA.B	Watine & Arnault—Berthune
L.SG	Louiseau—Saint Germain-en-Laye	PL	Phillips—Leeds	WK.M	Galerie Wolfgang Ketterer—Munich
L.SM	Lerond—Saint Maur	PS	Phillips In Scotland—Edinburgh	WSW	Warner, Sheppard & Wade—Leicester
LE	Locke & England—Leamington Spa	PWC	Parsons, Welsh & Cowell—Sevenoaks	WW	Woolley & Wallis—Salisbury
LM	Lalonde Martin—Bristol	PX	Phillips—Exeter	WWL	Warren & Wignall—Leyland
LP	Lalonde Brothers & Parham—Bristol	R.G	Rosset—Geneva	YG.P	Youngs Gallery—Portsmouth,N.H.
LS	Love & Sons—Perth	R.I	Renner—Issoudon	12.P	De Cagny—Paris
M.LA	Massart—L'Isle Adam	R.K	Rasmussen—Copenhagen	15.P	Cornette De St. Cyr—Paris
M.LF	Manson—La Fleche	R.M	Regis—Marseilles	16.P	Ferri—Paris
M.NO	Mortons—New Orleans	R.V	Rijaud—Vernon	17.P	Lemee—Paris
M.V	Martin—Versailles	RB.HM	Richard Bourne—Hyannis, Mass.	21.P	Pillias—Paris
MA.V	Maynards—Vancouver	RG	Rowland Gorringe—Lewes	23.P	Jozon—Paris
MC.A	Martin & Courtois—Angers	RG.M	Raynaud & Gamet—Marseille	28.P	Morelle—Paris
MCB	McCartney, Morris & Barber—Ludlow	S	Sotheby—London	29.P	Ledoux-Lebard—Paris
MCC	McCartney, Morris & Barker—Ludlow	S.BM	Skinner—Bolton, Mass.	32.P	Chalvet De Recy—Paris
MM	Morrison, McChlery—Glasgow	S.D	Sadde—Dijon	33.P	Boisgirard—Paris
MMB	Messenger, May & Baverstock—Godalming	S.J	Sausverd—Joigny	35.P	Ader, Picard & Tajan—Paris
MS.P	Martinot & Savignat—Pontoise	S.O	Savot—Orleans	36.P	Deurbergue—Paris
MV.LH	Mabile-Vankemriel—Le Havre	S.Tr	Strange—The Rocks, Australia	37.P	Englemann—Paris
MVT.L	Mercier, Velliet & Thullier—Lille	S.W	Sloan—Washington	4.P	Le Blanc—Paris
MW.A	Mak Van Waay—Amsterdam	SB	Sotheby Belgravia—London	40.P	Tilorier—Paris
N	Neale & Son—Nottingham	SBA	Sotheby Beresford Adams—Chester	42.P	Libert—Paris
N.M	Neumeister—Munich	SKC	Sotheby, King & Chasemore—Pulborough	45.P	Oger—Paris
O	Oliver—Sudbury	SMG	Shakespear, McTurk & Graham—Leicester	50.P	Binoche—Paris
O.F	Osenat—Fontainebleau	SPB	Sotheby—USA	54.P	Delaporte—Paris
OL	Outhwaite & Litherland—Liverpool	SY	Sotheby Parke Bernet, O/S of USA & UK	56.P	Ribault-Menetiere—Paris
OT	Osmond, Tricks—Bristol	SYB	Sotheby Bearnes—Torquay	6.P	Audap, Godeau & Solanet—Paris
P	Phillips—London	T.B	Thierry—Brest	60.P	Rogeon—Paris
P.LF	Pillet—Lyons-La-Foret	TH.B	Thelot—Blois	61.P	Millon—Paris
P.M	Phillips Ward Price—Montreal	TL	Lawrence—Crewkerne	62.P	Renaud—Paris
P.NY	Phillips—New York	TRS	Thomson Rose & Spenser—York	63.P	Laurin, Guilloux & Buffetaud—Paris
P.T	Phillips Ward Price—Toronto	UA.Z	Uto Auktions A.G—Zurich	66.P	Loudmer & Poulain—Paris
PB	Sotheby Parke Bernet—USA	V	Vost's—Colchester	7.P	Robert—Paris
		V.LH	Viel—Le Havre	73.P	Labat—Paris
		V.P	Verhaeghe—Poitiers	75.P	Couturier & Nicolay—Paris
		VMB.H	Van Marle & Bignell—The Hague	77.P	Delorme—Paris
		VN.R	Vendu Notarishuis—Rotterdam	81.P	Boscher—Paris

INDEX

Pages 1-330 are found in Volume I; pages 355–688, in Volume II; and pages 713–1046, in Volume III. Where more than one page number is cited for an artist, the first citation refers to the main biographical entry; subsequent citations refer to additional color plates.

Hays, William Jacob, 238
Heade, Martin Johnson, 186, 30, 367, 368
Healy, George Peter A., 159
Held, Al, 1041
Hennings, Ernest Martin, 852
Henri, Robert, 612, 733
Henry, Edward Lamson, 318
Herzog, Hermann, 256
Hesselius, John, 50
Hetzel, George, 215
Hibbard, Aldro Thompson, 854
Hicks, Edward, 89, 36
Hicks, Thomas, 200
Hidley, Joseph H., 237
Higgins, (W.) Victor, 841
Higgins, Eugene, 761
Hildebrandt, Howard Logan, 675
Hill, John William, 153
Hill, Thomas, 236
Hinckley, Thomas H., 160
Hirsch, Joseph, 980
Hirst, Claude Raguet, 516
Hitchcock, George, 470
Hoeber, Arthur, 499
Hofmann, Charles C., 191
Hofmann, Hans, 811
Holahan, Mary F., 13
Holdredge, Ransom G., 276
Holty, Carl Robert, 934
Homer, Winslow, 280, 370, 377
Hope, Thomas, 253
Hopkin, Robert, 248
Hopper, Edward, 830
Horton, William Samuel, 614
Howland, Alfred Cornelius, 293
Hubbard, William James, 137
Hubbell, Henry Salem, 658
Hudson, Grace Carpenter, 615
Hunt, William Morris, 206
Huntington, Daniel, 174
Hurd, Peter, 955
Hyde De Neuville, Baroness, 86
Indiana, Robert, 1042
Inman, Henry, 125
Inman, John O'Brien, 227
Inness, George, 212, 390
Inness, George, Jr., 501
Insley, Albert, 417
Irvine, Wilson Henry, 647
Jacobsen, Antonio, 472, 359, 362, 363
Jarvis, John Wesley, 88
Jenkins, Paul, 1025
Jennys, William, 111
Jensen, Alfred, 950
Johns, Jasper, 1045
Johnson, David, 223
Johnson, Eastman, 209, 378
Johnson, Frank Tenney, 684
Johnson, Joshua, 105
Johnson, Lester, 1009

Lawrence, Jacob, 1005, 408
Lawson, Ernest, 677
Leavitt, Edward C., 324
Lebduska, Lawrence, 904
Leigh, William Robinson, 623
Leighton, Scott, 460
Leith-Ross, Harry, 855
Leslie, Alfred, 1037
Leutze, Emmanuel, 169, 717
Johnson, Marshall, 433
Johnson, William H., 939
Jones, Francis Coates, 534
Jones, Hugh Bolton, 455
Kacere, John, 1011
Kane, John, 571
Karfiol, Bernard, 850
Katz, Alex, 1036
Kaula, William J., 666
Keith, William, 295
Kelly, Ellsworth, 1026
Kennedy, William W., 181
Kensett, John Frederick, 170, 369, 386
Kent, Rockwell, 831
Key, John Ross, 252
King, Albert F., 506
King, Charles Bird, 101, 24, 714
King, Paul, 629
Kingman, Dong, 986
Kline, Franz, 981
Knaths, Karl, 888
Knight, Daniel Ridgway, 311
Koch, John, 982
Koeniger, Walter, 817
Koerner, William Henry D., 791
Krafft, Carl R., 840
Krasner, Lee, 988
Krimmel, John Lewis, 102, 374
Kroll, Leon, 846
Kronberg, Louis, 676
Krushenick, Nicholas, 1044
Kuehne, Max, 812
Kuhn, Walt, 783
Kuniyoshi, Yasuo, 876
La Farge, John, 270, 29
Lambdin, George Cochran, 239, 28
Lambdin, James Reid, 139
Lambert, Ted R., 959
Lane, Fitz Hugh, 131, 367
Lathrop, William Langson, 564
Laurence, Sydney, 616
Lauritz, Paul, 875
Laux, August, 443
Lever, Richard Hayley, 776
Levine, Jack, 1000, 751
Lewis, Edmond Darch, 269
Leyendecker, Joseph Christi, 687
Lichtenstein, Roy, 1027
Lie, Jonas, 806
Lindner, Richard, 942
Lippincott, William Henry, 464
Little, Philip, 538

Longpre, Paul De, 507
Looney, Robert F., 383
Louis, Morris, 992
Low, Will Hickock, 495
Lucioni, Luigi, 933
Luks, George, 626, 734
Lumis, Harriet Randall, 659
MacLane, Jean, 795
MacDonald-Wright, Stanton, 883
MacIver, Loren, 977
MacKenzie, Roderick D., 617
MacMonnies (Low), Mary L.F., 550
Mader, Louis, 323
Maentel, Jacob, 71
Major, Ernest L., 609
Mannheim, Jean, 596
Marca-Relli, Conrad, 994
Marcius-Simons, Pinckney, 624
Marin, John, 660
Marsh, Reginald, 919
Martin, Agnes, 990
Martin, Homer D., 275
Mathews, Arthur Frank, 575
Matulka, Jan, 882
Maurer, Alfred H., 637
Maurer, Louis, 257
Mayer, Frank Blackwell, 221
Mayer, Peter Bela, 856
McComas, Francis, 682
McCord, George Herbert, 449
McEntee, Jervis, 225
McLaughlin, John, 924
Meeker, Joseph Rusling, 220
Melchers, Gari, 570
Melrose, Andrew, 277
Metcalf, Willard Leroy, 543, 723, 727
Mignot, Louis Remy, 242
Millar, Addison Thomas, 568
Miller, Alfred Jacob, 147, 394
Miller, Richard Emil, 764
Miller, William Rickarby, 183
Millet, Francis Davis, 432
Minor, Robert Crannell, 299
Mitchell, Joan, 1034
Moeller, Louis Charles, 512
Mora, Francis Luis, 685
Moran, Edward, 234
Moran, Edward Percy, 590
Moran, John Leon, 605
Moran, Peter, 314
Moran, Thomas, 290, 389, 396
Morris, George L.K., 962
Morse, Samuel F.B., 106, 15
Moses, Anna Mary Robertson "Grandma", 576
Moses, Forrest K., 899
Mosler, Henry, 319
Motherwell, Robert, 1001
Moulthrop, Reuben, 70
Mount, Shepard Alonzo, 132
Mount, William Sidney, 138